WINCHESTER
HEART OF A CITY

ANDREW RUTTER

P & G Wells Winchester

© 2009
Published by P & G Wells
11 College Street
Winchester SO23 9LZ

ISBN 978-0-90079-604-3

Ordnance Survey maps reproduced by permission of Ordnance Survey on behalf of HMSO – Crown Copyright (2009), all rights reserved.

Inside covers © English Heritage. NMR. Aerofilms Collection (1947).

Text © Andrew Rutter.
Chapter 10 © Richard Whinney.
Illustrations © Andrew Rutter, Keith Leaman, Nick Bourne, John Reynolds and John Crook.

The acknowledgements on p. 293 constitute an extension of this copyright page. Every effort has been made to contact copyright holders; any omissions are inadvertent, and will be corrected in future editions if notification of the amended credit is sent to the publisher in writing.

All rights reserved. No part of this book may be reproduced in a retrieval system or transmitted in any form or by any means, electrical, mechanical or otherwise, without the permission of the copyright holders.

The right of Andrew Rutter to be identified as the author of this work has been asserted in accordance with the Copyright, Designs and Patents Act 1988.

Sponsored by the City of Winchester Trust.

Design and typesetting by Judith Blake. Printed by Sarsen Press, 22 Hyde Street, Winchester SO23 7DR

CONTENTS

FOREWORD		v
PREFACE		vi
CHAPTER 1	Winchester Conservation Area	1
CHAPTER 2	Access Roads into Winchester	21
CHAPTER 3	The Walled City	27
	1: High Street/Southgate Street area	27
	2: St Swithun Street/St Thomas Street area	38
	3: Little Minster Street/Great Minster Street/St Clement Street/The Square	47
	4: Cathedral Close/Wolvesey Palace	57
	5: Eastgate Street/Union Street/St George's Street/ Silver Hill/Friarsgate	72
	6: St Peter Street/Parchment Street/the Brooks/North Walls/ Abbey Gardens	82
	7: Colebrook Street	102
	8: Tower Street/Cross Street/Staple Gardens/Jewry Street	106
	9: Law Courts/Barracks/The Castle	115
CHAPTER 4	The Northern Suburb: Hyde	129
CHAPTER 5	Eastern Winchester: St Giles' Hill, The Soke, Wharf Hill, Riverside	143
CHAPTER 6	Western Winchester: The Railway, Westgate	179
CHAPTER 7	Winchester College	203
CHAPTER 8	Christchurch Road and St Cross	225
CHAPTER 9	Importance of Detail	251
CHAPTER 10	Archaeological and Historical Development of Winchester *Richard Whinney*	267
GAZETTEER OF INTERIORS		285
FURTHER READING		291
ACKNOWLEDGEMENTS		292
ILLUSTRATION CREDITS		293

The Cathedral from Southgate Street

FOREWORD

In the early '60s a campaign by the Civic Trust led to government legislation that created the first conservation areas. This represented a major advance in heritage thinking for two reasons: it recognised the importance of whole areas of towns and cities rather than only individual historic buildings, and it introduced the concept of enhancement in partnership with preservation. Places change over time and generally it is these changes that give so much character to the areas we love. But in the post-war era the damage caused by bombing, and the desire to create a brave new world upset the pace of change, and great harm was done by wholesale demolition and unsympathetic renewal. Conservation of precious areas has largely put a stop to this.

Winchester is one of the best examples of the benefits of conservation area legislation. It is a tribute to the Council and its officers that the city was one of the first to designate conservation areas and to apply the balanced policy of preservation and enhancement, so that this world famous city has been spared the worst of the damage done in many other places. Amongst those officers who rose to the new challenge, Andrew Rutter is an outstanding example, as I learnt during my Chairmanship of English Heritage, when we had the responsibility of monitoring and encouraging the process. It is a great pleasure for me, therefore, to introduce his book and to commend it not only to Wintonians, but to all cities, towns and villages that value their heritage and wish to manage change so that it enhances rather than only preserves their character.

It is also fitting that this important book is sponsored and edited by the City of Winchester Trust, which has done so much to help in the conservation of the city. One of the first local civic societies, it was founded in 1957, the same year as the Civic Trust. It is very sad that as I write we have just had the news of the end of the Civic Trust, which means that the burden of heritage protection fails more than ever on the shoulders of local societies like Winchester's Trust.

Andrew Rutter's meticulous study of the city to which he devoted much of his working life, and the honest way in which he sets out both successes and failures, is a credit to his architect's eye and his planner's overview, which have both been supported by his ability to draw. It is good to have many of his sketches, originally produced to assist the City Council in reaching decisions, alongside the wealth of historic illustration in the book. An additional pleasure comes from the watercolour illustrations by Keith Leaman of the Trust, which emphasise the often overlooked importance of the setting of a city. Winchester is unusually blessed by its intimate relationship with the surrounding countryside, which can be seen from many of its streets, and from which one can look down into the city without the interruption of careless modern development.

Montagu of Beaulieu

Lord Montagu of Beaulieu
May 2009

PREFACE

This book is the culmination of 24 years enjoyable practical work in Winchester, with its historical buildings, rather than any sustained academic research. Consequently, I have first to thank those who by example and encouragement in my developing years helped me to acquire the judgement necessary for me to do the work and, secondly, those who turned a survey into a book.

I grew up in the wonderful countryside on the Dorset/Wiltshire border, where my Quaker father, William Farley Rutter, a solicitor, was also town clerk in the Saxon hilltop town of Shaftesbury. He was aware both of the continuity of the historic legacy and the unpretentious townscape qualities of his home town and its landscape setting. He set me the example of interest in community affairs of all sorts, backed by hard work. Later, as a county councillor, he made use of new conservation legislation to reverse the planned destruction of the south side of Shaftesbury's shopping centre in order to promote through traffic, which would have been disastrous for its future.

My mother, Hester Elisabeth Fox, encouraged artistic endeavour of all sorts, and I was fortunate to find at Sidcot Quaker boarding school in the Mendip Hills in 1944 an outstanding art master in John Newick. Eventually with his help I gained entrance to the Architectural Association School of Architecture in London.

Freehand drawing in ink was very much on the curriculum as a discipline to make us both observant and accurate in recording the environment and presenting our designs. Andrew Carden was a studio master and he invited me to work for Carden & Godfrey where I became architect for new buildings in Rochester and Hove and conservation architect on projects in Sussex. Subsequently, on the Urban Design Course at Edinburgh University, I was given the opportunity by Professor Percy Johnson-Marshall to join a multidisciplinary planning team working on the rejuvenation of Kilmarnock.

In 1969, I came to work for the Hampshire County Council on forward planning, with the special task of giving architectural advice to their officers in south east Hampshire. In 1974, local government was reorganised and Winchester District was created with local planning and development control powers under the direction for the first time of an architect, Jack Thompson. He appointed me to the new and unknown job of 'Conservation Officer' in which I could use all my talent for architectural design, drawing, and interest in landscape.

Winchester had experienced a period of planned demolition to facilitate structural change and eliminate 'slums', and our remit, promoted by the local Civic Society, was to raise the standard of design in any environmental changes. There were many challenges: the town was threatened by a destructive motorway alignment; proposals for a dual carriageway, three-quarter inner ring road; pressure to build thousands of square feet of offices for firms moving out of London with their parking demands; and many key historic buildings in disrepair.

One major challenge came in the form of a large development on the Chesil Station site owned by the City Council. If that had gained planning permission it would have made sensitive control of development elsewhere very difficult. A very good team of planners, landscape architects and support staff worked together to steer Winchester development in a positive conservation direction. We were helped by the constructive criticism of the Winchester Preservation Trust (now the City of Winchester Trust). Planning decisions were aided by local architects who voluntarily gave time to a monthly architects' panel to assess new proposals. Not only did they help to keep our architectural appreciation alive to different ideas but they also helped to give confidence in negotiation by showing that criticism, based partly on my test drawings of context, was not just the personal whim of one council officer.

In September 1997, Simon Birch, successor to Jack Thompson, backed by the City Council, asked me to undertake a formal 'Conservation area appraisal' of Winchester, using the current English Heritage guidelines before my retirement in March. This was a statutory requirement that we never had time to accomplish for all conservation areas because of the number of planning and listed building applications that had to be considered.

It is a false assumption that everybody sees the town in the same way. I came to realise that people do not look at a town in an architectural way unless guided, which I hope this book facilitates. I believe it to be imperative that a study of the Winchester Conservation Area has to be made with a high regard for its landscape setting.

Richard Whinney and Graham Scobie at the Hyde Historic Resources Centre have provided a chapter on archaeology, drawing on archaeological work that has been undertaken in the last 40 years. This offers a better grasp of the town's origins and development.

The City of Winchester Trust, led by Mrs Patricia Edwards, their chairman and formerly planning committee chairman, consulted Robert Cross, a retired publisher, who believed that it should be turned into a book with some additional historic research and a different balance of historic/modern illustrations to make it visually interesting.

The result is this book which I hope offers an understanding of, and insight into, the many factors that have shaped Winchester's landscape, streets, spaces, buildings and activity. It provides a template that could be applied to villages, towns and cities across the country.

Note on conservation areas

The 1990 Planning (Listed Buildings and Conservation Areas) Act places a duty on every local planning authority to determine which parts of their area are 'Areas of special architectural or historic interest, the character or appearance of which it is desirable to preserve or enhance' and designate them as conservation areas.

The Act and recent Government Advice (Planning Policy Guidance Note 15) also states that the local planning authority should, from time to time, formulate and publish proposals for the analysis, preservation and enhancement of these conservation areas.

This book began as a technical appraisal of the Winchester conservation area, which was originally designated under the 1967 Civic Amenities Act as three separate areas, the Town Centre, Hyde Abbey and St Cross, first published with the Town Centre plan in 1968.

It is based on a detailed visual analysis of the area supplemented with reference to historical maps and a number of published books. It defines and records as many as possible of the distinctive features of Winchester and its setting, giving wherever possible an idea of the evolution of the townscape that one can see. It attempts to be factual and as objective as possible although comments are made about the design of buildings from a townscape and personal point of view.

To achieve this in a manageable form, the assessment is divided up into:

An analysis of the setting of Winchester using maps, drawings, watercolours and descriptions.

A description of the qualities of the access routes into Central Winchester (the walled town) with some supporting drawings.

A description of some of the main character areas based on the historical evolution of the town.

An archaeological chapter, included because Winchester was originally listed by the Council for British Archaeology as one of the forty most important towns from an archaeological point of view. It has since been selected by English Heritage as one of thirty of these for more detailed study, and was fortunate to have detailed archaeological studies for ten years made under the direction of Martin Biddle. The broad archaeological picture is set out in map form supplemented with text to give some idea of the evolution of key Winchester features. A great archive of detailed material is held by Winchester City Museums, and new discoveries are constantly being made.

The book examines the various elements that comprise Winchester's special character and appearance. However it should be recognised that it is the combination of these features which justifies the designation of the conservation area and the proposals to revise these boundaries.

The information contained in this assessment was collected during the period November 1997 to January 1999 and then updated in 2005. Of course the city has gone on evolving since 2005 but the study had to be terminated at some date or it would never have been finished. The omission of any feature from the text and/or accompanying maps should not be regarded as an indication that they are without significance or importance in conservation and planning terms. It should be stressed that this book is a personal view and not intended to be a scholarly study with academic references to historical information discovered. A list of further reading is given at the end of the book.

ANDREW RUTTER

Hyde Street seen from the junction with North Walls

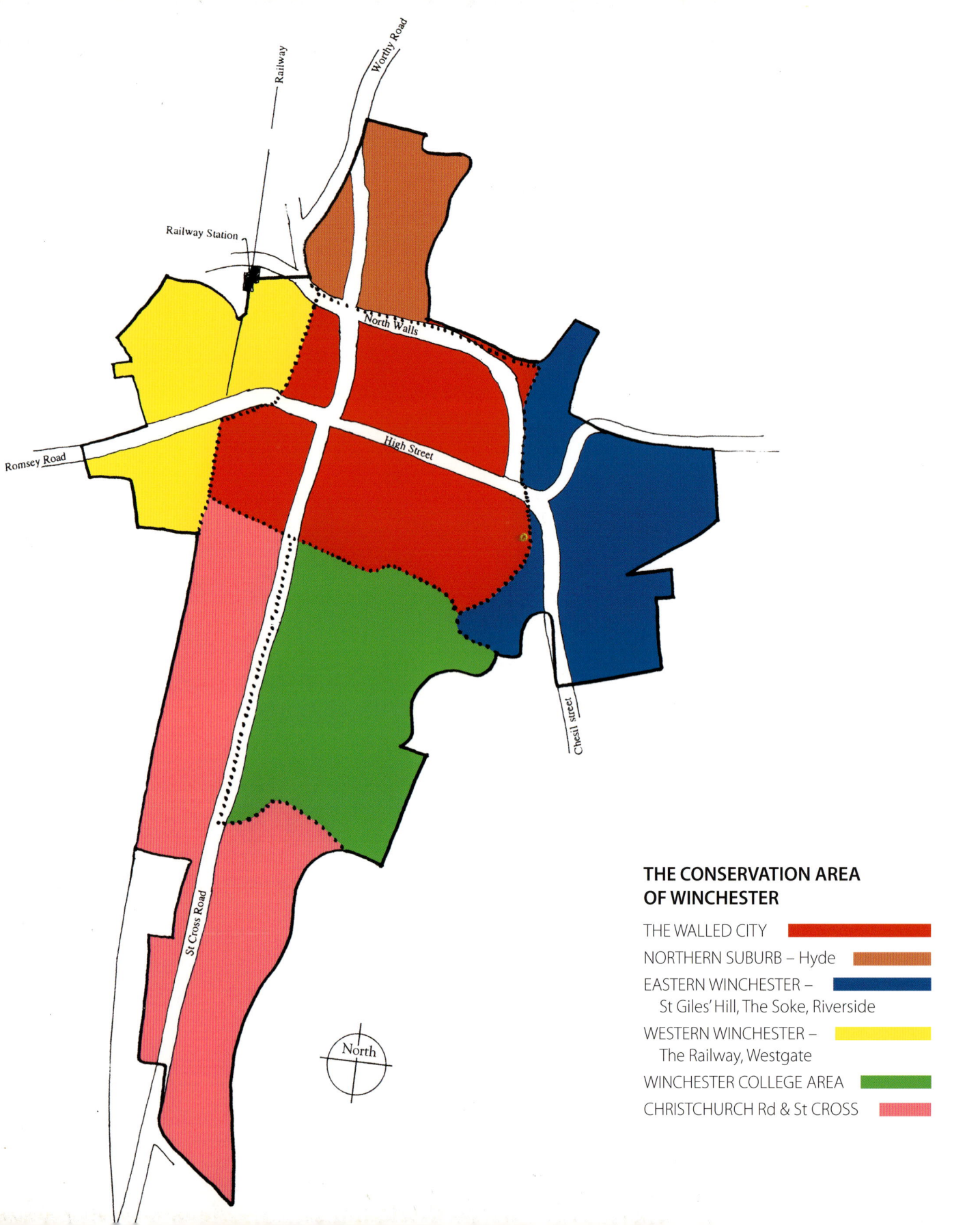

CHAPTER ONE

Winchester Conservation Area

Winchester is a beautiful, yet puzzling city. It is rooted in English history, a county town, but within commuting distance of London. Winchester has within it and its setting a combination of timeless, spiritual qualities, as well as the conflicting pressure for constant change.

The city has survived depopulation from the Black Death, the Plague, fluctuations in the economy, and major destruction from two civil wars. It has also survived the worst excesses of post 1945 planning policies promoted by Sir Patrick Abercrombie, the results of which can be seen in the Brooks area.

Despite its relatively prosperous economy the city is nonetheless dependant for the upkeep of many of its most important historic institutions on outside finances. Its townscape represents the relative power of different sections of society through the ages, within a setting of great character that has changed considerably over the last century.

Winchester is an 'urban palimpsest' that can only be understood by patient study, analysis and exploration, through all seasons of the year. This conservation area appraisal sets out to undertake this.

Origins and setting

The city is located at a point in the chalk downlands where the very pure water of the westerly flowing River Itchen breaks through the downland to the south on its way to the sea. This made it an ideal position for an Iron Age settlement, having plentiful fresh water and high defensive ground on both sides of the valley. During the Roman period, Winchester (*Venta Belgarum*) became an

Railway cutting and station

important point on the east to west route from Dover to the Mendips using the high ground and avoiding the forests. The settlement was also well connected to the estuary harbour of Bitterne as well as having road connections to Silchester and Bath.

Winchester did not have the advantages that its rival London had, such as a navigable river with easy access to Europe, room for expansion and a rich hinterland, with the result that London evolved into being the capital of England while Winchester remained an important but subjugated centre, particularly for church and legal activities.

The arrival of the railway in 1838 helped to make Winchester attractive to visitors, but the city only regained some status by becoming an important administrative centre with the creation of a modern prison, a police headquarters for Hampshire in 1850, the County Hospital in 1863 and a centre for the Hampshire County Council in 1888. Winchester also became an important centre for other activities, having a large cattle market and a corn exchange.

As a result of a growth in local industry there was a strong working class presence by the beginning of the 20th century which amongst other things led to a demand for playing fields and helped to finance healthcare. Out of the expansion of local and county authorities, the law courts and the hospital grew the middle class sector.

With the electrification of the railway in the 1960s and the advent of the motorway in the 1990s, Winchester has come within easy commuting distance of London. The communication links have created the conditions for sustained pressure on the city to expand.

It is only in the late 20th century that the north/south route from the midlands to Europe has started to develop as a major axis with the upgrading of the A34 to high quality dual carriageway status linking into the motorway system to Portsmouth, Southampton and Europe. Southampton Airport now provides easy access to many places both in the UK and Europe including some of the major European airports for onward flights throughout the world.

In 1930 a town planning scheme prepared by the City Engineer and Surveyor, Mr Warwick, recognised the difficulty of anticipating future growth and said 'it cannot now be said that any land is safe from building purposes, owing to the increased transport facilities. The programme should be the preservation of all that is beautiful as far as is humanly possible, not necessarily by the sterilisation of land against building, where such land is admirably suited for building, but by the avoidance of haphazard development with no thought for the future'.

The insanitary conditions of the late 19th/early 20th century have been removed, together with the industries in the city centre. These have been replaced within the central conservation area with offices and dense residential developments. Central Government demands for considerable increase in housebuilding throughout Hampshire, with Winchester having to take its complement, is already having a dramatic effect on the city's sensitive environs. The potential damage to Winchester's setting as the Government's directives are fulfilled is only going to be exacerbated over the coming years.

The difficulty of making structural changes to the centre of Winchester without destroying its essential character has been clearly illustrated in the last 30 years of the conservation debate. The greening of the river valley connecting the water meadows north and south of the city has been achieved. The dual carriageway three-quarter ring road included in the town centre plan of 1976 has been abandoned as unacceptable. Trial positions for inner bypass routes further out have been studied and found not to be particularly attractive to traffic, and highly damaging to the environment.

The need to provide for thousands of parked motor cars has coarsened the townscape north of the High Street and has threatened the garden areas which are still a feature of Winchester, particularly to the south of the Cathedral. A major park and ride system has been established at Bar End to absorb cars off the motorway. Debate continues as to how and where alternative park and ride facilities on the periphery can be sited. The way in which society is willing to deal with movement and the facilities to go with it will be crucial to the development of the character of the conservation area and its setting. In many ways this is equivalent to the long running debate in the 19th century over main drainage and who should pay for it. It is intended therefore that this conservation area appraisal will form a basis for the future management of what survives of this ancient city.

Relationship to its surroundings

Historically the story of Winchester as a settlement starts on the surrounding hills with Bronze Age culture. Particularly important is the Iron Age encampment on St Catherine's Hill which is visible from many parts of the conservation area, the larger Iron Age settlement within the town at Oram's Arbour and the Saxon development on St Giles' Hill.

Some of the best viewpoints from which to grasp the development, character and layout of Winchester are located on adjacent hills and ridges. Complementary to this, many buildings and public spaces in Winchester enjoy wonderful views of the countryside which add immeasurably to the quality of these spaces.

The historic access routes into Winchester from Roman and medieval times gain an identity from the

View to St Catherine's Hill. Drawing from *The Itchen Valley* by Heywood Sumner, 1881

way they relate to topography and how they approach the conservation area itself. There is a remarkable consistency in the way these approaches have not yet been visually spoilt by unattractive modern commercial developments as is so often the case with our towns and cities.

Because trees form an essential component of the conservation area, the aggregate effect of these can only be appreciated from higher ground outside the conservation area. So, for example the Christchurch Road area has the appearance of a wood when seen from St Giles' and St Catherine's Hills.

The medieval buildings of the Cathedral, College and St Cross are built of materials which stand out very white against trees and landscape, and one of the best views of all three together lies outside the conservation area at Bushfield Camp.

Because of the particular topographical nature of Winchester's setting, trees well outside the conservation area provide a setting that emphasises the character of the buildings within the conservation area, rather than visually competing with it as housing and commercial developments would do.

Equally, because of the topographic situation, principal buildings like the Cathedral are also seen against the landscape of arable land stretching miles away to the north and east, as well as grazed chalk

View South from St Catherine's Hill. Drawing from *The Itchen Valley* by Heywood Sumner, 1881

downland that is closer. Changes to the husbandry, management or use of the surrounding land could alter the characteristics of this sensitive setting.

The quality of the river valley, with its great variety of water elements from main river to small channels and including an early canal, the vegetation, flowers, birds, trees, mammals, and the enclosing downland combine to provide an atmosphere of peacefulness and harmony which forms an essential contrast to the density and bustle of both the central conservation area and its historic suburbs. This rich environment is within walking distance from the centre.

There are many public footpath routes available both in and around the immediate countryside which enable both residents and visitors to enjoy this countryside with its fabulous views back to Winchester. To complement the fascinating sequence of townscape within the conservation area, there is a great variety of experiences to be obtained within just one or two miles from the centre.

The particular orientation of the setting of Winchester gives a great range of lighting effects on the landscape, varying according to the seasons, so that features such as St Catherine's Hill which can be seen from many places, look quite different at different times of day and with different seasons. Some of the characteristics are inherent to Winchester's setting and have been for centuries. It is not difficult to think back in time when confronted with such views.

Some of the characteristics depend on actions taken by past generations which are finite. Some depend on continuing management and on visions for the future. But they are under threat because of the intensity of the pressures that are growing from economic activity, population growth and modern technology. One can list the main issues as follows:

(a) Although archaeological remains have been deliberately destroyed on Twyford Down, and adjacent to the M3 roundabout at Winnall, the careful excavation which took place complemented excavations in 1933 on St Catherine's Hill, increasing our understanding considerably.

(b) One building in particular (the Police Headquarters) has damaged the scale of the tree skyline to the east. It is the first building that you see when you come down the motorway or from Three Maids Hill.

(c) The motorway and its associated dualled A34, although skillfully inserted into the landscape has brought elements of a quite different scale to anything previously introduced into this small-scale countryside. It brings its attendant visual and noise pollution which is contrary to some of the essential characteristics mentioned and now affects much of the conservation area. If the motorway were ever to be lit to reduce accident risk, this would be exceedingly damaging to the character of Winchester.

(d) Motorway junctions normally provide strong economic pressure for the sort of commercial developments that have disfigured the approaches to so many other towns. Because of the route chosen for the M3, of necessity commercial development is positioned within, or very close to, the essential setting of the Winchester conservation area. Examples of such pressure are already taking place at Winnall and it would be a tragedy if the same thing happened south of Winchester.

(e) The Southampton Airport development has resulted in noise pollution from the flight path, which starts over St Giles' Hill and follows the valley down towards the airport. This has increased significantly in recent years and continues to increase with the improved airport facilities and the advent of low-cost flights.

(f) Extra housing at Bushfield Camp could impinge very directly on the setting of St Cross, a rare survivor of a medieval institution which is still in use for the purpose for which it was set up. The Structure Plan is asking for extra housing in the vicinity of Winchester.

(g) Extra housing also produces a demand for road space and parking which will affect both the conservation area and its setting. One of the transport problems in Winchester is the small number of river crossings, arising out of the very nature of its setting.

(h) Development has for years been approved and implemented too close to trees which not only potentially shortens their life, but also makes it unlikely that in the future large trees of the species that we now enjoy will be replanted, unless positive action is taken. Consequently, one of the major features in the 20th century which we have relied on for disguising the extent of development around the setting of Winchester's conservation area may be degraded.

(i) Telecommunications are producing a continuing demand for masts, which would cause disfigurement to the setting of the conservation area.

The following analysis looks in much greater detail at the dangers and opportunities arising from the above.

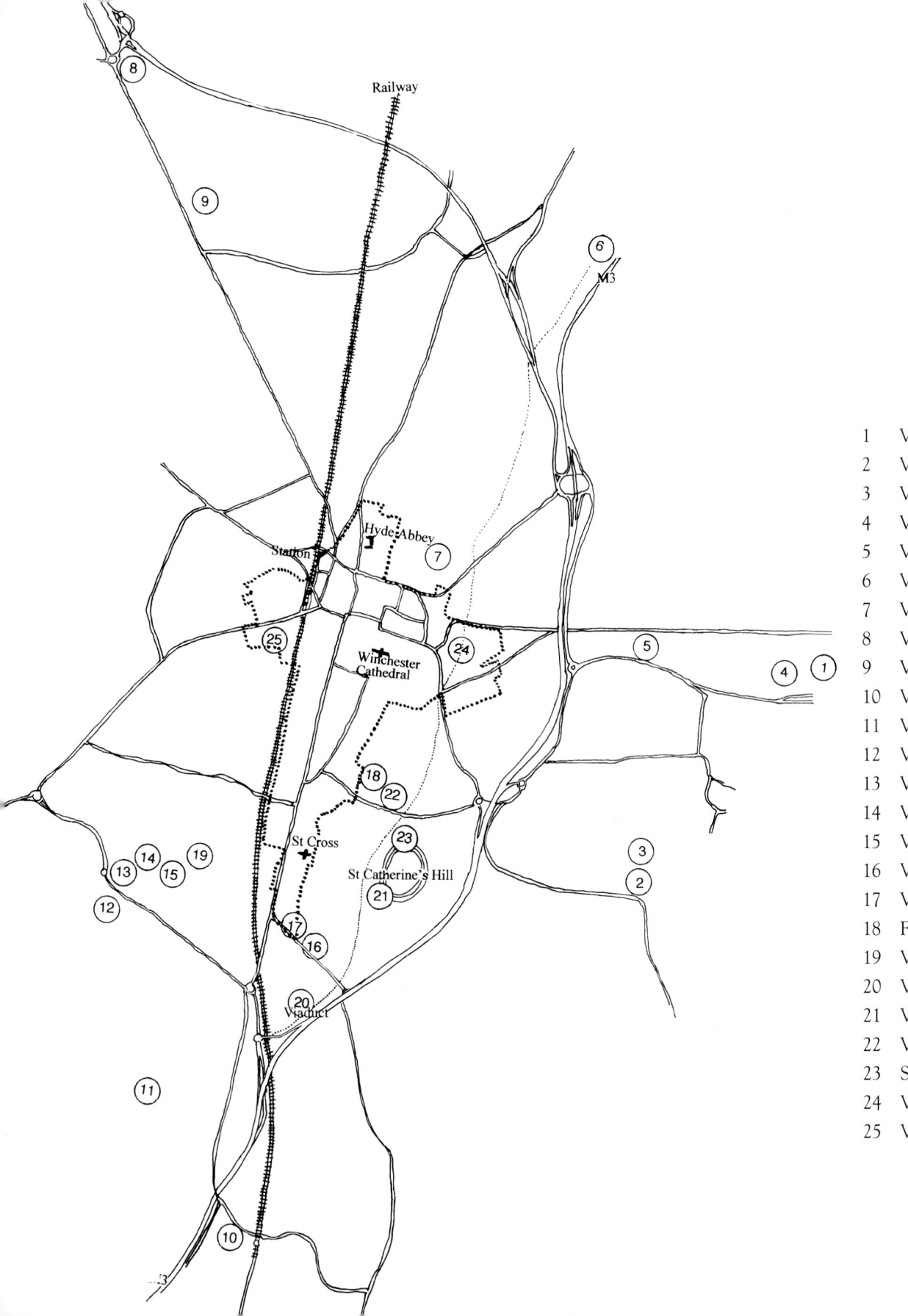

1   View from barrows adjacent to South Downs Way on Telegraph Hill
2   View from Morestead Road
3   View from Chilcomb Saxon church below Deacon Hill
4   View from the east end of Magdalen Down Butterfly Reserve
5   View from Magdalen Down Butterfly Reserve
6   View from Easton Down Farm looking south west
7   View from the Winnall Moors Nature Reserve, looking south
8   View looking south near Three Maids Hill
9   View from the ridge near Three Maids Hill – further south
10 View from Shawford Down to the south
11 View from Compton Ridge
12 View from Oliver's Battery Primary School
13 View from footpath extending from Whiteshute Ridge to Yew Hill
14 View from Whiteshute Ridge – public open space
15 View from the southern field at Bushfield Down
16 View from Five Bridges bridleway/cycleway, looking south west
17 View looking north and east from Five Bridges bridleway
18 From the Clarendon Way north of Garnier Road
19 View from Bushfield Down, north slope
20 View from Hockley Viaduct
21 View from the edge of the old bypass cutting, Twyford Down
22 View from the Canal by Garnier Road
23 St Catherine's Hill – view looking north east
24 View from the southern viewing point on St Giles' Hill
25 View from West Hill Cemetery – St James' Lane

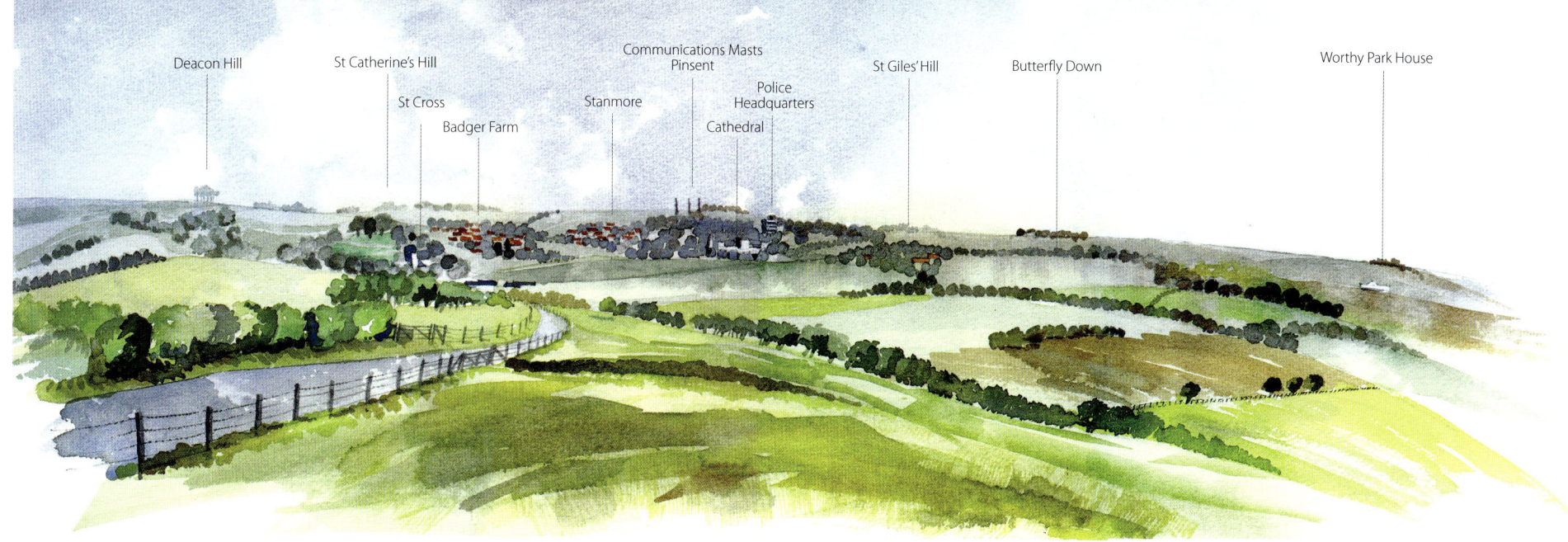

View from Barrows adjacent to the South Downs Way on Telegraph Hill

Analysis of the Winchester conservation area setting

1 View from Barrows adjacent to the South Downs Way on Telegraph Hill

This view is within sight of Cheesefoot Head, the highest point on the local downs within an Area of Outstanding Natural Beauty. It shows how St Catherine's Hill and St Giles' Hill are quite low compared with the surrounding downland. The conservation area is very small within the overall landscape. The Cathedral stands out because of its whiteness. The Hampshire Police Headquarters, St Thomas's spire, the Butterfield building and the maternity building at the County Hospital are all prominent features.

The wooded background created by the trees on Sleepers Hill is an important feature at this distance and is of even greater significance closer to as a background to both Winchester College and the Cathedral when seen from St Giles' Hill.

The housing developments at Stanmore and Badger Farm are split up by the open spaces associated with 'the valley' and Whiteshute Ridge, which is important for the setting of the conservation area.

The trees associated with the railway and the Christchurch Road Victorian suburb, now the southern part of the conservation area, make a spine through the landscape, so that medieval St Cross is still very much isolated in its setting.

The M3 coming out of Twyford Down cutting crosses downhill across the valley to the cutting made through the Magdalen Hill ridge between St Swithun's School and St Giles' Hill. This pushes noise up the dry valley into the conservation area.

2 View from Morestead Road

St Catherine's Hill and St Giles' Hill both look small compared with the surrounding downland and Winchester's western suburbs.

The Cathedral is much more important, dominating the central conservation area with a background of the County Council buildings, and punctuated by the spires and vertical features around the town.

The southern part of the conservation area appears like woodland.

Sleepers Hill is an important wooded area, separating development into sections.

The great dry valley, which comes into the conservation area from the east, is a valuable area of Grade 1 farmland (comparatively rare in this region) with the County Council sportsground at its western end on a little terraced platform.

The sewage treatment works, with its terracing and lake, are an important foreground feature and a good place for the study of birds.

The M3 is a prominent feature where it swoops down from St Catherine's Hill, across the valley and through the ridge, introducing a restless flow of movement to accompany the noise.

3 View from Chilcomb Saxon church, below Deacon Hill

St Giles' Hill becomes more important as a wooded feature on the skyline.

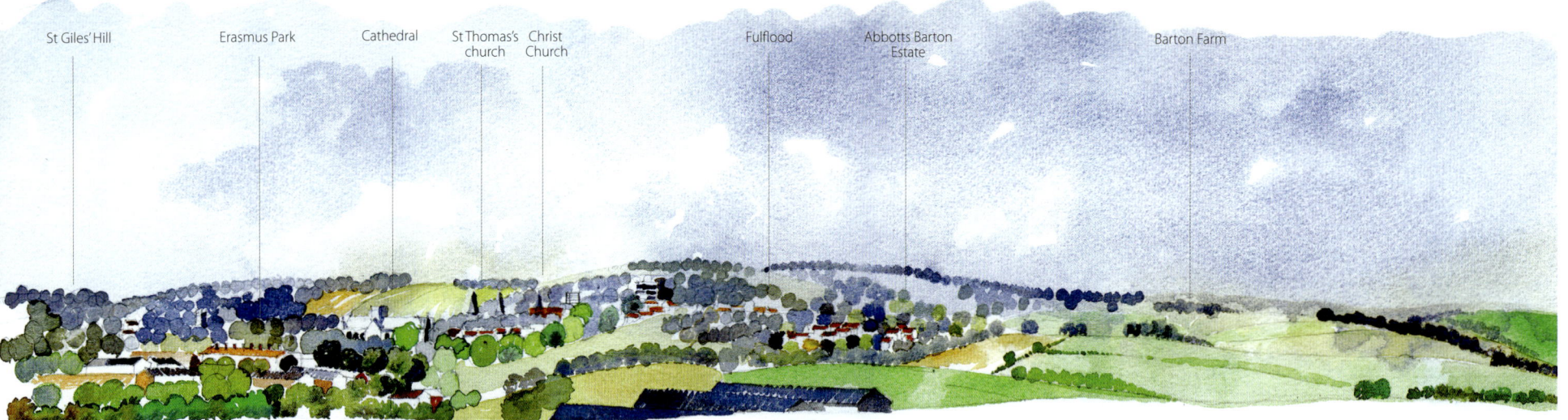

View from Easton Down Farm looking south west

The shape of the hill and its trees are much more important than those within the conservation area. The Cathedral dominates the outlook and is one of the few views seen directly from the east. The other church spires and the buildings of the hospital on Romsey Road form a supporting framework.

The factory in the foreground has a good landscape framework so that it does not significantly detract from the view. The M3 is still apparent within this view.

4 View from the east end of Magdalen Down Butterfly Reserve

St Catherine's Hill and St Giles' Hill with their trees are very important in framing the view into the southern part of the conservation area.

The College tower is set against the background of trees.

St Cross tower and Chapel are seen emerging out of the trees that visually connect it to the town via the railway line and the conservation area.

The line of trees at the top of the valley on the east side of Bushfield Camp, and the fields associated with Bushfield Camp to the south and south east, are very important as a countryside background to St Cross, as is the landscape feature of Whiteshute Ridge defined by the tree- and hedge-lined medieval route into Winchester from the west. This is the route along which King William Rufus' body was brought to the Cathedral after a hunting accident in the New Forest.

The M3 is again prominent as it passes through the landscape.

5 View from Magdalen Down Butterfly Reserve

This is a splendid view of the dry valley coming down from the east into Winchester and the downland that is the end of the Area of Outstanding Natural Beauty, finishing with the distinctive semi-detached feature of St Catherine's Hill itself. This feature shows up markedly different in contrasting light, because one is looking south.

St Catherine's Hill and St Giles' Hill frame a fine view of St Cross which again appears wonderfully isolated as a medieval building group, despite the development on higher ground on the west side of Winchester.

Note the importance of the area immediately behind St Cross leading up to Bushfield Camp as a way of separating it from development at Badger Farm.

Note too how even a four metre high thorn bush on Chilcomb Ridge looks significant in this relatively small scale landscape, because it is seen in silhouette. In the foreground the County Council playing field is an important element in the landscape, but still needs the shelter which trees provide. The sheer alien scale of the motorway and associated roads becomes very apparent in this view even though it is slotted into the landscape. The restlessness of the constant traffic is a major visual intrusion by day, and with the lines of lights at night.

In the 1950s the Government explored the idea of using the underlying geology as a safe place to store gas. This was not popular locally and Winchester MP, Peter Smithers, defeated legislation in Parliament.

6 View from Easton Down Farm looking south west

This is private land which is very important to the setting of the Cathedral when seen from Whiteshute Ridge, Bushfield Down as well as other views into Winchester.

The Cathedral stands out a powerful silhouette along with the College tower and spires in the bottom of the valley, between the wooded St Giles' Hill and the wooded ridges rising up to the south west of Winchester.

The Whiteshute Ridge open space is significant as a visual background to the silhouette of the Cathedral.

View from Shawford Down to the south

The Winnall Moors with substantial areas of open space and woodland form a notable middle ground feature.

The very large factory buildings (by Winchester standards) adjacent to the old GWR Newbury Railway line at Winnall are absorbed into this view because they are tucked in under the hill but this area needs planting more than ever to break them up visually now that roofs are becoming lighter to prevent solar gain. This is also important when seen from the footpaths on the other side of the valley.

The railway through Winchester on the other side of the valley is disguised by virtue of being either in a cutting or tree-lined.

7 View within the Winnall Moors Nature Reserve looking south

The Winnall Moors is a large area with the River Itchen on the east side and two parallel but smaller streams on the western side and the 17th century system of water meadows in between. There are considerable areas that are reverting to woodland. This is one of the best sites for observing birds in Hampshire in terms of the number of different species.

The trees round the three coarse fishing lakes adjacent to the Itchen Way public footpath visually cut off the industrial estate from the Nature Reserve which lies adjacent to the river.

In the 19th century the main buildings of central Winchester including breweries were very prominent in silhouette. Over the last thirty years, trees have obscured these views.

8 View looking south near Three Maids Hill

This is a skyline view of downland and the wooded ridges forming the setting of Winchester from the north. Note how the trees on St Catherine's Hill just pop over the top.

The buildings of the police headquarters, the prison and the hospital divulge the presence of the town.

Very noticeable is the strong tree-lined feature of the straight Roman road going towards the Hyde gateway into the centre of the town.

9 View from the ridge near Three Maids Hill, further south

This again shows the importance of the tree-lined feature of the Roman road going towards the centre of town, whose position is marked by St Catherine's Hill. It also just shows the police headquarters at the highest point of the conservation area and how the ridge goes on much higher to the west to Pinsent marked by three masts.

The substantial housing developments of Harestock and Weeke and the new army camp are hidden within the landscape features formed by the well-sited perimeter trees that are notable in this area.

10 View from Shawford Down to the south

The Cathedral and St Cross are very visible despite the distance, the Cathedral appearing to 'float' on a bed of trees.

View from Compton Ridge

The scale of the memorial beech avenue planted along the Roman road going towards Compton (after the 1914-18 war) helps to alleviate the effects of the motorway and the railway.

St Catherine's Hill prominently marks the edge of the area, which is the immediate setting of St Cross. The hospital and prison on Romsey Road are very visible as skyline features in the distance to the north west.

11 View from Compton Ridge

From this view, one can see clearly both the Cathedral, St Catherine's Hill and the Compton conservation area around the church.

The trees along the Roman road running in to the south gate of the Roman town, play an important part in making the dramatic cutting for the motorway look comparatively insignificant.

The police headquarters on Romsey Road breaks the skyline; this is an unfortunate intrusion as this building destroys the scale. There is a large area of farmland in the middle ground, which is part of the local plan's strategic gap essential to the setting of the Cathedral and the conservation area.

12 View from Olivers Battery Primary School

This is the highest point to the west where one can get a very broad view of the conservation area in its setting of St Giles' Hill, St Catherine's Hill and the ridge on which the hospital and police headquarters are set.

The Cathedral is very prominent, lighting up in afternoon or evening light, dominating the new development at Badger Farm in the middle ground with its broken roofscape and dark tiling. It is accompanied by the vertical features of the other churches and the College chapel, all of this seen against the arable farmland of Easton Down which makes an essential setting for the Cathedral.

The traffic on the motorway is just visible threading itself above the long ridge of the nave of the Cathedral. The railway makes a spine of trees going out towards St Cross.

Most of the conservation area buildings are still hidden by trees. In the distance the ridge with the Butterfly Down in front of St Swithun's School and the whole eastern valley at Chilcomb are important components of the view.

13 View from footpath extending from Whiteshute Ridge to Yew Hill

This is a view looking south east, which shows visually how the Cathedral and College tower are very much on a level with the old buildings at Bushfield Down. This emphasises the sensitivity of Bushfield as a site in its relationship to Winchester.

The beech trees to the north of the existing Bushfield Down are very important as a landscape feature in the foreground of the views which look right out over to the Butterfly Down by St Swithun's School.

The power lines going into Winchester are a dominant feature in the landscape and lower down very much affect the setting of St Cross. It would be good if they could be placed underground as a contribution towards the development of Bushfield Down.

View from Whiteshute Ridge public open space

14   View from Whiteshute Ridge public open space

The Cathedral and central conservation area look much closer and details of the buildings in the conservation area, surrounding the Cathedral, can be seen more clearly. The Cathedral still shows up light against the farmland of Easton Down area. Unfortunately recent factories at Winnall show up too and affect the clarity of the Cathedral silhouette. Again the M3 is just visible with moving traffic seen over the ridge of the nave.

Trees on the edge of Sleepers Hill are important as a skyline feature visually containing the developments of Stanmore and Badger Farm.

Whiteshute Lane, now the Clarendon Way, the long distance footpath from Salisbury, runs behind the hedge on the right hand side, pointing at St Giles' Hill, with views from either side before the walker plunges down into the conservation area itself.

15   View from the southern field at Bushfield Down

A broad view in which St Cross, the College and the Cathedral can all be seen close together in one unique view looking north east in their setting between Easton Down and St Giles' Hill. These buildings light up wonderfully in the afternoon and evening sunlight.

16   View from Five Bridges bridleway/cycleway, looking south west

The viaduct in silhouette effectively blocks out most of the traffic and some of its noise from this peaceful scene, except on the west side, where the M3 climbs to go over the railway line. Note the line of memorial beech trees along the Roman road to the right.

17   View looking north and east from Five Bridges bridleway

This shows the junction of the stream which passes the St Cross Almshouses to feed St Cross Mill and the lovely, clear River Itchen, where otters roam, a scene that cannot have changed much since medieval times. What an amazing sight it must have been for soldiers and pilgrims who landed at Southampton as they approached Winchester and caught their first view of St Catherine's chapel and its tower on top of the hill to the right. The chapel is now replaced by a copse of trees.

The central conservation area shows up with the top of St Giles' Hill in the distance. Because of the height of the trees, the medieval buildings in the valley cannot be seen. There is a well-used footpath which continues up the river valley past St Cross (where it is joined by the Clarendon Way) and the College, to the High Street, and beyond to Winnall Moors north of the central area or, alternatively, to the Itchen Way on the eastern side bound for New Alresford.

18   From the Clarendon Way north of Garnier Road

This area of the valley floor is predominantly used by Winchester College for playing fields, although there is an important section between the river and the canal, managed for wildlife, which is designated a Site of Special Scientific Interest.

The footpath runs towards the south end of St Giles' Hill public open space which has a number of pine trees in the distinctive planting style carried out at the end of the 19th century. It is separated from the inner playing fields called Riddings Mead by the Lockburn stream which issues out of the Cathedral Close. This used to convey foul water in medieval times. It is now planted with bullrushes, different sorts of cornus, and other plants, their stems most colourful in autumn and winter. The River Itchen flows roughly parallel at the lower level.

The Cathedral and College buildings are visually important in this unfolding vista in relation to St Giles' Hill on the right, and with the great view of St Catherine's Hill. In preparation for encountering the walled town, the old lime trees and the carefully mown grass on the left introduce a much more urban feel. The fields still flood occasionally.

The importance of the Butterfly Reserve on Chilcomb Down as part of the downlands ridge which then extends away behind St Catherine's Hill and Twyford going eastwards, is emphasised.

The relative dominance of the motorway is very much played down in this view which has enabled much of the peacefulness of the relationship between St Catherine's Hill, the water meadows by St Cross, Winchester College and the conservation area (originally interrupted by the GWR railway line, and the 1937 dual carriageway bypass) to be restored.

St Cross is still very much isolated as a medieval building group in its own setting, although it is probably best appreciated from St Catherine's Hill.

The view looking on down the Itchen valley is important, with Twyford church showing up strongly in this landscape with Shawford Down to the west. The farmland with its Roman villa pushes up onto the downs and the site of the Twyford water pumping station. The former is an Ancient Monument, which is still visible, and the latter is the best place to appreciate our Victorian industrial heritage, both within cycling distance of Winchester.

View looking north and east from Five Bridges bridleway

View from Bushfield Down north slope

19 View from Bushfield Down north slope

The Cathedral appears to be suspended over trees and encloses the conservation area which leads down to St Cross. St Cross again appears very isolated, but the importance of the Butterfly Down on Chilcomb ridge is quite crucial to its setting.

20 View from Hockley Viaduct

This reveals the wide shallow river valley dominated by trees, and the Cathedral and St Catherine's Hill on the eastern side rising up over the line of trees that marks the old railway line.

The Police Headquarters and the important listed hospital building on Romsey Road show up on the other western side.

The Viaduct is doing a splendid job in shutting off the noisy motorway from the peacefulness of the valley in which St Cross, Winchester College and the Cathedral stand. It would be marvellous if this structure could be restored as a public walking and viewing point connecting with Bushfield Down and Badger Farm.

21 View from the edge of the old bypass cutting, Twyford Down

Note how prominent the Bushfield Camp land is. Viewed from St Catherine's Hill, this forms the backdrop to St Cross Almshouses.

Whiteshute Lane (Clarendon Way) again appears a very important landscape feature isolating the large Badger Farm development from St Cross, even though much of it on the upper slopes is only a hedgerow.

The trees on Sleepers Hill ridge combine with those in Christchurch Road conservation area to form the setting for St Cross Almshouses. To the left note the importance of the memorial beech trees along the Roman road entrance to Winchester.

To the right note how the central conservation area climbs steadily up the slope to the Iron Age fort at Oram's Arbour, next to the Police Headquarters.

The Cathedral is the centre piece of the valley with its tower silhouetted against the sky, but at this point the view is not as striking as from Bushfield Camp.

22 View from the canal by Garnier Road

St Cross is seen as an isolated group of buildings, much larger in its relationship to the fields of Bushfield Down and therefore vulnerable to the effect of development in this setting.

In this view, the very simple silhouette of the Norman tower of St Cross is seen against the beech trees to the north of Bushfield Down.

The 17th century Itchen Navigation canal with its boat turning area and the plane trees planted in the 1860s is an obvious man-made feature within this landscape which is now rich in wildlife habitats.

23 St Catherine's Hill, view looking north east

This gives an intimate view of the old walled town conservation area, dominated by the Cathedral which is seen against trees on the Bereweeke Road ridge, Park Road and that area of high ground coming into the old cattle market site in Andover Road, which are essential settings to the Cathedral in this view.

Winter view from the edge of the old bypass cutting, Twyford Down

The trees along the railway and the St Cross Road conservation area show up as a single landscape feature running down towards the left of the view.

The College playing fields and water meadows in the foreground are an essential open space bounded by the trees along Garnier Road, originally planted to obscure the Victorian pumping station, and then extended to shut out the original line of the bypass (now M3) in the water meadows.

This is the best view of the 17th century canal running into what was a landing place at Wharf Hill. The canal is constructed in an angular way across the valley floor with a tow path and locks, in contrast to the natural curved path of the main River Itchen, which is less easy to pick out. This canal line has been reinforced by the planting of a line of plane trees when Winchester College acquired it.

Trees along the old Newbury/Didcot GWR line are still very important in placing the industrial area at Bar End within some sort of landscape framework although once again modern development leaves little space for proper tree management.

It is also noticeable that the park-and-ride car parks are not visible from this view.

The terraced buildings around St Catherine's Road and All Saints church, Highcliffe are prominent in this view as a foreground to the trees on St Catherine's Hill and make a sharp contrast with the more recent city housing.

Also note in this view the trees on the lower southern slopes of St Giles' Hill, at present outside the conservation area, which are a feature of its overall character, but sadly being encroached on by the development of large houses.

The playing fields at Bar End are an important continuation in landscape terms of the playing fields of the College and an introduction to the dry valley which stretches away to the east.

The trees along the Itchen valley also link up with those on Winnall Moors and the other side of the central conservation area, just beyond St John's church in St John's Street.

The view also indicates the importance of the open space which is West Hill cemetery in St James' Lane, together with Christ Church and its spire, both of which are visible just below the police headquarters skyline feature.

The whole hospital complex and its new large multi-storey car park is seen as a combined feature, but again contained by wooded slopes, while much of the development of the University of Winchester on the lower slope is also hidden.

24 View from the southern viewing point on St Giles' Hill

This is the best distant view of Winchester College chapel and Wolvesey Palace. It is interesting how the tower of the College stands up well as a foreground feature against development at Stanmore and Badger Farm and how important the open spaces between both these developments are in this view.

The wooded slope of Sleepers Hill acts as a background to the Cathedral and this

View from West Hill cemetery, St James' Lane

becomes even more important if one moves up to the classic viewing point on the top of St Giles' Hill. It is noticeable how the western slopes of St Giles' Hill form an area of woodland so close to the centre of the conservation area.

St Cross is isolated as if in the country, with the River Itchen meandering down towards it.

The St Cross Road area can be seen as a wooded feature following the spine of the railway. It shows up again the importance of Bushfield Down fields and its associated tree feature above St Cross and also the broad ridge of farmland over towards Compton in the strategic gap.

The noisy M3 motorway is just visible on the southern side of St Catherine's Hill, but again the memorial beech trees planted along the Roman road to Southampton help to put the motorway firmly in its place in the overall landscape scene.

In the foreground, houses line Chesil Street (The Soke). This scene relates well to Buck's Panorama of 1736.

25 View from West Hill cemetery, St James' Lane

Deacon Hill to the east is a feature in the background to the medieval Winchester College tower, the Victorian Christ Church spire and the central monument in the cemetery itself.

St Catherine's Hill is very dominant in the view out from the cemetery. The individual nature of trees making up the Christchurch Road conservation area become important as they lead down to St Cross, which again looks isolated in what could be a medieval landscape.

The motorway is visible climbing up to the north side of St Catherine's Hill spilling its noise pollution.

Visual Analysis

The topographical setting of Winchester is small-scale with the width of the valley representing the walled town only about 500 metres across. The extremely valuable water meadows north and south of the central area effectively restrict the expansion of the central area as well as affecting its visual character in a positive way.

This makes the small scale of Winchester's conservation area vulnerable to road works, car parks and large scale development.

From this study of the relationship between Winchester and the countryside, it is possible to define the essential setting of Winchester's conservation area within the important countryside beyond. It is this setting which gives Winchester its unique sense of place.

This variety of topography within which Winchester is set has largely determined the history of its development since it was first established as a Roman city and as the Saxon and Norman capital of England.

1 Built up residential areas such as Badger Farm and Stanmore absorb character from the views of the conservation area and the downland countryside beyond. In these suburbs the principal issue is the management of the tree stock which makes such a contribution to disguising the mass of housing as well as adding to the environmental quality of these estates.

2 Areas on ridges, for example, Sleepers Hill, Chilbolton Avenue, Bereweeke Road and Worthy Road have development which is generally at a low density enabling the tree stock to predominate. This creates a particularly high quality setting for the conservation area which has been achieved within the 20th century and therefore now poses new problems of management. The principal issue here is how to manage the tree stock to obtain continuity of forest species without substantial gaps appearing. This could be by neglect and tree loss caused by old age or, more likely, by intense development too close to the trees. In time, this would create a situation where buildings dominate and it would only be smaller trees that people would tolerate so close to their houses. This would have a detrimental affect on the view which one sees at present.

3 Extensive exposed areas of farmland like Easton Down which at present form a distinctive setting to the Cathedral. If any change were to be contemplated through the structure plan system, then it would be essential to plant extensive tree belts to provide both shelter and visual containment. In time a background would be created against which significant buildings like the Cathedral can still maintain their visual predominance, weathering in such a way that stone and lead roofed buildings appear light against trees which look dark.

4 Areas of river valley such as Winnall Moors, downland like St Catherine's Hill, and parts of Bushfield camp are important for nature conservation because they provide areas that do not suffer from modern farming methods.

St Cross Farm, which uses St Cross Park, the water meadows up to Garnier Road and takes in St Catherine's Hill contributes to the management of both water meadows and downland flora and fauna Farmland which covers the area of land on Winnall Moors outside the ownership of the City Council is managed in order to grow hay in conjunction with wildlife management of the streams and wetland.

The land of the butterfly conservation area on Magdalen Down which would be very sensitive to changes on the flatter land at the top of the ridge was purchased by Hampshire County Council and added to the reserve.

5 Bushfield Down. This is a unique area which, although it does not have any distinctive features, nonetheless by virtue of its elevated position on the west side of the valley plays a crucial part in the setting of St Cross, as well as providing a backdrop to the central conservation area. It also represents the best position to appreciate the three principal medieval buildings that give Winchester conservation area its visual character, the Cathedral, Winchester College and St Cross in their original downland setting, still amazingly unaffected by modern development.

If one considers that these three groups of medieval buildings are of both national and European cultural importance, as one of the best surviving groups of pre-reformation institutions, unblemished by subsequent development, then the desirability of retaining this open space – part of their setting – becomes essential and should never be downgraded.

There is constant pressure for development which Winchester has experienced since the conservation area was first designated in the mid-sixties. A motorway has been built of a scale totally different from any previous transport system around Winchester. This motorway is alien to the character of the countryside against which the conservation area is set.

Many of the views into Winchester from the surrounding downs are so important that a case should be made to include them within the conservation area. The views are important both historically and as the setting within which the conservation area is located. If the setting was weakened the conservation area would be severely compromised. The areas of countryside to the north do have protection as they are covered by legislation in the form of 'sites of specific scientific interest'. However these sites do not have the visual impact that the sites to the south and east have.

6 St Catherine's Hill, Plague Pits Valley and the Downs up to the motorway

This is both historically and visually important. Historically as it was amongst the first concentrated Iron Age settlements in the area. This is the site of a medieval chapel used by the Crusaders, a 17th century maze and 17th century plague burial pits. Visually it forms a distinctive outline when viewed from the city. The views into the city from the slopes and summit are also dramatic.

7 Hockley Viaduct and the trees associated with the railway line that this served

Both help to screen the motorway traffic as well as contributing to the peaceful character of the river valley.

8 The Itchen Navigation Canal and associated structures

This is an early canal (started in 1665) making use of some man-made construction and some sections of river which adds significantly to the character of the valley, as distinct from the riverside landscape. The section from Tun Bridge on Garnier Road to its terminus has important trees along its banks.

9 The north and south fields at Bushfield Down

These fields form an important background to the setting of the medieval St Cross Hospital, a remarkable institution still used for the purpose for which it was first built.

Irrespective of any other consideration it should be the aim of both planning and highway policy to maintain the seamless relationship between Winchester and its countryside by landscape means and avoid the downgrading of routes into and out of the town by unnecessary commercial clutter.

Winchester has a timeless relationship with the countryside and it is surprising how well one can still pick up the routes of the basic Roman roads that were imposed on the landscape.

Wherever possible, these routes should be protected by having tree planting along their frontage so that the impact of suburban development is reduced.

Bushfield Down above St Cross church and Hospital

Overview of Winchester's townscape

The history of Winchester's townscape is dramatic. It has lost two Saxon Cathedrals, a major 12th century Abbey, a major Saxon Nunnery with a reputation for education, a Hospital and Chapel for illnesses requiring isolation, four Friaries, 50 Medieval Parish churches, at least four town Gateways, three quarters of its defensive walls, its enormous Castle, its Norman Royal Palace, the Cloisters, Chapter House dormitories and many service buildings of St Swithun's Priory, the medieval Bishop's Palace, and St Giles' medieval fair.

So to what extent is Winchester still a medieval town as compared, for example, with Salisbury with its planned 13th century layout, Cathedral complete with cloisters and Chapter House and completely walled close, or Wells with its medieval layout, Cathedral Cloister and Chapter House, moated Bishop's Palace, Canons Alley and market place still surrounded with extensive numbers of timber framed buildings?

The fact is that the Cathedral, Winchester College and St Cross still dominate the townscape of Winchester because of its small-scale setting. All three are still living institutions. These building groups have extensive gated enclosures and are supported by a range of historical, well-preserved buildings and constructions of various periods.

This legacy is also given added value by the fact that the evolving city has been influenced by features from the Iron Age and the Roman period whilst the road pattern is still basically Saxon.

Although the Saxon street pattern survives substantially intact it had a peculiarity in that the connection between the main spine of the east/west High Street and the side streets used to be by narrow passages as seen on Godson's Map of 1750. When the paving commissioners started work in 1777 these narrow streets were first paved with stone. Since then many of these passages have been widened to accommodate wheeled vehicles. Areas of paving stone remaining can be seen adjacent to the Hampshire Chronicle building and in the Royal Oak Passage.

It is difficult to find or see the Cathedral when one enters the walled town. It is such a dominant building but only when seen from adjacent hills and approach roads. Winchester is not a dramatic place; rather it has a range of quiet architectural qualities which have to be discovered on foot, with dramatic townscape effects occurring at the last minute, for example when one turns the corner into the Close, when one approaches the College tower from the south west, or when visiting the 'viewing point' on St Giles' Hill.

Winchester has been through great social and townscape changes within the last ninety years. Much of the riverside has been reclaimed from industry and housing to provide a landscape amenity. Considerable central area overcrowding and squalor has been replaced by council housing further out at Stanmore, Highcliffe and Weeke with primary schools from the central area following them. Even prime housing sites such as Wharf Hill, St Martin's Close, Eastgate Street, and the Riverside were all redeveloped for local people.

As a consequence by the 1960s, half the housing stock in Winchester was local authority housing. This tends to be overlooked by those assessing the relative wealth of Winchester's inhabitants. Within the central area there was even a pattern of local shopping nodes which included sub-post offices at the Broadway, Chesil Street, Kingsgate Street, Upper High Street, Romsey Road, City Road, Stockbridge Road and St Cross. In addition to the central shops, there was a cattle market on Andover Road with associated businesses.

A huge part of central Winchester was demolished in the 1950s in order to eliminate slums and adjust the town to modern transport, paving the way for new buildings such as multi-storey car parks, shopping centres, bigger offices and a hotel which was considered essential for the development of its economy. A good deal of St John's Street was demolished but luckily Canon Street was saved, even though the Ministry of Housing and Local Government cancelled the listing of eleven of the best properties at the east end of the street in 1962.

Winchester is a compact city with a range of eating and drinking places, with the garrison church on Southgate Street converted to the Screen Cinema and with the rejuvenated Theatre Royal in Jewry Street providing further activities.

From a shopping point of view, Winchester's basic street layout does not give much flexibility. Rents are high; the size of units is often restricted by listed building considerations, limiting the range of goods; and servicing the shops is difficult. However its compactness, character and ancillary facilities make it an attractive place to be in.

The Cathedral is the centre of the diocesan community, functioning as an administrative centre for a large area and a spiritual focus for the Anglican community, and also attracting in the region of 400,000 visitors a year. The nave forms a huge space for concerts as well as providing display areas for constantly changing exhibitions.

The development of the townscape cannot be fully understood without recognising the part played by major landowners which include the following institutions:

1 The Church Commissioners own significant areas of land inside the walled town as well as downland on the outside of Winchester.

2 St John's Charity has a history which goes back to the Saxon period. The Charity was intertwined with the City Council up until the 1850's. They own the freehold of a number of shop and office sites in addition to the land that their four groups of Almshouses occupy. St John's have developed many of their sites and have made major contributions to the city as a whole.

3 Winchester College land within the city walls has been relinquished but the College have since consolidated their ownership in the south east part of the conservation area, and have promoted residential development at Edgar Road, Wharf Hill and Domum Road. The College also has land ownership on the east side including the canal and St Catherine's Hill.

4 Winchester City Council acquired substantial areas of land within the walls during medieval times, and have expanded this further. They promoted a Private Members Bill in the House of Commons in relation to the redevelopment of the Brooks and St George's Street. In 1962 they commissioned the Garten Report with a brief to define buildings in central Winchester that were essential to its character. This formed the basis of a new form of 'Town Scheme Grants' used to fund and help save some key buildings. The city also encouraged a ten year programme of major archaeological excavations between 1960 and 1970. These excavations came under the direction of Professor Martin Biddle from 1970. The city has supported an archaeological section in the continuation of the work, creating a proper base for this and the Museum Service in 72 Hyde Street and its barn in 1976. Recently this facility has been disbanded.

5 Hampshire County Council is the largest employer, with responsibility for education, libraries, archives, transport, social services and many other related matters. Their buildings dominate the west end of the town, and they have built the only post war building within Winchester to be listed. They have also accepted responsibility for the Great Hall of the Castle and the redundant St Thomas's church, a key feature of the central area's silhouette, for which they have provided a new use. Since 1969, they have taken the lead in conservation advice and practice.

Winchester Cathedral

CHAPTER TWO

Access Roads into Winchester

The relationship of Winchester's conservation area to its very special countryside setting can be appreciated by using the extensive footpath network, some of which comes close to the rivers and the canal that pass through the middle.

This is a resource of priceless value from which one can appreciate fully the wide range of native trees, bushes, grasses, flowers and the wild life associated with them, despite the effects of modern farming practices on much of the countryside round about, as well as the effect of the changing light on the landscape through all the seasons.

Figure 1

Information is increasingly being produced by the County Council, such as leaflets on the Clarendon Way, Itchen Way, South Downs Way and by the City Council (Keats Walk), but these are resources still under used by residents and visitors alike. The best way to appreciate Winchester's quality is to walk the footpaths.

Unusually one can still approach Winchester conservation area by car from any direction, without being visually assaulted by the sight of cheap industrial buildings and competing petrol filling stations on either side of the road, all jostling for attention. Planning policies and good owner management have so far ensured that the landscape still predominates.

One can drive from the countryside proper through the suburbs which do not have any better design of housing than those of any other typical county town. The routes in are disguised and modified by roadside trees until one gets close to the conservation area.

These routes are now described in turn, in an anticlockwise direction.

From the north – A34

The Roman road descends from Three Maids Hill, with trees on the western side and farmland on the eastern side until one gets to Park Road which with adjacent land helps to provide the setting of the conservation area (**Figure 1**). Here, there are trees on either side up the hill and over the ridge near Ashbourne Lodge until you cross the railway line where there is a view over the city centre to the Cathedral, backed up with trees inside the old walls of the town (**Figure 2**).

Figure 2

Recently a very ugly individual building adjacent to the railway line has been replaced with a better, modern retail warehouse building, only to be disfigured by large signs at odds with what is normal on other routes into Winchester. Sadly the

Planning Department seem not to have thought of any architectural strategy to make signs a subservient part of the building design.

From the northwest – A272/ B3049

From Stockbridge, you come up the hill from the undulating countryside, passing down a tree-lined road to the suburban centre of Weeke, and then uphill, past the 12th century St Matthew's church and a wooded ridge to Bereweeke Road, before descending again down the gradient where trees have been somewhat eroded by recent development. You are then channelled into Winchester by late Victorian terraced developments, passing under the railway bridge to emerge into the conservation area along the 19th century road created to link the railway into the town near the old Northgate.

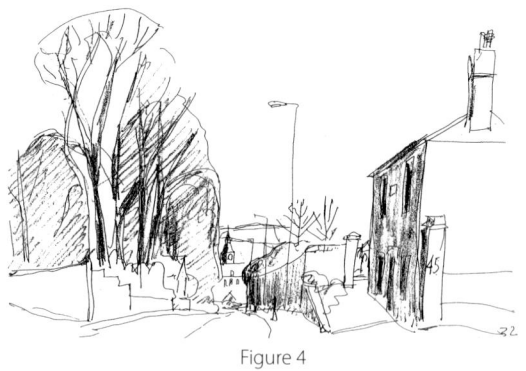

Figure 4

From the west – A3090

From Hursley, going through magnificent countryside, you come uphill to the first roundabout within a setting dominated by trees. A tree-lined ridge leads past a fine beech avenue (**Figure 3**) – with a gap on the other side originally reserved for upgrading to a dual carriageway – until the trees stop with a garden centre and prison car park on the north and the listed six-storey hospital building on the southern side with its clutter of lower out-buildings.

From the south – A33

From the south, on the old Roman road, a glimpse of the medieval building of the Cathedral is seen from a distance. The road then goes up and down along a route lined with beech trees before arriving at the roundabout on the outskirts of Winchester. The route passes over the railway and continues downhill to St Cross. The trees again re-establish themselves through the Christchurch Road suburb which forms a gently twisting route into the centre. The road rises towards the walled town marked by the imposing spire of St Thomas's church, and framed by a very large copper beech tree on the right-hand side.

Figure 3

From the motorway – M3

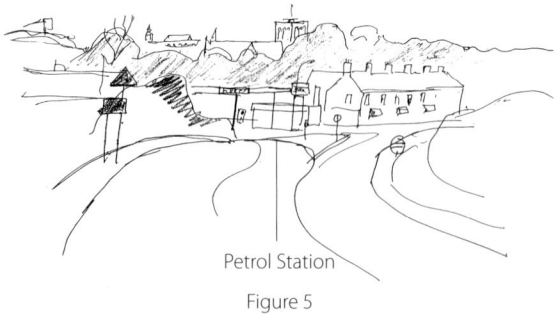

Petrol Station

Figure 5

After this, the trees are re-established on the north with a strong terraced form on the southern side, until one proceeds steeply down West Hill (**Figure 4**) where the beech trees on the left-hand side complement the massive wall of the old cemetery and water reservoir on the right-hand side to frame a view of the Queen Elizabeth II Court, the County Council office with its fine brickwork, tiled roof and clock-tower, silhouetted against the countryside beyond. This all makes a powerful statement at the beginning of the conservation area.

From the motorway, St Catherine's Hill appears at the end of its supporting downland. Approaching along a switchback section it is possible to see the Hockley Viaduct on the left before rising up into the cutting through Twyford Down. Re-emerging on

Figure 6

the other side it peels off downhill with a fine view of the wooded St Giles' Hill in front. The motorway spur brings you to Winchester via a roundabout. This is Bar End where the Cathedral tower with its setting of trees is seen rather uncomfortably over the top of the most garish petrol station in Winchester. Some of these trees are located on the route of the old GWR railway line (**Figure 5**). The route passes along a rather bleak street which could be improved by tree planting before rising over the old GWR railway line into the Soke (**Figure 6**).

Alternatively, if you approach along the Roman road over the hills from Wickham, you have a striking climb between the beech trees on the western side with a south westerly view to Fawley. At the edge of the ridge the road suddenly changes direction to run along the ridge towards St Catherine's Hill. From here there are spectacular views over the whole length of Winchester with the Cathedral at the centre, before plunging down the road with its new tree line.

From the east – A31

Figure 7

This entry into Winchester has a whole sequence of views; the approach is along the Roman road, now a dual carriageway, which terminates at the Morn Hill roundabout, the start of Magdalen Down (**Figure 7**). The road splits to the right where the original road runs along the ridge into Winchester, or left, a more gentle Victorian route that passes down into the valley. The motorway now cuts through with the scarp of Magdalen Down (the Butterfly Reserve) on the right-hand side and opposite an opening onto farmland.

Returning to Magdalen ridge, the route passes the municipal cemetery established in 1916 with its cover of trees and then emerges along the ridge with views out to the countryside. This Roman road is marked by a sequence of fine beech trees (**Figure 8**).

Figure 8

After passing Victoria Hospital and St Swithun's School and onto Magdalen Down, you suddenly come across the bridge over the gash of the motorway. Here you can appreciate the wooded outline of St Giles' Hill with St Catherine's Hill away to the south west and the long stand of beech trees sheltering the Winnall estate (**Figure 9**).

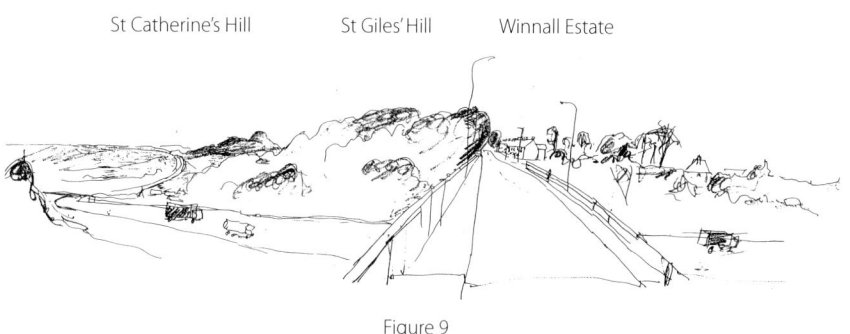

Figure 9

This suburban route continues toward the town centre and still has fine trees, though these are missing in places where modern houses have been built. In some cases small trees have been planted but in other cases, where there is a service road, it should be possible to re-establish a tree line into Winchester (**Figure 10**).

Figure 10

The road then proceeds downhill passing a steep bank on the left. There are Victorian terrace houses on the right past which glimpsed views of Winchester can be seen where the road abruptly swings left.

Here you have a particularly fine three quarter view of the Cathedral with a whole range of typical townscape features on display that make up the character of central Winchester. You see the wooded backcloth of Sleepers Hill, the spire of St Thomas's church, the varied rooflines of buildings, chimneys and individual trees (**Figures 11, 12**).

Figure 11

Figure 12

The steep descent passes down the wooded slopes of St Giles' Hill on the left but provides a view out to St Catherine's Hill with a foreground of residential buildings in the Soke which, in townscape terms, mark another bend directly into the urban streets of Winchester leading to the bridge over the River Itchen.

Winnall entrance – M3 Motorway

This route passes along an avenue of trees which frame the Cathedral tower before plunging abruptly over a scarp where the whole three quarter length of the Cathedral is picked up rising above buildings from the 15th to the 20th centuries (**Figure 13**).

Figure 13

An entirely new road layout proposal associated with extensive car parking on the water meadows was rejected following a public enquiry in 1976. The road now has to wriggle downhill past an area of light industrial buildings and ends up aiming at Parmeter House, a five-storey building that as a townscape feature guards the access to the town without achieving any architectural distinction.

At the last moment the road swings round this building and the listed First In Last Out public house, to pass through an area of three-storey buildings of which those on the left hand side are not of any distinction but those on the right have succeeded in recreating the townscape quality of a medieval street as a foreground to the Cathedral in a simple and direct way (**Figures 14, 15 & 16**).

Finally, the road turns over the River Itchen across a brick causeway, recently constructed to mark the County Council's centenary, which replaced an 18th century mill demolished in 1967 but leaving hatches for water control. The sight of the Cathedral is lost, and the landscape is once more dominated by local riverside trees before passing through what was the Durngate into the town (**Figure 17**).

Figure 14

Figure 15

Figure 16

Figure 17

Conclusion

There are signs that this seamless transformation between the countryside and the centre of town is being eroded by developers who fail to understand the very special nature of the setting of Winchester, and the features required to maintain this.

The highway authority should be made aware of the importance of the valuable landscape along the access routes into Winchester, and adopt a policy of planting trees. It should be a matter of planning policy when negotiating on sites affecting these access routes to protect and reinforce the way in which trees frame the view of people arriving into Winchester. This will help to maintain the sensitive but very important setting of the Winchester conservation area.

Winchester City Centre Map

Northern area (top of map):
- Tumbling Bay, River
- Pol Sta (Police Station)
- Coun Offs, Tower Street, Sussex Street
- Liby (Library), North Walls
- PW markers throughout
- F Sta (Fire Station)
- Durngate Pl
- Wales Street, Moss Road, Ebden
- Beggar's Lane, St Martin's Close
- St John's Road

Central streets:
- Cross St, Staple Gardens, B3040 Jewry Street
- St Peter Street, Parchment Street
- Upper Brook Street (B3331), Middle Brook Street, Lower Brook Street
- Park Avenue, Union Street, Lawn St
- St George's Street (B3040), B3331
- Cross, Car Park, Friarsgate
- HPO, Tanner St, Offices (B3331)
- St Clement Street (B3335), High Street
- Bus Sta, Eastgate Street, Water Lane
- Blue Ball Hill, Chester Rd
- St John's St, Magdalen Hill
- Tunnel (dis)

Cathedral/Close area:
- The Square, Market Lane, The Broadway
- Mus (Museum), War Meml
- VENTA BELGARVM
- Old Minster, Cathedral
- Statue, YH
- St Thomas Street, Southgate St, Symonds Street
- Close Wall, St Swithun's Priory (remains of)
- 35m, Coun Offs, Iss
- G Hall, Bridge St (B3404)
- Colebrook Street
- Recn Gd
- **The Soke**
- Sks, Chesil Street (B3330)

Southern area:
- Deanery, **The Close**
- Castle Wall, Wolvesey Castle
- St Cross Road, Friary G, Canon Street
- St Swithun Street
- PW, Sch
- Close Wall
- Wolvesey Palace
- Castle Wall Paths, Path
- Culver Road, Kingsgate Street
- PO, College Street
- St Michael's Rd, Eastcliffe Rd
- Highcliffe Rd, Canute Rd
- Meml, PW
- FB, Wharf
- Hare Hill
- St Catherine's

CHAPTER THREE

The Walled City – 1: High Street/Southgate Street area

Winchester High Street (Magno Vico)

In origin this is a straight Roman street running from the bridge over the River Itchen and the associated Eastgate of the walled town up to the Westgate adjacent to the fortified camp on the high ground at the other side of town. Following the collapse of the Roman Empire the strategic layout of Winchester did not really change, so that the fort became the castle and the walls and gates remained in the same position. However the street has become subtly changed over time to a meandering route so that one cannot see from one end to the other. But with modern development, the sword of King Alfred in the Broadway relates visually to the cupola on Barclays Bank and the fleche on top of the clocktower of Queen Elizabeth II Court.

The subtle change in geometry enables the street to be a continuous entity that creates the backbone of central Winchester both visually and as the main street for shopping and professional services. It also reads as a strong townscape feature when seen from St Giles' Hill.

All sections of the street are affected by its east/west orientation with the strong contrast of light and shade depending on the sun's movement. And yet it falls into distinctive sections each with different characteristics. This was emphasised when the narrow central section was pedestrianised in 1974.

The Broadway

The Broadway (earlier known as Cheap Street), which is the main point of arrival, was created in its present form about 1800 when a whole street was demolished to reveal the town house of Mr Pescod, the Winchester Recorder, now Abbey House. Abbey House was given a new battlemented front and became the Mayor's House

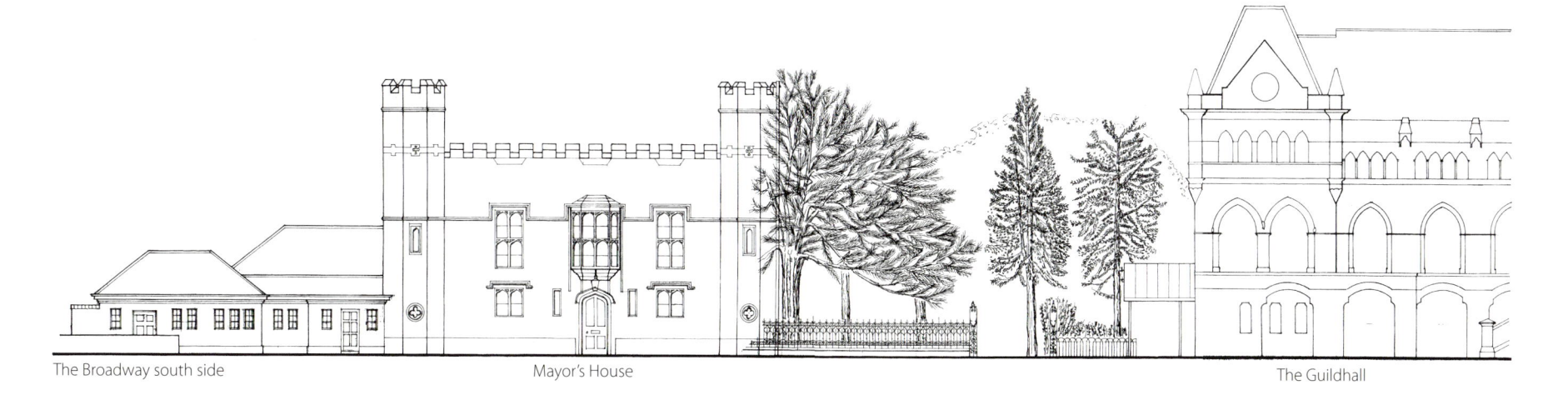

The Broadway south side   Mayor's House   The Guildhall

after the grounds had been acquired for pleasure gardens. A major water feature of the old High Street was moved southwards thus creating the potential for the elliptical form that is its present shape. At the eastern end, the continuity of the urban design was reformed with the development of the fine Almshouses at St John's South with their gothic gateway in 1834, and the speculative development opposite undertaken after the demolition of Mildmay (Eastgate) House in 1847. The elaborate gardens were subdivided to provide a group of townhouses, three with shops on the ground floor, together with the creation of Eastgate Street parallel to the river, with a hotel and shop on the corner and some residential units.

St John's Hospital South, mid 19th century, lithograph by Owen Browne Carter

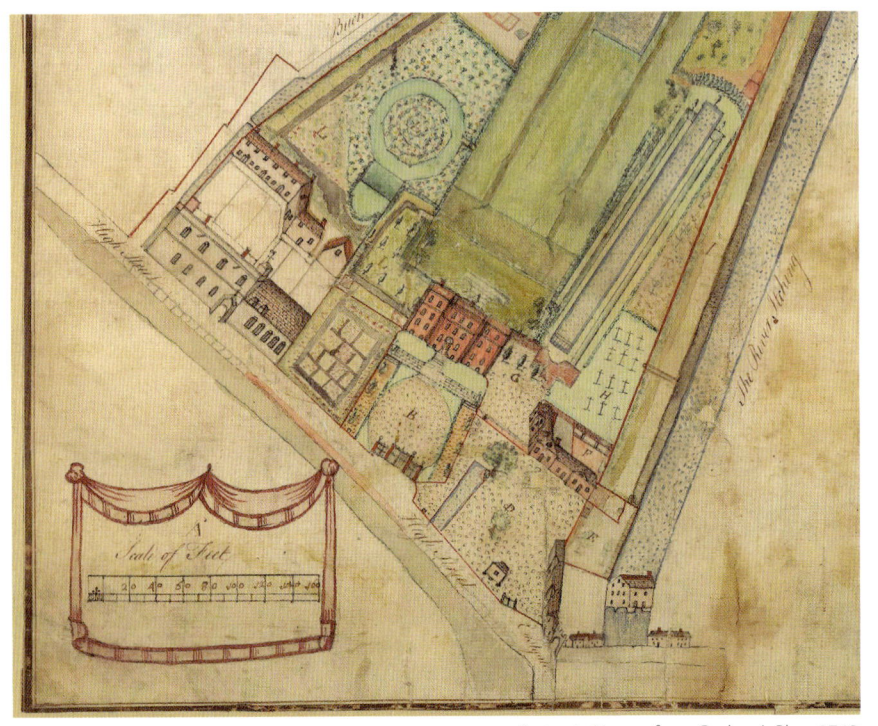

Eastgate House, from Godson's Plan, 1748

St John's House, first floor assembly room. Lecture to Archaeological Institute, 1845

The Broadway is the only part of the High Street to have tree planting on either side and is now dominated by St John's House and its chapel. These buildings have been continuously modified since their origins as a 13th century hospital and then developed as important buildings for the governing of the city. In 1769 a new first floor assembly room was added. In 1873 a new Guildhall was built opposite and St John's House reverted back to St John's Trustees.

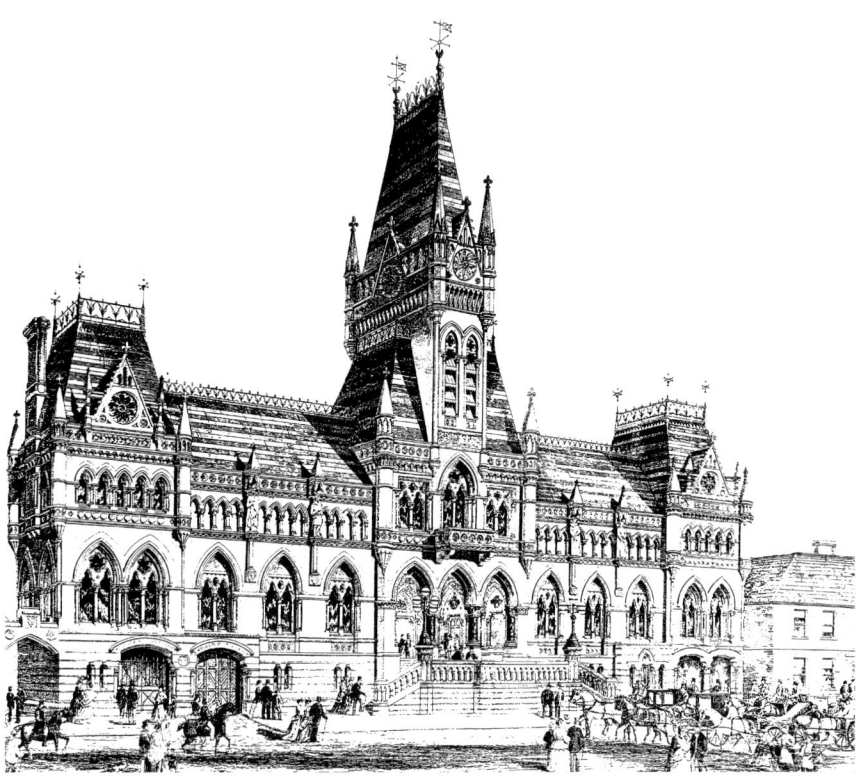

Perspective sketch of the Guildhall 1873

The Guildhall has a first floor entrance and steps forming a platform for formal civic occasions. It is interesting that its clock tower is a feature that is designed to be particularly effective in three quarter perspective viewed from east and west in the High Street, where it is seen against the hill, rather than on the north/south axis.

A key feature is the statue of King Alfred by Hamo Thornycroft erected in 1901. The statue is seen against the wooded hillside of St Giles' Hill and from the diminishing perspective views from the High Street.

On the south side, enclosure of the street at pedestrian level is made by a very handsome and elegant set of cast iron railings to Abbey Gardens. They were put there in 1890 by Richard Moss, a popular Winchester MP and benefactor, to replace the original walls now that the gardens had been opened to the public. This was once the site of a major medieval Abbey, St Mary's, which was demolished by Henry VIII. It is now a public space in which one can enjoy peace away from the bustle of the street and obtain a view of the east end of the Cathedral.

Colebrook Street West to Market Street

The second section of the High Street from Colebrook Street west to Market Street is more or less parallel to Market Lane, with a three-storey development on the south side contrasting with the more irregular features of the north side which include listed buildings from medieval times. These were starting to be replaced in the 1930s by mostly undistinguished commercial buildings with living accommodation over some of them.

This section of the street is terminated by the 18th century design of 25/26 High Street with its windows looking towards St Giles' Hill, now painted and often sunlit. This projects into the street marking the position of the kitchen of the Royal Palaces in the Saxon and early medieval period. It also marks a cross street from Upper Brook Street through to Market Street, site of the medieval Thomas Gate. On the south side this gives access to the Cathedral Close.

Pedestrian section

The third, narrowest section of the street is very uniform in scale and visually dominated by the Grade II* group of buildings with irregular skyline incorporating the late medieval planned form of the covered 'Pentice'. It contains the most important 15th century timber buildings to remain and the distinguished early 20th century building for Boots the chemist that respects the town form in this area. The opposite side of the street is mostly undistinguished architecturally apart from the Arts & Crafts building for W H Smith. The policy of asking for three dimensional shop signs has started to add a touch of visual interest above fascia level appropriate to an historic town.

Upper part of pedestrian section

The street widens out again and climbs up the hill quite steeply towards the medieval Westgate which can now been seen clearly at the end of the street. It is subdivided by cross traffic at the widened staggered junction of Southgate Street and Jewry Street. The eastward part of this section up to Southgate Street contains a wealth of the most important listed buildings in a range of architectural styles on both sides of the street, including three original shop fronts. Tucked into the south east corner is the 15th century Buttercross with its raised steps, pinnacles and sculptures, which helps to reinforce the medieval character of this corner with the adjacent timber framed buildings almost touching it. Alongside it the intriguing covered passageway leads through to the Square and the Cathedral Close with its lime avenue leading

spot in the High Street most favoured by protesters, musicians, buskers, morris and country dancing teams. It is also the site of the christmas tree. People of all ages enjoy sitting on the Buttercross watching others perambulate.

Further west and as a the result of widening to accommodate buses and modern traffic flows, the street surprisingly opens in to a square at the end of Jewry Street. This was formed as a result of the demolition in the 1950s of the splendid ancient coaching inn, the George Hotel, together with some adjacent buildings, replaced by the Neo-Georgian Barclays Bank building in 1956. This looks very much like a town hall in its design with a cupola on top of the entrance forming a townscape feature of significance. It was never thought of as a building which should provide architectural interest to 'turn the corner' or to provide a continuation of the shopping frontage at pedestrian level in the High Street.

High Street with Buttercross, by F P Barraud c. 1880

The 15th century Buttercross, drawing by Owen Browne Carter c. 1830

to the 14th century perpendicular west front of the Cathedral.

This section of the street which has some of the feel of a square is made exciting by the dark boldly cantilevered form of the 18th century clock that contrasts visually with the sunlit buildings on the north side and the double bow window and the painted brickwork of No 107 opposite the Buttercross which architecturally forms a hinge point for the eastern part of the street.

The space in front of the Buttercross contained stocks in medieval times, a pump up to the 18th century, a postbox in the 20th century and is a natural central meeting place, which the Town Crier still makes use of. It is now the

Statue of a horse and rider by Elisabeth Frink

Uphill towards the Westgate

After Southgate Street the road runs more steeply uphill and the street has a varied but moderate set of buildings on both sides containing some good listed buildings. Three quarters of the way up the street is broken by two spaces, that on the south side containing three weeping limes planted in 1980 to replace a huge holm oak that had become dangerous. The space also contains the Frink statue of a horse and rider, paid for by subscriptions from architects of Hampshire, and opposite an urban stepped paved area. This replaced the lawn of what used to be a surgeon's house erected in the 19th century and now marks an important pedestrian route through to the County Offices.

The High Street continues with three-storey buildings on both sides that visually frame the medieval Westgate through which one gets a glimpse of Romsey Road outside the walls beyond, opening up on the north side to allow traffic to circulate. This 'bypass' implemented in 1956 is dominated by the formal design of the red brick County Council offices of Queen Elizabeth II Court that is now a listed building and the more recent Mottisfont Court. The group of buildings next to the Westgate on the south east side are part of a major redevelopment by the architect Donald Insall that retained the centre of two of the original buildings and wrapped the new additions around them.

Westgate from the South East, c. 1800, unknown artist

The reverse journey West to East

Approaching the High Street from the west, the arches of the Westgate frame the street visibly as far down as the Buttercross with the Guildhall appearing over a varied roofscape. This view ends with St Giles' Hill where the historic viewing point is framed by forest trees. Moving down the street the 18th century clock becomes more important and is itself seen against the background of St Giles' Hill before you pass under it to arrive at the Buttercross. Here the buildings shut out the distant view, until it opens up through the central section adjoining the Pentice into the widening Broadway. The route out of town becomes constricted again as it passes over the narrow 18th century stone bridge beside the City Mill reconstructed in the same period, together with its flanking buildings.

One of the magical views of Winchester, where the trees on St Giles' Hill lit up by the southern and western sun used to come right down to the bridge, was lost when development was carried out on the railway line in 1978.

Barclays Bank

Royal Oak Passage

High Street north side
Jewry Street junction to St Peter Street

St Peter Street

High Street north side from Parchment Street towards Middle Brook Street

Upper Brook Street

Cross Keys Passage

Bus Station

High Street north side from Cross Keys Passage to Bus Station

Summary from a design point of view

The High Street is still the only street apart from the narrow North Walls where one can walk from one end of the walled town to the other. Although this only takes fifteen minutes the variety of the different sections, the character of many buildings in different styles, the wide range of materials used (though brick and tile predominates) and the varying natural lighting make this a fascinating experience, particularly if you also look above ground floor level.

Most importantly, the buildings are designed on quite narrow frontages typical of a medieval town. This combined with a very large number of vertical components contained within their design both above and below fascia level is an important component of the character and rhythm of the street. The elevations to the street are punctuated at regular intervals by a wide variety of strong gabled roof forms from medieval to the classical pedimented form, including some Dutch brick gable ends.

As an example the 1980s gabled building to replace the bland International Stores on the corner with Upper Brook Street (now occupied by Laura Ashley) does respect the historic rhythm and pattern, and introduces quirky features with its fenestration and balconettes that contribute interest to the overall pattern of the street. From the Cathedral Close the repeated gables attract attention, as well as forming an important foreground to the Cathedral seen from Upper Brook Street.

Where new replacement buildings have not been designed to take note of these principles of rhythm and style, they have noticeably devalued the character of the street. For example, Marks & Spencer's westward extension and 9-11 High Street where the 19th century Mercantile Stores of James Cooper had infinitely more character than the supermarket of a similar scale and floor area that surprisingly replaced it in the 1960s, as can be seen particularly in the acute three-quarter view. This is because the modelling of the vertical elements on the original is so much stronger and the powerful horizontal effect of the first floor window on the replacement is entirely out of place.

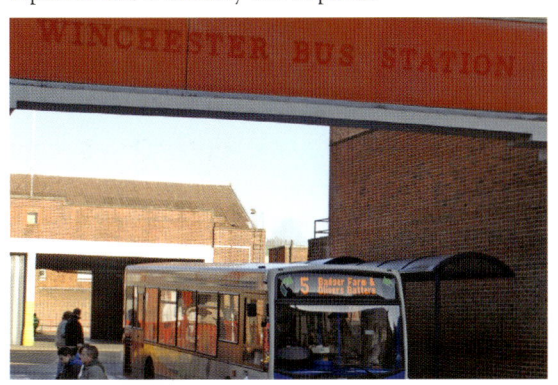

The gap provided to give egress from the bus station for double decker buses in the 1930s destroyed the continuity of the street, even though the buildings have some detail and have been increased in scale to three stories, to form an architectural 'frame' to try to compensate for the 'gap'. The bus station seen through the gap is unattractive and depressing, but the whole site is currently the subject of planning negotiations. Hopefully there will be a major improvement to an area desperately in need of regeneration.

The 1990s building on the site of Woolworths (118-121 High Street) uses good materials for pitched roofs and walls, and introduces more architectural rhythm than its bland flat-roofed predecessor. It is however very indifferent in its handling of architectural detail to the windows and the frames separating the shopfronts and just does not live up to the important position that this frontage occupies within the street.

Southgate Street (Goldestret)

Historically Southgate Street was always an important, mostly level, street on high ground leading from the Roman South Gate to the High Street, although the modern position of the street is slightly further east. For centuries the street would have been dominated by the Castle on its mound to the west. In modern times it is predominantly a commercial street.

Serle's House, Southgate Street

In the 17th century, after the Civil War which led to the Castle's demolition, land alongside Southgate Street was acquired for King Charles II to act as a parkland setting for his proposed new palace on the Barracks site. When this was

Grand staircase in Serle's House

abandoned in 1685, four fine new houses (long since demolished) were built at the start of the 18th century which are clearly illustrated in Buck's panorama of 1736 and Godson's map of 1750. The latter still shows garden land until Serle's House was built in 1748 for the Sheldon family. It was not until the very narrow Southgate was demolished at the end of the 17th century that it became a major road. This street, in typical Saxon fashion, had distinct narrowing between St Clement's Street and the High Street where there were inns like the Black Swan. This was widened first in the early 19th century on the east side, then in the 1950s on the west side.

Since the early 19th century the eastern side has been steadily infilled with a series of early and late 19th century town houses with railings in front. The last timber framed house was on the site of the 'Green Man' and was demolished when Stopher designed the present public house around 1886.

The western side has had a more chequered history, first with a building for the local militia erected on the line of the old Saxon Gar Street behind Serle's House (a building later used by the judges sitting in the court in the Great Hall). In 1845 St Thomas's church was moved from its site in St Thomas Street to a much larger site to the south of Serle's House built to the design of EW Elmslie. Then the lower barracks was built with its guardhouse on one side of the church, a school/chapel and headmaster's house on the other side and a four-storey barrack block adjacent to the militia building overshadowing Serle's House entrance, by now acquired by the Army. At the south end there was a substantial stables joined to a Victorian brewery. The stables later became a motor car repair garage with a showroom in front.

Approaching from the south a three-storey 18th century building opposite a 19th century composite terrace marks the medieval Southgate but the dominant spire of St Thomas's church has replaced the gate in townscape terms, signalling from afar a distinct change between the suburbs and the inner city. This gains in

St Thomas's church

importance as you progress northwards, past the car showroom and the Screen Cinema, converted from the garrison church, only to find that it is, in fact, set back away from the road behind its own lawn and plane trees. At this point the Guardhouse to the Lower Barracks becomes the important visual feature.

Guardhouse: entrance to the Barracks

After the Guardhouse there is now a formal space in front of Serle's House, which Pevsner rates as the most ambitious 18th century house in Winchester. The building was designed by Thomas Archer, together with its interesting interior. This space was rearranged after the second world war by taking down the mature lime trees and the boundary wall on Southgate Street, creating a bus layby, and building formal entrance gates to produce a memorial garden to the Hampshire Regiment. Its formal setting of trees includes evergreens to help blot out the Law Courts. Since the original main entrance to Serle's House had been rather overshadowed by the Lower Barracks, a new entrance was designed on the semi-basement floor by the architect, Peter Sawyer, to complete the formal memorial garden with its central flagpole. This garden, in turn, is bounded on its northern side by the three-storey Grade II* Hotel du Vin erected in 1712. The building was converted into a hotel with a new extension in the 1930s, and rejuvenated and extended again at the back in the 1990s, by taking in the eastern section of the barracks leading up to the militia building. The Hotel du Vin is a fine house that was only just saved from collapse by having a frame put inside it in the 1970s. This is followed by a three-storey terrace of rather less significance which has been saved by rebuilding the end property onto St Clement Street to form a 'book end' to the whole terrace. During rebuilding an opportunity was taken to incorporate blind window openings, to improve the appearance of St Clement Street. No 8 has the only art nouveau railings in Winchester.

Hotel du Vin

Green Man public house post-1886 and pre-1886

Returning to the site of the Southgate, on the east side is the Green Man public house and Devenish House (three storeys) with a modern glass infill on its north side between it and the adjacent Victorian terrace giving a hint of the surprisingly modern building on backland, which has curved balconies and a high level glazed sitting room. The building was designed and built by Plincke Leaman & Browning for St John's Trustees. It is partly a new building grafted onto a refurbished one, the whole complex now a purpose built nursing home. In front of this infill in Southgate Street, there is an excellent example of a small tree that gives added quality to the street in an unpromising situation.

Adjacent to this, going north are two terraces of different heights forming Chernocke Place, both designed by Owen Browne Carter in about 1848 in yellow brick and stucco and now separated from each other by a projecting office building, replacing a single-storey car showroom in the 1970s. Although Meadow House was constructed in brickwork that is much too dark to make an attractive building, it links the two terraces better than a flat building would.

The northern terrace of four townhouses is the more elaborate of the two in its detailing (No 35 still retains its fine internal lotus-leaf plasterwork). After the war the porches on this terrace were demolished to save repair costs and reinstated by the Winchester Preservation Trust with help from English Heritage in the 1970s. After the first world war the Employment Exchange was sited here and queues would stretch along Southgate Street, and down the High Street as far as the Buttercross and men would cycle after delivery lorries hoping for payment to unload them.

North of this the three-storey Fiennes House is one of the few buildings in Winchester to make extensive use of terracotta as a building material, and was originally built for the Hampshire Club in order to provide a meeting and dining place for lawyers during the course of trials at the Law Courts.

This marks the position of the medieval St Thomas' Passage which steps down from Southgate Street and provides for the public a splendid distant view of the west elevation of Winchester Cathedral arising over the roofs of other houses and also seen against the backcloth of St Giles' Hill beyond.

Two doors to the north is an early 18th century townhouse with side wings (similar to 26/27 St Swithun Street) now sadly subdivided into three units. Further north again, opposite the Hotel du Vin, is an 1870s Victorian terrace which shows the change that comes about when buildings use materials brought in by the railway from elsewhere in the country. This terrace contains an excellent shop-front in the art nouveau style which complements the railings on the other side of the street.

Further north again, the varied height and detail of the buildings is interesting. This section of the street is greatly enhanced by the attractive window of No 11 and the hanging scissor sign above. The street ends with a building by Owen Browne Carter in the Egyptian style which makes a strong statement on the High Street corner.

The western side was widened to improve traffic flow in the 1930s leaving a set back terrace of shops in neo-Georgian style with two floors of offices above (now converted into flats), only the carving of the Black Swan on the corner being saved from the demolished stuccoed inn.

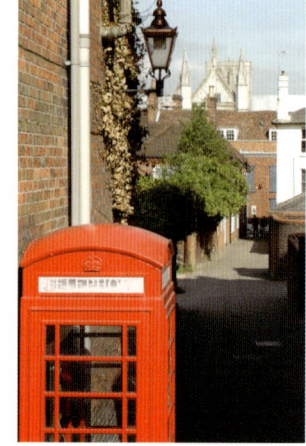

Nursing Home entrance, Southgate Street

Chernocke Place

Telephone box by Giles Gilbert Scott at top of St Thomas' Passage

Southgate Street shops, east side

Chernocke Place

The Walled City – 2: St Swithun Street/St Thomas Street area

St Swithun Street

St Swithun Street is a residential street, squeezed in between the line of the old city wall and a two and a half storey high outer close wall.

Looking down St Swithun Street to Prior's Gate

The western end starts in Southgate Street just inside the city gate adjacent to the Green Man public house. On the south side of St Swithun Street the corner is made by a set back three-storey office building built in the 1960s with cheap, badly stained, calcium silicate bricks, very thinly detailed aluminium sash windows, weak sills and a mock Mansard roof trying to disguise the fact that it is really a three-storey building – the whole a quite unsatisfactory design for such a prominent position. In the parking area underneath there is a flint panel marked out which, in fact, is the line of the city wall adjacent to the Roman Southgate.

Walking down St Swithun Street, three-storey buildings frame attractive views out to the downland beyond Chilcomb. The street then widens out into the start of St Thomas Street where the white painted 17th century cottages form an arresting block before the street narrows down again and looks onto the Close wall. Here visible over the top of the wall are a number of large trees in the gardens which link up with those of Wolvesey Palace. The medieval Prior's Gate closes the east end of the street.

The road slopes downward towards the east with the Cathedral boundary wall on the north side. At the eastern end is the 14th century Prior's Gate made of flint and stone with battlements and a grey, weathered oak gate under a stone arch. The gate still retains a horse mounting block to one side and has a coat of arms over the arch.

Looking back through this gate during the day (it is still closed at 10.00 p.m. every night) one sees the long, slightly wavy line of the Close wall made of rough coursed flints with a clay tiled capping on the north side of St Swithun Street. The wall is devalued by a row of insensitive lamp standards. It terminates at the southern bay of the 17th century mellow red brick almshouses with clay tiled roofs and distinctive diagonal chimney stacks. Here the road makes a little jig southwards before rising uphill into the western section.

The trees in the Close gardens top the wall, visually linking up with the trees planted on the old castle mound on the other side of Southgate Street. It is also just possible to see the spire of St Thomas's church on the right hand side.

When the sun is shining, the silhouette of the houses and their chimneys on the south side of the street make a strong pattern of shadow across the road and up the Close wall.

On the left hand side of the street is a good range of unlisted two-storey buildings, mostly representing different 19th century dates and styles. These buildings have retained their original materials and detail including a pleasing chimney-scape.

The area was badly damaged during the Civil War. Three houses at the east end have recently replaced a two-storey light industrial building and the old Winchester College Yard has been replaced by another new building. This whole terrace has been given vitality by the three-storey rendered and painted building at No 5 with its attached stable block. The most important building, three quarters of the way along, is a splendid 17th century listed building, St Aethelwolds, with a fine doorcase. This house incorporates part of the city wall at its rear and it has a little garden on the western side over which one can see the three-storey Hamilton House in Canon Street.

Outside the Prior's Gate at the eastern end is a little medieval space dominated by the three-storey listed 18th century brick town house with parapet and sash windows, built against the tile hung stair to St Swithun's church. This is located over the Kings Gate which leads to Kingsgate Street and College Street.

Brick pedestrian arches were inserted either side of the stone gateway in the 18th century to facilitate the constant pedestrian traffic. Underneath the left hand arch a shop has incorporated a delightful 18th century bow window recycled from the old George Hotel on the site of Barclay's Bank. At night the light in the shop radiates a distinctive pattern of lines from the glazing bars which becomes an added attraction.

No. 5 St Swithun Street with stable

St Swithun upon Kingsgate

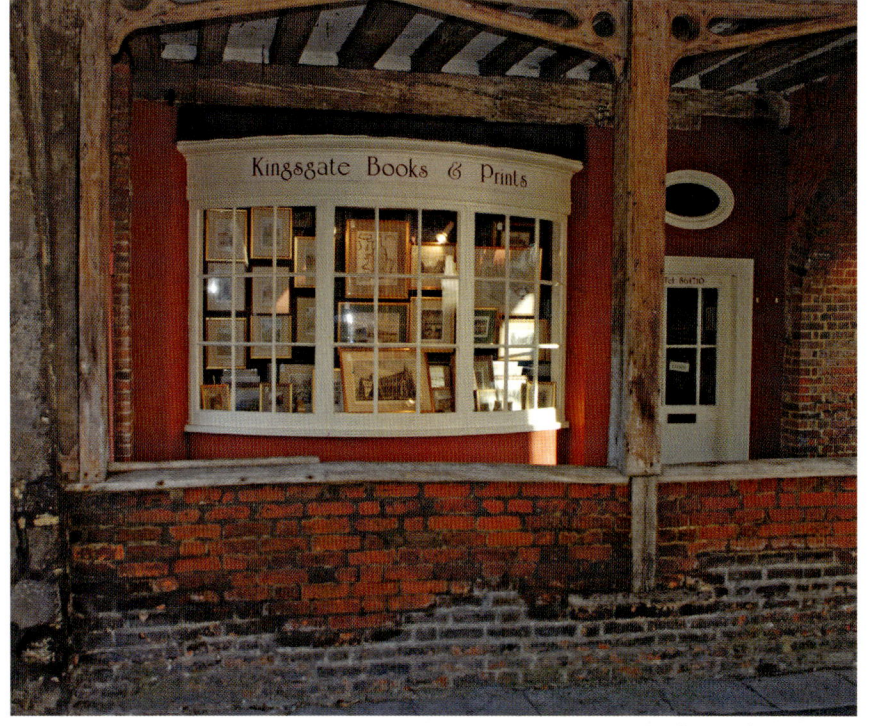

St Aethelwolds

Shop under Kingsgate

Christs Hospital

Wayneflete House

Christs Hospital Almshouses

Christs Hospital gardens, Symonds Street

Walking up towards Symonds Street and arriving at Christs Hospital you look north along the return Close wall of Symonds Street to the trees and the striped brick and stone wall of Minster House. Facing Symonds Street is the 18th century Wayneflete House set back from St Swithun Street where the road bends before climbing up the western section to Southgate Street.

Looking up this section of Symonds Street, a pair of neo-Georgian houses has been inserted on the left; there is also a glimpse of the back of the houses in Canon Street and the wonderful copper beech tree in the garden of Beech House, which is part of the end of the 17th century town house which terminates St Thomas Street.

On the right the almshouses have a very strong gabled end with diaper patterned dark headers in brickwork incorporating a wall plaque. At the back of the almshouses one gets a glimpse of the powerful 17th century projecting stone chimneys with rebuilt diagonal brick shafts above.

Moving westwards there is the original stable block to No 11 St Thomas Street which in the 1970s housed an arab horse which was exercised in the garden! Following this building is the gable wall of the 17th century cottages which form the beginning of St Thomas Street. At this point, diagonally opposite, is the main entrance to the 1980s Lions Court, a brick-built housing scheme for older people, arranged around an internal courtyard which now occupies the site of one of Winchester's original car repair garages. This building does recreate the street scene but has its corners chopped off to comply with the road engineer's requirements. Within St Swithun Street the repeated gables help to integrate this large building into the street scene, and at low level the railings add some interest. The street finishes at the Southgate end with a brick and stone stable block, beyond which can be glimpsed the totally surprising aluminium-clad form of the extension to a nursing home in Southgate Street and, beyond it, the cupola on Barclays Bank in Jewry Street. Finally, the confident design of the Green Man public house, designed by Thomas Stopher, with its decorative dormer windows gives emphasis to the corner entrance. Closing the vista on the other side of Southgate Street is the end gable of the cinema, formerly the Garrison church, and the gables of the housing beyond.

St Thomas Street (Calpe Street)

This is Winchester's finest cross street, starting at Lloyds Bank in the High Street (the old Guildhall) with its bell tower from which the curfew bell is still rung every night. This forms a vertical feature in the High Street but, with its white boarding, domed lead roof and fine weathervane projecting from a distinctive lead ball finial, is an important landmark in St Thomas Street, both in views from the south and from nearby buildings in Southgate Street.

St Swithun Street seen from the southern end of St Thomas Street

The High Street seen from St Thomas Street

The street curves subtly toward the west, dips down to Minster Lane, rises again and dips down to St Swithun Street where it ends in Nos 26 and 27 St Swithun Street, a three-storey brick town house with wings put up in 1730, over a great cellar which takes advantage of the steep change in levels. Built on the line of the southern town wall, it was originally one dwelling. It has not been a single house for some time and it now has an Edwardian projecting bay window (almost identical to one on the back of Pilgrims School) with 18th century doors on either side, in place of its original entrance.

St Thomas Street is a street of mixed use with commercial buildings at the north end and residential at the south. There have been planning problems over the need for parking to encourage continued residential use of large houses, while trying to limit parking that would be damaging to the character of gardens attached to offices.

St Thomas Street is lined by a whole series of fine listed buildings dating from the late 17th and 18th centuries which replaced medieval buildings at the north end, although in the garden wing of No 24 there is the 11th century vaulted undercroft that was used as a mint.

View of St Thomas Street from the gardens of Nos. 23/24

The listed buildings south of St Clement Street mostly retain their beautiful walled gardens. These enable wonderful specimen trees to grow, such as the copper beech seen over the new garage courtyard to No 24 and the sinuous forms of the weeping ash in No 23. It is noticeable in the street scene that the large cupressus in St Thomas graveyard and the ash tree and robinia in No 10 frame views along the street each way, although considerably separated by the distance between. From the north the cupressus makes a wonderful jagged silhouette behind the roofs of No 23. The walled gardens also ensure that a number of buildings are seen as three dimensional villas rather than in their terraced form; this is essential to the character of the immediate townscape. No 12 has decorative pedimented features to its walls on either side of its entrance elevation.

Looking in more detail at the north end: opposite Lloyds Bank is a very fine 19th century building, with a turret to turn the corner and projecting two-storey gabled bays in a timber framed wall. This was erected by the architect Thomas Stopher to accommodate the Dolphin public house and some ground floor shops with residential units above. The fire surround from the interior of the medieval timber framed building that used to exist on this corner was moved to the boardroom over the gateway of St John's Hospital South.

The Dolphin Inn

In the 1980s this building and its neighbours in the High Street were refurbished by the architects Plincke Leaman & Browning for St John's Charity in order to provide better long term income. In the process they converted the public house to a shop, reinstated traditional shopfronts along St Thomas Street and created a two-level courtyard behind of some character in place of a squalid yard. This permits the High Street shops to increase in depth and has the effect of providing separate access to upper-floor areas for residential and office use doubling up as a fire escape. It is interesting to note that this is a rare example of a refurbished mixed use scheme in the late 20th century.

On the opposite, east, side of St Thomas Street there is a row of 17th century cottages in one of which John Lingard, historian and Catholic priest, was born in 1771. A break was made to this side of the street in the 1930s so that motor traffic could circulate between Little Minster Street and St Thomas Street without having to negotiate the very narrow Saxon lanes into the High Street. This break has now revealed a view of a timber framed wall and the twin gables of buildings in Little Minster Street. In the reverse direction there is a better view of the attractive front of No 24 St Thomas Street and its splendid Tuscan door case. This is the house in which Cromwell is reputed to have received the keys of Winchester Castle after his successful siege in 1645.

No. 24 St Thomas Street

The next block on the east side of St Thomas Street used to contain, amongst other things, the Bendicks chocolate factory. When this moved out to the Winnall Trading Estate the City Council acquired it and the frontage in St Thomas Street, with the idea of building a museum. Instead, however, it was decided to draw up a development brief for the area including a vacant section of Little Minster Street and a section of St Thomas Street which had become very dilapidated.

This went out to competition for mixed use development in the early 1980s and resulted in a high density scheme by the architects, Plincke Leaman & Browning, who produced the best analysis and perspectives to show how the townscape would be respected and developed. The scheme was implemented to provide offices, town houses, flats and two corner shops. This also rejuvenated King's Head Yard to serve as a paved service area with its own plane tree, seat and decorative lamp-post on the north side. Twenty years later this has all been removed together with a restaurant and replaced by Mozzetta, a four-storey block of flats by architect Huw Thomas with projecting balconies in steel and glass inspired by medieval timber framed buildings. On the south side there are two almost Dutch-style gabled four-storey brick town houses with a keyhole slot, through which there is access to houses at the rear. These provided the contrast in scale so typical of the best historic streets. The corner building to St Thomas Street has an unusual design which cantilevers out over the footpath to satisfy the engineer on sightlines while tightening up the townscape from a visual point of view. It also has an angled chimney to add interest to the skyline.

Further east the rendered white building No 8, which has retained its railings, provides a glimpse through to the Cathedral from the upper floors of listed houses opposite. This is followed by the rather surprising bulk of the four-storey 19th century terrace of Penarth Place with unusual access to the front doors up a flight of steps to the first floor level, all set within arched openings off the frontage.

The corner site onto Minster Lane, which provides a link with the Close walls and a glimpse of the Cathedral, was for years a specialist garage, with a standard single-storey industrial building occupying all of its site, although it incorporated stones and bricks from an older building in its side wall to the lane. In 1996 this was redeveloped as a town house which enabled a garden area to be reclaimed and trees planted to the benefit of Penarth Place.

Sketch of the old St Thomas's church based on a painting by G F Prosser

Opposite Penarth Place is an amazing almost secret garden space that was the site and graveyard of the medieval St Thomas's church (shown clearly on Godson's 1750 map). This was demolished in 1845, when the new St Thomas's church was built in Southgate Street. This lovely space with its trees and bushes in between the graves, is beautifully looked after by the owners of the two fine 17th century town houses at the back of the site. The churchyard is bounded on the south side by an old medieval wine store on which was erected a distinguished stable block for Mulberry House opposite and which was converted into a residential development in the 1980s by Masons, the builders. Its twin gables contain oval windows, arches

Site (now a garden) of old St. Thomas's church

with 18th century style entrances on either side of a pedimented gateway, and fine railings that guard the courtyard, Masons Yard. It forms a feature from Minster Lane and defines the eastern entrance to St Thomas' Passage which runs up to Southgate Street.

From this point on, the west side of St Thomas Street has changed considerably in recent years whereas the east side has remained virtually untouched except for small adjustments. At No 18 two Edwardian houses were converted to a single office in the 1970s and given a new central entrance with steps, thin railings and a

Mulberry House

Lee House/Carlisle House

glazed porch. However the garden space has become a parking area with just one or two trees left, and the building has now been changed to two houses.

Next door, Lee House/Carlisle House has had a chequered career, starting life as a 17th century private house with stable yard and garden arranged rather like No 12 opposite. In the 19th century it became the first external boarding house for Winchester College (when it was called Chernocke House). It then acquired a substantial wing which swept away the stable block. With the late 19th century College building programme it became redundant as a boarding house, becoming a nurses' hostel and lastly a hostel and office for the Probation Service. By this time more additions had been made, the garden area had been lost, leaving these substantial buildings with only a squalid yard reached by a hole punched in a barbarous way through the front building.

Lee House and Carlisle House (ex Chernocke House) were themselves rehabilitated in 1996. This followed the abandonment of the probation hostel and the publication of a development brief that sought to separate the 18th century house and its front garden from the adjacent building by introducing a new access to the land at the rear. This involved substantial demolition, which now enables the spire of St Thomas's church to form a part in the street scene here. The main house, which commands wonderful views of the Cathedral by virtue of the walled gardens to adjacent properties to the east, has become an architects' office. The subsidiary buildings have become houses with two studio flats at the back. Three new single-aspect houses have been introduced to the north side of the courtyard, which is set out for parking and also incorporates trees and hedges to create a new townscape.

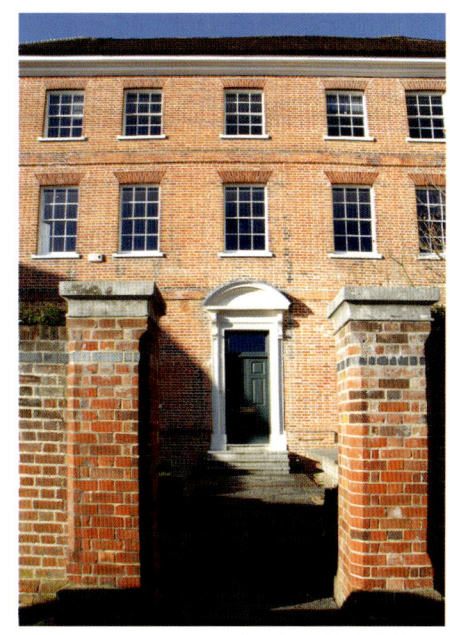

In the 1970s the garden area next door was about to be redeveloped as an office building and parking area but this was resisted at appeal and a dense residential scheme agreed which led to the loss of a very fine yew tree. From a townscape point of view this development incorporated a gabled front and a projecting bay window hard against the pavement at a point where the road changes level, the bay window therefore maximising its effect.

On the corner site since the 1930s there had been a motor repair garage and petrol pump in an ugly series of industrial buildings. The site was redeveloped in 1987 as Lions Court, using the change of levels to incorporate underground parking. Rather unusually it has entrances at both corners.

On the east side of the street returning northwards, Nos 14, 15 and 17 are of colour-washed brick with a datestone of 1695, leaded light windows and rather heavy three-light dormers. There is a section of original stone paving remaining outside. No 11 is a fine late 18th century design with slate roofs and a long garden wall. The owners negotiated an agreement for a new service area through this wall into the vegetable garden and a fine second-hand wrought iron arch and gateway (that came from Northington) was incorporated. These frame a view of trees and, diagonally, the 15th century tower of Winchester College chapel.

No 12 was given a new gate to its parking yard and the stable was converted to offices, but parking in the wonderful garden was refused.

Looking further northward after the knuckle point of Masons Yard the mostly colour washed buildings on the east turn the corner opposite two red brick houses and help frame the view of the curfew tower. The urban quality of the street derives from the listed buildings on the west side and the complicated Dutch gable of No 99 High Street with its two-storey bays projecting over the shop.

The northern section of the street has been repaved by the City Engineer with dark grey concrete blocks to a small-scale diamond pattern to reinforce the visual message that this is a one-way-street that is not suitable for through traffic.

14, 15, 17 St Thomas Street

Walled City – 3: Little Minster Street/Great Minster Street/St Clement Street/The Square

Little Minster Street (Mensterstret) – Symonds Street

These two streets follow on from each other, but will be considered in turn.

Little Minster Street leads directly to the gate of the priory and was originally the nearest to the Cathedral. It starts, as was typical of a Saxon street pattern, with a very narrow lane at its northern end between two three-storey listed shops. When it reaches St Clement Street it widens out considerably and becomes a curved street which dips, then rises up to a point where there are two gaps in development and then falls towards the corner of the Cathedral Close.

It is still a narrow street which used to be primarily a service street to Great Minster Street, and once contained a chocolate factory, garage and two public houses, but is now largely residential.

The northern end is terminated by the attractive 18th century front of 105 High Street, whose intricate fanlight and round-headed windows face down the street. At its southern end the Cathedral Close wall can be seen leading round to a view of the west front of the Cathedral, framed by yew trees.

As a street, its continuity was broken in the 1930s when the King's Head public house, a twin gabled timber frame building with first floor bays, was demolished to create a vehicular connection between Little Minster Street and St Thomas Street. This allowed access for fire fighting and servicing, but the frontage has now been reinstated following a planning brief and competition in 1982. The winning scheme

NatWest Bank from Little Minster Street

Mozzetta, Little Minster Street

consisted of two four-storey gabled brick town houses with garages below, and shop units at either end, the one in Little Minster Street being three-storey, and the one on St Thomas Street corner being two storeys high.

The four-storey units have provided the contrast in scale so typical of the best Winchester townscape and it is interesting that the higher roofs, which are actually quite shallow in depth, fit very successfully into the townscape as seen from the Cathedral Green. In 1984 the development incorporated the re-paving of the yard and the introduction of a plane tree next to the Minstrels restaurant (which was the only street tree), a curved brick seat and a restored traditional Victorian street light. The north side of Kings Head Yard was then demolished in 2005 and replaced with a prominent four-storey block of flats known as Mozzetta to a design by architect Huw Thomas.

In architectural terms, Little Minster Street is now a fascinating one because of the range of architectural styles encountered. At the north end the 18th century listed shop unit in the High Street was occupied by Hunt's the Chemist from 1850-1976. This building still retains its 18th century wooden shutters and a service building in Little Minster Street, a building that has a complete Mansard roof to the first floor. This is an unusual little building slightly marred by the size of the garage opening but it terminates this part of the street in an attractive way and could so easily have been swept away and replaced by a modern flat roofed storage building.

Apothecary House

Opposite to it on the east side is a modern glazed café extension to No 13 the Square in place of some poor quality outbuildings. This refreshing addition has given the whole area a lift by virtue of its careful use of contrasting materials, sophisticated detailing and a modesty, which is in such a contrast to the normal fussy, so-called 'Victorian' conservatory beloved of many restaurants.

This modern cafe adjoins a service building resting on a 13th century stone cellar that is the only building left in central Winchester with cast-iron window frames. Two doors down is a close-studded 16th century timber framed building which creates a strong visual pattern despite rather odd windows. Its neighbour on the other side of the passage to the Square is a modern, tile-hung service extension to a restaurant in Great Minster Street. This is followed by the rear of the Old Vine public house and No 23 Little Minster Street which has been adapted with external stairs to three small workshops for specialist retailers.

Opposite No 23 on the west side a shop unit with its town house above turns the corner. This adjoins the building that was once Bendicks chocolate factory. Though not beautiful, this building has been turned into four town houses, altered and refurbished to incorporate ground floor garages and second floor roof terraces that command views to the Cathedral and the Close.

Café extension to the rear of No 13 The Square

Adjacent to the 'chocolate factory' is an old hall building opposite which is a pair of small 19th century mews cottages. Behind the old hall building is an internal commercial development with semi-basement rooms lit from a surprising glazed elevation within a courtyard, known as Calpe Yard, between Little Minster Street and St Thomas Street. This development is served by a paved parking area which, looking to the west, gives an attractive view past a three-storey flint gabled building in St Thomas Street to the large cupressus tree in St Thomas graveyard. Looking east there is a view of the copper beech tree in the Close and the top of the west end of the Cathedral, illustrating the value in townscape terms of having some low development in Great Minster Street.

To the south of this, on the west, there is a terrace of five three-storey town houses which replaced

Small workshops in Little Minster Street

demolished cottages. The design exploits the subtle street curve with the west elevation accommodating windows and a door overlooking the yard.

From the north these buildings help to close off the street, stepping down in scale to the white two-storey Victorian neighbour and the much smaller 17th century cottage which ends the street. This cottage is also the key townscape feature looking from the Close.

From the south the composition steps up in scale to be equivalent to the rear wing of Minster House and yet the terrace is not too overpowering even though it is three storeys high, because the top storey is within the steep roof pitch and lit by dormer windows above a very bold eaves line.

Three-storey town houses

The garage doors, by being set back, are played down so that in perspective one notices the pedestrian entrances in both directions and one house is compensated for its lack of a view of Cathedral Close by a first floor bay that looks up and down the street, adding to the complexity of the townscape form. This building is also interesting at the back where projecting asymmetric gables are tile-hung and contain small balconies and a staircase for access down to the small walled gardens. Looking back up this street, the Mozzetta building on the site of Minstrels helps to turn the corner.

The beginning of Symonds Street, at the north end, is at a conjunction of several walls, of which the five-metre high flint Close wall on the east side is an important townscape feature running the whole length of this narrow, but straight, residential street that drops gradually to St Swithun Street. The street is terminated by the 18th century Waynflete House in St Swithun Street, with its lovely doorcase and fanlight set back behind a low wall, topped with vigorous, rhythmical railings in a wave-like pattern.

On the west side there are three sections of high brick wall that front onto the road, the easternmost one sweeping round and stepping up in Minster Lane so as to enclose the garden of Mulberry House, with its cherry tree that overhangs Symonds Street. Built into the wall of this garden is a pediment with a door under a four-centred arch. On the garden side this turns out to be a 'decorative eye catcher' with a central entrance and two niches for sculpture. This effectively breaks up the

17th century cottage at the end of Little Minster Street

strong upper line of the Close wall that is seen with the Cathedral over the top. Following this section of wall there is an entrance to a service courtyard between walls through which one sees the rear view of No 12 St Thomas Street with its attractive staircase window with Gothic pointed glazing bars. At the top of the service yard there is a lovely view south westward to Lee House in St Thomas Street and northwards to the yew tree and very old mulberry tree of the garden in Mulberry House.

Going back to Symonds Street, the garden wall reasserts itself, here as a retaining wall to both the service and the garden sides of Symonds House, a Regency rendered house. The entrance elevation is set back behind railings with a simple high Tuscan porch. This forms a dramatic contrast with the smooth light painted features to the walls on either side.

Further down the street, the two remaining buildings, a 19th century house and a row of 17th century almshouses, are set back with attractive open rose gardens to the front, the latter enclosed by 19th century railings with a central brick and stone gabled gateway. (The railings are a 1990s copy of the original that were lost during the war.) These buildings are seen against the backcloth of spectacular oak, ash and copper beech trees in the gardens of St Thomas Street, with the spire of St Thomas's church peeping above the roof line.

At the south end of Symonds Street, the long two-storey bulk of the almshouses punctuated by a three-storey gabled pavilion topped by a cross, is that of Christs

Hospital, founded in 1607 by a wealthy merchant, Peter Symonds. This has mellow 17th century brickwork in Flemish bond with diamond patterns created out of dark headers and stone quoins all set on a flint and stone base (from recycled buildings) with arched doors for each pair of almshouses, roofed with old clay tiles. The central block, added by Butterfield, has a main central chimney stack with six columnar flues and one can also see the tops of six chimneys which are built of stone with brick tops turned at an angle to the base. It is interesting how this has been added to at the north end with a similar design but in darker 19th century bricks. The adjacent 19th century house (Upper House) by Butterfield is designed in a similar style with a decorative brick detail to the front doorway.

In this street three stone plaques are inserted to the almshouses with Peter Symonds' coat of arms of three trees and a shield repeated on the stone 19th century porch. The inscription which sets out the terms of the endowment is set into the wall between the original almshouse and its extension. There are also good examples of painted Roman lettering on the doorways of Waynflete House and Symonds House.

Great Minster Street

This is a fine street, residential at the south end, with shops and businesses at the north end. It is still medieval in character arising out of its very tight south entrance between the walls of Minster House and the Close. The road continues past the two houses on the eastern side with their narrow two-storey frontages, terminating with the view of the 15th century stone tower of St Lawrence's church. The church is hemmed in by buildings with steep, tiled roofs and a flying frontage over the narrow passage which links through to the Buttercross. Inside this passage there is a pillar which was once part of the Norman palace. There are other remains of both the Norman and the Saxon palace that preceded it incorporated into other buildings and cellars in the vicinity.

Many of the listed buildings in this street have a timber framed core as can be appreciated if one looks at the southern side of the passage through to Little Minster Street. The timber framing can also be seen at the rear of the restaurant adjacent to the shoeshop, a building originally made up of five timber framed tenements which now has a rebuilt 18th century brick front. Nos 15 and 16 on the west side have mathematical tiles on the face and timber quoins to make them look like a brick building. This type of finish was first brought in to modernise timber framed buildings when the fashion changed to brick and, in later examples, used as a facing to keep the weather out of brick buildings. No 16 has the upper part of a wonderful sinuous 18th century shop-front and fanlight, the window modified in the 19th century, as was the restaurant opposite.

Minster House

The restaurant at No 9 has an exposed timber frame in the wall flanking the passage through to Little Minster Street and an 18th century oriel window on the front.

The Old Vine public house has the best medieval stone-vaulted cellar in central Winchester plus a fine 17th century staircase and good 17th century panelling upstairs. It is one of the few buildings to have Gothic-arched ground floor windows and door. Nos 6 and 7 have 18th century brick fronts with attic floors complete with blind windows. These buildings, including Nos 8 and 10, disguise their original overhanging fronts which were similar to that of the bakery next to the Buttercross. No 4 has had added a two-storey 1930s bay window.

Great Minster Street is unusual in having a pair of shallow 17th century houses with end yards but no gardens. The houses back onto the Cathedral Close and replace the wall that enclosed the cemetery after 1350. These houses were known as the 'Constables Houses' because the land originally formed part of the estate that came under the control of the 'Constable' (or administrator) of the adjoining King's Palace. Close to the southern end is a Victorian cast iron lamp that at one time burned off sewer gases.

Constables Cottages

These characteristics ensure a wonderful sequence of views as you walk along this street from south to north. After the direct view down the yew avenue to the war memorial and the statue of William of Wykeham on top of the west front of the Cathedral, two magnificent beech trees frame a superb three-quarter view of the west front of the Cathedral with its row of pinnacles and nave buttresses culminating in the Norman tower. There is also a long view, which particularly in winter opens up the aspect towards the Wessex Hotel with the Guildhall tower behind, terminated by the trees on St Giles' Hill as a background.

A copper beech then closes the street in with houses on either side, framed by the dense foliage of the Chinese privet tree on their north side, before the view opens up again on the east side towards the main west front of the City Museum and the view down the Square to the cul-de-sac leading up to the St Lawrence's church tower. This must be one of the most painted and photographed views of Winchester.

In the opposite direction, running south, the street has an intimate feel as you emerge from the passageway from the Buttercross with the traditional striped canopies and tall narrow buildings. At once a magnificent three-quarter view of the Cathedral opens up above the lime avenue, framed by the museum to the north and the Chinese privet to the south.

From the passage alongside No 9 there is a spectacular view of the Cathedral

The Old Vine

and Great Minster Street looking south with the large beeches overhanging the 17th century houses and also east down Market Street to the Wessex Hotel. This view illustrates the stark contrast between the urban quality of the Square and the greenness of the Close as well as the narrowness of the buildings between the two.

After this point the street curves round and is terminated by the tile-capped Close wall, with the Refectory appearing over the top of it, along with trees in the gardens of the Close. The magnificent front of the late 17th century Minster House (Winchester's first bank) with its lovely doorcase and modillion eaves ends this sequence of views.

St Thomas' Passage and Minster Lane
Often in historic towns minor passages are more interesting than major roads and this is particularly true of this route. From the top of the steps in Southgate Street is a lovely view of the Cathedral tower and the pinnacles of the west front seen against the sky. In front is a little walled lane leading down to Mulberry House with overhanging shrubs either side. As you walk down the lane the Cathedral disappears behind the 17th century Mulberry House, incidentally one of the few houses in Winchester with a set of shutters.

At St Thomas Street the whole of this attractive elevation can be seen with its doorcase and blue shuttered windows. Turning left is a view along St Thomas Street to the curfew tower on the old Guildhall, between buildings rising two storeys from the pavement down Minster Lane. Here the Cathedral suddenly reappears on the left hand side, before slowly disappearing as you move down this street past an old chapel. To the left are visible the asymmetric tiled gables of the 1980s curved terrace in Little Minster Street. These buildings have corner windows and external staircases that run down into their back gardens. Architecturally this is one of the best 'backs' in Winchester. Towards the end of the lane the small-scale angular tiled roofs and twisted chimneystack of No 40 Little Minster Street become the most important feature. This turns out to belong to a little white painted house on the corner. Round the corner an avenue opens up to the west front of the Cathedral beyond the silhouette of the War Memorial.

On the return walk, starting at the west front of Winchester Cathedral past the War Memorial a dark yew avenue frames the white 17th century cottage at the end of Little Minster Street. Emerging from this avenue you are led between the flint walls of the Cathedral Close on the left (where there may once have been a major gateway) and the lower brick-and-flint garden wall of Minster House on the right. This allows a long perspective down Symonds Street before the road turns into the narrow Minster Lane which runs uphill with a high brick wall on the left and much more varied townscape on the right. At the west end there is an old stone wall

Corner shops at junction of St Thomas Street and St Clement Street

with a new house perched on the top of it. This house replaced a repair garage in the 1980s. Note the strategically placed Sarsen stone probably placed to ward off carts rounding the corner. The old 'u' shaped stable block of Mulberry House, now Masons Yard, closes off the view from the street. Close to St Thomas Street there is an intriguing glimpse on the right into the old St Thomas's churchyard overlooked by two attractive 17th century houses. Beyond, rises up the lead-clad gable of the law courts.

Turning left into St Thomas Street, you see down to the 17th century house at the end before turning right into St Thomas' Passage. This rises uphill between garden areas (now car parks) to steps which are flanked by two large buildings in Southgate Street, Fiennes House on the left and an 18th century house on the right. Here is located Winchester's only remaining Giles Gilbert Scott cast-iron red telephone box. At the top of the steps is a three-quarter view of Serle's House, its memorial garden to the right and the spire of St Thomas's church to the left, dramatic by day but even more so at night.

St Clement Street
This is the only surviving narrow service street from Saxon times. The street runs parallel to the High Street crossing Southgate Street and must have originally been connected right through to the Square and Market Lane.

It is a very narrow sloping street running from west to east, and informally lined with two-storey buildings. The street terminates at the widest end at the 18th century Trafalgar House and at the other end with the interesting back of No 15 Little Minster Street. Walking downhill and looking over the roofs, the green copper roof of the Guildhall tower comes into view set against the trees of St Giles' Hill with the interesting slate pattern of the end building showing up in full light. Because of the narrowness of the street the south side is in deep shadow so that at the crossing with Southgate Street the corner buildings stand out distinctly.

Walking eastwards, the most distinguished part of the street is the corner with St Thomas Street where two early 19th century rendered buildings, designed in the Greek idiom, formally 'turn the corners' in a delightful curved design. Adjoining this on the north side is a new development, St Clement Yard, carried out in the 1980s with the insertion of a residential building, entrance and carefully designed gate looking into an attractive courtyard. This is one of the best examples in Winchester of new buildings using traditional forms but reworked in the modern idiom with careful detailing so that it enhances the street with the simple curved brick wall leading into the courtyard via an iron gateway.

On the south side, the prunus tree in a little garden enhances the area. The Hampshire Chronicle printing works is a robust commercial building which with its rooflight contributes to the roofscape of central Winchester, though printing is no longer carried out here. Hammonds Passage, the alley beside the office, is one of the few stone paved alleys left untouched and also contains the 18th century shutters for the bow-fronted Chronicle building in the High Street beyond. These Hampshire Chronicle buildings have recently been sold for development. It is hoped that a well-designed creative result can be achieved on this sensitive site. Crossing Southgate Street, the little display window built into a blank wall on the south side creates a welcome point of interest. At the west end of St Clement Street there is an example of how the City Planning Department, by insisting on keeping the corner Victorian building when most of the street was demolished, has enabled the character of this end of the street to be maintained.

Nos 2 to 5, Aquitaine House, illustrate clearly the problem of access in a hilly historic town for disabled people. At the time that the building was erected the use of a semi-basement seemed a rational and acceptable use of space. It is the semi-basement that has necessitated the flight of steps up to the front door. Note the extensive work to create an acceptable disabled access on the site opposite.

This street tends to be used as a bypass and has been repaved to indicate low traffic use with bollards to discourage parking.

The Square
This straight tapering commercial street has evolved out of the very complex history surrounding the Saxon and Norman royal palaces, the market and their relationship to the walled Cathedral Close. It has now been proved that the Norman kitchen was located at the eastern end round the corner in the High Street. By 1350 the Square had become a series of public markets, walled off from the cemetery. This led to a market house being built on the south side at the western end in 1615 with a frontage of stone pillars and arches and an entertainment room over, used for plays from 1690 to 1784. By the end of the 17th century the south side and the east side were fully developed with buildings and this became the Town Square.

Eclipse Inn

After her trial in the Great Hall of the Castle conducted by the ruthless Judge Jeffreys in 1685, Lady Alice Lisle from the New Forest was executed here outside what is now the Eclipse Inn (formerly St Lawrence's Rectory) for the crime of sheltering supporters of the Duke of Monmouth's rebellion. This was also the site of the town pillory. In 1875 two buildings on the south side of the street were amalgamated and given a rendered front and sash windows to create Winchester's first dispensary (now a shop). In 1902 the market building was replaced with a

The Square   Museum   Cathedral   Great Minster Street

public museum to house collections built up since 1848, that had moved from Hyde Abbey School to the Old Debtors Gaol in Jewry Street, then to a wing of the Guildhall. With flint and stone walls the Museum has the architectural grammar to make it a strong and confident building.

The townscape of this street is interesting because the north side is made up of thirteen relatively narrow but deep frontages backing onto the Pentice, producing buildings of irregular height, including the gable-ended timber framed Eclipse Inn and Nos 23 and 24, a fine 17th century building which marks the western junction with Great Minster Street. The south side by contrast has only five wide frontages with very shallow depths, consistently two or three storeys high, producing a totally different and much more uniform architectural entity.

The street widens towards the west giving the Museum prominence; the view is terminated by three-storey 18th century brick buildings with good ground floor shops. These make an attractive composition, although no single building looks precisely down the street. Unfortunately the three gables of Mozzetta in Little Minster Street devalue this group seen from the eastern end. Looking eastwards down from the Square is an oblique view of Colson's 19th century rebuilding of Morley College, the 17th century almshouses for clergy widows. This rebuilding destroyed the feeling

The Square, late 1970s

Gilbert's Bookshop in the Square, 1976

The two modern reconstructions and alterations to the north side of the street have retained and enhanced its character, in one case by reconstructing the front of No 32 and allying it to quite a different back and in the other case by constructing a double-gabled building with large first-floor oriel windows, and linking it to a roof that comes down to normal two-storey height. Internally this building has an interesting section with half-landings connecting floors within a modern exposed structure. This development has also upgraded the notion of a 'service yard' to buildings in the High Street, making it into an attractive space with some planting.

This street forms part of the rather tortuous west/east traffic link south of the pedestrianised High Street which spoils its character from a pedestrian point of view because of the continuous traffic which easily gets blocked.

The street has been repaved in an attractive manner and advantage taken to widen the pavement on the sunny north side, making it possible for people to sit comfortably outside the two restaurant premises with umbrellas for summer shade.

Experiments have been made in closing this street to motor traffic for short periods when it has taken on a more traditional character with market stalls, even including trees amongst the stalls. There has been a suggestion that trees should be planted permanently in this street. However, part of its essential character is that like the High Street it is an urban space in its own right, with attractive architecture on both sides, which is a total contrast to the grass and trees of the Close just round the corner. Cellars and passages under the space outside the Museum rule this location out for tree planting as well.

Market Lane

This is basically a service street to the High Street and to buildings fronting the Close. It starts at the west end with the potentially interesting rear of the stone Market House.

From a townscape point of view the difficulty is to encourage a design mentality that turns servicing requirements into townscape that is worth looking at, either when looking down the street or going across it through to the Cathedral Close.

Winchester Museum

Rear of the Market House

of a Square by eliminating the wings, for a more formal composition. Consequently the street is now terminated by the west elevation of the Wessex Hotel with St Giles' Hill in the background beyond. Continuing eastwards there is a magnificent three-quarter view of the north side of the Cathedral glimpsed through trees.

Looking west the street is terminated by fairly new small shop buildings and roofs with views to distant trees on Romsey Road, though in some positions the tower and fleche on Queen Elizabeth II Court also adds interest to the skyline.

Closing the street, looking east, are the City Council offices, combining two pavilions with an arched entrance in the centre to give access to the back of the Guildhall yard. The colour is unfortunate, the detailing is too flat and even devices like combining windows and solid panels together look better on drawings than they do in practice.

The holly tree in the garden of Morley College makes a welcome break to the buildings and signifies the way through from the High Street to the Cathedral. This cross route has been made interesting by the distinctive paulownia tree in the Wessex Hotel yard, the incorporation of St Maurice's church tower into the composition with Debenhams, and tombstones set into the paving. Here a brave attempt has also been made to upgrade the image of public toilets, with large windows giving an attractive view out to the Cathedral and an interesting three-dimensional symbol sign.

One other surprise is the little yard behind the Baker's Arms, where the landlord, by roofing it over and planting a wisteria, has created a popular outside sitting area, although the substitution of imitation cast-iron lace for a simple, modern, elegant structure, is regrettable.

St Maurice's church tower

The Baker's Arms

The two-storey extension to Debenhams is intrusive. The first building adjacent to the tower represents an overscaled domestic type of neo-Georgian brick building with giant sash windows which look boring both here and in the High Street. It also has flat roofs and water tanks on top that look ugly from the Cathedral tower. The recent rear extension is an attempt to produce windowless architecture except in the staircase hall. This does incorporate pitched roofs that contribute to high level views and at street level an attempt is made, by the use of specially shaped bricks and brick patterns, to provide interest for the pedestrian walking by. In practice this is not bold enough to be entirely satisfactory. The back of the former supermarket next door is hideous.

Walled City – 4: Cathedral Close/Wolvesey Palace

Winchester Cathedral Close

> 'Places give roots to people.
> Buildings can either threaten and destroy, or add to and create places.
> Their first responsibility must be to add to places, to nurture the spirit of the space, which in turn nurtures us.
> The interiors of buildings also create inner places. Each room has a spirit. It starts with the architecture and develops with usage'.
>
> Christopher Day – *Places of the Soul*

This area forms the spiritual heart of Winchester as defined in Saxon times by the Old Minster in 662, the New Minster in 900, and redefined in medieval times by the building of the Norman priory and monastery from 1079 to 1093.

Fortunately, from the townscape point of view, it is not yet surrounded by car parks, so that the Cathedral and its Close still have to be discovered on foot.

Maintaining the Cathedral within its walls and gates does create many headaches. For example, routes in for fire engines and ambulances can easily be blocked. Any damage by modern lorries to the Prior's Gate, such as happened in 1998, creates access problems and the roadway through this gate has in recent times been lowered to allow fire engines through.

The whole area is dominated by the great stone Norman Cathedral, which is still by far the largest single building in Winchester with its simple and austere tower, long and powerful nave and spectacular interior. This building is also a focus for the whole river valley beyond.

The building, through its fabric, exhibits the continuity of an idea, adjusted, damaged even, and elaborated by generations of very able people and their craftsmen down through the centuries. This process of development is still going on with the addition of sculptures and furnishings such as the symbolic figure by Antony Gormley in the crypt, icons at the east end and the furniture in Izaak Walton's chapel in the south transept.

Although the ruthlessness of the Commissioners at the Dissolution in 1538 led to the destruction of the cloister, chapter house, communal dormitories and refectory, it left the Cathedral largely intact. The Cathedral came close to being wrecked at

The Deanery, Cathedral Close

The Cathedral and Wolvesey Palace

the time of the Commonwealth in the 17th century. In the 19th and 20th centuries the Cathedral again was threatened but this time by natural causes.

In 1905 great raking shores were erected as first aid. Walls had to be strengthened by grouting, underpinning was necessary under much of the Cathedral, ties were put in between the transepts, new buttresses erected on the south side of the nave, and repairs carried out to the west front all of which took until 1912 to complete. During this process, the diver William Walker undertook the job of underpinning and worked for six years for six hours a day in the dark, under water. The number of other craftsmen employed at one time reached 187 and the total cost of the work was £113,000, a cost well beyond the resources of Winchester without outside help.

The surrounding Close is also the most obvious medieval townscape within the area of the Roman walls, because every part of it, except its northern interface with the town, is contained by impressive flint and stone walls. These define the space inside and create a palpable separation from everything outside. There is a different quality inside the enclosed space which has a sense of peace, tranquillity and continuity.

Replica of raking shores (2008)

The Cathedral and Close together have the potential for inspiring a sense of awe, wonder and beauty, all reflected in its buildings and landscape spaces, which combine to promote a spiritual atmosphere.

The Close provides a strong contrast with the different architectural qualities and bustle of the town and the outside world. It remains the largest green area in a densely built-up city. The Close contains some wonderful trees which in winter act as a lace-like foil to the great bulk of the light coloured stone Cathedral. In other seasons, it is more their shape and colour that complement the building. Some of the trees, such as the planes planted in the 1740s, are of an individual size that is awesome when viewed from eye level, and also show up individually from St Giles' and St Catherine's Hill. Like the Cathedral itself, they also exert a particular influence on the spaces in which they grow.

Within the walls, buildings from medieval times to the present day are arranged in tight clusters separated by gardens, the nature of each cluster depending on its origin and present use. Trying to understand the building layout is complicated by the fact that the original monastic establishment of the Priory was changed at the Dissolution to a different administrative set-up. Whilst the Cathedral still retained much of the income from a large part of southern England, the newly appointed Dean and Chapter of twelve canons were each entitled to individual houses, rather than the dormitory accommodation provided for monks.

The Dean took over the Prior's Hall which was separated into different floors and extended with a library wing to the east. Other buildings were converted and new canons' houses built amongst the monastic buildings. Several of these were destroyed during the Parliamentary occupation in the 1640s, leading to the construction of the fine set of houses in Dome Alley in the 1660s. This helps to explain the extraordinarily rich townscape sequences reflecting a long history which can be experienced when examining the Close.

The Close is divided into distinct areas, each of which has its own characteristics while contributing to the quality of the whole. There is the northern area of the Cathedral graveyard, the only burial place allowed in medieval times within the City walls. This graveyard became very full by 1389 at the time of the Black Death, when around 6000 people died in the city. This area used to be subdivided from east to west by the Paradise Wall, a remnant of which is still to be seen on the east side of the Close. There was probably a main entrance gate at the end of Great Minster Street. The profusion of gravestones was cleared away in favour of grass that was easy to maintain. It is now subdivided north/south by railings. This followed a decision in the 1930s which led to the western area being made available to the town and the eastern area including the foundations of the Saxon Minster retained as an enclosed space.

There is the central area south of the Cathedral leading through to the Prior's Gate which gives access to the working part of the Cathedral community. Here are accommodated the houses, the offices for the Diocese, the Cathedral and the Friends of the Cathedral, the Education Centre, the maintenance yard, the Judges' Lodgings and the Pilgrims' School.

The Pilgrims' School is a preparatory school and choir school for the Cathedral which has both boarders and day pupils. In total there are over 1600 people who live or work full- or part-time in the Close. It must be remembered that this is a spiritual and administrative centre for its Diocese, and a focus for pilgrims from around the world as well as a national treasure.

Since the 17th century the Close has been a busy pedestrian route between the High Street and Winchester College, the Canon Street area and through the watermeadows to St Cross. It is the constant flow of people passing through on foot or on bicycle going about their daily business which gives such a vibrant quality to this space.

There are also three other areas of interest. The Dean Garnier Garden to the south of the Cathedral's east end, the Visitors Centre with its shop and refectory to the west, and the ruins of Wolvesey Castle to the east of the present Bishop's Palace.

Private Areas

Here in the heart of Winchester, are extensive areas of private land. They include recreation areas used by Pilgrim's School, maintenance yards for the Cathedral and various private gardens.

These private gardens vary greatly in size and character. There is the great L-shaped garden of the Deanery which pivots around the two enormous plane trees planted about 1740 on the east side. The garden has one arm alongside the mill stream that comes through from Abbey Gardens and the other on the west side running up past the library wing, added onto the Deanery by Bishop Morley in the 1680s. This garden commands wonderful views of the Cathedral. There is also a walled vegetable garden to the south adjoining the new Pilgrims' School classroom block.

South east view of the Cathedral from No1 The Close, 1870

The simple walled garden of No 1 is dominated by the proximity of the Cathedral which looms over the 17th century house.

On the west side of the Inner Close the front garden of No 11 has a magnificent diagonal view of the nave, tower and south transept rising over the remaining core of the Norman west tower.

Then there are the smaller, but still substantial, gardens of the houses in Dome Alley, those on the north side looking to the Cathedral and those on the south side self-contained within the high flint perimeter walls. The garden of the Judges' Lodgings abuts the Prior's Gate and has an ancient yew tree spreading across the wall.

Public Areas

One of the great advantages today is that the full bulk of the Cathedral can be seen from all angles close to. This would not have been possible on the south side in monastic times because of the residential buildings, nor on the north side, because of the boundary walls separating the graveyards from the city.

From the north its entire length can be seen and, in winter sunlight, a view right through the Cathedral nave to the windows on the opposite side.

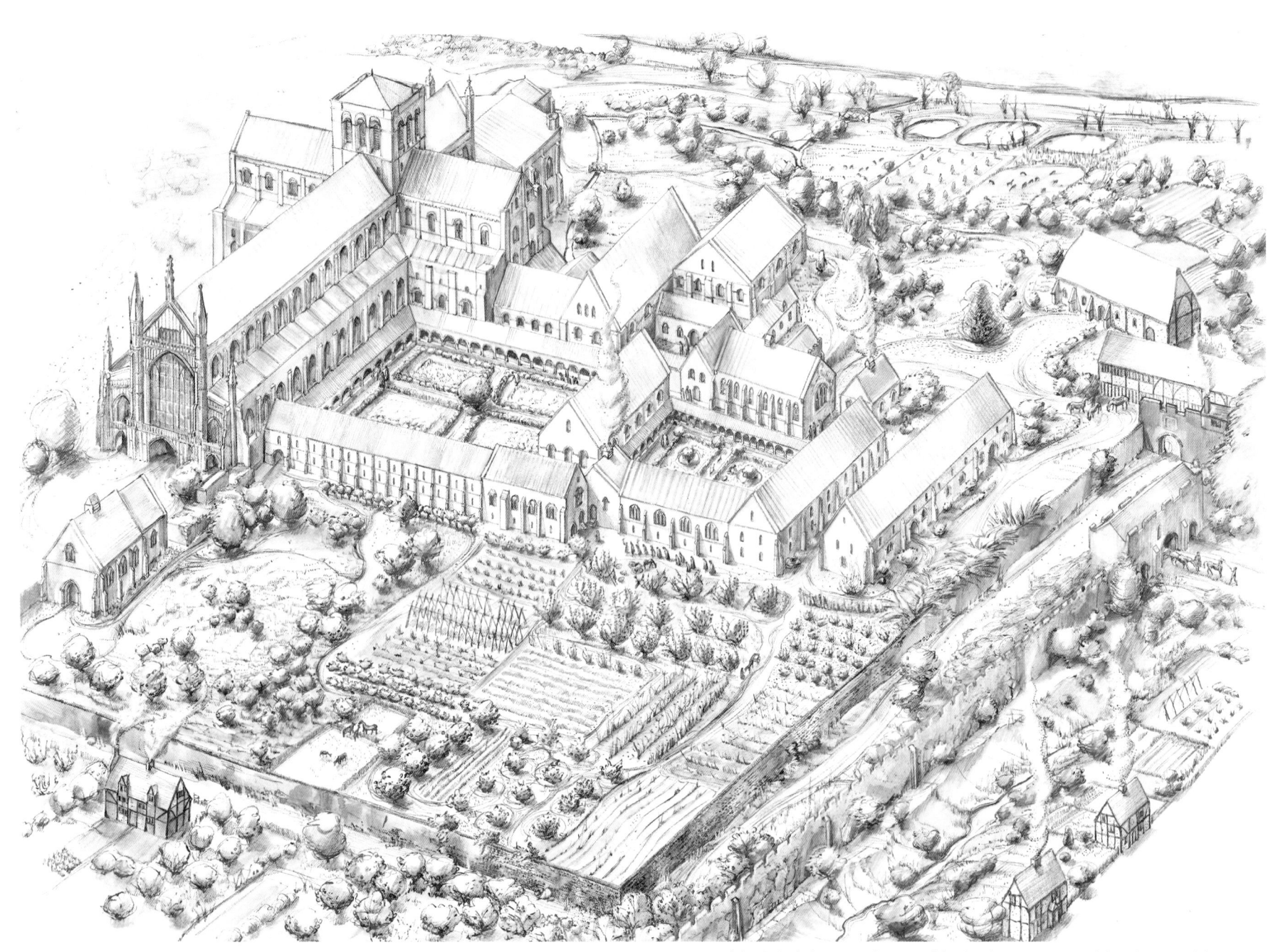

Reconstruction of the Cathedral priory at the time of the dissolution, c. 1540. Judith Dobie ©English Heritage

1980s drawing by Andrew Rutter based on Judith Dobie's original

From the west can be experienced the full drama of the 14th century great window and main entrances that replaced the Norman towers. The window is 34 feet wide and 53 feet high containing a mosaic of fragments of stained glass, broken up during the Commonwealth period and randomly reassembled creating an abstract picture.

On the south side of the Cathedral, after walking through a small doorway, cut through the buttress to the 14th century west front, you can experience the sheer perspective and power of the nave, tower and south transept. Walk through the slype to the east end and very clear signs of the movement in the retrochoir can be seen, the result of extending the building eastwards, off the tufa 'island' and onto the alluvial subsoils of the flood plain.

From the east there is the exciting build-up of the two beautiful east windows, the lower one under a crenellated parapet, the upper one with its two side turrets and arcaded gable with the Norman tower over the crossing.

From the north east corner, viewed from the vicinity of Colebrook Street, the east end rises up like some great ship at its moorings.

Passage between Outer and Inner Close

Outer Close

The Cathedral, despite its great size, is virtually hidden from the High Street but, when approached via St Maurice's Covert, the majestic length of the nave explodes into view.

The building of the Wessex Hotel in 1960 on the northern part of the Close was believed to be on the site of the Saxon Minster. The initial excavation sparked off an eleven year programme of archaeological excavations under the direction of Martin Biddle on sites across the City.

Comprehensive excavations in 1960 as part of this programme revealed a great deal of information about the Saxon Old Minster founded in 648 and extended westwards to encompass St Swithun's shrine in 993, and the New Minster founded in 900. The Old Minster was destroyed to make way for the Norman Cathedral which was built on a slightly different alignment as can be seen in the floor plan, now laid out in brick in the Outer Close.

Reconstructions of New Minster (left) and the west-works of Old Minster, covering Swithun's tomb, from the north west, in their most magnificent state c. 993-4 to 1093
Winchester Research Unit

The three avenues of trees leading up to the west door of the Cathedral, and the other trees along the north boundary are clearly shown in the Bucks' drawing of 1736 and Godson's map of 1750 (see pages 277-8). It is these trees, plus an avenue of yew trees planted on the western side after the First World War, which guide visitors from the edge of the Close to a point much closer to the Cathedral where the great west window can be appreciated.

Just as parts of the fabric of the Cathedral have to be renewed so too does tree planting. In their maturity, the lime avenues created a space articulated by trunks and branches and with a canopy of leaves which was a natural preparation for the glory of the stones, piers and vaults of Wykeham's nave inside. When the time came in the 1980s to replace the lime avenue some thought it better to leave the view of the Cathedral opened up. This would have made for an uninteresting open space, devoid of summer shade and seasonal change, and would have diminished the scale and impact of the west front.

On the edge of this space are two pieces of sculpture. Firstly, the bronze statue of a soldier (by J Tweed, 1922) commemorates the members of the Kings Rifle Corps who died in two World Wars. This is seen against the sky from this position but also can be seen silhouetted dark against the receding geometry of buttresses on the north side of the Cathedral in low western sunlight.

Secondly the formal cross and supporting base of the main war memorial is in memory of members of local regiments killed during the First World War.

From Great Minster Street, this cross is seen framed by the yew trees, set against the great west window, whilst from the Cathedral the yew trees give a dark formal and dignified background that contrasts with the whiteness of the stone.

West front of the Cathedral before gravestones were removed and the ground lowered, 1882

These avenues also show up the form and visual interest of other types of trees in the Outer Close like the contorted weeping ash and the evergreen Chinese privet that flowers in winter. The most significant are the two beech trees on the western edge which frame the view of Minster House. The copper beech to the north is a particularly fine and vigorous specimen with a height of some 20 metres. This tree was planted in about 1838 at the time when Owen Browne Carter's Corn Exchange in Jewry Street was built.

The buildings surrounding the Outer Close are variable in quality but interesting. Starting at the west side is Minster House, a fine early 18th century building. In contrast, the two narrow houses of similar date in Great Minster Street turn their backs on the Close to make an attractive background to the trees. The City Museum marks the north west corner and has attached to it a range of buildings along the north side whose entrances are in the Square. No 3, The Square is an early 18th century, three-storey house with good red and grey brickwork and early sash windows; unusually the main entrance opens onto the Close. The adjoining building has a projecting oriel window of great townscape value when walking down the northern path. Next is Morley College almshouses for widows of clergymen.

This is a good Victorian rebuild by John Colson, with a steep roof and prominent chimney stacks, but lacking the detailed character of the 17th century building that it replaced.

Morley College before 1870 rebuilding

The surviving 15th century tower and Norman doorway of the former St Maurice's church in Market Lane visually fill the gap between the almshouses and the Wessex Hotel. The hotel is a flat-roofed 1960s building with visible roof tanks and which is articulated into two separate blocks. The main block, which expresses a framed structure, has a base of large rough flint and brick facing, next to the pedestrian footpath. The square bedroom block, supported on dark, brick-clad columns, to accommodate guests' parking underneath, is less successful. This lacks the quality of detail one would expect in such an important location, although Pevsner in his Buildings of England series applauds the decision to build a modern design. What the two blocks do achieve is to frame a view of the copper-roofed Guildhall tower set against St Giles' Hill and prominent in views from the west front of the Cathedral in winter. The hotel also accommodates the heating plant for the Cathedral, allowing demolition of the former rather awkward building in the graveyard but leaving a mound in the corner of the Close, now planted with holly trees.

On the east side are two cottages and the remains of a bakery to which has been added an extension with modern flats hard against the remaining Close wall that provides a charming, quirky, small-scale domestic contrast to its enormous neighbour and the two huge plane trees in Wolvesey Palace garden to the south east.

Inner Close

The route to the Inner Close passes the west door of the Cathedral and the remaining rubble core of one of the Norman west towers (now built into the garden wall of No 11), and through the gateway formed in the south west buttress of the Cathedral by Bishop Curle in 1632. Before this date the way into the Inner Close from the west was through the nave and south aisle of the Cathedral itself. This new diversion is commemorated by an epigram inscribed, in Latin, on the west side of the buttress, separating "those who would worship and those who would walk". A similar message, in the form of another Latin epigram, is given in an inscription set into the garden wall on the right, with additional words, translated as "private property has yielded to public utility", recalling the fact that part of the garden was given up to create this public thoroughfare.

Curle's Passage provides a perspective view under the arches of the buttresses, which were added to the south nave aisle in 1912 to resist the thrust of the nave roof. This narrow 'slype' opens out into the beautiful grassed space of the former cloister garth, which is bounded on its eastern side by the arcaded screen, all that survives of the Norman chapter house. Extending southwards from this is a stone wall, containing two doorways, and then the mass of the 14th century Prior's Hall, now the Deanery, with its two-storey windows, steep tiled roof, dormers and chimneys. At the southern edge of this space lies the much lower 17th and 18th century, brick-built Judges' Lodgings with its sunken pedimented entrance porch and large sash windows.

Cheyney Court

The road follows around both sides of the cloister garth, on the west side skirting the garden wall of No 11 and the front wall of No 10, rebuilt over the vaulted 13th century buttery which marks the position of the west end of the south cloister, demolished, together with the chapter house and other priory buildings, in 1563. Continuing southwards, after passing the windowless north wall of the Judges' Lodgings with its two chimneys arched together, the footpath separates from the road. Here the Close narrows where the striking early 16th century former stable buildings step forward and, with the side wall of the Judges' Lodgings, its garden wall and the three picturesque towering gables of Cheyney Court, appear to close off the space completely. Cheyney Court, which once administered the Bishop's laws governing the Soke outside the City walls, displays close timber framing, projecting leaded-light windows, ornamental barge-boards and lead rainwater pipes above a stepped stone-and-flint base incorporating stone-mullioned windows of varying shapes and sizes. The right-hand gabled bay of this building is occupied by the Close Porter's Lodge, which also extends at right angles and includes an upper-floor room cantilevered out from the Close wall, next to the Prior's Gate.

The undercroft to No 10

It is only when near to the Prior's Gate that it is apparent that there is a way out of the Close at this point. Looking out westwards through the wisteria-clad gateway, there is a view of the length of St Swithun Street, which is defined on the right by the great height and uninterrupted length of the flint Close wall. To the left is the church of St Swithun upon Kingsgate, built over a gateway in the City wall, which ran parallel to the Close wall between the gardens of the houses in St Swithun Street and Canon Street. The church is reached by a stair enclosure attached to the side wall of the end house in St Swithun Street.

Prior's Gate

The Inner Close is protected against entry from St Swithun Street by two large iron-studded oak gates under an arch surmounted by battlements and a coat of arms. These gates, as with the smaller gates to the east and the west of the Cathedral, are locked each evening, cutting the Inner Close off from the outside world. Going back into the Close from St Swithun Street, the daytime visitor enters a confined space, with the timber-framed walls of the former stables (now serving as a music school for the Pilgrims' School) in front and the three- and four-storey Cheyney Court on the right.

Moving north, the space which opens up in front of the Pilgrims' School makes an impression because of the mixture of architectural styles, forms and materials of the buildings which surround it and its framing by cedar, beech and magnolia trees. The whole is, nevertheless, completely harmonious. The south front of the stone Deanery has a 13th century entrance wing, with three narrow pointed arches on the ground floor and a mixture of medieval and sash windows above. The battlements at the top of this meet the back roof slope of the wing of the Prior's Hall, whose stone gable has had large sash windows inserted, and an earlier roundel high up in the apex. These and the delightful iron basket balconies were introduced when the Prior's Hall was subdivided and upper floors were inserted, including attic bedrooms.

To the east of the main and entrance wings of the Deanery are the long lines of Bishop George Morley's library and gallery of 1662, with its red roof tiling, brickwork to the upper floor and the classical stone pediment above Gothic window tracery all visible over the garden wall. Soaring behind and above this are the lead roofs of the Cathedral and the huge 14th century presbytery windows, flanking the powerful architecture of the early Norman south transept gable. Above it all rises the later Norman tower, with its decoratively carved belfry openings and its straight parapet 45 metres above the ground.

The area in front of the Deanery entrance has over the years changed to a hard surface but, to the east, grass and trees predominate, surrounded by brick, stone and flint walls. Over these there are views, in the winter months, across the Deanery gardens and the grounds of Wolvesey to the tree-clad slope of St Giles' Hill beyond. Significant in the foreground space is the variety of trees, including a cedar and a tall lime tree, planted in the early 19th century at about the time of Jane Austen's death. This space is important, both as a setting for the buildings and as a link to the rest of the Cathedral Close. The sculpture on the lawn, depicting the Crucifixion, is by Barbara Hepworth, from the period when her work was influenced by the Dutch artist, Piet Mondrian.

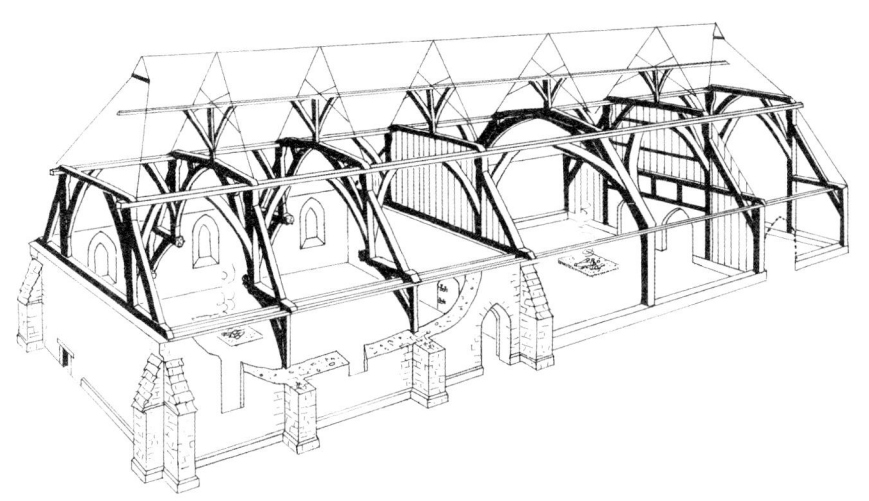

The Deanery by Owen Browne Carter, c. 1830

The Pilgrims' Hall range, dated to 1310/11: reconstruction drawing by John Crook, 1988

Set back behind this area, on its eastern side, is the main range of buildings housing the Pilgrims' School, a preparatory school providing education for, among others, Cathedral choristers and Winchester College quiristers. The red-brick Georgian entrance block is a re-casing of a 17th century house, which itself enclosed the southern three bays of the medieval Pilgrims' Hall, which was built to accommodate travellers making the pilgrimage to the Cathedral and the shrine of St Swithun. The northern bays of the Hall survive and contain the earliest hammer-beam roof so far identified (1310-11) under a large tiled roof which sweeps down to low eaves over stone walls and deep buttresses. This end of the building now serves as the school hall. Despite the mixture of building styles and forms, the whole presents a satisfying harmony.

Built behind the brick wall forming the southern boundary of the open area in front of the Pilgrims' School is a range of flat-roofed music practice rooms. These face a playground enclosed by modern two-storey ancillary buildings, some with flat roofs to keep below the top of the Close wall against which they are built. Above this the buildings of Winchester College can be seen, in particular the Headmaster's House and the Chapel tower. Framing this view on the right-hand side is the timber-framed end wall of the former Cheyney Court stables, now part of the Pilgrims' School.

Turning westwards, past the sunken entrance elevation of the Judges' Lodgings and the length of brick wall enclosing the new Cathedral workshops and yard, a diversion may be made into Dome Alley, formerly known as 'Dumb Alley'. The significant buildings in this cul-de-sac are the four long, shallow, red-brick houses, built for Cathedral canons at the time of the Restoration in the 1660s. The pair of houses on the south side have their main windows overlooking the private gardens at the back, so that they originally presented mainly windowless elevations and chimney stacks to the roadway, whereas the northern pair of houses have a mixture of 17th century cross windows and later sash windows looking over the road. There are vestiges, on the chimney stacks of the southern houses, of the curved brickwork which was originally employed in the form of Dutch gable parapets to all the houses on both sides of the road. The later introduction of straight gables and barge-boards has cut through the deep decorative brick cornices, which were originally continuous on both pairs of houses. The ornamental leadwork of rainwater goods and the lead aprons at the junctions of the barge-boards were reused from earlier, Tudor, buildings. The four houses retain original panelled doors set behind projecting brick porches. Internally, the houses have sets of 17th century oak panelling incorporating mantelpieces, some with carved figures. These fittings were purchased by each canon when he took over the house and then sold to his successor, at a set rebate, at the end of his occupancy.

The view along Dome Alley is closed, rather disappointingly, by a garden wall and garage doors but does have a distinctive, and distant, focus on the spire of St Thomas's church in Southgate Street.

When the Dome Alley houses were built (after 1660), the chapter rebuilt a fifth house, No 9 the Close, this time faced in stone. This house, known as Church House, and until recently serving as offices for the Diocese of Winchester, stands at the entrance to Dome Alley, with its main three-gabled elevation facing east into the space in front of the Deanery across its own grassed forecourt. Most of the windows are sash-windows inserted in the 18th century but 17th century stone mullion-and-transom windows survive in each of the gables and in part of the ground floor.

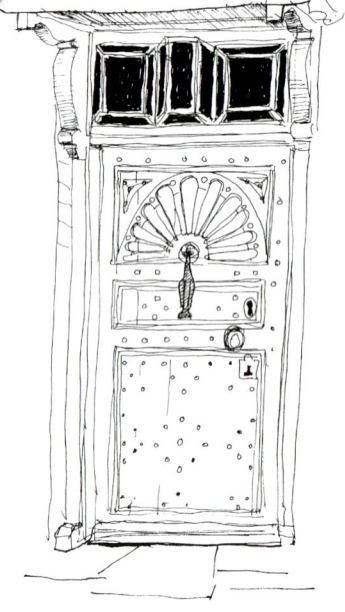

Original door, Dome Alley

Mantelpiece, No 7 The Close

Church House

East front of No 11 The Close

Adjoining Church House to the north is No 10 The Close, partly built over the vaulted undercroft of the cellarer's quarters of the Priory. This building also houses the Cathedral Education Centre whose entrance is approached under a lean-to porch roof. In front of the house is a small paved parking area with small-scale planting but, further north, the detached house No 11 The Close has its own front garden and sweeping drive enclosed by a stone front wall overhung by a large yew tree.

No 11 is another 17th century Close house re-fronted in the 18th century and the original symmetrical house has had a later extension added on the north side, now a separate dwelling. The main part of the front of the house has a fine oak doorcase with a bracketed stone canopy. The segmental pediment over the slightly projecting central bay is also of stone.

The lawn of the cloister garth, with its trees and surrounding buildings, is probably the very heart of the Cathedral Close. Viewed from the south the Cathedral is, of course, dominant to the point of being overpowering. Coming closer, the great scale of the building, its height and its three-dimensional quality, increases and then changes with the impact of the Edwardian buttresses. Between the Deanery and Church House a magnificent lime tree, some 25 metres high, softens the view of the nave and tower from the south. Other trees have been planted here at various times, eventually to grow up and succeed the lime, creating over the passage of time a subtly changing scene.

The open area of grass now serves as the site each winter of the ice-skating rink and this, with its surrounding temporary market stalls, brings a new life and change of pace to this part of the Close. At other times of the year, the seats between the south aisle buttresses allow quiet and contemplation of a slower pace of life, as a refuge from the traffic and bustle of the town and away from the crowds of the Outer Close.

Looking eastwards from the garth, the Norman arcaded screen of the former chapter house frames, across a lawn, the west elevation of No 1 The Close. Built in 1699 of brickwork in Flemish bond with dark-blue headers, this has a top-lit, single-storey entrance lobby set between projecting wings. It was the home in the 1880s of Archdeacon George Sumner, later Bishop of Guildford, whose wife, Mary, founded the Mothers' Union here in 1885. Their son, Heywood Sumner, was an artist of national standing, an exponent of sgraffito work in plaster, who produced some of the best engravings of Winchester and the surrounding countryside. He later became an archaeologist in the New Forest. Examples of his sgraffito work are to be found in the interior of No 1 The Close.

Emerging from the long, dark 'slype' passage under Bishop Morley's Cathedral library, there is another, diagonal, view of the west side of this house, before continuing past it into the listed footpath of the Water Close. Here a central paved section, of mainly Purbeck stone, between margins of flint leads past a high boundary wall of flint, brick and stone on one side and railings bordering the bishops' burial ground on the other. Looking back from anywhere along this length of the path towards the east end of the Cathedral, the settlement, which occurred in Bishop de Lucy's retrochoir of the early 13th century, is very evident in the undulating horizontal lines and the leaning window jambs and columns. In the bishops' graveyard, the pencil cypress and other trees provide a foil to the expanses of stone on the Cathedral behind. Towards the south west, the view is of the roof and chimneyscape of the back of the Deanery, seen over the Dean Garnier garden.

As the open feel of the path by the railings is compressed into a passage running between two high walls, the tiled mansard roof of No 34 Colebrook Street becomes visible over the northern wall around its garden. This wall is built of a mixture of brick, flint and re-used stone, including several exposed sections of Purbeck stone column. Boundary walls are a special feature of the Winchester Conservation Area but few are better than those in the Water Close. Under the path, but audible through a grating, rushes the Lockburn, the underground stream commonly associated with the Saxon Bishop Aethelwold and serving to flush the sewerage system of the whole of the medieval monastic community. Visible over the walls are two great plane trees, nearly 30 metres tall and planted in about 1740.

The path appears to end in a small oak door set in the dressed stone wall ahead, but this serves only as the bishop's private walk to his palace at Wolvesey. The public route is, in fact, through a small gate hidden in the left-hand wall and then into a slightly wider space, before Colebrook Street, its car park and a return to the noise and hurry of central Winchester.

On the left, the gap in the wall by the water garden (created by the Winchester MP, Sir Peter Smithers, after pulling down a terrace of cottages) allows a final glimpse, through the foliage, of the windows, gables, turrets and pinnacles of the east end of the Cathedral.

Dean Garnier's garden

This garden was created in the 1990s to commemorate Thomas Garnier, who was Dean between 1840-1872, and founder member of the Hampshire Horticultural Society. He was also greatly interested in City affairs, and influential in securing drainage improvements in Winchester, including the sewage pumping station in Garnier Road which helped to banish cholera from the City.

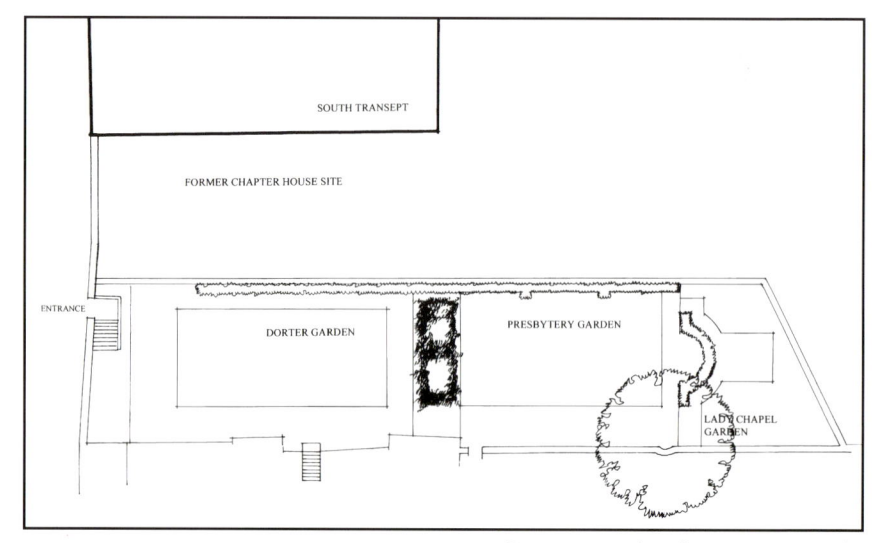

Diagrammatic plan of Dean Garnier's garden

The garden has been designed in three sections, the Dorter garden, the Presbytery lawn and the Lady Chapel garden. There is also a view out north east towards St Giles' Hill. At the western end part of the garden is set aside as a quiet place that catches the morning sun. This area also provides a beautiful view out over the Deanery garden to the Pilgrims' School and its new Stancliffe Building erected in the 1980s and beyond again to the Winchester College tower.

Closer to, there is a view down into the courtyard north of the Deanery and the 'Bakehouse', an interesting building of which the east part only is in stone which was probably the monks' lavatory over a branch of the Lockburn. This courtyard also contains a two-storey garden building entered at low level which protects an important piece of stone masonry showing the corner of one of the medieval buildings beneath its roof.

Looking at the Cathedral, it is worth noting that the windows of the transept illustrate the historical development of stone church windows, starting with the round headed windows of 1080, continuing with the geometrical windows of 1300, the decorated windows of 1350 and the perpendicular windows of 1400, all within one elevation. Since ordinary householders would be criticised by the Planning Department for selecting such a variety of windows in one building, why should it be considered acceptable to have them here? The reason is partly that Winchester Cathedral is large and the whole geometry of the building is so strong and powerful that it is able to contain such a range of historical windows.

The Dean Garnier garden requires time to reach full maturity so that the hedges and the pergola constructed in the middle can gain their full effect. It also has one

Dorter garden looking towards to the Deanery

or two details like the decorative spyholes in the door, and the finials to the simple railings, that lift them out of the ordinary.

Visitors' Centre

The Visitors' Centre is located on what was once the kitchen garden of No 11 behind its 17th century coach house which had fallen into disuse. The new building was constructed on a raft to avoid destroying the archaeological heritage beneath.

The Visitors' Centre in the Close

This building, designed by Plincke Leaman and Browning, has a modest entrance marked by steps rising up in front of the Cathedral, which lead past the shop into an outdoor space. The Refectory has strongly projecting gable roofs and looks out at the wall of the Close. (Note the pattern of ventilators for the roof on the north side). From this tapering space can be seen the west end of the Cathedral rising up over the tiled roof of the shop which has a cantilevered external staircase casting a pattern of light and shade on the ground.

The building is a good example of a design that is traditional in form but modern in detail using the structure to provide interest. The colour scheme selected for the structure and flooring was based on the traditional Benedictine colours of grey and white. From high-level views in the town, its lead and slate roof fit well into the overall townscape. It readily accords with the modesty of colour and experience of some of the best townscape in Winchester, whilst sitting in a building which is of the late 20th century in its internal arrangements.

Wolvesey Palace

The history of this site is only partially understood. It was certainly a Saxon site from 964 when Bishop Athelwold founded the monastery of New Minster under strict Benedictine rule and then discovered that he required a separate house in which to carry out wider duties as the lord of the great estate as well as being a courtier. This area was defined by the line of the western wall that still divides the Deanery from Wolvesey Palace.

Already in ruins in 1680 it was used as a quarry for the new bishop's palace and the ruin of Wolvesey Palace became scheduled as an Ancient Monument in 1915. Evaluated in 1921-32, repairs were executed then and again from 1963 to 1974. It is now accessible to the public, under the care of English Heritage.

Wolvesey Old Bishop's Palace 1171 by Terry Ball © English Heritage Photo Library

The present footpath access, alongside the 1680 Palace and the 14th century chapel that replaced an earlier Norman one, gives especially good views across the playing fields and to the best surviving section of battlements on the city wall against the background of trees on St Giles' Hill. In the middle ground can be seen the tower of St Peter Chesil, the highest point of the multi-storey car park behind Chesil Street, and the Soke with its characteristic 17th century chimneys.

Wolvesey Palace and old palace ruins

From within the ruins can be seen the 14th century chapel attached to the wing of the 1680s Palace, which was designed by Sir Thomas Fitch.

It is hard to imagine that the medieval palace was moated and preceded by Roman and Saxon development and that there used to be a busy medieval trading courtyard adjacent to College Street inside the medieval gatehouse, pulled down in the 18th century. Its great wool house was converted in 1716 to a coach house and stables with a mill to the west. The tower of William Giffard's West Hall, built in about 1110, was higher than the present chapel and the great East Hall, built by Henry de Blois, 1135-1138, was of a similar height, thus making a really impressive set of medieval buildings to complement the Cathedral and Winchester College.

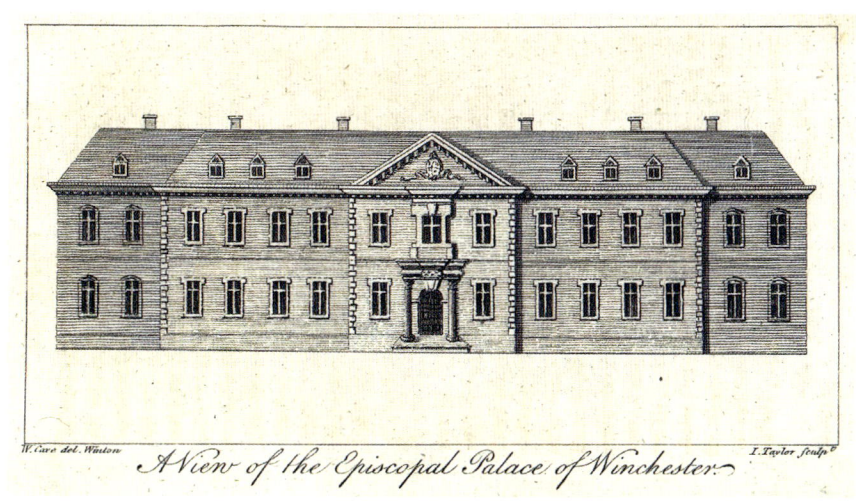

Wolvesey Palace from a drawing by William Cave in Wavell's History and Antiquities of Winchester, *1793*

The Bishop had another major palace with a great hall, courtyards, a well known jail tower and gardens, adjacent to Old London Bridge, on the south bank of the Thames. This was where he lived when attending the King's business or Parliament. It was at its most magnificent later on in the 14th century, but was sold in the 17th century for warehouses. It is now a ruin standing close to Southwark Cathedral, with one fine rose window remaining.

Nor is it easy to grasp that the present Wolvesey Palace, although a large building, is, in fact, just the east wing of an enormous baroque palace whose upkeep became too costly. Built in 1680 and demolished in 1786, this would have filled up much of the width of the present courtyard garden. Farnham Castle became the preferred residence of the Bishop until the 1920s when the Guildford diocese was separated from Winchester. Door canopies from the 1680s building were salvaged and appear in places like the Friary entrance in St Cross Road with some stone possibly going to Shawford House.

The ruins of Wolvesey Palace look most impressive either from the west end of St Giles' Hill or from the playing fields inside the city walls. In June 1908 this was the scene of the Winchester National Pageant which was used to gain publicity and money towards the cost of repairing the Cathedral. Wolvesey Palace was used as a background to a series of nine episodes in British history from King Egbert through to Walter Raleigh. Many prominent national figures including the King and Queen were invited and the Great Western Railway put on a special train to Chesil Station. Local people from aldermen to school children dressed up in Elizabethan attire and the event raised £2,500, a considerable sum at that time.

Wolvesey Palace from a drawing by Owen Browne Carter, c. 1830

Walled City – 5: Eastgate Street/Union Street/St George's Street/Silver Hill/Friarsgate

Eastgate Street/Union Street

Eastgate House (from Godson's map of 1750)

In 1750 North Walls ended at the Durngate. The road went on past a substantial collection of buildings, across a bridge at Durngate Mill and then divided into Welsh Street (Wales Street) and Water Lane. Similarly the High Street passed out through the Eastgate. No street connected the two bridges inside the walls.

The land in between belonged to St John's Charity, and the Black Friars. (St John's built St John's House and chapel and, in 1862, St John's Hospital North.) The Black Friars' land was acquired by Winchester College and leased to Sir Robert Mason, a courtier of the Stuart period, to build his mansion. By 1759 the elegant Eastgate House had become the home of the Penton family, who were MPs for Winchester from 1741 to 1796. This was the place where King George III and his Queen stayed when they visited Winchester in 1778.

Godson's map shows the house set back from the High Street, behind a courtyard formed by magnificent gates (resited in 1846 in front of Kingsland House, Chesil Street). At the east and to the rear were remarkable water gardens, known as 'The Lawn'.

In 1844, the house and grounds were divided and sold at auction as 46 freehold building plots. A local builder, Newlyn, laid out a new street in about 1850. This was at the time when the Government imposed a brick tax. The builders avoided the tax by using chalk from St Giles' Hill to build the walls of the buildings before finishing them with rendering.

Nos 1-3 Eastgate Street

Thus was created, on the west side, probably the most original formal townscape in Winchester. It was designed to turn the corner from the High Street and, until 1851, was called 'High Street Eastgate' so that there was no loss of prestige in the address. It comprises three sections: the first, a group of three houses over shops probably using the first plate glass windows in town; then five bow-fronted houses with little cast iron balconies, stone parapets and charming oval, dormer windows; followed by a terrace of 11 units. These have sub-basements and use shallow pilasters to divide off the narrow entrance bays from the wider window bays, thus creating a rhythm along the street. The terrace has bold eaves under a slate roof with prominent chimneys. The visual strength of this terrace and its companion to

Eastgate Street terraces

the north is reinforced by the repetition of gate piers and hedges. It also forms a noticeable piece of townscape when seen from St Giles' Hill above.

This whole group is also important when viewed from Abbey Gardens, where the play of light on the rounded facades is very successful. At the rear, the terrace has three storeys, each of which has large windows and creates a strong sense of enclosure with the range of almshouses of St John's Hospital North. The almshouses are built in a vigorous late Victorian Tudor style with decorative windows, porches and chimneys, and parapets divide up the roof. The main entrance to the almshouses is through cast-iron gates adjacent to St John's Chapel and has its own lawns, containing cherry trees and bedding flowers, appropriate to a private space. It forms a peaceful residential environment for elderly people, although close to all the facilities of the High Street. Its service road emerges to the north in Eastgate Street, next to a lower terrace of nine houses, designed in similar style, but with a string course arched over the window openings and combined chimneys which show up strongly in perspective. These buildings have small front gardens with walls and some railings.

St John's Hospital North

Eastgate Street (Mazzini Terrace on the right), 1907

brewery, the houses and workshops adjacent to it, on the west side of Union Street, were all pulled down to make way for a comprehensive development as recommended by Sir Patrick Abercrombie in 1957. This covered twenty-nine acres, although he did recommend the retention of the west side of Eastgate Street. The rest of the

Union Street flats

The next section was once dominated by the Lion Brewery, which was taken over later by the Co-op. The east side of the street was at that time completely filled with late Victorian townhouses apart from a group of five larger houses in multiple occupation, called Mazzini Terrace. This had decorative plaster details, including the heads of kings and queens at the front. It was a striking building, with a complicated section, that proved almost impossible to convert in a practical way.

In the post war period, this street came under conflicting pressures. Demolitions along the waterside had made the river potentially much more attractive. The demolition site was redeveloped with three-storey council flats, low-pitched slate roofs and shorn-off (but prominent) eaves details, designed by Peter Shepheard. The flats were designed to have shared amenity land between them containing forest trees and service courts. They do not create formal street architecture, apart from the high boundary wall running behind the pavement in Union Street. The buildings do, however, frame views towards the Cathedral Tower and work particularly well along the deep-set, winding brook running from Durngate through to Friarsgate and Buskett Lane. This area is not so attractive in Lawn Street, where a combination of single-storey garage blocks, balcony access for disabled residents and brick paving (to reduce maintenance costs) create a less satisfactory environment.

Lawn Street garages

The junction with Friarsgate is particularly weak, with a parking court next to the road, and even the windows overlooking the area are unattractive.

Much of the east side of Eastgate Street was pulled down, in order to construct a three-quarter ring-road which was included in the Town Centre Plan of 1968 and scheduled for re-construction.

Friarsgate junction

After the proposals were abandoned, the City Council's new development brief of 1978 for the St John's Street area suggested a riverside walk behind new housing on Eastgate Street. However, the land did not belong to the City Council, in fact the developers wished to exploit both frontages. This meant that Nos 62 and 63 Itchen Court set the pattern of development that followed including the Council's own development of Nos 66-74 Eastgate Street for elderly residents.

For this scheme, the architects Underdown & Brealey set out to recreate the informal pattern of roof profile and elevation, typical of many Winchester streets. However, within the constraints of a public sector housing scheme, which had no requirement for chimneys, they were not able to recreate the bulk or the visual interest of the old Mazzini Arcade at the front. The scheme with gables over a ground floor common room is bolder at the back.

North of the former 'Mash Tun' public house on the east side, one section of the street is a planted open space with a hawthorn hedge against the road. This was to extend the amenity of the riverside for pedestrians walking to and from Winnall. Seen from the south, this becomes a significant aspect of the street.

Union Street on its east side contained the Moorside

Itchen Court, 62-3 Eastgate Street

Moorside House, Union Street

Garage and some indifferent housing. This site has recently been developed by St John's Charity to provide two types of specialist housing. An impressive Roman watergate in dressed stone was found here during an archaeological dig in the 1980s. The London practice of Phippen, Randall & Parkes were appointed to undertake these buildings. With their design they created a sculptural effect on the west side, with a tower on the corner.

Returning south past Union Street buildings are the trees in the riverside space, beyond which can be glimpsed St John's church tower against the trees of St Giles' Hill. At the south end of the street, King Alfred's statue, the Broadway and Abbey Gardens come into view.

The group of buildings at the south east end, including the former Mildmay Arms public house and Eastgate House on the corner, are important in townscape terms because they close off the High Street in the west/east direction and act as a focal point where Eastgate Street opens out.

St George's Street/Silver Hill

Historically, this was a narrow Saxon street climbing up the hill and similar to St Clement Street on the south side of the High Street. However St George's Street was once much longer, connecting Lower Brook Street to Staple Gardens.

Former Mildmay Arms, Eastgate Street

St George's Street looking east towards junction with Parchment Street, 1955

When the street was widened, on its northern side it had to avoid demolition of the substantial 18th century building at the end of St Peter Street. This introduced a curve in the line of the road and created a pedestrian pinchpoint which was overcome by a ground floor colonnade.

The opportunity was taken of creating a small urban space behind Godbegot House, which shows off one of Winchester's most important surviving timber-framed buildings in the High Street. Recorded in the paving pattern is the floor plan of the medieval church of St Peter in Macellis.

In townscape terms, St George's Street finishes disappointingly at its western end, at the junction between two terraced buildings in Jewry Street, with the attractive copper fleche of Queen Elizabeth II Court showing over the roofs. The City Council acquired No 5 Jewry Street with a view to creating an entrance to a major shopping development. At its eastern end, St Giles' Hill and its trees form a backcloth against which to see the buildings.

Of crucial importance to the character and scale of the street was the decision to keep and refurbish No 5 Upper Brook Street (the former Echo building) with its attractive tile hanging above a stone wall. This incorporates carved stones from the medieval church of St Ruel and bricks from an earlier Roman building discovered underground.

The adjacent development, for the City Council of the three-storey building by Casson & Conder (attached to but subservient in scale to No. 5), created a pedestrian pentice of shops away from the traffic, enclosing a space planted with six trees, paved with granite sets. At the western end, the building projects forward to emphasise the junction with Parchment Street.

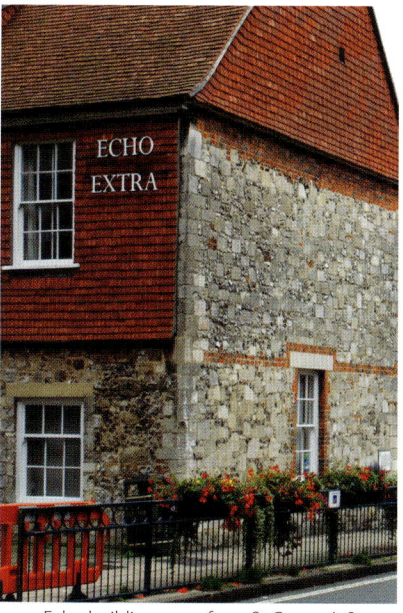

Echo building, seen from St George's Street

Unfortunately, the detailing of this building was ill-conceived and so its windows have had to be replaced, damaging its character. One of the trees had to be removed in order to provide room for lorries to service the shopping development on the other side of the street. Increased awareness of the needs of wheelchair users led to a ramp, which severely compromises the design of the space. However, the trees remain an important feature for the character of St George's Street, looking from either east or west.

The space behind Godbegot House

St George's Street was widened as far as Jewry Street, as the result of a private Act of Parliament of 1953, to by-pass the narrow section of High Street containing the Pentice and the Buttercross. This was to cater for east/west traffic including delivery vehicles and buses. The north-facing side of the street was primarily given a service function, without as much design effort given as for the buildings opposite.

Moving west up the hill, traditional buildings have been replaced with a series of flat-roofed buildings. These exhibit standard mid 20th century commercial practice with either horizontal or vertical bands of different materials and projecting flat canopies.

St George's House has an all brick elevation, with closely spaced vertical piers, and a mock-Mansard roof at the top to achieve maximum lettable floorspace. This does not achieve the subtlety of buildings in the High Street; the chunkiness of the canopy and the way that it copes with a steep change in level are not in character with Winchester. The RMC building at the top of the street exhibits no sense that its designers grasped its importance in the townscape as a corner building and the infilled frame and basement entry are visually poor. What this street demonstrates is the unimaginative overall quality of commercial architecture for shops and offices, particularly in the 1960s and early 1970s, which was driven at the time by the requirements of commercial agents and traffic engineers.

St George's House, St George's Street

There are architectural problems in fitting shop buildings with large floor areas into any traditional street pattern. From the operator's point of view, they require the maximum shelf space without windows and have demanding service requirements. Offices occupying upper floors tend to produce endless rows of windows on the outside to serve deep-plan floors.

In the 1930s Sainsbury's and Marks & Spencer established themselves in the High Street, on either side of Middle Brook Street, in mock classical buildings. Sainsbury's then abandoned their main entrance in the 1960s and built a large store behind. This presents a bald servicing aspect to Silver Hill, with a strong horizontal design emphasised by its flat roof, deep fascia and string course. The canopy rounds the corner, above large plate-glass windows, and provides views of shopping trolleys and crude lettering.

Middle Brook Street entrance to Marks & Spencer built in the 1930s, with St. Maurice's church beyond

Marks & Spencer added lumpy extensions to their High Street building, with its flat roofs and tile-hung upper-storey. Although the building in St George's Street incorporates shop windows and there is a half-hearted attempt to make patterns at first floor level, the whole design makes no positive architectural contribution.

The King's Walk development was designed to attract pedestrians away from St George's Street into a small shopping mall. This results in a service elevation to Silver Hill. Above, office floorspace was provided on three storeys linked to a multi-storey car park. The developers were required to use good quality materials. The resulting buildings have horizontal bands of tile hanging to give a more three dimensional quality than the adjacent post office building in Middle Brook Street but are completely out of character with traditional streets.

At the time of writing, the buildings described in the Silver Hill area and in particular Sainsbury's and King's Walk, still exist, but it is expected that there will be major changes to this whole site. Hopefully this run-down indifferent area of Winchester will be vastly improved.

The redevelopment of No 126 High Street in 1986, running through to St George's Street, provided a building with strong roof designs, more character in detail and in the choice and use of materials. This emphasises the important passage at the north end of Upper Brook Street and also allows views of the Cathedral.

This was followed in the late 20th century by the demolition of an ugly Woolworth's store and its replacement by a building divided into separate shops with gables in the vernacular style and using good materials but lacking convincing detail. The building has a corner turret that provides a focus when viewed from Upper Brook Street and a large loading bay in St George's Street for internal servicing. The design of the scheme improves the roofscape.

Further west, W H Smith has created a large shop, running through from the High Street to St George's Street by incorporating the former Masonic Hall. This has been achieved by using its interesting eastern elevation as the key to providing a new building that again uses good materials to break down the scale. It is designed with an attention to detail, which makes it interesting to walk past in either direction. Fascinating archaeological information concerning the medieval "John de Tytyngs House" has been incorporated inside the building, but it is doubtful how many people notice this and it might be more effective as part of its window display.

National Westminster Bank destroyed most of a listed building, apart from the attractive facade in the High Street, and created an indifferent elevation onto St George's Street. This now has a recessed lobby with cash machines, a poor solution, compared with, for example, the Lloyds Bank equivalent in the High Street.

King's Walk

Atrium, the Brooks Centre

Junction of Upper Brook Street and St George's Street

Former Masonic Hall, St George's Street

The Brooks had an ambitious floorspace brief. At its eastern end, it has been modified, with double-height windows, giving a hint of an exciting shopping interior. The St George's Street elevation is punctuated by a tower which gives it prominence in views up and down the street. It was intended as the entrance to an area of small shops, which proved not to work financially and had to be replaced with a department store.

As a tower, it fails to reflect the essential modesty and understatement of many Winchester buildings. In hindsight a more modest solution, responding to the character and grain of the town would have been a stronger contribution to the town centre.

The attempt to design good streetscape has not been successful, because the role of St George's Street/Silver Hill is ambiguous. The eastern end is terminated by the Marks & Spencer warehouse, and is almost entirely a service area. The central paved section between Middle and Upper Brook Street, gives the idea of a pedestrian area, though it has a flow of buses and taxis through it. In many ways, the rest of St George's Street is more successful, particularly if the pentice in front of the Casson & Conder block could be comprehensively redesigned.

Friarsgate

This post-war street was created primarily to take east/west traffic. It bypasses the High Street and provides access to the bus station and the central car parks.

In townscape terms, Friarsgate has the three-storey extension to the telephone exchange, with its Mansard roof, as a western terminal feature. This virtually cuts out the sight of Ashburton Court at the top of the hill. At its eastern end, the views are of St John's church silhouetted against St Giles' Hill, then the gables of Itchen Court in Eastgate Street, followed by St John's Croft, St John's Street leading up to trees on St Giles' Hill.

Because of its recent origins, Friarsgate has given rise to a variety of building types on its southern side. These comprise a two-storey health centre, a three-storey office block, a six-storey car park, and a three-storey shopping centre. In contrast, on the northern side is a mix of housing which consists of three-storey flats set within gardens, followed by an open car park and a 1930s windowless picture palace, now a church. This is visually important, but lumpy and made of poor materials that have recently been upgraded with new windows, painted, rendered walls and a much more sophisticated entrance canopy.

Within the last 15 years, trees have been maturing and now help to pull the whole area together and have given variety and attraction to the street. The trees have gone some way to offset the loss of the copper beech that used to terminate the street in Eastgate Street. They start with a group of limes on the corner of Eastgate

The tower, Brooks shopping development

Returning to the eastern end, a surface car park surrounded by compact sorbus trees was replaced by the Brooks shopping development, completed in 1991. It actually gives the same number of parking spaces, by placing them beneath the water table and introducing natural daylight right down into the car park. It created shopping at two levels, round an atrium, making use of diagonal pedestrian flows. This building has an inflexible design which if required will be expensive to modify radically. The development did, however, promote an archaeological dig that has given the town important information concerning its Roman past.

Street, then the large alder outside the Health Centre, where the stream crosses under the road. This was the site of the town's first fulling mill called Coitbury in the early 15th century; beyond are the trees in Middle Brook Street. On the north side, trees have defined the line of the street and helped to give the street some interest.

It is worth noting that much of this area is likely to be changed dramatically in the near future. A scheme is being considered which will comprehensively redevelop Kings Walk, the post office, multi-storey car park and Friarsgate through to the bus station site. As a result of this many of the existing trees in Friarsgate and Middle Brook Street are under threat. Every effort needs to be made for their retention or replacement wherever possible, to maintain one of the qualities that is the essence of Winchester, that is the co-existence of large trees and buildings.

View from Friarsgate

Friarsgate multi-storey car park

Walled City – 6: St Peter Street/Parchment Street/The Brooks/North Walls/Abbey Gardens

St Peter Street (Alwarene Street)

This is a straight street running from north to south and situated on a terrace below Jewry Street. It represents the edge of the firm ground overlooking the marshy land in the river valley, and which was originally inhabited in the Iron Age and later became part of the first Roman town.

St Peter Street started in the High Street alongside the timber framed Godbegot House as a narrow alley which was partly built on the site of the butchers' shambles. Following an archaeological dig at the time when St George's Street was widened in 1958, an open space was created in which is marked out the foundations of St Peter in Macellis, a church whose origins go back to the early 11th century.

In terms of levels, St Peter Street rises up to No 6, Avebury House and then slopes steadily down to North Walls. Its length is broken by the large forest trees on either side of the street that appear to form a tunnel view in summer, even though the trees are well separated.

From a townscape point of view, St Peter Street north of St George's Street roughly divides into three sections. The southern section contains mostly listed buildings built hard up against the pavement, with the southern vista terminated by three-storey buildings in the High Street. The middle section is rather indeterminate, with a wide range of building types and styles including buildings associated with the Roman Catholic community. The northern section consists of two three-storey terraces facing each other, a 19th century terrace on the east and a 1970s sheltered housing scheme, Richard Moss House, on the west (which replaced a large cinema building), all creating a formal street character. The northern end of the street is closed off by a tree spreading over the wall built on the line of the original city wall.

In land use terms, this is a mixed street of offices, hotel and housing – although historically, since the Reformation, St Peter Street has had a special association with the Roman Catholic community.

North of St George's Street, the eastern side of St Peter Street starts with an unusual listed 18th century building, with wide door-case and twin two-storey

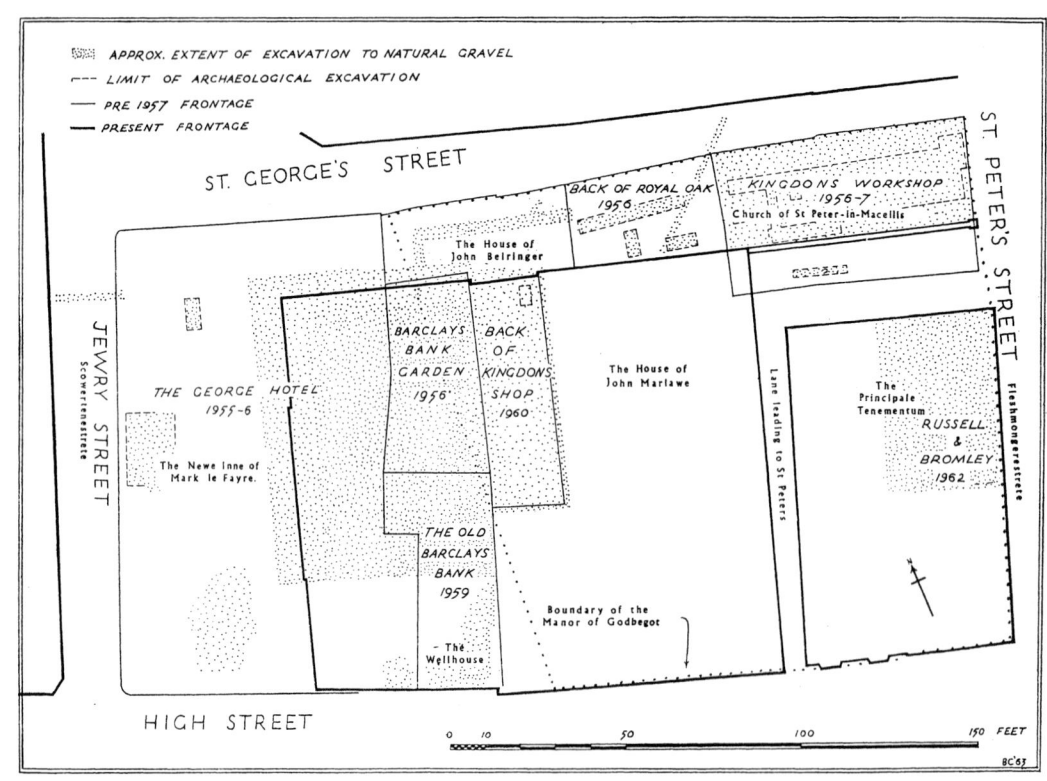

Historical pattern of area between St Peter Street and Jewry Street. From *Winchester Excavations 1949-1960*, Vol. 1 by Barry Cunliffe, Winchester Excavations Committee

splayed bays. There follows a 19th century gabled building which, in fact, hides a medieval detached timber-framed kitchen and the extensive frontage of the Royal Hotel. This commences with a storage-type building over the entrance into the hotel yard. (This is the best point from which to see the extent of timber-framed buildings remaining at the south end of Parchment Street). The painted brick storage building has many blocked up window openings and an internal hoist surviving from its earlier use as a silk mill.

No 23 St Peter Street

The rendered and painted entrance front of the Royal Hotel, with its slate roofs, is an interesting asymmetrical composition with a modest single-storey doorway between projecting wings leading into a top-lit vestibule of some charm. In 1583 this was the site of Lady West's House, so called after a Catholic recusant. Then from 1795, a refugee order of Benedictine nuns from Brussels occupied the house until 1857 and the upper front bedroom is believed to date from that period. Two years later, a local business man Charles W Benny turned the building complex into the Royal Hotel, as it appears today, with a major elevation and conservatory facing north into the sunlit garden. Along the street, this garden is defined by a stone, flint and brick wall; behind are planted three major forest trees. The garden is at a lower level than the street and is a survivor of gardens that used to exist north of the High Street. It is bounded by the high south wall and roof of the Methodist Chapel. Sadly, this garden was narrowed to accommodate the two-storey bedroom block, needed to expand the hotel in the 1980s.

Royal Hotel

St Peter Street, by Heywood Sumner

two-storey, windowless store behind No 4. This has now been transformed into a modern office building, with its own car park behind with access from St Peter Street. In townscape terms, it is important that No 4 retains its character as a free-standing cube and the temptation to add infill offices, between this and No 5, should be resisted. No 5 is a good Victorian Gothic building, with stone mullioned-and-transomed windows that fits the townscape sequence well.

North view of the Benedictine Convent, St Peter Street

On the west side of this section of street, there are two little 18th century town houses with delicate doorcases (with a brutal 1970s office building slapped on the end), with basement car parking access from the rear.

Next door is a fine house, with a central chimney stack and particularly strong modillion eaves, supposedly designed for the Duchess of Portsmouth by Wren's office in the mid 17th century. It was later significantly modernised, with a rendered front, 19th century windows and slate roofs, and painted white. For many years this and the adjacent building had been occupied by the Probate Office, who had a

No 4 St Peter Street

No 5

Entrance to Avebury House

No 6, Avebury House, is an important Grade I listed building erected in 1690 with tiled roofs, strong modillion eaves and soft red brick, slightly set back from the street. Built probably for Sir Charles Norton, the two wings were added soon after.

The southern wing contains an excellent arched cellar and the north incorporates an entrance gateway (with very fine wrought iron gates), through which one can glimpse Milner Hall framed by a yew tree. Unfortunately, the walled garden of this fine building is completely given over to car parking, apart from three trees. The windows of this house appear to have been modernised with Georgian sash windows, in place of 17th century cross windows.

It has one of the most beautiful doorcases in Winchester, leading through into a panelled entrance hall. Internally the passage is defined by delicate Corinthian columns. This doorcase may possibly have been added when the windows were modernised in 1740. It remained a private house for 249 years, getting its name in 1790 from a vicar retiring from Avebury. In 1817, it became the house of Dr Charles Mayo FRCS, a surgeon to the County Hospital in Parchment Street, who helped to establish the reputation of the hospital as a teaching centre. He also became Mayor in 1840, 1845 and 1852. It has been in office use since 1939 having been purchased by the Government and used by the Inland Revenue, before being sold to Mr Rothman for his accountancy practice in 1964.

The next section of the west side of the street illustrates the resurgence of the Winchester Catholic community led by their outstanding French-trained priest, John Milner 1752-1826. He was also a noted antiquarian and published in 1798 'The History, Civil and Ecclesiastical, and Survey of the Antiquities of Winchester' which became a best seller. John Milner took up residence in the house next to Avebury House, called St Peter's House, built by a cavalier named Roger Coram. It was used by Catholic priests, who celebrated Mass in a flimsy building in the garden.

Interior view of St Peter's Chapel (Milner)

Outside view of St Peter's Chapel (Milner, 1798)

On this site in 1792, Milner built a fine chapel, which was to be the first Roman Catholic church built in England since 1585. It was designed by John Carter as the first ecclesiastical building of the Gothic Revival in England. Inside, the church was decorated with paintings by William Cave and had important window glass and fittings, including, in the centre of the altar, a tabernacle modelled on the west end of York Minster. The 12th century stonework of the street entrance was brought from the demolished leper hospital of St Mary Magdalen, to the east of the city, where it had formed the west doorway. This was taken down to be incorporated in the new St Peter's church in 1926 and replaced by the present stonework of the gateway. After the Emancipation Act of 1829, the Catholic community grew and acquired more buildings and land to the north as well as in Jewry Street. The attractive gabled Peterhouse was pulled down and three terraced houses erected in 1826, with cast-iron railings around the area at the front. Adjoining this was a school, and a fine brick wall with an elaborate brick coping and pineapple gate-pier finials. These mark the entrance through to the early 17th century convent. In

1926 a new much larger St Peter's of yellow iron-stone construction was erected to the design of F A Walters, the chancel of which, with its chequer-board pattern of flint-and-stone panels, and tower, form an important visual contribution to this part of St Peter Street.

By the 1960s the Roman Catholic estate had become very run down. A presbytery was constructed alongside the church and later converted into a Parish Hall when a new Peterhouse presbytery was built behind the brick wall. Major repairs were undertaken to the convent and Milner Hall (the original church) was given back its vaulted interior. This former chapel had been vandalised and stripped of its vaulting in the 1950s due to dry rot, an upper floor inserted and used for electrical appliance repairs. A modern wrought-iron gate has been introduced at the street entrance, to replace a heavy studded wooden door, so that after 200 years the church porch can be seen from the road. The opportunity was also taken to redesign the landscape of this charming courtyard garden to unite all these buildings.

Opposite, on the eastern side, is the strong gabled form of the Methodist church. Built around 1880, of flint with stone dressings, with twin entrance doors, plate-tracery windows above and a slate roof, this church was recently converted into twelve flats.

To the north of this, Sutton Gardens (once a 19th century market garden with greenhouses) was made into a residential development, with attractive Sussex bricks, of two storeys on the road side and three storeys behind. This creates two paved courtyards dominated on the east side by trees. At this point in the street, one gets a fine view eastward to St Giles' Hill, seen over the trees and buildings of Parchment Street in winter. On the roadside are two infill domestic Victorian buildings, of no particular architectural merit. Next door, at Albion Place, an ugly flat roofed extension to a Victorian rectory has been replaced by a tall three-storey extension using classical details which enrich the curved south end, making a distinctive townscape feature. Behind, a courtyard development has been created with two square, three-storey towers, and a ground floor veranda which returns on the west side as mews flats over garages. St Peter's church tower is very dramatic seen from this point.

Gate piers to Peterhouse with pineapples

The northern section of the street comprises one of the biggest and deepest terraces in Winchester, Princess Court, three storeys high with a semi-basement, and a slate roof containing attics and chimneys. Erected to a rather austere design, with sash windows that have very slender glazing bars, a central carriage arch, a later bay, and cast iron railings to the front areas, these houses are built in pale yellow Beaulieu bricks at the front, which became the fashion for a short time in 19th century Winchester. As they complement the stone of the Catholic church yellow bricks have been specifically encouraged by the Planning Department for new development in this area.

Albion Place

Princess Court, St Peter Street

A modern yellow brick has been used on the upper storeys of the social housing opposite, which has three gables with slightly projecting bays to break the length, effective in perspective. Railings on top of a brick wall add privacy to the ground floor and interest to the street, mirroring the fine set of Victorian railings opposite. However, the difficulty of matching bricks and railings is apparent and the combined effect makes this a rather severe section of street, too narrow to be softened by the planting of trees.

Royal Oak Passage

This is primarily an access to the Royal Oak public house, which has a 14th century cellar. On the east side, it is flanked by a 15th century timber-framed building, known as Godbegot House. Historically, this was a Saxon site which came under the jurisdiction of the church, rather than the town, allowing people to seek sanctuary there. It was originally designed as a series of small properties entered from the passage with a grander house at the front. The house has a fine panelled upper room. Godbegot House was converted into a hotel in 1908 and an American financier, J Pierpont Morgan, paid for the new timber-framed front which replaced a skin-deep 18th century rendered facade. The building is now a restaurant.

The upper room in Godbegot House

It is the best place in Winchester to get some idea of the architectural power of a double-jettied, timber frame, which almost covers the passage. Through this, from the north there is a view across the High Street to St Thomas Street. The passage is paved with old limestone.

Parchment Street

This is the one street on the northern side of High Street now forming a complete townscape entity, despite being cut through by St George's Street. Looking northward, the view at the end of Parchment Street is closed by two-storey, terraced houses on the line of the former city wall.

The street has a substantial commercial/shopping component. Because it links in so closely with the Buttercross on the High Street, it stands a reasonable chance of succeeding commercially, despite the barrier to free movement represented by St George's Street.

It is made up of properties that are predominantly two-storey, although the height increases at the southern end, where three-storey buildings are introduced. Significantly, there are contrasts of height and form along the street to make it visually interesting. Looking from the

Southern end of Parchment Street

High Street, the bulk and chimneys of No 71 on the east, the pinnacles and roofs of the Methodist church, oriel windows, symbol shop signs and a variety of shop fronts give Parchment Street an air of some significance.

The northern, predominantly residential, end has front gardens, making this in summer a 'green' route into the town.

At the High Street end, W H Smith built their strong corner building in 1927 as a ground floor shop with a tea room above in a modern interpretation of a barn, with internal wall paintings depicting the life of King Alfred. The architects used an Arts and Crafts style, with oak detailing and decorative lead work. Its service end, designed as a medieval stone building, is so much more attractive than the banal utilitarian approach adopted in many mid-20th century buildings. Smith's have taken up the full length between the High Street and St George's Street by acquiring the Masonic Hall at the back and retaining its characteristic gable. This sizeable shop helps to keep alive this section of Parchment Street together with the smaller shops opposite.

Terrace on east side of Parchment Street

Parchment Street, west side

On the western side of Parchment Street beyond St George's Street, the brick fronts of numbers 6 and 7 disguise earlier timber-framed buildings. No 9 not only has a splendid shell door canopy, coved eaves and sash windows, but internally has a fine staircase and a set of panelled rooms, one with a decorative plaster ceiling. When the ground floor was taken over by a wine merchant in the 1930s, the building was mutilated by the insertion of wide shop-window openings. Sash windows matching the originals replaced these when No 9 was upgraded to office use in the 1970s. However there was a price to be paid for this change which brought the attic rooms into use together with the introduction of two central chimneys with a plastic replica at roof level.

When the wine merchants moved from No 9 into the former counting house next door with its extensive cellar, an enlarged window was put in on the ground floor. With the recent alterations to this part of the building (in conjunction with the conversion of the adjoining chapel to residential use) this window has been replaced with a single large sheet of glazing fixed to the external face of the building.

On the opposite side of the road was the large house, stables and garden of Sir John Clobury, a 17th century soldier, who assembled the site from 16 medieval properties. In 1758 this was acquired for Winchester's first purpose-built hospital, designed by John Wood, an architect from Bath. This was a substantial classical building, 224 feet long, three storeys high, containing six wards and a chapel. It had a grand entrance approached by two flights of steps and a pediment over, and projecting end wings, the whole set behind railings with a garden at the rear. The three townhouses Nos 12 to 14 on the west side were erected at about the same time and occupied by staff in the hospital. After 100 years, it was eventually abandoned due to poor drainage and lack of sewers in the area, in the belief that an elevated site in Romsey Road would be more suitable for a modern hospital. Here the architect William Butterfield designed and built the present County hospital in the 1860s. The Parchment Street site was sold and redeveloped for terraced houses both in this street and Upper Brook Street. There was no thought of converting the building to any other use. Meanwhile the argument between the 'Muckabites' (city ratepayers who refused a sixpenny rate to build a sewerage system) and the 'anti-Muckabites' (led by the doctors, and including the Bishop and those from the Close and College who did not have to pay rates) continued until 1875 when the new sewerage system was completed.

Former County Hospital, Parchment Street, east side. Photograph by William Savage c. 1865

The brick, Gothic Methodist church on the west side was built in 1903, with fifteen foundation stones. (Until recently it was occupied by the Samaritans but now houses the Winchester Business Centre.) It has two gabled entrance porches, battlements and pinnacles, and tall pointed windows, all of which give very strong vertical emphasis to the building. This is important to the townscape character of Parchment Street when looked at from both directions. It is better built than the Salvation Army building at the far end of the street which, whilst contributing equally to the skyline, was structurally poor and had to be replaced with a replica. The original Methodist church has now been converted for housing with a modern five-storey tower block behind using a boarded finish and topped by a white penthouse.

Opposite the church is what was Winchester's first post office, a yellow brick building with elaborate detailing; next to it was Will Short's car repair garage, later taken over by Blackwell & Moody whose business activity is commemorated in the name of Stonemasons' Court. The community of small businesses grouped around this paved courtyard creates an attractive space off the main street. Directly opposite, at No 11, another courtyard but less tightly enclosed is Kingdon's Yard, taking its name from the ironmongers who once occupied the site.

Former Methodist church

Stonemasons' Court

Former Post Office

The main building, which used to be timber framed, has been substantially rebuilt retaining the same elevations to the street, including the unusual shopfront with its curved glass and wooden detail. This was recycled from a liner being dismantled at Southampton in the 1930s. It also still retains the interesting wrought-iron sign on the first floor, which casts strong shadows as a result of the street's north/south alignment. This building now has a bay window at the southern end, to adapt it for residential use over the shops, and has an office building wrapped round the courtyard at the rear, with modern railings at the entrance. The tree planted in the courtyard needs time to grow to form the focus of this composition. Next to the entrance to Kingdon's Yard is the rear access road to the Royal Hotel.

On the opposite side, British Telecom has an entrance for high lorries to service the back of the telephone exchange in Upper Brook Street. Near the north east end of Parchment Street there is a fine late-Victorian Gothic terrace, made interesting partly by using repeated building forms such as gabled bays and partly by varied treatment of decorative elements such as bargeboards. This terrace successfully merges into a lesser design to the south that nevertheless has striking windows. Opposite, a new building has been inserted on the site of a prefabricated hut, re-forming the line of the street and providing a day centre with flats above. This repeats the gabled form but without the interest in detail that would improve and suit its prominence. The courtyard contained within the development gives a fine view of the Roman Catholic church tower in St Peter Street through the canopy of important trees on its western boundary.

Between this development and the Salvation Army citadel, a row of failing shops and a group of industrial garages (which totally covered the backland) have now been replaced by two rows of town houses that reinforce the scale of the street. These show considerable attention to detail, so that the varied silhouette typical of this sort of street has been maintained.

Kingdon's Yard entrance

The Brooks

The Brooks are a low lying part of the city which the Romans drained when they wanted to expand their town. The Saxons organised the three open brooks running through the area, which remained the principal means of drainage until the 19th century. These brooks are now mostly underground. Over the centuries the area has had widely fluctuating fortunes, following variations in commercial prosperity and population changes in Winchester as a whole.

The street's character has been transformed at the southern end by modern development including the Brooks Shopping Centre so that it is now a residential street at its north end and a commercial street at its south end. Looking north, the street has lost its terminal feature in North Walls by the pulling down of town houses and the creation of a car park. Looking south, the street relates to the Cathedral in three different ways. From the north section one gets a view of the very long, lead nave roof sailing serenely above all other roofs. In the southern section, there is a good three-quarter view of the Cathedral tower and north transept, with its rose window seen over the modern development in St George's Street. Crossing over St George's Street there is the first sight of the full height of the buff stone nave and two tiers of windows.

The Brooks from Lower Brook Street, 1955

23 Upper Brook Street 1955

There is evidence of settled housing in Roman times, after the Norman Conquest and in the later Middle Ages, with stone and timber houses and often with small industrial activities such as textiles and tanning mixed in.

In the 19th century it contained markets, a wool warehouse, a flax factory, an iron foundry, a timber yard and slaughterhouses. There was an expansion of high-density brick houses, plus churches and a school. As the result of post-war planning policy, large sections have been redeveloped.

Upper Brook Street/Market Street (Sildwortenestret or Shieldmakers)

This was originally a Saxon street on low-lying land, which had a brook running through it, and which connects North Walls and the High Street. It used to have a group of fine 17th century townhouses, virtually opposite the Echo building. The controversial demolition of these, as part of the City Council's comprehensive development proposals, led to the founding of the Winchester Preservation Trust in 1957 and to their subsequent successful application to have Nos 30/32 listed in 1978.

The Echo building

The west side is given strength by the retention of the Echo building, and in the northern half of the street by the long, two-storey, red-brick Victorian terrace, with well-designed windows and doors relieved by an attractive string course. Near the North Walls junction there is an interesting three-bay 'Gothic variation' with roughcast walls, inset entrance and prominent decorative fascia over, Gothic casement windows and good chimneys. At its southern end, the street's scale and integrity has been destroyed by the bulk of the 1930s

'Gothic variation' house, Upper Brook Street

telephone exchange and its somewhat more interesting northward 1970s extension which, despite its modern Mansard roof and recessed ground floor shop windows, has a very two-dimensional elevation. This extension was curtailed in size by the presence of the existence of the listed building next door. The Porthouse and the 1960s Casson Conder block, extending round the corner from St George's Street, both adopt flat roofs to keep down the height and scale of three-storey buildings.

On the east side, at the north end, the graveyard of Holy Trinity provides a contrast to the continuous line of buildings opposite. With its attractive gate, flint walls and the avenue of lime trees leading up to its west front, the church entrance is flanked by a Gothic flint-and-brick corner lodge to the north and the gabled end of the 19th century church hall to the south. The controversial decision by the Secretary of State, in 1980, to refuse demolition of Nos 30/32 (two 1846 artisan dwellings) has enabled the north end of the street to retain its two-storey character. The area between the church and Nos 30/32 was the subject of a development brief and resulted in a modern development which succeeds in fitting into the scale of the area. No 30/32 became the Winchester Heritage Centre, headquarters of the City of Winchester Trust which provides a watching brief on development proposals in the context of the overall historical background of this great city.

The adjoining open car park site behind Winchester Family Church (a former cinema and bingo hall) has an expensive telephone cable underground which limits any development. The area has lost two important sorbus trees – those that remain were part of the planting around the old central car park created under Abercrombie's plan in the 1950s.

The Porthouse, Upper Brook Street

The Brooks shopping centre abruptly marks the change in scale of the central area, and introduced a building type foreign to Winchester, covering a whole street block. Here it presents huge openings for servicing, capped by a smaller scale third floor, with a gabled roof treatment. The new road which has been introduced linking Friarsgate with St George's Street illustrates how the geometry required for modern traffic fits ill with traditional townscape. However, the scheme does enable street trees to be incorporated, of which the plane tree outside the winestore is the most important contribution to the street perspective.

West side of the Brooks shopping centre

Whatever the merit of the Brooks scheme, the south west corner is possibly the least successful single element. It incorporates a main entrance (including one for disabled people) and gives the shops some sort of external balcony. It has already been modified to incorporate the needs of the larger British Home Stores shop in St George's Street but the falsity of the large blank shop windows is all too obvious.

South end of Upper Brook Street

On the south side of St George's Street, the gable of the Jaeger building and the brick tower of McDonalds mark the narrow southern end of Upper Brook Street. Unfortunately, plot sizes on the east side are too narrow to permit shops on both sides of this important link and on the High Street and St George's Street frontages as well. The compensating decoration of the side wall in bays is very half-hearted, making the character of shop fronts, blinds and hanging signs on the west side all the more important.

At the south end, the rather teasing junction with the High Street and its busy pedestrian activity, the attractive building at No 25 High Street, the glimpse past its colonnade to the classical stone and brick Market building, the Cathedral and trees in the Cathedral Close all contribute to a rewarding townscape.

Market Street

This is a short, straight street leading to what was Winchester's enclosed Market Square until the late 19th century. Now it looks into the Close along an avenue to the buttresses and pinnacles of the Cathedral's west front with the dark silhouette of the gable-end and the impressive set of chimneys of No 11 the Close rising over the flint boundary wall beyond.

Market Street, looking south

The western side with the pavement has a recent set of small shops, with better detailed shop fronts than many in Winchester – crying out for good symbol signs. The Market Inn on the corner is of a 19th century design and conceals the remains of a substantial timber building. The eastern side now has the flank of the stone and brick market building of 1857, hard on the road edge and recently converted to provide flats and shops. Beyond that is the end elevation of Morley College almshouses behind the brick wall.

Middle Brook Street (Wunegrestret)

On the line of the major Roman street running under the Cathedral to Kingsgate this is a straight link between North Walls and the High Street, and on the axis of the north transept of the Cathedral which (with its rose window and the tower above) is the most significant townscape factor in the street.

Middle Brook Street 1813, painting by Samuel Prout

Clearly, it was a grander street in medieval times, as the watercolour in the City Museum by Samuel Prout illustrates. This shows its central open brook, a number of gable-ended timber-framed houses, some adapted as shops with first-floor projecting windows, with carved brackets under the decorative barge-boards (as can still be seen on Cheyney Court in the Cathedral Close), together with St Maurice's church and the forest trees behind, over which the Cathedral dominates.

A comparison with the same view today illustrates how the scale of central Winchester has changed in the late 19th and 20th centuries. Although the trees in the Close can still be seen, they are mostly hidden by the shop extension to Debenhams, which completely hides the tower of St Maurice's church. A new tower containing lifts to offices and car park at the junction of the multi-storey car park and Middle Brook Street, starts to intrude on the Cathedral tower and the skyline.

Market stalls in Middle Brook Street

Looking northwards, where the two-storey scale of the Victorian housing predominates, this street is continued by the avenue of lime and plane trees beyond the line of the northern city wall to the art school campus and the recreation ground. This avenue is complemented by the trees in the Holy Trinity churchyard on the western side. The eastern elevation of Holy Trinity, with its flint walls, great east window and needle-like copper fleche dominates this space.

In terms of use, the southern end up to Friarsgate is a shopping street with market stalls offering a variety of produce, adding an attractive venue to Winchester's shopping experience. The northern end of the street is residential, the site of the former King Alfred Boys' Club having been redeveloped as two terraces of town houses set at right angles to each other.

Terrace on site of Boys' Club

On the eastern side, where there used to be a Franciscan friary until the Dissolution, there is an Edwardian terrace with large windows, making use of flint in its main walling. This is followed by Victorian houses with attractively detailed bay windows. This section of the street ends with No 36, a 16th century timber-framed building that was disguised by Victorian trappings and discovered as it was about to be demolished in 1975 as part of the comprehensive redevelopment of the adjacent site. Permission was given for an office building to be added, forming a small courtyard, provided that the original building was restored, including the well-preserved 17th century wall paintings inside. On the western side, the Victorian housing next to the bingo hall was similarly reprieved from demolition, though the potentially attractive space opposite No 36 (Prince's Buildings) is disappointingly just grass and a telephone pole.

No 36 Middle Brook Street

In the shopping area, the section of the street between Marks & Spencer and Sainsbury's is dull and featureless. The next section adjoining the Brooks and containing the market stalls is much more lively.

On the eastern side, the set-back Kings Walk shopping centre is a three-storey building, designed in bands of tile hanging and windows, which leads through to an inner courtyard in front of a brick warehouse adapted as a retail market and one of the few buildings in this clearance area to be retained. Kings Walk is the sort of building that is very difficult to modify and the added entrance canopy is hardly an improvement. The bland office elevation of the Post Office next door, is about to be changed along with the multi-storey car park. The car park tower affords one of the best views of the northern aspect of the Cathedral from its staircase window.

View of the Cathedral from the car park tower

Lower Brook Street/ Tanner Street

This is a curved, level street, most of which has been affected by compulsory redevelopment. It is primarily residential as far as Friarsgate. At its junction with Union Street, there is a view of the Cathedral tower above the multi-storey car park, softened by the foliage of the special ash trees planted on the north side of Friarsgate.

From the junction with Silver Hill, at its southern end, the Cathedral tower is seen again over the modern shops in the High Street where distinctive chimneys add interest.

Looking north east, the street is terminated by the trees to the east of the police station. Approaching Union Street, the tower of Moorside (St John's care home) becomes a focal feature.

At its north end, the street starts with the traditionally designed fire station, fronting Union Street with its yard behind, through which can be seen the east end and fleche of Holy Trinity and a beech tree. There follows a pleasant, curved row of late-Victorian brick houses, with slate roofs, ground floor bay windows and a small garden space in front, defined by low brick walls. On the east side is a brick

Kings Walk shopping centre

terrace of flats, built for the fire service, with balcony access on the top floor and projecting staircases. These look rather awkward as street architecture and have a flat roof because the planning authority at the time did not want the Cathedral tower challenged by higher buildings. They have their garages to the south, creating a weak corner with Garden Lane.

Cossack Lane House

On the south side of this is Cossack Lane House, a four-storey block of flats which projects into the street in both directions. This was, in fact, a warehouse, virtually square on plan, converted by Bendall, a local firm of developers, with rendered first and second floor walls, totally modern windows and a steep, 'mock Mansard' slate top storey, with as many dormers as the windows below. This was, at the time, a typical 'conservation area' type of application, but a comparison with Wharf Mill (developed by the same team) demonstrates how much more successful the latter was in retaining an industrial character.

To the south of this, and set back behind a low wall and front gardens, is a three-storey block of flats, Godson House, with low-pitched slate roofs, inset balconies and Sussex stock bricks. This has rather pleasant proportions, typical of architect Peter Shepheard's housing in this area. It contrasts

Godson House, rear elevation

with the rear elevation which is obscured by timber-framed walkways. These overlook a sunken car park bounded on the other side by No 36 Middle Brook Street and the Winchester Family Church. This car park site was the subject of a major archaeological excavation in the 1960s, uncovering the churches of St Mary and St Pancras, together with a variety of house foundations and evidence for the cloth industry that flourished until about 1400 in central Winchester.

South of Friarsgate, in Tanner Street we find the traditional brick, three-storey, tiled-roofed NHS Coitbury House, its neighbouring square brick box St Clement's Surgery, with blue panels and a flat roof on the east, and the five-storey car park and the postal sorting office (now closed) on the west. This has a large opening for lorries together with the service bay to Kings Walk shopping centre. Altogether, this does not make for good townscape.

The two-storey building at the end in Silver Hill, contains Hunts the Chemist, which moved from No 45 High Street, following the doctors' surgeries when they relocated from the Trafalgar Street area.

Wool warehouse, north elevation

On the east side of Tanner Street, surrounded by parking, is a large, well-built four-storey brick wool warehouse, used as such well into the 19th century. This used to have a continuous window along its north elevation to light the workspace. It is currently used as a store by Marks & Spencer. To get an idea of its true importance in the townscape, it is necessary to view it from Joyce Gardens or St Giles' Hill, (where it is seen to have a much larger bulk than the medieval St John's Rooms) since it is almost hidden from the High Street by the buildings flanking the Bus Station. Its retention is proposed as part of the Silver Hill comprehensive redevelopment scheme which will see the demolition of nearly all the other buildings in this area.

Cross Keys Passage

This is an important pedestrian link between Lower Brook Street and the High Street, through a small arched opening next to an old timber hall house that has been much altered. The rear wing on the east side is a pleasant, 19th century building; on the west side of the passage, the flat roofed extension to No 153 was intended to be a series of small brick kiosk shops, but never used as such.

Beyond the R.A.O.B. Club, the passage opens out into a yard which contains an electricity sub-station and a series of unattractive buildings with flat roofs and unpleasant windows on all sides. The sudden emergence through the little arch into the High Street, opposite the 19th century Welcome Gospel Hall entrance, comes as a complete contrast.

Cross Keys Passage, looking south

Looking north

North Walls

This straight street, probably of Roman and certainly Saxon origin, has always been inside the city wall and ditch which separated the town from the lowlands and waterways to the north – making a strong 'edge' to the town. Since the late 19th century the development of suburbs has blurred this edge.

In the 1750s the North Gate with its chapel above was demolished after part had fallen down on a christening party. The only evidence of the medieval wall is a very small section of ancient monument near the end of St Peter Street, now incorporated in a 19th century wall. The 19th century terraces have replaced the medieval wall and Holy Trinity church, on the other side of the road, with its steep slate roof and copper fleche, is set back behind a low flint wall within its own landscape of trees.

The change in levels at the west end of North Walls is quite dramatic and can be appreciated from the footpath and small open space in the recently completed housing on the former Marston Brewery site.

North Walls looking east, c. 1900 from Warren's *Winchester Illustrated*, 1905

Odeon Cinema and former St Swithun's School, September 1944

Winchester High School for Girls, North Walls c. 1890

bay and balconies. Note the range of attic windows which command superb views. North Walls provides quick access to the one-way system and the motorway, as well as to the central streets of Winchester. It is very narrow for the volume of traffic that uses it, but it works better as part of the east/west one-way system than the previous two-way traffic system that created enormous delays in the 1960s. It gives little amenity to pedestrians and cyclists, although it is important as the only street (apart from the High Street) to go all the way through the city centre.

It is a street of mixed residential, office and service use, with the two-storey police and fire stations at the eastern end. The scale is larger with predominately three-storey buildings at the south western end, which was non-residential for nearly a hundred years. When St Swithun's Girls' School moved out to Morn Hill in 1932, the site became an art school and later served as the County Library Headquarters and Reference Library until recently. These impressive buildings have high floor to ceiling heights, steep gabled roofs and carefully detailed windows. Proposals are under consideration for conversion of the building to houses and apartments retaining most of the exterior fabric of the original school building. Already returned to residential use in the 1980s was the site of the former Odeon Cinema, demolished to build Richard Moss House on the corner of St Peter's Street. The 19th century terrace in St Peter Street on the opposite corner has an arresting scale with its end wall rising up sheer four storeys from the pavement, enlivened by its east facing

Richard Moss House, North Walls

In townscape terms, the eastern view with the flint-and-brick wall on the north side and a succession of three-storey buildings on the south side drops steeply down to the roofs and chimneys of the late Victorian terraces facing south that then line the road as far as Middle Brook Street. For a short distance beyond, there are terraces on both sides. The ones facing south are early 19th century built using the cream Beaulieu bricks. These are followed by the two-storey 1960s police station with two lime trees marking its entrance. The terrace facing north Nos 60-66 is late 19th century with good two-storey bays, well-detailed entrances, and small protected gardens in front.

The street is terminated by the tower of Moorside, attached to a strongly modelled residential building that defines the change in the road's direction. This is seen against the background of pleasant buildings on high ground in Beggars Lane and the trees of St Giles' Hill beyond. With the combination of the trees along the waterway north of the police station and the tower, the street effectively signals a 'gateway' to the riverside and the streets beyond, which still contain one or two remnants of the medieval town.

Looking westward, the road rises up from Parchment Street (the effective edge of the first part of the Roman town) and ends with the substantial corner buildings on the west side of Jewry Street. Here there are two linked portions of an office building over the flint-walled car park, which replaced the picturesque late 19th century Crown and Cushion public house, designed by Thomas Stopher. The flint walls combine with a small tree to make successful townscape at that end of the street.

Abbey Gardens

The space that is now Abbey Gardens, was originally protected by being the site of the Saxon Nunnaminster founded by the wife of King Alfred, Queen Ealhswith in 903. It was rebuilt in 1100 when it became St Mary's Abbey. By the time of its dissolution in 1539, it was an important religious house supporting 102 people including 26 nuns, and providing education for children. It had its own mill, brewhouse and bakery and also had a responsibility to maintain the East Gate of the city.

After the Dissolution under Henry VIII, the site was given to the City Corporation, the western part becoming an industrial sector. The eastern part was sold in 1699 to William Pescod, a lawyer, who built his house here and created a garden with avenues and tree planting. The house had its entrance on the south side within the garden, probably because the Bridewell that used to be looked after by the nuns was still in existence in the High Street, before it was widened into the Broadway. At some time in the 18th century, a pedimented gateway was added to the front of the mill building as an 'eyecatcher' feature within the garden.

The house and garden are clearly shown in Bucks' engraving of 1736, Godson's map of 1750 (which includes an avenue on the site of Abbey Passage) and Milne's map of 1791. The 1873 Ordnance Survey map shows two pairs of houses adjoining the east side of Abbey House, called Folkestone Place.

Abbey Mill

When the Corporation acquired Abbey House and garden for use by the Mayor, the Bridewell was removed and a new entrance was made from the High Street with decorative towers on either side. In 1880 Richard Moss (brewer and Winchester Member of Parliament) had a highly decorative cast-iron fence erected in front to protect people from the waterway that fed Abbey Mill and to enable the 'public pleasure ground' to be controlled. By 1887 Folkestone Place had been demolished, opening up the space that has become the Broadway.

Abbey Gardens now has a complicated pattern of use. People living in houses in central Winchester bring their children to play here as a central park. It is used by visitors to the town as a place to relax and as a meeting place. The eastern part has been set aside as a children's play area with swings and a splendid red train.

Abbey Gardens

In townscape terms, the garden offers a delightful three-quarter view of the east end of the Cathedral from the little riverside that runs through to Abbey Mill (now an office). The Cathedral rises up over the City Council offices, the adjacent houses and the yew trees planted down the western side. To the east, there are good views of St Giles' Hill rising up over the 1970s wing of St John's South, the almshouses that enclose most of the eastern side of the garden. At ground level there is a diagonal view up part of Eastgate Street.

Typically of Winchester, Abbey Gardens does not have a formal architectural setting. Nonetheless, standing under the mill portico a range of historic buildings can be seen, including the medieval St John's House, Abbey House from the 18th century, and the 19th century Guildhall and almshouses. There is also a view of the Broadway, at this point used as a coach stop, seen through the cast-iron railings.

The mill stream in the garden is an attractive feature, overhung with weeping willows, alder and oak trees which create an attractive centre piece. Also in the garden there are some specimen trees of particular significance, like the handkerchief tree.

This park is highly manicured with beds of roses and annuals. There is also a scented garden, designed for the particular use of the blind.

Abbey Passage

This interesting pedestrian route, containing a whole series of surprises within quite a short distance, starts next to Abbey House beneath the porch of the Guildhall Saxon Suite. It is a path that continues with visual interest at both low and high levels.

To the east the trees in Abbey Gardens overhang the path while, to the west, the space opens out around a sunken area. This is one of the few places in central Winchester where archaeological discoveries are displayed below ground level. It is disappointing that the information boards have faded – more could be made of this area showing the remains of the Abbey. Around the excavations can be seen the strongly patterned brickwork of the Guildhall.

From here, the passage closes in with a row of five cottages, with slate roofs, rendered flint-and-brick end walls on the west side, and glimpses out to Abbey Gardens on the east.

Medieval gateway to Water Close

The path continues with brick walls on either side, broken by access points, and gives an end view of the three-storey City offices, before a three-quarter view of the east end of the Cathedral and its tower opens up. To the east, the path is closed by buildings until, at the end, the magnificent plane trees in the Dean's Garden can be seen. On the other side of Colebrook Street is Water Close. This is a wider space, with a small-scale, medieval doorway leading through into the Cathedral Close. Here on the right is a classical water garden, with a large magnolia, stone balustrade, water lilies and a pencil pine as a foreground to the great east window of the Cathedral chancel. This is one of Winchester's most intimate and admired views.

Walking back to the Broadway, note the variety of trees on either side of the Passage and the strong contrast between the yew trees on the edge of Abbey Gardens and the views of lawns and flowerbeds opening up within it.

Classical water garden, Water Close

Walled City – 7: Colebrook Street

Looking west, Friends' Meeting House in foreground

From the High Street looking south, with St John's Almshouses South on the right

Looking east

The U-shape of this street, which used to have its own church of St Peter at the east end, derives from its position between St Mary's Abbey, the City walls to the east, the ground occupied by Wolvesey Palace on the south and the Cathedral Close walls on the south and west. Its relative spaciousness at the western end is due to a process of demolition of slums in the 1950s as part of Sir Patrick Abercrombie's plan for an administrative centre for the city. It was felt that a great ecclesiastical building should not be hemmed in with lesser buildings in medieval fashion, but be 'opened up' to the river by straightening Colebrook Street. In this case the river is too far away for this to be successful in townscape terms and fortunately the south side of Colebrook Street and its listed buildings remains intact.

Starting at the eastern end, a two-storey brick Victorian public house stands on the site of the City's old East Gate. On the western side, there is a harmonious group of buildings stretching right along this section of the street, starting with the listed Gothic revival almshouses designed by William Garbett in 1848, constructed in dark header bond with orange diaper designs and stone window surrounds. There is an attractive bay at the southern end of the almshouses which exploits views towards St Giles' Hill. The rest of the street consists of two-storey Victorian terraced houses, with a strong string course, placed either side of a three-storey listed 18th century house. This building has bricked-up openings at each end under arches with carved heads on the keystones. It was possibly used as an armoury for the local militia close to the East Gate or as an additional storage place for grain for the City Mill. The shallow curve of the street emphasises the taller listed building which looks out onto Scott Gardens.

On the eastern side, the city walls have disappeared to allow views between

garden provides an elevated platform from which you can look across at the backs of buildings in Chesil Street and to St Giles' Hill beyond. The most significant buildings in this view are St Peter's Chesil church with its 15th century tower, and the 16th century house 'The Soke', built against it. This retains stone walls and massive stone chimneys with diagonal 17th century brick shafts on this elevation and yew topiary in its lovely garden. At the south end of this part of Colebrook Street is an entrance yard to St Mary Magdalen almshouses which were extended in 1976. This is unsatisfactory as a final stop to the street partly due to the prominent roof lights and the removal, for a car park, of the tree that was supposed to form the focal point.

Scott Gardens

St John's South almshouses

the houses on this side of the street. The most important of these views is through Scott Gardens (dedicated in 1952) with railings, shaped trees (echoing the topiary on the other side of the river), and a terrace with steps down to the river walk. The

Two-storey terraced cottages

East view of Cathedral from Colebrook Street

East view of Cathedral from Colebrook Street by Owen Browne Carter, 1830

The east end of the road is closed in by three 18th century town houses with good doorcases, followed by Colebrook Place, and a 1912 art nouveau cottage, whilst on the right-hand side there is a row of late 19th century two-storey cottages. However, the principal building is a three-storey 18th century town house that used to be the rectory for St Lawrence church but is now the Friends' Meeting House. This has a long flint wall on the road frontage and two major beech trees growing behind. The entrance drive now leads to a new rectory and another house, both of nondescript design.

Round the corner, the distinguishing feature of the southern section of Colebrook Street is the contrast between the scale of the houses and the dominance of the east end of the Cathedral. The south transept roof is first seen pale above the house roofs, then the tower and both transepts rise above trees. As the street curves, the Cathedral disappears behind houses, leaving only the north transept in view by the Mill House. Further on, after walking past curving garden walls, the east end of the Cathedral is seen once again over the Close wall, re-emerging with a dramatic close-up view as you turn into Water Close. This sequence of views lights up strikingly in early morning sunshine, contrasting with the attractive orange roof tiles and brickwork of the houses which form a foreground to the Cathedral.

The Friends' Meeting House is attached on its west side to a Victorian terrace, three houses with slate roofs and four houses with tiled roofs that link up to two major 17th and 18th century town houses.

The street is then closed in by the 19th century building of Abbey Mill and, beyond it and set back, the Mill House which has a slate-clad southern elevation. Abbey Mill is the building into which, in 1793, William Shenton moved his spinning and weaving business, which had employed up to 300 people on the site of the present Royal Hotel in St Peter's Street. This is also the point at which a feeder stream crosses under the road from Abbey Gardens into Water Close.

View of Cathedral from the garden of the Friends' Meeting House

From this point onwards, the central Victorian primary school and the rows of timber framed medieval buildings, one of which housed the first County hospital, were swept away in the slum clearance scheme. This was intended to prepare the way for new city offices and an entertainment hall to replace the Guildhall, as promoted by the 1950s Abercrombie plan. In the event, a car park has been created, behind which is a steel-framed building with tile hanging accommodating City Council offices.

The western end of Colebrook Street is now closed off by Paternoster Row, a group of houses and flats formed out of a building that was once a bakery (with five circular windows between cast-iron small pane windows) and adjoining cottages. It has a three-storey extension abutting the Close wall, with diagonal slatted timber balcony fronts and a tiled Mansard roof. There is a passage under this building leading to the wall and railings around the Outer Close. On going through the passage, the Cathedral suddenly looms up rather reminiscent of a liner in dock. From here there are views out across the Close to trees and buildings on the west side of the city above the roofs of the Square. The Wessex Hotel is screened by trees and an arch and remains of an earlier Close wall that divided the town graveyard from that of the monks. On the right-hand side there is a pleasant small garden to two small Victorian houses.

At the end of the street, the view is framed by the Welcome Gospel Hall with its gable and high chimney on the western side, and the three-storey wing of the Guildhall and attached public house on the east. This public house has two steep slated gables over the windows, flint walls with dark mortar and red brick dressings and attractive tiled fascia lettering.

Returning to the Wessex Hotel, which replaced a line of houses, the building is designed as two linked blocks which fail to enhance the urban quality of this area. An attractive three-quarter view of the east end of the Cathedral opens up beyond and on the eastern side across the car park the beautiful listed building, No 34 on the south side of Colebrook Street, can be seen. This is a fine classical fronted house, with two scalloped arches over windows and a delicate fanlight over the central door. This house, which used to have cottages adjacent to it on both sides, is now flanked by its own garden entrances and walls with a background of the Close wall and the magnificent plane trees in the gardens of the Deanery. The car park opposite has been enclosed with a wall and a hedge at low level and contains small trees to maintain the perspective line of Colebrook Street; any redesign of this area should take account of the position of this outstanding house.

No 34 Colebrook Street

Continuing back down the road, first Colebrook House and then Preston House, with its projecting oriel window, a row of cottages and the Friends' Meeting House come into view.

The next view is of the rendered common room block of the Magdalen Almshouses in the foreground with the glinting stainless steel weathervane on Chesil church beyond. You then turn the corner to look back north along the curving street towards St John's South almshouses which, with their gabled roofs and decorative chimney stacks, make a bold end to the terrace.

One of the most important features of Colebrook Street is the series of walled gardens. For example, the 1930s White House with pantile roofs and shutters, adjacent to Abbey Gardens on the north side, is set in a beautiful garden with carefully selected trees and shrubs, many from Australia, and the Mill House has a dramatic front garden with the mill stream rushing through.

All the buildings on the south side have gardens running down to the Wolvesey Palace outer wall which was built in 1377.

Colebrook Place

This is a narrow unmade road on the south side of Colebrook Street that used to have terraced housing on both sides. The west side was pulled down in 1912 when Colebrook Cottage was built, opening up a stunning view of Wolvesey Palace and St Catherine's Hill. The east side retains early 19th century terraced cottages with strong chimney stacks, and a pair of Edwardian semi-detached houses set hard against the perimeter flint wall of Wolvesey Palace. The new entrance and conservatory to No 8 Colebrook Street has enhanced the junction of the two streets.

Colebrook Place

Walled City – 8: Tower Street/Cross Street/Staple Gardens/Jewry Street

Tower Street (Snidelingestret)

Snidelingestret means literally 'a place overgrown with coarse grass'. It is now a street of mixed use that rises up from the Westgate and then descends gently northwards, where it turns corners and runs steeply down to Jewry Street within the new sector of the walled town. The area was entirely transformed by the building of the County Council offices. First came the brick-built Queen Elizabeth II Court in 1959, then the Ashburton Court extension in a prefabricated concrete system (on the line of the old city wall). The building is entirely different in size and character to the two-storey residential terraces that preceded it, but probably not dissimilar in scale from the castle ramparts of the pre-Commonwealth period. This building has recently been refurbished.

This development has had an enormous effect on the character of Winchester's townscape; in the views from Joyce Gardens and St Giles' Hill, from Water Close and Colebrook Street, and far outside the conservation area, from Peter Symonds' playing-fields and St Catherine's Hill. Such a concentration of employment has also generated traffic and led to the modification of surrounding streets including the new dual carriageway in the northern part of Sussex Street. A multi-storey car park has been built under Ashburton Court.

Georgian terrace, Tower Street

Tower House, now demolished

Tower House once stood at the north east end of the street, a tall, square Gothic rendered flint building with crenellated top, that had many of the qualities of a tower. This stood close to a mound covered with trees that marked the north east corner of the city defences but it was insubstantially built and in an unstable condition. An original scheme for the replacement of Tower House was not carried out and the present four-storey design with a separate three-storey building lacks the silhouette of the 19th century house or the visual interest of the original design. On either side are two terraces of a quite different scale. These are the listed three-storey 19th century terrace of town houses, Portland Terrace, with fine porches, and the unlisted but attractive two-storey 19th century houses, Nos 69-83, that step down the hill eastward toward the Theatre Royal in Jewry Street.

Stepped early 19th century buildings

Portland Terrace, Tower Street

Returning on the east side, Tower Street has two interesting terraces of different design; one Edwardian with linked bays and good railings, and the other with three-storey early 19th century buildings. A further group of four town-houses and a Christian Science reading room now fill the gap on this side of the street and help to modify the overpowering effect of Ashburton Court.

Terrace of three houses

Mottisfont Court, corner of Tower Street/High Street

Terrace opposite Ashburton Court

Semi-detached 19th century houses

Corner building replacing Tower House

20th century terrace and Christian Science Church

East side of Mottisfont Court, behind Tower Street

In 1988 the County Architect's department designed a new office building, Mottisfont Court, on the east side of Tower Street. This building narrowed the street to make a better townscape composition, and reintroduced the idea of a pentice with columns to create a better environment for pedestrians. The building makes good use of the different levels to turn the corner. Within this plan is an open space resulting from the need to keep a mature holm oak tree. On its eastern side this building has a totally glazed elevation that looks out over central Winchester using a traditional repeated gable form.

The southern view down Tower Street leads the eye round to the north elevation of the Westgate, which marks the original town wall. The plane trees on the eastern side arch over the street and divide it into two sections, providing both visual interest and delight. Sadly, the horse chestnut tree that used to stand so proudly at the north end of the street at Five Corners was not replaced when the new development was agreed. The dull area of parking enclosed by a wall now has only a small tree to compensate.

Cross Street

Cross Street runs diagonally from Tower Street to Staple Gardens. On the north side is the new Treasury Court housing development and on the south side is the service yard behind Mottisfont Court. Visually the street is dominated by the five-storey Queen Elizabeth II building with its Danish inspired tall casements and attic windows in a steep pantile roof.

At the west end of the street a Victorian terrace makes a strong corner by incorporating two large arched head casement windows on either side of a splay, now a blocked entrance. The overhanging bushes in the end garden disguise a set back half-pebble-dashed Edwardian house, set at an angle to the frontage. At the junction with Staple Gardens the corner is formed by Bilberry Court, a housing scheme designed by C H Design. It was one of the first buildings to comply with the conservation officer's policy, introduced in the 1970s, to incorporate pitched roofs on new developments.

Staple Gardens (Brudenestret)

This is a narrow street of mixed office and residential use running from the High Street to Cross Street and then gradually down to Tower Street. In townscape terms it finishes at the south end with the gable end of No 72a High Street framed between the three-storey office, formerly the Talbot Hotel (on the site of the medieval Star Inn) and Westgate Chambers.

Minter's Court, Cross Street

Staple Gardens looking south (left) and north (right)

Next to it, a former car-park which could have been purchased as an open space by the City from its accumulated 'open space fund', has instead been overtaken by a new housing development using a fashionable curved aluminium roof. This is part of a development which incorporates four-storey flats with balconies on backland, uncomfortably close to the plane trees in Tower Street. On the opposite side is an area behind Mottisfont Court that provides two pedestrian links, one to the High Street and one to Staple Gardens. Unfortunately this has not been comprehensively developed to produce a cohesive and attractive addition to this part of the conservation area.

Looking back down Cross Street from Tower Street, the infill scheme with its repeated square windows and crudely detailed curved roof lacks charm, despite attempts at modelling the frontage to relate it to its Edwardian neighbour. The road is effectively closed off at its east end by a Victorian public house, the New Inn, in Staple Gardens now converted into three houses.

The street divides roughly into two sections: the southern mostly built up hard against the pavement, and the northern section where the character of development on the west side was blighted in the 1960s by a building line to allow for proposed road widening that did not take place. Subsequently this line has been relaxed to allow the street form from the south to be extended.

On Godson's map of 1750 the area is shown as gardens with few buildings. At the junction with Cross Street a market place for the sale of cloth and wool is indicated. This was where the King's office governing the entry of wool into Winchester and export overseas was set up in 1326, and where weighing and bagging wool, adding a seal and collecting tax (the wool staple) took place. It was one of only ten such sites in England. There was also an annual sheep fair just outside the walls on Oram's Arbour.

In the 19th century, the east side of Staple Gardens was developed with printing works, warehouses, an upholsterer, a gas works and a dairy, interspersed with public houses, housing and servicing for the properties along Jewry Street. The north end backed onto the cattle market with a high flint wall hiding a change of levels at the back of the Corn Exchange. By the early 1970s, following the movement of factories out to the Winnall estate, this had become a run-down area. After the building of Ashburton Court and its large car park, a study was commissioned by the City Council from Donald Insall & Partners into the possibility of a major redevelopment of the area with a 100-bed hotel by the Westgate and a shopping centre of 4,000 sq.m. with pedestrian access from Jewry Street into a square.

There were alternative proposals for an ambitious cultural area, which included a similar hotel, a theatre of national significance with a 1000-seat auditorium, and a city museum at the back of the United Church which could be turned into a conference hall. Staple Gardens would have become part of a loop road system with City Road and Sussex Street.

These ideas foundered and a modest brief for the area was then formulated in 1981 by the Planning Department. This resulted in the selective development and refurbishment of the best buildings, including No 33 and the adjoining warehouses, a new architects' office with large loft windows by Househam & Henderson, and some mixed development. This has created Charlecote Mews, an intimate, varied townscape and a series of pedestrian lanes with shared parking areas, block paving and some small-scale planting. Although it is unlike any other part of the city, it is well integrated. The south end of Staple Gardens has been regenerated by new development, the upgrading of terraced houses and the introduction of a pedestrian link to Ashburton Court.

Jewry Street (Scowrtenestret)

Scowrtenestret was the street of the shoemakers until the 13th Century. Jewry Street runs along a terrace of land connecting the City's North Gate to the High Street. It was within the old Oram's Arbour enclosure and it is of at least Saxon origin. It is interesting to note that on Godson's 1750 map it is shown as a straight street with a kink round an important courtyard building, probably an inn just inside the North Gate. The Gate was pulled down in 1755.

In the modern street plan the resulting curve gives the street added townscape interest in both directions. The predominantly slate roofs of the street draw the townscape together with the cupola on Barclays Bank, the large glazed lantern on the United Church, the tower of St Peter's church, the turret on the Library and the roofs of the De Lunn Buildings are all important features.

The street rises noticeably from the High Street to a point opposite the United Church and Sheridan House and then gently falls to North Walls. In terms of use, it serves as a secondary shopping street with an increasingly wide range of activities: restaurants, public houses, churches, offices, the Theatre Royal and the Library. In

Charlecote Mews, Staple Gardens

Charlecote Mews

Old Gaolhouse, Jewry Street

Former Roman Catholic presbytery

A timber framed hall house (now the Loch Fyne restaurant), which belonged to Nicholas Waller, remains from 1509. Almost opposite is No 29, the 18th Century house that was the Catholic presbytery. In 1785 a theatre was built at No 40 Jewry Street; most of it was demolished in 1863, and the one bay that survived collapsed during building work in 1980 and has been reconstructed (with a phoenix under the eaves). In 1788 a county gaol was built on the west side of Jewry Street and this was extended in 1805. George Moneypenny designed a classical building with a powerful stone pediment on its central pavilion, which was attached to two side pavilions all having heavily rusticated quoins. It originally had a front boundary wall and an arched street gate.

traffic terms it is a part of the town centre one-way system and is heavily used. It has recently been redesigned to give more space to pedestrians.

In medieval times the Jewish community established themselves as money-lenders in this area, with their own synagogue near the corner of St George's Street. Although they were expelled in 1290, the name has persisted apart from a change, for a short time, to Gaol Street in the 19th Century when the prison was erected on the west side.

The Library, formerly the Corn Exchange

St Paul's church, Covent Garden

Corn Exchange

St Peter's Catholic church

Doorway from the Magdalen leper hospital

In 1835 the architect Owen Browne Carter won a competition to build the classical Corn Exchange on the west side in front of the cattle market. He based the portico on Inigo Jones' design for St Paul's church, Covent Garden. This is the most distinguished building in the street. Completed in 1838, it was soon followed by the Market Hotel (converted into a theatre in 1914), and the Greek-style terrace that turns the corner into the newly constructed City Road to connect up with the station. The design of the hotel is repeated round the corner and still survives, as a restaurant.

It is interesting that both the Corn Exchange and the gaol have proved to be adaptable to new uses. The gaol was replaced in 1849 by a larger prison in Romsey Road and the site was divided and put up for sale as separate lots. This led to the situation where a Victorian church in early English Gothic style, designed around an octagonal plan, was inserted between the pedimented central section of the gaol (for many years a furniture shop, now a public house) and the north pavilion, now a furniture shop. The southern pavilion was taken down and redeveloped as a stuccoed Victorian terrace containing ground floor shops, with a further brick and stucco terrace linking up to the High Street. There is a narrow passage next to No 5 where the Saxon street (now St George's Street) continued to Staple Gardens.

In 1926 the growing Roman Catholic community built their new, larger church to a design by F. A. Walters on the east side, opposite the Corn Exchange, now the library. Although a considerable building with a tower, it forms a relatively low-key townscape feature element in Jewry Street because it is built within the gardens of No 29 at a much lower level than Jewry Street itself. It incorporates a doorway and a statue taken from the Magdalen leper hospital, a fine building located on the Alresford Road that was demolished in about 1790.

A new scheme is in the process of replacing the single-storey shop built quite outrageously on the front of Northgate House, retaining the courtyard and tree. Adjoining this is a courtyard containing a tree which now frames a good diagonal view of the Library. Beyond the De Lunn Buildings was another flamboyant building by Thomas Stopher, the Crown and Cushion public house, which has been replaced by commercial offices.

The townscape character of Jewry Street is one of a great mixture of buildings of different types, styles and eaves height. In addition to those mentioned, these include the Greek-style stuccoed Nos 34-37 with stone ground floor columns, the highly elaborate De Lunn Buildings with steep gables and balconies. Opposite is the Theatre Royal, a conversion of the Market Hotel, which used to have a glazed canopy along the street, whose removal accounts for its rather weak elevation. Other distinctive buildings are Century House, a stone-fronted classical revival building designed by T. D. Atkinson in the 1930s (now an Evangelical church) and Sheridan House, Winchester Design Partnership's 1980s shop and office buildings, which replaced a garage and tyre store. The latter has large brick arches and a recessed clerestory marking the highest point in the street and is striking in views from both the north and south.

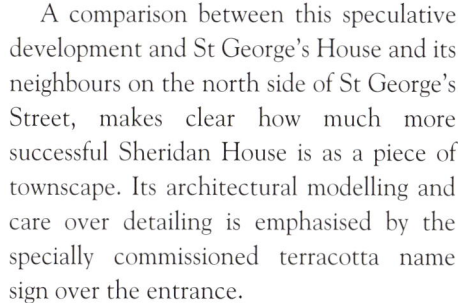

A comparison between this speculative development and St George's House and its neighbours on the north side of St George's Street, makes clear how much more successful Sheridan House is as a piece of townscape. Its architectural modelling and care over detailing is emphasised by the specially commissioned terracotta name sign over the entrance.

The major transformation at the southern end of Jewry Street was the demolition in 1957 of the George Hotel. This had a history dating back to medieval times and was a favoured place for social activities. When the railway reached Winchester the hotel proprietor supplied horse-drawn cabs for visitors. Before 1957, Jewry Street had a narrow (Saxon) link to the High Street which required a policeman to control the traffic to let buses into the High Street. Widening the road enabled traffic, including buses and delivery lorries diverted from the High Street, to flow freely around the area. In rebuilding the east side, Barclays Bank's architect, William Curtis Green, took the opportunity to make a bold architectural statement in neo-Georgian style, with special narrow bricks, complete with pediment and cupola on the top. This has a civic presence similar to that of a town hall in relation to the space created. It forms a strong contrast to the narrow-fronted buildings on the south side of the High Street and the buildings on the west side of Jewry Street. Unfortunately the north side of the 'square' is weak. No 45 is an Edwardian building that was not intended to have its end wall as a focal elevation, while the flat-roofed 1960s RMC building with its unfortunate proportions, lacks any interest in its detailing,

De Lunn Buildings

Theatre Royal, formerly the Market Hotel

Century House

Sheridan House

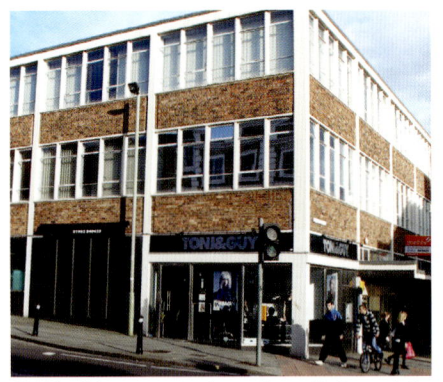

has poor materials and relatively short ground-level windows. Such an ill-favoured building indicates how an area can be weakened by insensitive design, no doubt exacerbated by traffic engineers' sight-line demands. A traffic reorganisation scheme led to the resiting of a horse trough (a memorial to the horses killed in the Boer War), seats and a new tree which has improved the character of this corner.

RMC building, junction Jewry Street/St George's St.

Barclays Bank

At the south end of Jewry Street the present corner building is significant because of an earlier proposal to create a three-storey flat-roofed building that would have demolished the first purpose-built bank building in the High Street, Nos 91-93, to create a wide 45 degree engineering splay. This had to be re-negotiated following a change to conservation area legislation status in 1968 which then brought demolition of unlisted buildings under control within a conservation area. The 19th century building finally removed was so riddled with dry rot and, being on the corner, so difficult to repair structurally that a replacement building was accepted. This introduced a short colonnade for pedestrians with a projecting bay window to close up the width of Jewry Street in townscape terms. The architect selected a local bright orange brick to strengthen this effect. This was much more acceptable as a corner building than any previous development proposals although the coat of arms over the bay is not bold enough and the blank wall designed for cast aluminium lettering lost its purpose when the owners decided on an illuminated corporate image sign. The building is now being marred by poor signs over the display windows.

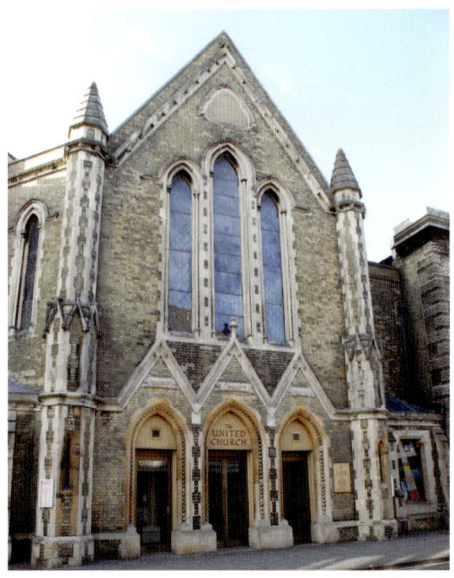

The covered passage between Nos 12 and 13 has unusual reused decorative gates placed well back for reasons of access.

The transformation of the United Church in 1989 changed it from a forbidding dark building to a lighter one with ground floor reception rooms and a hall and access behind.

The northern end of Jewry Street is in the process of being revitalised, led by a refurbished theatre and an extended library.

United Church

Walled City – 9: Law Courts/Barracks/The Castle

The Law Courts and the Castle

Because it also relates to the Great Hall, one of Winchester's foremost buildings, the area in front of the Law Courts should be one of the most attractive spaces in the City. However, despite the large investment in buildings, floorscape, building repair and archaeological investigation, the whole area is visually disappointing; it is tucked away and, unlike the Cathedral Close, does not have strong pedestrian flow through it.

Castle Avenue offices from the north

Three Minsters House rear view (south), mid 1970s

The nature of the space is dictated by the buildings that surround it: the Law Courts and Hampshire County Council offices. This creates a rather bleak square, made necessary by security considerations.

The new buildings on the north side are overpowering even though they use good materials. Three Minsters House, which is mirrored by the rear extension to Trafalgar House on the east side, is a reflection of the period when it was built, with its large areas of lead cladding and narrow vertical fenestration. The area is not uplifting and the silhouettes of the buildings are uninteresting. Nevertheless there are glimpses of architectural features in the town, such as the cupola on Barclays Bank, St Giles' Hill and the countryside beyond.

Sallyport in retaining wall on line of original Castle defences

The middle terrace is vast, with a daunting cold-coloured granite wall on its western side – an odd choice of stone when so many of Winchester's great buildings are in a much warmer softer limestone. The old sallyport passage of the Castle has been unimaginatively presented; this historic element could have been made much more interesting. Even the flight of steps adjacent to the Law Courts is daunting, monumental and overpowering in scale.

Castle Hill between offices and Three Minsters House

The lower terrace is not designed to be 'used' and its design, with the centrepiece of a rose, looks more effective when viewed from above than it does from eye level.

Great Hall and Castle Hill offices from lower terrace

Law Courts from entrance to courtyard

The upper terrace, leading from the Westgate, uphill past the early 18th century offices, does give the feeling that you may be approaching an important building. The approach also has ash, holm oak trees and the remnants of the base of the castle round tower; finally there is the Great Hall doorway across a beautifully laid-out area of granite setts.

It is difficult to obtain any real grasp of the size of the castle destroyed in the Civil War and the fact that the surviving Great Hall was only one small part of it.

Over the last twenty years this space has been softened by extensive planting, the hornbeam in front of the Law Courts being of particular importance. The County Council has recently created a permanent exhibition to introduce visitors to the Great Hall with interesting material on the history, scale and scope of the castle. They also promoted a competition for a sculpture on the middle terrace to commemorate the Queen's Jubilee. This was won by Rachel Fenner and unveiled by Her Majesty the Queen on 21 November 2003. It has introduced colour and symbolism in a powerful group which contributes to this public space.

It might be helpful to visitors if there was a sculptured model of the castle at the height of its development to help interpret this historic site. And, additionally, the County Council could replace its 'rose' with a simple decorative fountain which would have the effect of introducing something living that catches the light in the sunshine seen against the dark north face of the Law Courts. Such a fountain would contribute to the view from all levels. This is a classical townscape feature of which there are no really successful examples in Winchester.

As an exhibition space, the area has been used for sculpture displays by major 20th century artists such as Elisabeth Frink, Henry Moore and David Pye. The Frink horse at the High Street entrance has remained since the 1975 exhibition. One of the good things about locating sculpture here is that it can be seen from various levels and viewpoints.

Sculpture by Rachel Fenner

The Barracks

Chapter 10 illustrates the importance of the Peninsula Barracks site, first as a Roman fort, then as a royal castle area, with fluctuating fortunes until the 17th century. Cromwell's agents then laid waste to the buildings which, together with the Cathedral, had been such a dominant feature of the Winchester townscape up to that point. The castle buildings were replaced by a baroque palace, later used as a prison during the French and American wars, paving the way for the army to acquire the site in 1793 and use the partly finished and damaged King's House as barracks. Further buildings were added; the garrison church/school and the rebuilt barracks were all largely completed after the fire in 1894 that destroyed the King's House.

The only building that has remained relatively unscathed through this long period is the Great Hall, built 1222-36 with its Purbeck marble columns and Round Table (1250-80), and judged to be the second finest medieval hall in the country after Westminster. The Great Hall has had a continuing use for ceremonial occasions and also major state trials such as Edmund, Duke of Kent (1330), Sir Walter Raleigh (1603) and Alice Lisle (1685). In 1642 it was sold to the Hampshire Justices of the Peace resulting in the addition of a new Grand Jury Chamber on the

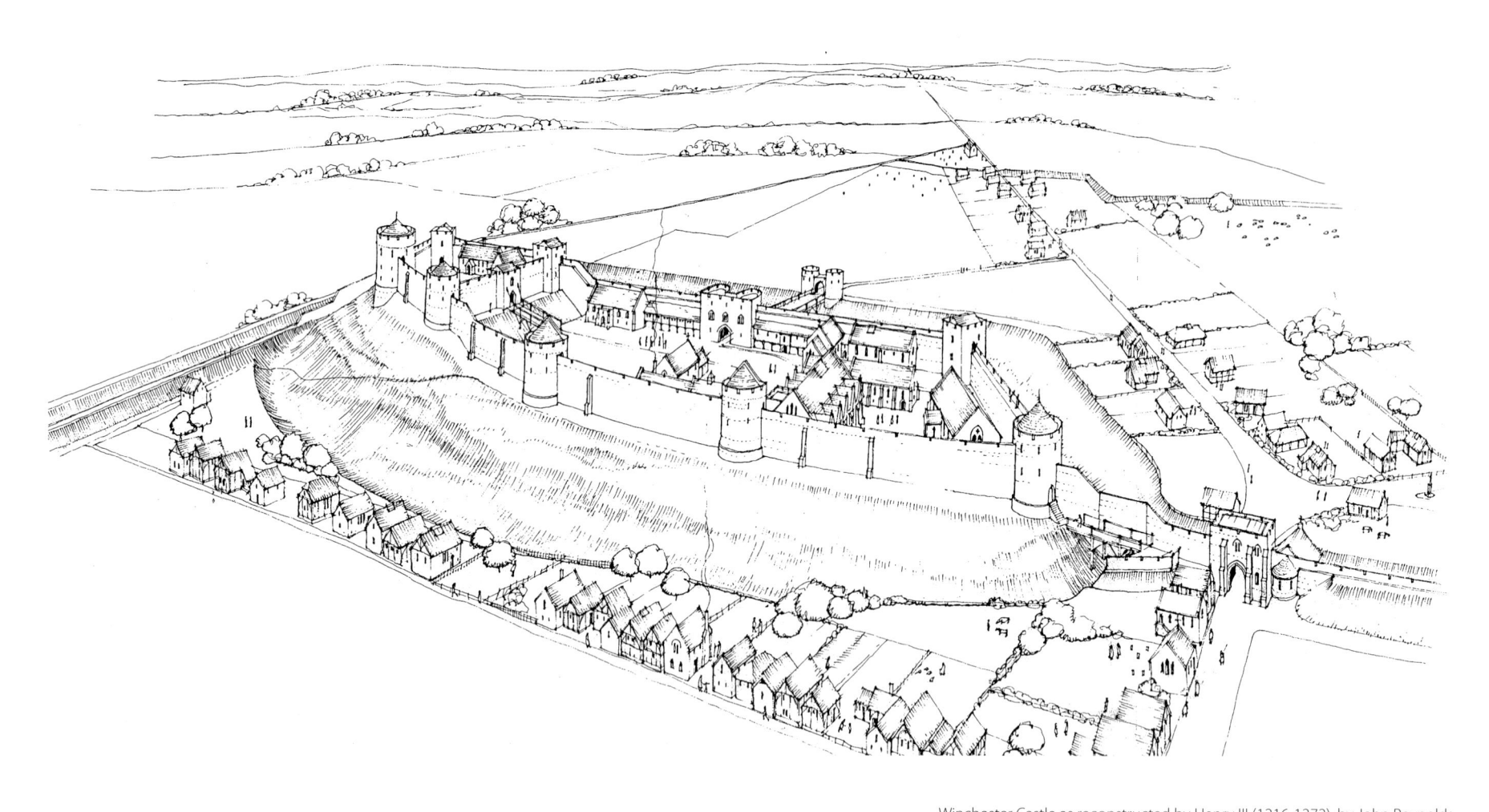

Winchester Castle as reconstructed by Henry III (1216-1272), by John Reynolds

west side, completed in 1774 and reconstructed in 1849. In 1870 new courtrooms were built on the east side, cutting through the enormously thick external wall of the Great Hall with a Gothic-arched opening. The roof was remodelled, windows glazed with stained glass and new internal decorations implemented, including a list of Knights of the Shire in an overall pattern. By 1938, T. H. Wyatt's court building had developed serious failure because of poor mortar and had to be vacated and demolished. New courts were proposed but the outbreak of war intervened and the present courts were not completed until 1974.

The architects Louis de Soissons Partnership had to reconcile the brief's requirements of increased accommodation and keeping the height down to the level of the parapet of the Great Hall. They separated the large courts and offices on the south side from the ancillary accommodation on the north side with a great central curved corridor from the openings in the east wall of the Great Hall bending the axis around to face the Cathedral. Consequently its huge east window obtains one of the best views in Winchester. The architects then redesigned the adjacent space to the north with terraces to accommodate underground car parking and adding an heroic flight of steps linking the levels of the entrance and the Great Hall forecourt.

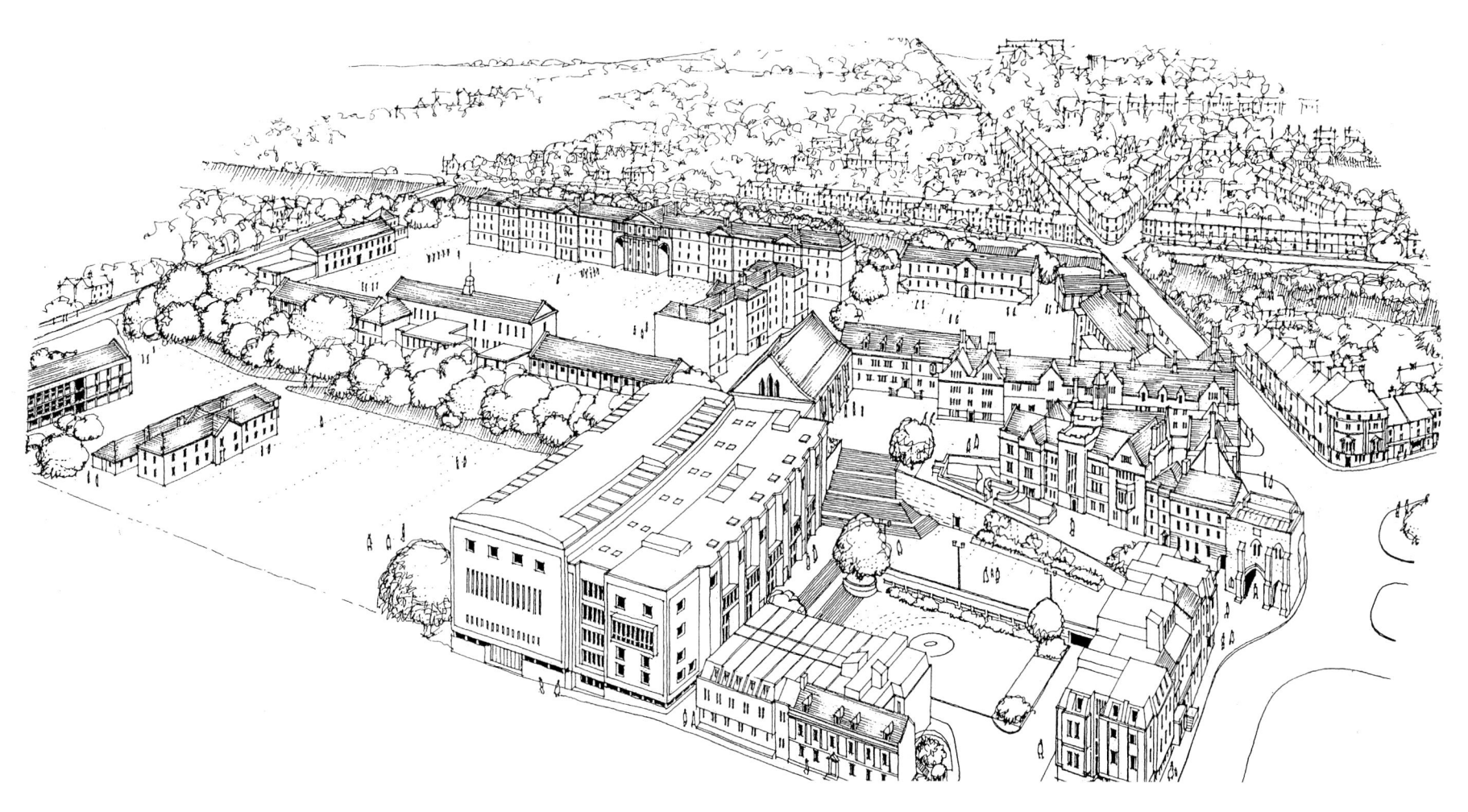

The Barracks, Castle and Law Courts, 1983 by John Reynolds

As with any major building, once the main design is completed, artistic alterations follow. In 1979, high-level roof lighting was installed in the Great Hall for the Queen's Maundy Thursday visit. In 1981, the striking stainless-steel gates were installed at the east end to commemorate the marriage of the Prince and Princess of Wales. These have a security function, and also help to disguise the awkward internal junction of the two buildings.

During 1986, a replica medieval garden was created in the tiny triangular space on the sunny south side of the Great Hall to form a surprisingly interesting space surrounded by large buildings. From this, Queen Eleanor's garden, can be 'read' in the wall the architectural changes to the Great Hall and also, on the south side can be seen the only visible in situ remains of King Charles II's Palace.

Throughout the 20th century the Barracks, rebuilt after the fire destroyed the King's House in 1894, has been an area set apart from the town and from which people have been excluded. The high walls, and the cranked concrete posts and barbed wire that surrounded St Thomas's church were required for military security but disfigured this part of the conservation area. This was particularly true after an IRA trial in the 1970s, which emphasised the partition of this area from the rest of Winchester.

The ruins of the Kings House from Clifton Hill, c. 1897

The Assize Courts by T H Wyatt, 1872

The Great Hall and Grand Jury Chamber. Watercolour by Owen Browne Carter, c. 1849

Adjoining St Thomas's church is the 18th century Serle's House by Thomas Archer. The building was acquired by the Hampshire Regiment as a Headquarters in the 1860s, and some unfortunate remodelling took place in the 1950s. At that time, the memorial garden was created along Southgate Street.

The new buildings, erected after the Second World War at the south end of the upper barracks by Booth, Ledeboer and Pinckheard to replace a Victorian block, were too bland to add anything distinctive to either the barracks space or the town. The single storey NAAFI building (now demolished) inside the north gate and its adjacent residential block were most unattractive.

Window on south side of Great Hall with evidence of architectural changes

end which are occupied by Army museums. It was the intention of the City and County Councils that the Upper Barracks Square (all of whose Victorian buildings were listed) should come into public use. The brief drawn up for development in 1985 assigned them this role but suggested that there was a possibility for change on the Lower Barracks (mainly unlisted) following the then current thinking that this was one of the few acceptable positions for a car park on one of the principal roads into town.

St Thomas's church seen from the Barracks

Queen Eleanor's Garden

In the 1970s the Army considered developing higher, wider and bulkier buildings with the likelihood of increased road traffic and helicopter activity over the town centre. But in the event it was decided to move the Barracks to a new suburban site. The new Sir John Moore Barracks opened at Flowerdown in 1984 and the buildings in the town barracks were left virtually derelict, apart from those at the northern

A limited design competition was held by the owners of the site, the Crown Estate Commissioners, and in 1989 the Ministry of Defence selected for the Lower Barracks a scheme by architects, Siddell Gibson, and the developers, Arundell House, for submission as a planning application. This scheme proposed demolition of all the existing buildings, except for the Garrison church and the guard house, and freed the Lower Barracks area for a series of courtyards above underground parking using a classical design theme. This was a typical 'big town' approach and would, for example, have hidden the Garrison church behind an office block, thereby changing significantly the character of Southgate Street. And it would also have hidden the south side of the Law Courts and a big section of the Castle mound. However, it would have provided a classical setting of more appropriate scale to Serle's House and made it possible to see the Cathedral from the original position of the King's House in the Upper Barracks Square, over the top of Serle's House, which would have been a striking townscape view. The scheme also proposed a statue of King Charles on horseback looking out at this vista.

Potentially, it would have enabled the City Council to have an enlarged museum on the east side of the Barracks Square, exploiting views out over the whole of Winchester, and a design was prepared for this. The City Planning Officer investigated the possibility of much-needed accommodation for King Alfred's College and the Winchester School of Art in the Upper Barracks blocks, which would have added a vibrant public space to the city.

In the end, the amended scheme on the Lower Barracks foundered on the high cost of providing underground car-parking, which included the undertaking of a detailed archaeological investigation.

Meanwhile, interest nationally had been focused on commemorating the country's military heritage. Winchester Barracks, the ordinary buildings, as well as the grander ones, were seen as a significant 19th century development during the heyday of empire and this led the organisation 'SAVE' to produce an alternative conservation scheme inspired and designed by the local architect Huw Thomas. This was predicated on the idea of retaining most of the remaining buildings, the spaces and the tree planting but exploiting the new development potential along St James' Lane. By being of a comparatively low density, with surface parking, the scheme largely avoided archaeological complications.

It proposed to convert to housing the existing buildings on both the Upper and Lower Barracks. The 'jewel in the crown' would be the development on the Upper Barracks Square of a formal garden of the sort that King Charles II and Wren would have appreciated, with a significant water area reflecting the existing buildings in place of the tarmac parade ground. A watercolour perspective sold this idea, and the architect hoped that the pond would be used for sailing children's boats.

This scheme was, however, inflexible as far as alternative use for individual buildings was concerned. It was unfortunate that the City Council (which ironically had owned the site some 300 years earlier) lacked the finance to acquire and implement a museum building. Nor were the different regimental museums able to secure a site for a restaurant and a building where topical exhibitions could complement their permanent exhibitions. Eventually part of the Romsey Road guardhouse was converted for this purpose.

Most of the Barracks has an Ancient Monument designation, so that English Heritage can control the archaeology relating to the castle. As a consequence, any work on the parade ground had to be built up to avoid damage to the archaeology underneath. During the course of the implementation of the conservation scheme on the Upper Barracks, archaeological information has been gathered concerning the castle and one of its round towers at the south end and a reputed tower and buildings inside the wall at the north end. None of the walls excavated was of a quality that could be left exposed, as is the case in Castle Hill. The underground remains have restricted the footprint of building at the north end inside the Romsey Road entrance including a rejected proposal based on a Welsh castle surrounded by trees.

The completed scheme for the Barracks site has provided a network of walkways that link different parts of the city. It has created three open spaces that are totally different in quality to any in other parts of central Winchester with fine views out over the town. It has provided a range of different housing types, and has allowed views of the spire of St Thomas's church from the newly created townscape.

These spaces combine with retained and new buildings, routes and features to create a change of use of the barracks site that has extended the public domain of the city. The site can be approached from many directions.

Mons Block, formerly the Barracks Hospital

Queens Court from Romsey Road

The Romsey Road entrance opens into a formal square, on one side of which are original barrack buildings (now a museum) and on the other a block of flats, Queens Court, which wraps around an inner square. The flats are built around the footings of what was probably Queen Eleanor's quarters in the castle – hence the shape of the new building. The front elevation picks up the formal 'military' theme of vertical pilasters, the module of which is reflected within the square, and emphasises the view into the inner courtyard. This building exemplifies an unfortunate weakness in the procedure for monitoring the construction process which frequently happens in Winchester and elsewhere. In this case the building was designed up to planning stage, at which time the detail requirements are minimal. Details generally follow the planning stage but are then not subject to the planning process. Once planning permission is granted, the land value increases dramatically and sites are often sold at considerable gain to the speculating developer. The second developer has a narrower financial margin to play with so the building is cheapened, less good materials are used and the all important detail disappears. More often than not, the architect is dismissed as being too expensive so there is no guiding hand from the designer. This is a process that happens only too often and one can generally recognise the gulf that exists between buildings that are developer-led and those which have design detail continuity from the original concept to the completed product.

From Castle Avenue it is possible to pass through the Great Hall out into the delightful Queen Eleanor's Garden, up steps onto the podium of the King's House and then out onto the great Barracks Square.

In Southgate Street, the outer wall has been reduced to reveal the three-quarter end view of Garrison church, now a cinema. The trees along the frontage to Southgate Street will, in time, improve the setting looking towards St Thomas's church spire. The Guardhouse has been refurbished as a home and made more attractive by the renewal of the glazed canopy to the entrance.

The Hotel du Vin has incorporated the old quartermaster's house, creating a new entrance including one for disabled people. This footpath continues past the hotel garden to give access to the Barracks site at the converted militia building, the earliest military building on the site.

On St James's Lane, the old barracks walls have been opened to create a new access known as Constable's Gate, beyond which are terraces of rendered housing. An arch frames views in and out from Beaumond Green; beyond are brick terraced houses and a view of the wooded mound on which the castle once stood.

Circling around the base of this mound, and looking up at the new southern block, gives some idea of how dominant the old castle must have been. Steps lead up into the southern part of the Barracks Square with the three water rills and formal planting leading up to the great reflecting pool. The alternative route is from Beaumond Green, via a diagonal path up to the castle mound and then out into the centre of the old Barracks Square. Following around this, the route passes the Gurkha Museum, Queens Court, with a formal square, and out past the Green Jackets Museum, through the gateway and on to Romsey Road. Either way, the sequence of views both in and out is well worth the walk.

It is worth making the following observations on the main public spaces:

Beaumond Green
This is enclosed by new two-storey housing taking its cue from the existing dining building on the east side using two-coloured brickwork with arches to create a distinctive front door treatment and a repetitive brick pattern. It is essential over time that the design can be retained unaltered because the addition of porches and other modest changes would ruin the cohesive effect, as has happened to many other terraces in Winchester.

The green space with its formal pattern flowing into the centre is an effort to play down the visual effects of car parking, although it does not have the change of level that the architect had proposed.

Long axis of Barracks Square looking north

Between this and the Lower Barracks open space is a route centred on the spire of St Thomas's church. This creates an exciting open space leading through to the start of the principal ramp up to the Upper Barracks Square.

Lower Barracks Square
This is a large enclosed green space (70 m x 95 m) in the centre of Winchester with the west side formed by the castle mound, with its tree and shrub planting, and the south and east sides by plain red brick buildings. Each house has a small walled garden in front of it and the paired slate-roofed garden stores contribute to the townscape. The north side is closed by the formidable four-storey elevation of the Law Courts. The tree and shrub planting moderate the view of this building at ground level, though its facade with its lack of detail and unrelenting horizontal roof line will always look out of place in Winchester.

From the sitting space in the north west corner, there is a view of St Thomas's church and a glimpse of the Cathedral tower.

Long Block and water feature

Upper Barracks Square.

Measuring 70 m by 150 m this is the most formal architectural space in Winchester in the sense that it has a range of red brick buildings with stone dressings on all four sides.

This is a grand scale for Winchester which, with its tarmac parade ground, once made a wonderful background for military set-piece displays. Because of archaeological implications derived from the original castle buildings just below the surface, the scope for tree planting was limited as levels had to be built up above ground.

This space has been transformed by landscaping and water features. Round the perimeter there is formal planting to provide some privacy to the ground floor flats.

Because of the historical development of this Square, the buildings on each side, although designed with the same formal classical language, are handled with

East Block (formerly officers' mess)

varying degrees of skill. Unlike most successful Georgian squares, it has weak corner gaps. However, these afford good views out.

With a formal layout, the axes on which buildings are designed run through their central pediment and if these had been designed as a single entity, they would have related to each other precisely. This is not so in the north/south direction, making a formal layout of the garden difficult. The architect has tried to disguise this by incorporating three rills in the southern section of garden to reconcile the asymmetry.

The Long Block running parallel to the railway, is built on top of the old castle ditch on very deep piles. This is the most ambitious of the buildings with thirty-five window bays and a powerful centrepiece made up of great columns and composite capitals salvaged from Sir Christopher Wren's palace for Charles II. This building is four floors high and there are two large openings on either side of the centre piece through which can be seen glimpses of woodland lining the railway cutting and an elegant cast-iron fence on the railway boundary.

The first floor windows and centre piece have decorative head mouldings and the composition is surmounted by a pediment with a revised George III coat of arms and a pair of formal chimneys. The long wings on each side are then broken up by two projecting bays with stone quoins and a subordinate pediment above. These projecting bays have a good proportion of Flemish bond brickwork between the windows. Further decoration is provided by the cast-iron hopper heads and down pipes. This military building is now converted into flats.

Former gymnasium

Short Block on the north side is thirteen bays long and slightly higher than Long Block. It has a central projecting pavilion with an entrance and stone facings, two orders of shallow stone pilasters supporting a strong string course and above it a pediment with a central coat of arms. This is now used as a military museum for the Hussars and the Gurkha regiments. The former gymnasium in the north east corner has retained its external character, despite the problems of converting it into housing.

The eastern block (the old officers' mess) is fifteen bays, consisting of two storeys with sash windows and fan lights above. It repeats the same formal design as the Long Block. This building has a clock in its pediment and a small cupola on its roof with a weather vane of a gunner on top. It is now converted into houses.

The south block, recently constructed, was designed to contain town houses. It is twenty-two bays long with a central porch over a public footpath. This adopts the same format of a central pavilion and two side pavilions but the central pavilion is too wide to make a well proportioned pediment. The roof silhouette is uninteresting with an apologetic asymmetrical chimney.

Although this block is of appropriate colour and size, it is let down by its proportion and detail. The walls are stretcher bond, which produces a less interesting texture of brickwork. The mouldings lack conviction and examination of the central archway shows that the style is only skin deep, with a flat ceiling and down-stand beams close inside the arch, indicating that the construction is not traditional. However, it creates a strong closure to the south side of the square.

The weapons shed adjoining is not an easy building to sub-divide into residential use. However, here the design adopts the feature of dark glazing set back behind the light columns, preserving its townscape role as well as giving marvellous views out across the Barracks Square. The projecting modern balconies at the back also allow good views over the town in winter.

Former weapons shed

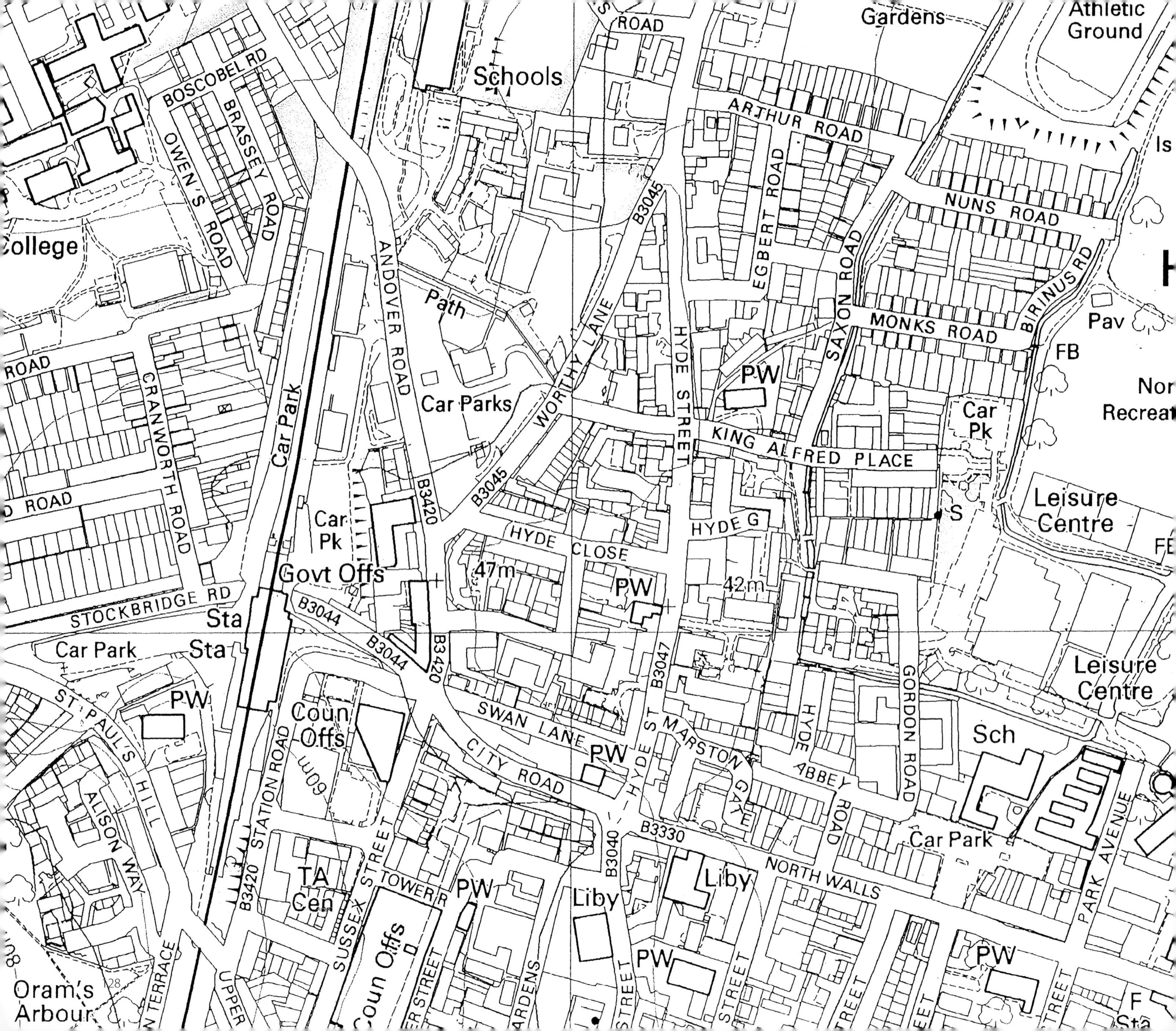
Gardens
Athletic Ground
Schools
ROAD
BOSCOBEL RD
BRASSEY ROAD
OWEN'S ROAD
College
ARTHUR ROAD
EGBERT ROAD
NUNS ROAD
SAXON ROAD
BIRINUS RD
MONKS ROAD
Pav
FB
B3045
ANDOVER ROAD
Path
WORTHY LANE
HYDE STREET
PW
Car Parks
Car Park
ROAD
CRANWORTH ROAD
KING ALFRED PLACE
Car Pk
Nor
Recreat
Leisure Centre
S
B3045
D ROAD
HYDE CLOSE
HYDE G
B3420
Car Pk
Govt Offs
47m
42m
STOCKBRIDGE RD
Sta
B3044
Car Park
Sta
B3420
B3047
GORDON ROAD
Leisure Centre
ST PAUL'S HILL
PW
Coun Offs
SWAN LANE
HYDE ST
MARSTON GATE
HYDE ABBEY ROAD
Sch
ALISON WAY
STATION ROAD
60m
CITY ROAD
PW
B3040
B3330
Car Park
PARK AVENUE
NORTH WALLS
B3420
TA Cen
SUSSEX STREET
TOWER R
PW
Liby
Liby
Coun Offs
TERRACE
UPPER
STREET
GARDENS
STREET
PW
STREET
STREET
PW
STREET
Oram's Arbour
28

CHAPTER FOUR

The northern suburb, Hyde

This was one of the largest areas of Roman burials outside the walls and there is evidence of Roman suburban development as well.

The suburb of Hyde beyond the North Gate (which was still in existence at the time) is still recognisable today, from the view seen in Bucks' panorama of 1736. By then the area had recovered from the great drama of the destruction in 1538 of Hyde Abbey, which with its tower and spire had dominated the townscape, much as St Cross does to the south today. The Abbey had become a purely residential area with a wealthy 'Gentleman's House' that had elaborate gardens and used Hyde Abbey's 14th century gatehouse as its entrance. However, the area had not yet experienced the building of the County Bridewell in 1769 or the invasion of Victorian breweries or 20th century service industries, which had come visually to dominate the area by the 1950s. This is a trend which has been reversed both by economic regrouping and the planned resiting of industries by the City Council onto redundant railway land at Bar End in the 1960s and 70s, so that in townscape terms the street has regained its integrity.

Having lost its Abbey, Hyde lacks the distinction of St Cross, but still has a strong sense of community, and Hyde Street is the key to its identity.

Medieval stone bridge under Hyde Street

Niche in garden of Hyde Abbey House

Hyde Street looking south. Photograph by C E S Beloe, 1910

Hyde Street

Hyde Street drops sharply away from the North Walls junction (in fact over a hidden medieval stone bridge which can be seen from the garden of No 86 attached to the south side of the Swan public house) and twists through a low lying section of mostly modern buildings, before rising up past the most important listed buildings in the street, Hyde Abbey House on the west side and the former Historic Resources Centre on the site of Hyde House on the east side. The street then turns the corner with the trees in Worthy Road (outside the conservation area) making a terminal feature.

It is this low middle section which has been most affected by Victorian industry and still provides the vestige of a service function to the town centre with a group of small businesses. Most of what was a fairly extensive office and light industrial centre has only very recently departed.

On the north side the small-scale Baptist Hall (1991) with its green copper roof forms a foil to the considerable frontage of Homerise House in two buildings, with its projecting upper storeys, followed by the setback offices of South East Employers, a witty enveloping of a bland 1960s flat-roofed office building that used to be the office of a dry cleaning firm, using mathematical tiles and a provocatively decorative doorway. This is followed by the stodgy mock-Georgian Wyeth House that replaced a very tall, decorative brewery building and contrasts with the domestic feel of the group of gables on the adjoining office premises to the north.

Welsh's (formerly Wyeth's) Brewery, Hyde Street c.1905. Photograph by W T Green

On the south side, the one remaining medieval timber framed building is incorporated into the Swan public house. The gable end of the Victorian counting house is followed by affordable housing lacking significant detail, a business centre and a row of new terraced houses that frame the two-storey Historic Resources Centre.

On the west side, Hyde Abbey House, once an important school, is an 18th century building. This is complemented on the other side of the road by the Dutch brick gable from the 17th century and the attractive southern elevation of the tile-capped stone walls of the former Historic Resources Centre, with its imposing wrought-iron gates. This quality of urban design continues on the west side with two three-storey 18th century buildings, one a public house and the other an excellent flint-and-brick 19th century terrace. It is then interrupted by the rather odd setback of the arched entrance to Rosewarne Court and a section of indifferent rendered buildings on both sides of the road. This continues until the crossroads at King Alfred Place is reached.

This point in the street, with St Bartholomew's church tucked round the corner on the east side, marks the residential nucleus of 18th century urban buildings which includes a shop. Here Hyde Street flattens out and beyond the shop is a good early 19th century red brick terrace with simple details on the west side, opposite a series of three fine 18th century houses. The characteristic double gable of the Hyde Tavern public house with its decorative bargeboard and fishscale tiling, is followed by the quite different 1902 parish hall with its stone-mullioned windows. These form an excellent townscape group.

Hyde Abbey House

Dutch brick gable, Hyde House

Beyond this the road changes character with a series of individual houses in good-sized gardens with boundary walls, incorporating major trees in front which dominate the street scene and compete for space. The road then closes in with a short and much altered terrace to the north before joining Worthy Lane with yellow-leafed robinia trees acting as a foil against the dark green yews and sycamores of Hyde Lodge and Worthy Road.

In the reverse direction the street starts on the western side with Beaufort House, a handsome double-fronted Victorian house which, with its rendered counterparts on the other side of the road, frames the fine trees growing in the grounds of Kingston House (once the home of the Hillier family, horticulturists). There follows the 1835 yellow brick vicarage, and on the west side, No 52, the listed centre-piece now incorporated into the group scheme with terraces and flats, with plane trees planted in front. These link up well with the street trees at the corner of King Alfred Place, where one can glimpse the tower of St Peter's church in Jewry Street.

The excellent 18th and early 19th century listed buildings that follow constitute the most distinctive section of Hyde Street which then merges into lesser rendered buildings. The flow of the street is interrupted by the setback entrance to Rosewarne Court to the west, and Hyde Gate to the east. A wide access reveals the plain rear elevation of the Historic Resources Centre, relieved by the quality of the low level garden wall and the small area of substantial timber framing at high level, together with its decorative brick end gable. This is the only good example in Winchester of this characteristic 17th century design feature that gives a clue to the original design of the gables in Dome Alley within the Cathedral precinct.

Opposite, on the western side, is a 19th century flint and brick terrace, designed by Thomas Stopher, with paired Gothic arched entrances, very chunky gabled dormers and bye-law fire-stop walls in between each unit, that complements the adjacent 18th century listed building very well. Between this and Rosewarne Court is an historic forge that used to shoe the heavy brewery cart horses and performed a useful metalworking service until comparatively recently.

Silchester Place is a vast improvement on the old garage which it has replaced.

Hyde Tavern

Hyde Parish Hall

Kingston House

Flint and brick terrace by Thomas Stopher, Hyde Street

It re-instates the street grain. Unusually these houses make use of monopitch roofs with overhangs. Then the business centre and Homerise House close in the street again with rather boring flank walls that frame the view of the Swan public house. The view is terminated by the office building at the end of Jewry Street backed by the bulk of De Lunn Buildings, the yellow end pavilion of the Corn Exchange (now the Public Library) and the three-quarter view of the Theatre Royal with its attached terrace. These buildings indicate that one has arrived at the town centre, even though the medieval gate is no longer there.

Four courtyard developments have resulted from the moving out of industrial buildings. First there is the Marston's Brewery site where Richard Moss, late 19th century MP and great public benefactor, made his money with the Winchester Brewery Co. Here the Swan public house, whose listing in 1987 also protected the Victorian counting house door and the fine brewery gates, ensuring that the street form was not interrupted, has been retained. On the brewery site, a new street has been created with town houses on the north side and an 'L' shaped building on the south side which exploits the dramatic change of levels to enclose an open space overlooked by serried rows of balconies and probably the first loft houses in Winchester. There are also lower buildings toward the walls which hide the sweep of the Roman city walls.

Reused former Brewery gates

Secondly, there is a business centre on the east side which not only has a major frontage to the street, now with arched windows, but has a narrow parking courtyard behind with a thin building divided into small units with a covered first-floor access walkway that even winds round a tree. This has decorative green balustrade railings and access staircases.

Business centre courtyard

Thirdly, the resiting of British Telecom, who wanted to demolish the lovely 18th century barn and malthouse attached to the Historic Resources Centre (saved by the City Council with a central government grant), made possible a residential scheme for art students and elderly persons around a series of courtyards. Hyde Abbey Gate weaves together the remains of Hyde Abbey, Hyde House (the 16th century replacement), the 1769 barn and a series of stone boundary walls with tiled caps. This is designed with two-storey buildings using traditional plan, section and roof, but with modern windows using good buff bricks and plain clay tiles for the tile hanging and the roofs. These help complement the quality of the historic buildings. The courtyards are linked by footpaths with simple landscaping. On the east this has produced an attractive frontage along the Hyde Abbey millstream, but the scheme is not so satisfactory where it has to play a formal part in the historic street, as at the corner of Hyde Street and King Alfred Place, or adjacent to the gateway. Hyde Gateway itself is largely neglected. The footpath, however, from King Alfred Terrace, through the hostel, on through the barn with its Roman wall mosaic and out into the sunny courtyard looking towards the lovely 18th century Hyde Abbey House, is well used.

Gateway at Hyde Abbey, a farm in the 1930s. Drawing by Adrian Friston

Fourthly, Rosewarne Court on the site of SCATS yard is a new development with terraced houses placed around two linked courtyards with minimal back gardens. The housing creates a quiet environment partly around a worthwhile lawn containing fruit trees and partly round a lower paved parking area. The scheme uses concrete tiles, rendering and brickwork, and modern windows which do not build on the quality of the surroundings. The entrance gateway, which is an important component of the scheme, is unattractively large in order to accommodate the passage of fire engines and refuse vehicles.

Hyde Church Lane / King Alfred Place

Hyde Church Lane is a narrow, twisting service lane mostly between walls, which gives side access to the Lido Sports Centre and Rosewarne Court where a single tree produces welcome relief to the street. Then the street curves round, bounded by the rendered side walls of Clarendon House, to emerge suddenly into Hyde Street. Between Clarendon House and the 18th century shop is a view down King Alfred Place.

King Alfred Place drops away as a modern widened street giving a view out over the Winnall Moors to the group of tower flats in Winnall Manor Road and the line of beech trees that climb the ridge behind the Winnall estate, cutting off the sight and sound of the motorway. In the middle ground of this view are the complicated slate roofs, brick chimneys and yellow chimney pots of King Alfred Place. In the foreground to the left are the trees of St Bartholomew's churchyard and to the right Hyde Abbey Gateway. Right in the middle, on the site of the original gatehouse to the County Bridewell and close to the crossing of the Hyde stream, is a square white house with a slate roof and modern windows using a shallow bow design on the ground-floor. This building is just not of sufficient quality for the important townscape position that it occupies.

King Alfred Place

Looking east down the street, which is a main access into a considerable Victorian suburb beyond, there stands the squat, square 15th century tower of St Bartholomew's church, attached to the 12th century nave which was used by the lay people in the monastery. It is one of only four medieval parish churches in the Winchester conservation area (St John, St Lawrence, St Swithun and St Bartholomew) to have survived and still being used for their original purpose.

St Bartholomew's church

The tower has chequered pattern stone-and-flint-walling, angled buttresses and a hipped plain tiled roof. This is silhouetted against the dark foliage of the yew and lime trees in Hyde Church Path. The porch shelters very early carved capitals and there are more examples inside rescued from the Abbey. The churchyard has chest tombs, a low flint wall and holly hedge enclosing it which creates an important green space opposite the 14th century Hyde Abbey gateway.

As the road descends the hill it is closed in by a white painted house before the bridge over the millstream where there is another detached house. Both are disappointing in townscape terms. At this point the main access road turns left becoming Saxon Road, and King Alfred Place continues as a cul-de-sac.

Here on the site of the Bridewell are three groups of houses that illustrate the history of the development of

Door detail, St Bartholomew's church

133

terrace housing in the 19th century as the price of urban land increased. To the south, backing onto the millstream, is a group of six 1830s thin, wide-fronted terraces with gardens in front, such as one might find in a village, which have been little altered. To the north is also a group of five 1850s terraced houses, now having typical service extensions to the rear. This group has been mutilated, one with 'stone' facing and one with paint. Further east there is a row of three semi-detached houses with deeper plans, such as are built in Monks and Nuns Road, with service passages in between.

Viewed across the decorative bridge from the recreation ground to the east looking up the hill, King Alfred's Terrace is a mixture of splayed bays with hipped roofs, and square bays with gabled roofs and low walls defining miniscule gardens in front. This terrace faces a rather indeterminate townscape on the northern side which starts with a gabled garage that displays more attention to detail than is usual. The garage is backed by evergreen trees that are linked by a massive hedge to the end gable of the last house. This house, part of a group, has had the details of the chimneys and the windows changed out of all recognition.

This is followed by enclosed gardens which give only a glimpse of the setback terrace and then, close to the river, is a single house of poor design detail and materials for such an important location. Looking up the hill, St Bartholomew's church tower is a silhouette feature but only just, because it is not high enough to pull the whole townscape pattern together at a distance. To the south of the church, the council houses are a visual muddle because they incorporate white painted fascias and rather unfortunate white window details that tend to overpower the ancient Hyde Abbey gateway. Again, it is the white painted house, No 2 in its key position, that is lacking appropriate silhouette or detail in relation to the adjoining terrace in Saxon Road.

Coming over the river and passing the green footpath space to the south with its two remarkably high poplar trees set against the boundary wall, one comes close to the stone-built Hyde Abbey gateway. From here St Bartholomew's church appears larger, but fails to relate well in townscape terms to the gateway because it is obscured by the low holly hedge, two major cherry trees and some more recently planted memorial trees. These appear to have been planted with a view to giving this graveyard area a separate identity. Finally the listed buildings on the north side of Hyde Street close off the street rather well.

Hyde Church Path

This is an ancient diagonal path, starting more or less on the alignment of the Roman road from the North Gate, which runs behind Hyde Street. The path, with brick-and-flint boundary walls to the west and 19th century railings to the east,

Design sketch for housing in Hyde Church Path

curls round the churchyard and runs downhill to join the route of the Nuns Walk out to Abbotts Barton, part of the Pilgrims' Way to Canterbury.

This route gives an excellent close up view of the tower before passing through the trees and re-emerging beyond the church. To the north the path is closed in by a group of modern town houses built on the old Hyde Parish School site. These are designed in an unusual combination of three-storey bays with first floor oriel windows and interesting brick details at eaves level, separated by two-storey houses disguised by roofs that come in two sections down to ground-floor door height. This was designed to create a strong rhythm and ensure the link with the smaller 18th century stone houses beyond. Two of these are set back and the rest are hard onto the pavement. This part of the path feels like a West Country fishing village and leads on out to the King Alfred public house and a diagonal view of the Monks Road houses.

Hyde Church Path

In the reverse direction, Hyde Church Path and its trees at the other end are framed between the Victorian King Alfred public house and Bartholomew Court flats. The detailing and the materials of the flats do little for the townscape. The impact of these buildings should be reduced once the gingko tree on the corner matures to assist the series of columnar Irish yews which carry the eye on to an interesting brick-and-flint wall that defines the boundary of the churchyard. This links up with the two lines of railings beyond that define the path on the next stretch. Note the greater strength and subtlety of the 19th century railings. The three-storey town houses draw attention to the simple sculptural flint forms of the church walls and chimney and the very powerful roof, designed by Colson, which culminates in a huge catslide over the north aisle, broken into by three gabled windows that complement the squat bulk of the tower at the end. Once more the trees close in before the path turns the corner and leads back to Hyde Street.

Surrounding this core in Hyde there is a development of Victorian housing which illustrates a series of variations on a fairly simple theme of red brick and slate roofs with either brick or cast concrete lintels, wooden sash windows and one- and two-storey bays with interesting and well detailed doors.

St Bartholomew's church from the north

Saxon Road

This is a wide north/south road terminated at its north end by a pair of semi-detached houses in Arthur Road and at the south end by the distant view of St Peter's Roman Catholic church and tower and, in the foreground, the poplar trees beyond King Alfred's Terrace.

Unlike other roads in the area, it subtly curves along the line of the Hyde Abbey millstream flowing from the north with a footpath on its east side which comes from Kings Worthy via the splendid Grade II* listed Abbotts Barton Farmhouse (the old home farm for Hyde Abbey) and becomes the Nuns Walk. This was shown as a causeway on Godson's 1750 map and was notable for its large elm trees.

Housing in front of Abbotts Barton Farmhouse

In the first stretch of this walk from the boundary of the conservation area to Nuns Road, the footpath, grassy bank and stream are at a similar level with a substantial bank of trees along the west side in Saxon Road. Between Nuns Road and Monks Road the stream is set down and hedged in on both west and east sides by trees. This footpath gives access to an attractive small terrace before it reaches Monks Road. In the next section to King Alfred Place, the stream is enclosed by walls and railings but

The footpath leading to Saxon Road

the water is now so far below the level of the road that it ceases to be a major feature and there are only occasional trees on the west side. Beyond King Alfred Place the stream emerges once more into a pedestrian area and, although it runs past walls on its eastern side, on the western side a grassy slope runs down to the stream and bridges remain indicating the position of the Mill that was once part of the Abbey.

Architecturally this is a rather disappointing street, swinging round the King Alfred public house with its attached enclosed garden at the crossing of Hyde Church Path. To the north of the public house a pleasant group of semi-detached houses looks out onto the trees along the stream. These are set at an angle to the road, one having the most original treatment of any bay and roof detail within this area. They have wide enough gaps between them to accept garage extensions, though these would need designing with great sensitivity. To the south of the public house, local authority housing has been built on both sides of the stream, which sadly does not add to the character of the townscape, partly due to the choice of roof tiles, the colour of the bricks and window design. The houses do, however, have interesting chequerboard boundary walls. On the west side, part of St Bartholomew's Court is set back to form a green which enables pedestrians in Saxon Road to appreciate the east gable wall of the church even though the adjacent terrace to the south is poorly designed. On the east side, St Bede's Court, with its cropped hipped plain tile roof, black boarding and projecting balconies adjacent to the stream, does enhance the area despite its tight confined site.

house adjoining Nuns Walk has a delightful 19th century gabled porch with slatted sides which gives it a visual lift.

Nuns Walk. Photograph by George Roger Browne, 1897

Monks Road

This wide residential road is terminated by trees set in the North Walls recreation ground at the east end and the King Alfred public house with trees behind in Hyde Street, at the other.

The street is made up of semi-detached houses with such narrow passageways between that they have the appearance of terraces. They combine double-height splayed bays, with hipped roofs and square gabled bays, to create a strong rhythm on both sides of the street. There are brick arch details over windows and doors in yellow and red, and mostly low brick walls defining garden areas in front of each house.

Nuns Road

Parallel to Monks Road, this wide residential road has similar characteristics, its west end terminated by a house framed by trees along the river valley and at the east end by trees within the recreation ground. There is a curious detail consisting of a gabled roof over a pair of doors which repeats at intervals down the street. The

Egbert Road

This is a wide residential road running north/south with the back of the town houses on Hyde Church Path topped by trees in the churchyard terminating the south end. An ash tree has been planted to replace a fine yew tree in the garage courtyard. The road has retained the feature of a corner shop and post office, now converted to domestic use. The two houses at the north end with their paired arched door openings and two-storey splayed bay windows with hipped roofs would have formed a good terminal feature in townscape terms. However, an extension to create extra rooms in the roof of the eastern house upsets the harmony of the street design from a distance and this gets worse as one approaches, since the background trees disappear and it becomes a silhouette feature in its own right totally at odds with the rest of the design of the house. To repeat the same extension on its neighbour would compound the mistake.

Another noticeable townscape feature is the contrasting effect between houses in this street. At the south end they have a straight roof, ground-floor bay windows and hipped slate roofs, the whole creating a very emphatic perspective line. This line is reinforced by cast lintels over the first floor windows, the sills and in some cases the string courses. The chimneys, their cowl details and yellow pots also make a major contribution to the rhythm of the street. At the north end, however, two-storey gabled bays give a vertical emphasis. This breaks up the repetitive effect of the chimneys, making them less important in the street scene but still important on the garden elevation. Many of these houses have low walls in front defining the gardens. Where these walls have been replaced with other treatments the rhythm has been rudely interrupted.

Egbert Road

Arthur Road

Danes Road

This is a short sloping street unrelated to a frontage, in which the character of the small slate roofed outbuildings is visually quite important.

Arthur Road

This is another wide residential road running downhill from Worthy Road to Saxon Road in the east with tree planting making a feature at either end. There is Victorian development on the northern side but with only intermittent development on the other. It is interesting therefore to observe how the gable ends of two terraces and a pair of houses in between, seen in perspective on the south side, give the impression of a two-sided development.

The western end is characterised by a new block of flats which puts architectural emphasis on the corner and makes use of brick details and rendered panels to provide some rhythm and interest, although these variations do not seem three dimensional enough to be really effective. It also has different shaped dormers and decorative ridges to compensate for the lack of chimneys. This building succeeds in making its infill neighbour, with its pale bricks and indifferent design, look out of place in a way that a good three dimensional modern building would not. On the other side of the road there are pale infill houses that look equally out of place but they are divided off from the rest of the street by a hedge that even encapsulates a telephone pole!

This street also incorporates a building, set back from the frontage, built for elderly pilgrims in 1897 to commemorate Queen Victoria's Jubilee. It is interesting that houses to the west of this have brick gables with rather mean eaves over paired windows, while to the east the houses have more elegant splayed bays with hipped roofs. The houses have low brick walls and pillars between and it is noticeable how obtrusive white painted houses can be in such a context.

The Aged Pilgrims Home

King Alfred Terrace

This wide east/west residential cul-de-sac running from the trees planted in front of the Recreation Centre towards the Hyde Millstream is an important pedestrian link parallel to North Walls.

King Alfred Terrace

Built in the 1890s, it is a simple attractive terrace with long sweeping roofs only broken to accommodate a single change of level with chimney stacks located centrally on the ridge and square ground-floor bay windows with slate roofs and inset doorways. There are low walls in front of all the gardens. These houses used to face onto an industrial area which has been replaced by a residential scheme which contrasts interestingly in scale with the other buildings. Halfway along, it provides a new vista through to the Roman Catholic church tower and a linking footpath to a small scale playground in front of an electricity sub-station near the end of Hyde Abbey Road. These houses, which incorporate railings along the footpaths, suffer from a lack of refined detailing.

City Road

This wide, level curved road was created on the site of the ditch outside the City Walls as a link to the railway station and to Stockbridge Road. The road under the railway line replaced the route out of Winchester north westwards. This accounts for the very strange junction between Swan Lane and City Road on the western side, which makes building design here difficult.

Buildings were quickly erected at the junction at each end, both on the Jewry Street end where the Greek terrace turns the corner in style and at the western end, where the Eagle Hotel with its courtyard of outbuildings were added. It is a shame that the sculptured eagle that until quite recently topped its central gable is now apparently lost.

Swan Lane junction with City Road

The late 19th century three-storey terrace that occupies the corner opposite could be smartened if the parapet and window details were restored, fascias given a simple cornice and the walls painted. The Albion makes an appropriate corner feature.

Baptist church, City Road

The Baptist church, erected in 1862, is probably the most important single building. Residential buildings fill in the north and south sides of the road. A series of pale slate-roofed houses with prominent (and mostly double) gables encroach on the substantial mound and these houses disguise the steep change of level at this position.

The north side has been redeveloped in the 20th century. This became one of Winchester's car service and showroom areas together with a redevelopment area for offices.

In the 1970s, as part of the three quarter ring road, this was to be widened into a dual carriageway, but when that scheme was shelved investment could start again. A four-storey office block was built and occupied by the Department of Social Security. It has a pedestrian pentice at the front, a rendered flat face and a large gable projecting into the street. The scale of the building is accounted for by the precedent of an earlier three-storey building on the site. Having been designed as an air-conditioned office its windows are strangely blank and out of scale – a disappointing building.

In views looking west the geometry of the powerful asymmetrical roofs of the Record Office look very odd in conjunction with the rest of the buildings in the street such as the small terrace at the Sussex Street junction. In distant views, from say Joyce Gardens or St Giles' Hill, such problems do not exist and these fit well into the townscape.

A submission has recently been made for new development on both sides of the road, in particular a mixed development replacing the former car showroom space, which is likely to have some impact on the townscape of City Road, hopefully for the better.

Station Hill

The Station, built in 1838 in an elevated position, is a fairly simple building acting as a terminal feature framed on the northern side by a tree belt. Its prominent station clock is an important local feature. The Victorian public house that adjoins it on the west helps to anchor it into the townscape in its new guise as a Registry Office. With a new double-height bay window with specially commissioned stained glass, this is now linked to the town by an avenue of plane trees. These run alongside the County Council Record Office, expressed as glazed offices on top of three floors of brick strong-rooms.

Swan Lane *(Twychene)*

This is an ancient narrow east/west lane outside the city wall and ditch, clearly featured in Godson's 1750 map, interrupted by the railway line in 1838 and superseded by City Road, which created awkward building sites on the south side. It now has a dual function of servicing properties in City Road and a residential function on its northern side. Its eastern end is terminated by the white rendered front of the White Swan with St Giles' Hill behind. In the reverse direction it climbs uphill and the railway station is seen framed by the important tree situated in the corner of the Eagle Hotel yard. On the south side there is an interesting build up of scale with a mixture of relatively small-scale buildings along the street tending to disguise the four-storey building along City Road occupied by the Social Security offices. This is followed by another office building and the 1960s design of the car showroom and the adjacent warehouse building, neither of which does anything for the townscape. The street ends with a rather odd three-storey office on the awkwardly thin site with interesting 'knob' railings. The north side contains predominantly pleasant two-storey buildings and an infill block which illustrates a solution to the problem of trying to incorporate car access in the middle of such a small-scale frontage.

Victoria Road

This is a wide residential road, sloping steeply downhill from west to east, that lost its Victorian integrity when two good terraces were pulled down along Andover Road to widen the approach to the City Road junction in the 1970s so that only the north side of this road retains its Victorian terraces. Consequently, at its western end there are now two new large-scale buildings.

Swan Lane looking down to Hyde Street

On the north side are three-storey flats with an access tower to create a feature to turn the corner with a carefully detailed roof design. The general design is a deliberately tough, muscular approach with strongly contrasted hard bricks, small blue metal windows, some bent round corners and careful use of details such as the ventilators to create a decorative affect.

Three-storey flats in Victoria Road

On the south side is a four-storey office block, with a much deeper plan making use of levels to tuck cars underneath. It has a false roof design to obtain the maximum development on the site and this includes a mock turret which looks ridiculous from Sussex Street, particularly now that there are alterations to the roof to meet safety regulations. However it uses good materials and careful detailing to create part of the street corner.

Victoria House is a three-storey sheltered housing scheme to the east which fills in the gap between the corner and Technology House. It makes a rather undistinguished complex both in terms of design and materials. However the buildings do relate in scale to the Victorian houses opposite.

The three-storey Technology House is an 'L' shaped office building on back land with a very deep plan which closes the end of the street. It has a repetitive elevation involving Velux rooflights in a mock Mansard, but has a greater degree of brick modelling than many such buildings. Advantage has been taken of a change in levels to form a lower-level hidden car park. A very simple landscape scheme incorporating an evergreen tree helps to soften and lift the effect.

The end of Victoria Road closes with undistinguished three- and four-storey buildings. The remaining Victorian terraces on the north side are pleasant buildings which by the use of steep gables and two-storey bays build up the scale from east to west. The eastern terrace has good railings to the frontage and steps to the front entrances.

There is a second section of Victoria Road which runs north-south as a narrow service road containing three small attractive buildings. There is the converted modern office adjacent to Technology House with its enormous gable window that lights up the central circulation. Then there is a set-back brick-and-flint building, that was once a school attached to the church in Hyde Street, with circular headed sash windows. Finally there is the little Parkersell office building on the west side whose scale has deliberately been kept low by using traditional central valley gutters and three gables sitting on piers.

However the principal historic interest of this road is the appearance of the stone-and-flint 18th century boundary wall, erected originally for the garden of Hyde Abbey House, which incorporates the remaining 17th century sculptures from the original Paulet House on the other side of Hyde Street. Most visible in the street is the Jacobean doorway which has both an interesting silhouette and detail to it.

The value of these sculptural elements was severely compromised in the 1960s when a terrace of six standard developers' houses, with green tile hanging and concrete roof tiles, was allowed on appeal into Hyde Abbey House garden, destroying much of its character and the space to grow new substantial trees. The road terminates at the north end with an ugly prefabricated building for motor repairs, backed up by the rendered gable of Rosewarne Court.

Boundary wall

Hyde Close

This is a narrow straight street which slopes gently from west to east with a northern deflection at its eastern end. It is terminated at its western end by trees planted in front of the Worthy Lane car park (old cattle market site), the end elevation of Cromwell House and the trees on the railway land behind it, and at its east end by an extension to the three-storey listed buildings in Hyde Street.

The north side comprises two-storey flint houses with brick dressings and casement windows, clay pantile roofs and central chimney stacks. On the south side is a similar scale terrace with ground-floor bay windows and first-floor sashes with interesting detail to the arches above and with lines of red brick that break up the first floor. All these houses still have small gardens in front which enhance the street though the overall effect of those buildings and gardens is gradually being eroded by unfortunate changes in detail.

Hyde Close

At its east end, the lane kinks north and runs past the end of a listed building before the street emerges between two three-storey buildings, the one to the north being a former public house and the one to the south a hostel, opposite the Historic Resources Centre. The listed building was an annexe to the private school for boys established in Hyde Abbey House in about 1760 and later run by the vicar of Hyde, Charles Richards. Among those educated at this school were George Canning, later to become British Prime Minister, Thomas Garnier, Dean of Winchester and instigator of the City's main drainage system, and Henry Sewell, the first Premier of New Zealand. The schoolroom itself was designed by the nationally important architect Sir John Soane and opened in 1796. It consisted of a single open hall with a small, semi-circular, gallery at the south end. This building has acquired added importance because so much of this architect's work has been demolished elsewhere. Unfortunately, an enclosure for the original entrance lobby and the staircase to the upper gallery has been demolished, leaving a mutilated end elevation, and a crude extension has been built at the back, originally as a Territorial Army drill-hall but now converted into flats. The best view of the Soane schoolroom is obtained looking west from Hyde Street.

Worthy Lane

This ancient curving wide road, with a grass strip between the carriageway and the pavement on the eastern side, is a main distributor road for traffic moving north and south in Winchester and effectively marks the boundary of Hyde area. At its north end it is closed off by an indifferent modern office building in Andover Road, with infill panels and backed by the brick Cromwell House, and by the trees on the railway. From its junction with Andover Road the first section goes uphill adjacent to the old cattle market, which incorporates some trees in it. At the start is a good late Victorian terrace with unusual decorative cast window details and a strong rhythm of big ground-floor bay windows with flat roofs. This terrace is raised up in relation to the road with steps up to the front doors, originally paved with buff and red tiles some of which have been replaced with other materials that are not so satisfactory. The gardens to these houses are attractive as a group.

At the top of the rise there is a brick-and-flint walled open space in front of a large two-storey building known as the Lido Sports Centre. This used to have in front the City Council's open-air swimming pool which was closed in the 1970s. The building is visually striking by virtue of its scale, rendered walls and strong cornice detail rather than from the window proportion or the lesser details of pilasters, entrance and so on. It does represent important covered recreation space that is complementary to the Recreation Centre.

Worthy Lane

At right angles to this, and gable-end on to the road, is the 1980 St John's Ambulance Headquarters, a carefully detailed but rather dark building which is linked to the flint wall on the boundary with Worthy Road. This boundary wall flows on down as the street rounds the corner as far as Beaufort House at the corner of Hyde Street. This section of street is enhanced by the trees in front of the Moat House Hotel, and by trees in the grounds of buildings in Hyde Street. Beyond Beaufort House there are two Victorian houses on the opposite side and the Worthy Road then continues on as a tree-lined road into the distance.

Map of Winchester area showing the following labels:

- Car Park
- MID... / Lower Br...
- FRIARSGATE
- TANNER ST
- LAWN ST
- Offices
- B3331
- EASTGATE STREET
- Bus Sta
- WATER LANE
- CHESTER RD
- BLUE BALL HILL
- ST JOHN'S ST
- MAGDALEN HILL
- ST JOHN'S RD
- ...RMSTONE ROAD
- 60m
- PW
- THE BROADWAY
- B3330
- PW
- Statue
- YH
- Tunnel (dis)
- Cemy
- FB
- BRIDGE ST
- B3404
- 85m
- St Giles' Hill
- 90m
- G Hall
- Iss
- Sks
- Recn Gd
- The Soke
- BARING ROAD
- NORTHBROOK AVENUE
- Coun Offs
- Sls
- COLEBROOK STREET
- Iss
- B3330
- STRATTON ROAD
- Iss
- Sks
- Castle Wall
- QUARRY ROAD
- Iss
- Close Wall
- Wolvesey Castle
- Paths
- CHESIL STREET
- 50m
- PETERSFIELD ROAD
- Wolvesey Palace
- Castle Wall
- Sl
- 35m
- Path
- NELSON ROAD
- PW
- FB
- WHARF HILL
- Path
- EAST HILL
- HIGHCLIFFE RD
- B3330
- CANUTE RD
- PW
- DELL ROAD
- Sch
- VALE ROAD
- Wharf Hill
- COLLEGE WALK
- ST CATHERINE'S ROAD
- PW
- PORTAL ROAD
- Blackbridge
- Highclif...

CHAPTER FIVE

Eastern Winchester: St Giles' Hill, The Soke, Wharf Hill, Riverside

St Giles' Hill, on the eastern edge of the conservation area, is one of the chalk ridges radiating out from Cheesefoot Head. At the base of the hill is a Roman river crossing point on one of the less important radial routes. This ridge line approach is still a characteristic introduction to the modern city.

The Saxons used St Giles' Hill as a burial ground, possibly supported by a church, although the archaeological evidence has yet to be investigated. Because of its commanding position looking out over the town, it may have been a more important site to the Saxons than is yet recognised.

After the Norman Conquest, the Church of St Giles, the patron saint of sick and crippled people, was located next to the Saxon cemetery to serve the needs of travellers coming into the medieval city from the east.

In 1087 the son of the important Saxon Earl of Northumbria was executed on the west end of St Giles' Hill in reinforcement of Norman rule. The site is thought to be near the present 'viewing point'.

In 1096 King William II granted Bishop Walkelin a three-day fair to be held around the old site of St Giles' church, initially in order to raise money for the building of Winchester Cathedral, including the Chapter House, Great Cloister and the Scriptorium. The latter was to form a workshop for the illuminated manuscripts of the Bible for which Winchester became famous from 1155 and which can still be seen in the Cathedral today.

In 1155 the fair was extended to a 16-day event, one of only five such fairs in England and the only one south of the Thames. The Bishop offered protection, security and a

St Giles' Hill from Pilgrims' School playing fields

strong judicial framework. Named streets were laid out and permanent buildings erected including the Bishop's courthouse on the site of Palm Hall (more recently renamed Milesdown).

This fair steadily grew in importance with the wealth of the area, based on the use of wool for weaving and dyeing of cloth, and it became known as 'the New Town'. It was laid out on a grid-iron pattern as were many of the new medieval settlements, with different trades having different quarters. It was enclosed by a ditch and fence with entry controlled by toll gates.

The outer enclosure for animals probably extended as far as the present Percy Hobbs roundabout. This enabled the merchants who had travelled on horseback from London, the Midlands, York, Wales, Ireland (as well as foreign merchants from France, Italy and Germany) to have somewhere to keep their animals safe and fed while trading. So powerful was the Bishop that, during the time of the fair, no other trading could be carried out within a 10 mile radius. This included the centre of Winchester where the Mayor annually handed over the keys of the gates for the duration of the fair to the Bishop. The city's great weighing machine was taken up to the top of the hill and tolls were collected from the incoming traders.

However, by the time of the Black Death in 1348, the fair's monopoly had been broken and it lost the bulk of its overseas trade to London. The city's own economy was in decline and the city authorities were given the right by the King to hold two fairs, in line with similar fairs in many other towns. By 1540, after the dissolution, St Giles' church had been demolished.

Also in Norman times, a hospital called St Mary Magdalen had been set up further east, close to the site of St Swithun's School, to cater for lepers and others

Internal view of St Mary Magdalen Chapel by J Schnebbelie, 1788

requiring isolation. It was one of the three significant medieval establishments set up to minister to the sick (along with St John's House in the Broadway and St Cross Almshouses). Its Chapel was one of the most magnificent examples of medieval decorated architecture in Winchester. It first suffered at the dissolution of the monasteries, then in the Civil War in the 17th century; later it was used to house prisoners in the trade wars with first Holland in 1665 and then France in 1689 which resulted in extensive damage. It was eventually pulled down in the 18th century, although John Milner, the Roman Catholic historian of Winchester recorded it. One of its doorways and a statue were incorporated into the present St Peter's church in 1926.

By 1784 St Giles' Hill had reverted to downland with just two buildings and field boundaries relating to some old features remaining. There were also chalk quarries on the west and southern sides and an associated lime kiln used for repairs to the Cathedral.

The modern character of St Giles' Hill started with the upgrading of the turnpike roads – Magdalen Hill acting as a bypass to St John's Street, and the Petersfield Road from Wharf Hill which had a gentler gradient. Then came the railway in a tunnel under the hill from the north, and the building of the suburb of Highcliffe with All Saints church, designed by J L Pearson, in 1898. This took over the function of St Peter's church in Chesil Street (making the latter's future uncertain until

Hospital and Chapel of St Mary Magdalen

taken over as a theatre in 1966) with its new Rectory on the south west side of St Giles' Hill. A new vicarage for St John's church in the Soke was built on the north west side, close to the new terraced housing in St John's Road, and a new house, Coitbury.

View across St John's church

However, a crucial event was recorded in 1878 when the Ecclesiastical Commissioners who had inherited responsibility for the Bishop's lands proposed to sell off land for residential development on the west end of the hill. A petition signed by 75 people was sent to the City Council, urging it to purchase land for a 'public park' since they had become worried about the encroachment of development on the western hill, following on from the development of the railway.

This resulted in the acquisition by the city of the sloping land on the top of the hill, the steep slopes to the south and west with some additional land from the railway company. Some was also donated by Lord Northbrook on the northern side leading down to Morn Hill, while he developed the flatter land further east with roads like Baring Road and Northbrook Avenue. The park was laid out by Morrison, a landscape architect, with steps, paths, and gates and railings made in the Winchester foundry of Jewell and Company. Despite protests, trees were planted as part of the design and these are now are its chief and most valued characteristic.

In 1933, St Swithun's School moved out from its site in St Peter Street/North Walls to a site near Magdalen Hill where they already had two boarding houses. In 1937 one of the first dual carriageways in England was built as a bypass to the south and east of Winchester, which cut through the ridge. A pioneering arched concrete bridge was designed to carry the Alresford Road over this deep cutting.

The combination of the arch and a heavy parapet that protected pedestrians from the winds, had the visual effect of tying the ridge together and it later became known as the 'Spitfire Bridge' as the consequence of a wartime stunt flight under the bridge. The bypass was used in the build up of men and materials for D-day with tanks, guns and lorries stored along its length.

The first train to Newbury through Chesil Station, 1885

It was the line of this road which marked the boundary between the wooded town suburb and the open downland beyond, where the St Swithun's headmistress's house stood on its south eastern side (now a Masonic lodge). The line was made much more brutal with the routing of the M3 and a distributor road making eight lines of traffic through the gap under a bridge that is visually weaker and gives little protection to pedestrians in a windy location.

It is now the tree planting which gives St Giles' Hill its distinctive character. The sides of the hill in public ownership are interesting because they provide a series of woodland walks on sloping paths and steps with a dappled pattern of light and shade, varied tree trunks and the seasonal variations of the vegetation. It provides visual colour throughout the seasons, the songs of birds and their patter through the leaves, occasional woodland flowers and glimpses through the leaves of features in town seen in bright sunlight. All this within a few minutes walk of the busy High Street and the river.

The southern entrance is marked by St Giles' Cottage, with an unusual elevation in which standard windows are turned into an oriel on the first floor, supported by decorative wooden brackets.

The grassland over the old quarry provides a lovely sunny space with sloping sides. Rising up its eastern side on the very edge of a steep bank into the remains of the southern quarry, there is a path with a set of steps up to the pine trees on the summit. Three quarters of the way up, a path branches off and runs along a terrace enclosed by ash trees, through which can be glimpsed the 15th century Winchester College tower. Finally a wonderful viewing point is reached under the shade of a beech tree which gives a splendid panorama of St Catherine's Hill, Bushfield Camp and the tower of St Cross surrounded by trees. Closer to, there is the startling green of the Wolvesey playing fields, surrounded by the Bishop's Palace, the Wolvesey Castle ruins and the tower and principal buildings of Winchester College. Although now marred by motorway noise, this is an essentially green view with the hills capped by trees, the middle-ground water meadows mostly hidden by trees, the foreground view of the Wharf Mill and a series of new and old pitched slate roofs that complement it. The Cathedral tends to be hidden by ash trees but, from this viewpoint, the medieval buildings stand out because of the light colour of their stone picked out by the sun in contrast with the darker bricks and tiles of the buildings beyond. In this view the darker copper beech trees in St Michael's Road also help to highlight significant details of the College buildings such as the chimneys on the headmaster's house.

Moving round to the west, you can either go up to the Saxon viewing point and look out or see the green top of the hill rising up to the trees on its summit; or you can zig-zag downhill, looking at the view of St Catherine's Hill between the saplings, with blackberries, moths, and butterflies in the glades on either side, before plunging into woodland around the western side. Within this woodland, there is an open glade with a choice either of going downhill past the former station master's house into town or passing through a gate and up a path with restricted views until you reach the north side with more open views of Winchester College tower, the Guildhall and St John's church. The path emerges on Alresford Road opposite the unusual flint and brick house with decorative gables that marks the entrance, on the other side, to the open space of Joyce Gardens. Alternatively, the steps lead to an upper level through the trees and come out at the north west corner of St Giles' Hill where the path crosses diagonally to Earlsdown on the corner of Northbrook Avenue and Baring Road.

St Giles' Cottage

View of the Cathedral from St Giles' Hill

There is one other route off the hill on the western side which leads to Chesil Street. This starts through the trees with a good view of Winchester College tower and Wolvesey Palace ruins, and plunges downhill to the bridge over the old railway line, through another thin, but important line of trees, beyond which is a good view of the east end of the Cathedral rising up over nearby slate roofs and the bell turret of the former primary school. It then descends steeply between flint walls and emerges abruptly at Chesil Street. Unfortunately, the potential link to the river and the weirs footpath visible opposite, overhung by maple trees, was never completed, although there is a possibility that this link is once again under consideration.

The top of St Giles' Hill covers a bigger area than Oram's Arbour and slopes very steeply both ways. As a consequence, from whatever direction you approach, the views to be obtained are only gradually revealed. The variety of trees that surround the space ensures attractive changes of colour during the seasons.

From the south, the strongest feature coming up the steps is the great line of pine trees backed by limes along Baring Road. On reaching Northbrook Avenue, the view is dominated by St Giles' House and a 1930s roughcast house, both with beautiful trees in their gardens, and glimpses of the Winnall Moors and the valley on the Kings Worthy side beyond.

From the north, a narrow lane with brick walls rises with the land to the same prominent lines of pine and lime trees along Baring Road. In the morning on a good day in winter, these cast blue shadows across the frosty grass when the town lights up in a sunny glow. Approaching Northbrook Avenue, the top of St Catherine's Hill appears amongst pine trees planted along the edge of the hill. Moving on to the south end, the hill dramatically drops away to reveal St Catherine's Hill with the M3 tucking behind it to the left, the St Cross tower framed by trees with a background of Bushfield Camp in the distance. In the foreground, the former Bar End goods yard and the trees along the disused railway line visually hold the two together.

Alternatively going right, downhill from Stratton Road, past the curious foxy memorial seat, the Cathedral emerges, framed by cedar as well as beech trees. At the 'official' viewing point, under the single pine tree that stands out so prominently from the Broadway, there is a breathtaking view, the strong dark tree-lined horizon, the snaking view of the High Street flanked by the green copper roof of the Guildhall tower and the clocktower of Queen Elizabeth II Court and to the left, the pale stone bulk of the Cathedral.

View of Queen Elizabeth II Court, the County Council offices.

In townscape terms, it is important to analyse this view because it has a number of lessons for development control within the streets of the conservation area. It falls roughly into two. The view to the left southwards from the High Street is most satisfactory because it has a major focus in the 900-year-old Cathedral which is surrounded by traditional buildings of a much smaller scale with their pitched roofs, interspersed with trees. The view to the right and north of the High Street is less satisfactory, but it is fascinating because of its complexity. Although it has a visual anchor in the County Council's offices, the middle ground reflects the comprehensive development area of 20th century building types that fit less comfortably with the small-scale roofscapes.

View South of the High Street

This view is dominated by the Cathedral. The image is made all the more powerful by its setting among trees. This treescape setting is made up from those in the Cathedral Close and in the College grounds to the south, the trees in Abbey Gardens and particularly those along the mill stream, together with trees on the remains of the castle mound at the Barracks, St James' Lane, the grounds of the University and along Romsey Road. In addition to this are trees outside the conservation area on Sleepers Hill, West Downs School site and up to the wooded ridges right along the western edge of Winchester which play their part in the overall composition.

In the foreground is a range of pitched, mainly clay-tiled roofs, broken up by chimneys. There are also two buildings which are a contrast, the two-storey St John's Hospital South and the City Offices, both seen against the Cathedral. The former has a long ridge line in an appropriately coloured clay plain tile mixed with pantiles to cover varying pitches, a device that breaks down the apparent scale of the roof. The latter building has hard-edged flat roofs now being disfigured by air-conditioning plant vents and railings. In 1969 after a fire in the Guildhall, new city offices were built on a prominent site attempting to avoid challenging the cathedral; this has failed visually.

In the middle ground, the two spires of Christ Church and St Thomas's church and the Guildhall tower, all Victorian buildings, complement the Cathedral and act as a visual foil to its mass. Also behind the Cathedral are the long horizontal lines of Southgate Street and the lower and upper Barracks, though these are not intrusive because of the colour of materials used (red brick and slate), together with the detail and the trees which break up the line. It should be noticed that the Law Courts, which are very prominent, are broken down into two elements of different height. Their impact is further broken up by two trees in the Hotel du Vin car park west of Southgate Street.

The most notable detractor is the Hampshire Police Headquarters which not only breaks the tree skyline and destroys the scale, but also appears as an awkward slab of glass and concrete, eight storeys high with a hard flat outline. Unfortunately some of the trees which have been reducing its impact have been knocked out by storms and there has not been room to re-plant them.

It is interesting to contrast this with the large hospital building which is seen directly above the Cathedral tower. It does not appear above the skyline in this view, has a varied silhouette of pitched roofs (even though many of its chimneys have been demolished) and is of brick and slate so that it does not have any strong impact despite its distinctiveness.

View North of the High Street

North of the High Street from St Giles' Hill

The High Street forms a very strong townscape feature, particularly in certain lights when the shadows are strong. Sometimes it can seem to be full of people, even at this distance. It has remained an important feature because the new replacement buildings have reinforced the general townscape as seen from the top of the hill.

In the background, Queen Elizabeth II Court with its clock tower anchors the street in the distance and is seen against the silhouette of trees on the ridge of Chilbolton Avenue beyond. These trees even help to mask the extension of Ashburton Court. However this is a light coloured building with strongly emphasised hard horizontal lines. The windows are 'endless' and there are no features to break it down into smaller areas that help it to fit into the townscape. The building is currently undergoing a major refurbishment which addresses some of these issues. There is currently a sizeable mixed-use development being constructed in place of Northgate House (Staple Gardens) and it will be interesting to see how it affects the townscape in this area. The building that replaced the battlemented flint tower house at the north west corner of the walled city is disappointing in its contribution to a very important site.

In the foreground, St John's House, the Marks & Spencer warehouse, St John's Hospital North and the development of Eastgate Street along the riverside form a distinctive roofscape. In particular the latter has slate roofs broken up by chimneys, the rendered walls stand out boldly, and it is all reinforced by the trees along Water Lane and the Itchen.

The area north of the High Street is densely built-up in terms of ground coverage and the large trees which still exist mostly on backland are noticeable and visually valuable. These consist of the maples in St George's Street, the chestnut behind the Casson Block, the limes and the other trees in the Royal Hotel's garden in St Peter's Street, the sycamores between St Peter's Street and Parchment Street and the group of trees around Holy Trinity church, which isolate this building, with its copper fleche as an important townscape feature. The trees in Tower Street and Cross Street also help to break down the scale of Ashburton Court.

In practice, the comprehensive development area proposed by Sir Patrick Abercrombie and partially implemented in the 1950s and 60s has thrown up a whole range of new building types, all distinguished by the fact that they generally have bigger floor areas than any of the traditional buildings in Winchester up to that date. Since then others have been added. Kings Walk offices and the adjacent multi-storey car park are probably the most intrusive because of their long dark horizontal lines which are a feature of their elevations. A building like the St Clement surgery is not allied to any townscape concept and has been made more prominent with the introduction of a glazed atrium roof. It is part of a flat-roofed design and these never look attractive from high level views unless hidden or disguised. At the time of writing, this whole area is under review for redevelopment.

St Peter's church and tower is seen towards the edge of the walled town and could easily be swamped by the rising scale of development, as St Lawrence church just behind the High Street has been. The bulky Andover Road offices immediately outside the conservation area are alleviated by trees seen on the railway land behind.

On the whole, the Brooks Shopping Centre has not fitted into the roofscape too badly although the central conservatory is rather nondescript in form. It is interesting that the Brooks tower is a much less successful townscape feature at this level than either the cupola on Barclays Bank or the Queen Elizabeth II Court clock tower.

Whatever happens on the bus station site or to the Marks & Spencer warehouse will have a significant effect on the character of this area.

Residential development off St Giles' Hill

The overwhelming impression of St Giles' Hill in summer is of a wooded area within which there are houses. The most significant of these are the Victorian and Edwardian houses and the most disappointing are the modern ones on infill sites. They are generally of standard designs with mediocre materials and no sense of place, town design or interest in detail. The site density is such that there is a threat to both tree coverage on the hill and to the whole character of the area. Particularly unimaginative is the development won on appeal on the very steep southern slope which is crying out for good modern design to cope with the enormous changes of level, something which traditional housing was never designed to do.

Baring Road

This road has an avenue of lime trees set in grass verges with a gravelled road surface. Where it turns south to go over the hill, it looks out under the trees to the sloping grassy space and the lower trees on the western edge.

Northbrook Avenue

Similarly this has an avenue of pollarded lime trees with grass verges. The north side is characterised by a good set of mostly brick-and-flint walls that improve towards the eastern end where, beyond a gabled garage hard on the boundary, there is an interesting pierced wall made out of terracotta blocks. This is so much better than modern concrete screen block walls seen elsewhere on the hill. In this case, it forms a setting to an excellent cast iron gate to Rowanhurst. The gardens of this and the adjacent house contain fine trees on the high point. At the east end a converted water tower marks the end of this development. The most important single building is Milesdown, the site of the Bishop's House (Palm Hall) at the time of the medieval fairs, which has an unsightly modern extension on its south side. However, it has a lovely garden to the west containing a number of very significant trees, and holds the key to a potential footpath through to St Giles' cemetery and the Alresford Road.

On the opposite side of the road is Earlsdown, now subdivided but still an important corner building. On the footpath route to and from town, the houses along the south side are quiet and pleasant with the St Swithun's boarding house of Hillcroft being the most important early house at the east end. Opposite Rowanhurst the site has been redeveloped by retaining the north and south elevations and adding substantial three-storey housing on the roadside with part garaging underneath, a tower at its eastern end and an additional room in the valley between the gables. Lower units have been put in the garden adjoining Quarry Road and these have hidden first floor balconies and funny little turrets.

Stratton Road

Stratton Road from the east

This has an avenue of pollarded lime trees similar to Northbrook Avenue. On the opposite side is a single wide-fronted brick house with a projecting garage in dark brick. St Giles' House is one of the best traditional houses (in fact now split up), and has a good modern northern extension that complements the house without copying it. On the corner of High Mount Close, which drops sharply away to a lower platform, there are five individual modern houses designed to exploit the views out, with flat roofs to avoid interfering with the main house, whose gables are an important ingredient of the landscape character of St Giles' Hill. This is complemented by the two 1930s rendered houses whose gardens contain spectacular trees framing a view over the edge of the south quarry. At its junction with the western open space is an interesting square modern house designed by Plincke Leaman & Browning in 1984 as a corner house, with fully glazed walls that reflect the tree and leaf patterns, cream blockwork piers and a slate roof. It is one of the only recent houses built in Winchester to make a positive architectural corner statement. It attracted the attention of the national press which claimed that it would ruin views down the High Street.

Modern corner house, Stratton Road

East Hill

This rises up sharply from the railway bridge and contains a short Victorian terrace with only pedestrian access. The terrace is perched on the north side and is visible across town from the west. Behind are trees amongst which are set some suburban houses. On the south side the buildings make a rather forbidding urban edge, recently improved by an adventurous modern infill building terminating with two attractive cottages on the thin tongue of land leading past Sunnybank into Petersfield Road.

Successful modern infill to East Hill

Quarry Road

This starts with a remarkable parting of roads formed by flint walls which gives the effect of a boat, creating a raised garden to a late Victorian house. This is the only house in Winchester to have external glass shutters and an interesting roofed pedestrian gate on the north side. After passing five or so Victorian houses within the old lime quarry, this road climbs steeply uphill, with trees in the gardens to the north east making an anchor to the more intermittent trees to the south. The impact of these trees remains dominant up as far as Northbrook Avenue, when the nature of development changes.

Petersfield Road

The road is characterised by brick-and-flint walls on the north side; some of the modern ones take no account of traditional ways of construction. The principal building of note is All Saints church designed by J L Pearson, an eminent Victorian church architect. This is a high stone and flint faced building with a tiled roof, though money ran out before the tower could be built. Founded on steeply sloping ground, it is more impressive from a distance than near to.

Large trees line both sides of the road, with a particularly important belt of beeches to the east of Fivefields Road framing a view out to Magdalen Down and the butterfly reserve on its south slope. There are large new houses on the steep ground to the north which show little understanding of the importance of trees and tree belts running up the hill, or of the character of this area, in their design.

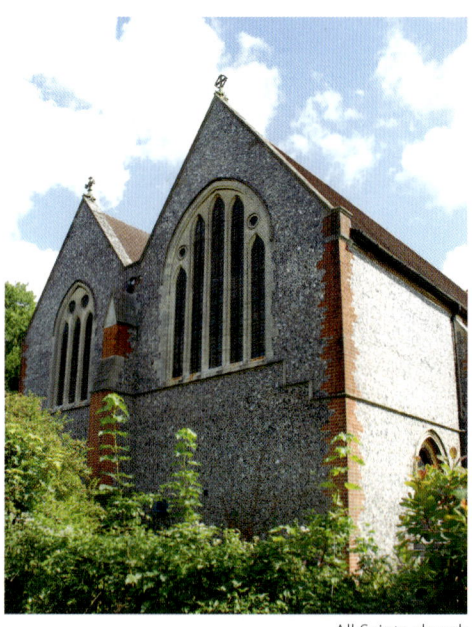

All Saints church

St Giles' Close

This is the first development off Alresford Road with a steep winding cul-de-sac edged by flint-and-brick walls overhung by bushes and trees. The cul-de-sac serves substantial Victorian/Edwardian houses on either side of the road, ending in a little

St Giles' Hill House (formerly Coitbury)

enclosed space in front of a fine lime tree with views of big cedar and beech trees in adjacent gardens. The most important house on the west side was Coitbury, designed and built by Alfred Frampton for his father, a Winchester builders' merchant. Now named St Giles' Hill House, it commands one of the best western view of the Cathedral.

Following demolition of the original All Saints Rectory, there has been some recent low-density development on the tricky west-facing slope, of which the most recent are constructed using tiled roofs and good bricks to provide mellow suburban style dwellings. The space given to trees on the periphery, including the railway bank overlooking Chesil Street, is very restricted. It could be that the pressure to alter the balance of the trees is likely to be high, but the best hope lies in the new tree planting on the central bank to help integrate this with the townscape seen from outside. The view of the east end of the Cathedral is particularly fine from this site.

New housing, St Giles' Close

St Giles' Cemetery

Not only is this important archaeologically, it also has a central spine of trees running from the Alresford Road up to the centre with a T-shape at the southern end. These trees are crucial to the character of the hill and also to the character of adjoining residential closes. The only building that directly relates to it is the lodge (70 Alresford Road) at the north east corner with its half timbered gables.

This space suffers from a lack of management so that the perimeter walls are gradually being destroyed, gates failing and gravestones damaged. Even its value as a wildlife space fails to reach anything like its full potential, though snowdrops poke up through the ivy in early spring and it is an important site for birds whose song is a local feature.

St Catherine's Road area

This was developed in 1884 and forms an integral part of the silhouette of St Giles' Hill because of its elevated position on a little plateau. It has its own unique pedestrian approach up steps from Wharf Hill which replaced Woolford's builders' workshop. From these steps, you can see St Thomas's church spire in Southgate Street.

At the top of the steps, this tight area of two-storey housing consists of four houses using slate roofs, brickwork and sash windows to form a distinct character. At the south west corner of Cathedral View is a good aspect of St Catherine's Hill and the trees along the disused railway line.

St Catherine's Road

St Catherine's Road

St Catherine's Road is a flat east/west road that has distinctive Edwardian terraced houses on its south side with paired gabled entrances and stone details to their elevations strongly emphasised by the flat strong course band inset with flint. These contrast with the carefully detailed brick elevations of the terraced houses on the other side of the road with their distinctive arches. Changes of levels on the south side at the east end are accommodated by semi-basements and steps up to the front doors.

At the end of St Catherine's Road, the land dips away suddenly to provide a good view towards Magdalen Down and the butterfly reserve and the foreground of the pitched roofs of Highcliffe proper beyond the school on the left hand side.

Turning into Canute Road, a shorter north/south road with a gradient, the same architectural theme as the south side of St Catherine's Road reappears, stepping up the hill with a fine view up to St Giles' Hill and the pine trees planted on the summit.

Highcliffe Road

This subtly curved road from the top of Wharf Hill steps, with narrow buildings on the north side, forms an attractive townscape. The terrace on the south side ends at Canute Road with a corner shop now converted to residential use.

The Soke

Because of the way that Winchester developed in the Middle Ages, there was always a shifting balance of power between the King, the Bishop and the emerging civic authority over ownership and jurisdiction of the land, with the town negotiating royal charters with successive monarchs. By 1200, Winchester had a charter confirming the privileges of the guild merchants and had acquired its own coat of arms showing five crenellated gates. In 1231, Peter des Roches, an outstanding Bishop who was also responsible for rebuilding the city walls together with one of the castle walls, was able, after a successful pilgrimage to the Holy Land, to set in place a new jurisdiction in the southern and eastern suburbs of Winchester called the Soke.

Bishop des Roches, not the mayor, became the Chief Magistrate and was responsible for criminal as well as civil jurisdiction. This was carried out from the Cheyney Court, just inside the Prior's Gate of the Cathedral Close, with prisons in the Bishop's palace and Cheyney Court, and stocks on the west side of St John's Street. He also owned the lucrative mills on the waterways outside the town. This administration continued until 1851 when the Church Commissioners were created to administer church land. Within the Soke there were substantial landowners who collected rents from their tenants, and these 'Gentlemen of the Soke' provided a bodyguard when the Bishop came to Winchester.

In the 13th and 14th centuries, a fair was held in September on St Giles' Hill which was the greatest market in southern England and attracted traders from all over Europe. Consequently, the eastern suburb became an important location with buildings up onto the hill. It centred around the two important medieval churches of St Peter Chesil ('chesil' being the name for a gravel beach which existed along the riverside close to the present bridge) and St John the Baptist on an elevated position in St John's Street which was the principle entry point to Winchester and the river crossing from London. St John's was founded in 1193 on a bluff above an area noted for extensive Roman burials. Entry to the church was originally from the north into the north aisle, and then transferred to a position beneath the massive tower probably added in the 14th century. The original scholars of Winchester College used St John's before their new chapel and rooms were completed, and it reached its maximum development in the 15th century when it gained three new east windows and internal rood screens.

It is clear from old descriptions and maps like Speed's plan of 1611 that the Soke was very densely built up, even though land inside the city might be available, and it had numerous merchants' cellars. It would seem that its popularity resulted from taxes being lower than those in the city in the later Middle Ages.

Last remaining stable block in Winchester: St John's Croft

Interior of stable block, St John's Croft

The Soke still does contain four of the best surviving timber framed buildings in Winchester, the Old Blue Boar of 1340, the Chesil Rectory of 1450, Tudor House in St John's Street and 42 Chesil Street. It also contains two of the most important large private houses in Winchester still in use as such. The first is No 12 Chesil Street on the site of the Premonstratensian order, founded in 1199, where monks offered hospitality to travellers arriving after the town gates were closed. The second house is St John's Croft at the top of St John's Street, an 18th century house complete with stables, walled garden, and an attractive summer house.

With the decline of the wool industry and the loss of the 'wool staple' in 1353 to Calais and the St Giles Fair decreasing in importance until it was little more than a cheese market by the 19th century (when Chesil Street became known as Cheesehill Street), the area, particularly St John's Street, became relatively poor. This accounts for the fact that St John's church is the best surviving medieval church in Winchester because there was not the money for it to be remodelled in the 19th century. Recently some of the 12th century wall paintings have been found. Because of its elevated position, St John's church tower (refaced in the 15th century), even though not very high, can be seen from Magdalen Hill as part of the composition with the Cathedral tower. It can also be seen clearly from large parts of the city centre, from St Catherine's Hill and from as far away as Bushfield Camp. It is therefore a townscape feature of considerable importance.

It was equipped with a wrought-iron-framed turret clock in 1559 which marked time by ringing bells and must have been one of the first public buildings outside the Cathedral in Winchester to have one. The clock's mechanism is now in the Museum.

St John's Street

St John's Street, with its narrow winding road rising uphill out of the valley, and its church in the middle is still very much a medieval street in character and contains two important timber framed buildings as a reminder that up until the 19th century it was this sort of building that predominated. It also demonstrates the value in townscape terms of modest changes in level to produce dramatic changes in views towards the Cathedral in a way not found elsewhere in Winchester.

By the end of the 19th century it formed a community with its church, school, rectory in the large house at the top, public houses, shops and open spaces. Despite recent changes, there is still a recognisable community.

Because of the post war desire of the City Council to eradicate 'slums' and the structural changes envisaged by published road proposals, the southern end of the street had been demolished in 1974 along with most of Chester Road. Some buildings had remained empty for fifteen years due to planning blight. The church was isolated on its little cliff and consequently had to be kept locked to combat vandalism.

St John's Street, early 20th century

View from St John's church into St John's Street

The area was the subject of planning briefs from both Winchester Preservation Trust in 1975 and the City Planning Department in 1977, which sparked off redevelopment during which further proposals to knock down the east side of the street were withdrawn in favour of a conservation scheme promoted by the Winchester Preservation Trust and the Hampshire Buildings Preservation Trust.

The start of St John's Street at the southern end is disappointing, partly because the trees shading the corner sitting area are not yet big enough to form a strong corner feature in their own right.

Although the fine 13th century chancel window is a prominent feature looking up the street, the silhouette of the church is not strong enough to make the white gable wall of No 13 seem a minor incident and the Victorian corner shop has lost character with its windows bricked up when it was converted to flats. The new houses on the west side of the street are worthy but uninteresting, while the east side contains two or three houses of individual character which help to make a more interesting townscape.

The 16th century timber framed building with its projecting upper floors frames the more interesting section of the street.

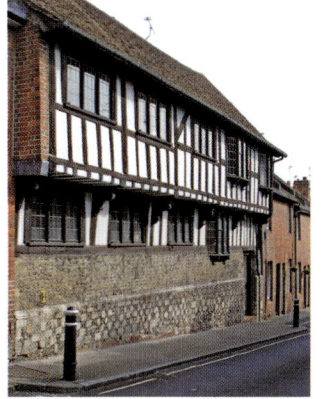

16th century timber-framed house St John's Street

As the view of the church recedes, the road is seen to go around it and the strongly gabled school, designed by Colson, built in 1848, with its decorative bargeboards, becomes important, as does the detail on the listed building adjacent to St John's Croft beyond.

Then the full design of the church, with its tiled roof, three gables in flint, and the flint-and-stone faced 15th century tower, 19th century brick porch and the 15th century entrance to the rood screen adjacent to the chancel window, comes into view. It is like looking into a raised-up country churchyard except that it is surrounded by the roofs of buildings on lower land on ground dropping away beyond the graveyard, with just a hint of the top of the Cathedral and the Guildhall beyond.

St John's church

Just beyond, a sarsen stone sticks out awkwardly into the pavement at the end of the church (like those to be seen in Abbey Gardens, which came from the foundations of the medieval church of St Ruel in St George's Street), hinting at earlier religious institutions. Here the street is closed off by No 35 Beggars Lane, St John's Croft and the tree in front of it. On the east side, set back from the Hall, there are two new gabled houses on the site of what used to be the school playground.

Beyond the school there is once more a view out over the northern graveyard and new flats in Chester Road to the Cathedral and its companion buildings.

Orchids are visible through the railings in early summer. A new entrance to cater for disabled people has been installed into the church.

Then the west side is shut in by a series of town houses ending with the 14th century Blue Boar with its jettied first floor. Here the road widens out into a triangular space to reveal the whole powerful elevation of St John's Croft, its Mansard-roofed neighbour, and its stables beyond, cutting into the hill, with its slate roof and unusual 18th century porch forming an attractive focus. This is one of the most important 18th century houses in Winchester which retains an original set of service rooms. Attached to it is a walled garden with fine trees, and an 18th century summer house. It also has a paddock with stables and an ancient group of beech trees at its southern end, making an important open space that is part of the setting of the house.

Beggars Lane

The lane terminates at a dramatic junction at the top of Blue Ball Hill with the Blue Boar, a jettied timber-framed building over a stone semi-basement. The building is followed by the end-on gable of No 35, a brick building with an end chimney stack and a true Mansard roof, not a common Winchester feature. Adjacent to this powerful elevation there is a small cottage, with a milestone outside its door and tiny dormer windows crammed in, before reaching the great brick wall, three and a half metres high, which encloses the garden of St John's Croft.

St John's Croft

The continuation of Beggars Lane is not unlike an old donkey path and commands a good view out over Winnall Moors and Abbotts Barton before descending to Wales Street, where there is another important 15th century timber framed building, No 53-55. On the western side is a row of three attractive Victorian houses with colour washed brick walls and slate roofs, prominent in views from Durngate. Returning past St John's Croft garden wall, there are good views out to the west to the Cathedral and Guildhall, despite the presence of two disappointing modern houses. The lane then dips to the Blue Boar, the view closed by the end elevation of this timber-framed building with its dramatic curved braces. Here a view opens up to the side of St Giles' Hill with Ashdene (the late 19th century Rectory) the other side of Joyce Gardens. The townscape quality of this area is particularly good and the triangular space used to be the site of Bubbs Cross, one of at least five city crosses.

Turning up the hill, the fir and holly trees in front of the library of St John's Croft link up with a group of beech trees on the land beyond which, in turn, link up with the trees on St Giles' Hill.

The Blue Boar from Blue Ball Hill

Joyce Gardens

St John's church from Joyce Gardens

This piece of land used to belong to St John's Croft and was given to the City Council in 1934 in memory of Ellen Joyce, wife of the Vicar of St John's in the late 19th century. Opposite St John's Croft there is an entrance to the path winding across the triangular space of Joyce Gardens up to Alresford Road, where the remarkable school caretaker's house is reminiscent of a lighthouse with more floors below Alresford Road than above. Walking up this path it is possible to appreciate the highly individual character of each of the town houses passed as well as gaining a view southwards to the tower of Winchester College standing out between the end walls of the school and St John's church.

As the path climbs steeply up towards St Giles' Hill beyond, individual trees become very important; the path then winds on round, still climbing, to reveal one of the most dramatic views over central Winchester.

The special quality of Joyce Gardens derives from the fact that the sloping grass and hedge forms the first side of a triangle. The second side is formed by St John's Croft and its neighbour with its rich palette of materials, including brick walls and chimneys, mathematical tiles, slates as well as roof tiles and carved wooden classical decorations to the porch. There is also a line of fine beech trees which are important to the immediate surroundings as well as being visible from afar. The third side is formed by a row of buildings, consisting of a 15th century church tower, a 17th century timber framed cottage (now rather crudely altered), an 18th century house, and the blank wall of the Victorian extension to the symmetrical building of 18th century design which has 19th century windows. Then there is a set-back 19th century house with slate roofs hidden by both planting and railings. Finally one sees the 14th century hall house and its distinctive clay-tiled roof, small carved timber-framed windows and oak plank door. This all gives a hint of the double-height 'hall' interior with a first-floor chamber and solar that a merchant would have enjoyed in the Middle Ages.

The Blue Boar from the east

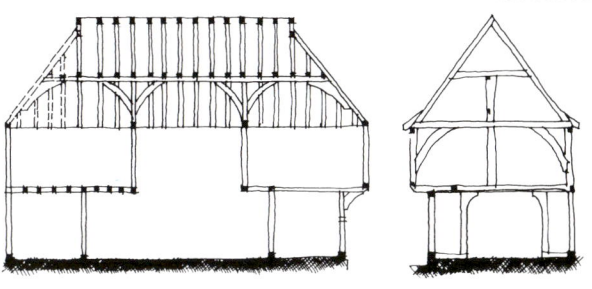

Joyce Gardens

Returning down St John's Street, there is first a glimpse of Blue Ball Hill above the delightful tiled roofs of the cottages in Water Lane at the bottom, with the great swathe of trees beyond in the river valley, the copper fleche on Holy Trinity church and then, half right, a view through to the Cathedral between the Chesil Rectory and No 23. Walking down the street, St Catherine's Hill becomes a major feature over the top of the tiled roof of St Peter Chesil church, which is seen against trees further west.

St Catherine's Hill disappears as you approach the old schoolroom where the two new town houses are set back and a view opens out around the corner to the group of listed buildings in Chesil Street at the bottom of the hill and the timber framed end wall and roofs of the Chesil Rectory Restaurant. Just before Tudor House to the right steep steps lead down to the 1980s flats which wrap around the end of the churchyard and, further to the right, the retaining wall of the churchyard with its stone and flint chequerwork appears.

It is noticeable, passing down the street, that traditional doors and windows have been retained. Some houses have double-plinth brick sills, others concrete sills and two of the buildings have Flemish bond brickwork, with dark headers creating a strong pattern.

The south end of the street is disappointing. The cottages next to the Chesil Rectory were demolished for 19th century road widening and have only recently been replaced with a tree which when mature will help to give interest to the space. Recently St John's Street has been upgraded by relaying the pavements with small-scale paviours, which has improved the quality of the street.

View from Joyce Gardens

Most towns have a characteristic silhouette and this view shows up one aspect of Winchester's. Firstly, there is the outline of the stone Cathedral, with its lead roof, rising above all other buildings in the town, but at an angle so that the light shows up its geometry. It even rises above the trees on Sleepers Hill to the west and is delicately complemented by the large spire of St Thomas's church in Southgate Street which is seen above the layers of the red brick and slate roofed barrack buildings with the lesser stone spire of Christ Church beyond. To the right of this is the bulk of the Law Courts, the gable of the Great Hall and the Victorian stone County Council buildings with their decorative chimneys and turret. To the right again is the large red brick and tiled Queen Elizabeth II Court, with its clock tower and copper fleche marking the end of the High Street. Attached to it is the bulk of Ashburton Court, which, at roughly the same length as the Cathedral, breaks the skyline of trees along Chilbolton Avenue/Bereweeke Road.

Ashburton Court introduced into the Winchester townscape a new building form which has always been found intrusive because, although it has the bulk of a castle, it has lacked the modelling and interest which such a building would have had. For the first 35 years of its life, Ashburton Court was clad with dull concrete panels with long, horizontal bands of repetitive windows, unrelieved by strong vertical elements visible at a distance. It had a hard roofline, emphasised by the long white rail serving as a cornice and completely at odds with the softness of the traditional Winchester roofscape.

The thorough re-shaping which Ashburton Court is undergoing at the time of writing looks very promising as an example of how a large building mass can be assimilated into a traditional townscape without a reduction in size. This is achieved by changing the facing materials between different parts of the building visible at a distance and by breaking up the horizontal line into strongly modelled vertical elements clad in a local red brick.

Another intrusive post-war building is the slab block of the County Police Headquarters on top of the hill which is becoming more noticeable with the passage of time as large beech trees surrounding it come to the end of their life. Further to the right again the tower of St Peter's Roman Catholic church and the slate roof and copper fleche of Holy Trinity compensate by adding interest. In front of these dominant buildings there is the rich texture of the small roofs of central Winchester and their dormers and chimneys; yet even this pattern has been coarsened by the long horizontal flat-roofed multi-storey car parks at King's Walk.

Police Headquarters, top right

It is interesting to notice how strongly buildings like the medieval St John's House, the 19th century Guildhall with its tower and green copper roof, the Marks & Spencer warehouse (an old wool warehouse not very visible from the High Street), and the three new white gables of the 1998 'Bird in Hand' development in Parchment Street, show up from this distance. Also how effective as a visual feature is the cupola on Barclays Bank and how ineffective the bell tower on the Brooks.

It is also noticeable in this scene that, whereas central Winchester is dense with buildings, trees form an important feature. They surround the Cathedral and make a strong contribution to the southern area of the city and provide a backdrop to the Brooks area. Again, looking north towards the Recreation Ground and in the nearer foreground, a line of trees marks the river valley.

This view changes dramatically from morning to evening light and, according to the seasons with winter mists and the cycle of vegetation colours, in an uncanny way the Cathedral seems to come closer or move away. At night, when the Cathedral is floodlit, the darkness of the trees on Sleepers Hill adds to the effect of the lighting in a way that a housing estate full of street lights without trees would not.

Chester Road

A wide, straight Victorian road cut into the side of the hill, this has residential development on its east side and rather indifferent garages and fences on its west side.

It closes at its southern end with the outline of St Catherine's Hill rising up behind two linked housing units. At the north it ends with the attractive tiled roofs of the 18th century Rosemary Cottages, built on top of a bank with large trees adjacent and behind them.

Apart from the striking brick-and-flint, gable-fronted Edwardian house and a Victorian house next door at the north end, Chester Road was rebuilt in the early 1980s with houses and flats in a comprehensive redevelopment around St John's church, with the end blocks set back to accommodate a turning head. This is in an area where a significant Roman cemetery was located.

The south end of Chester Road connects with the footpath system rising up from the riverside. There is a choice of two routes to St John's Street. Either you proceed through a grassy open space containing silver birch trees, on round below the churchyard and up steep steps to St John's Street, coming out opposite the half timbered Tudor House. In this case there is a continuous range of houses round the south side of the wall, but on the north a dramatic sunlit view of the flint-and-stone St John's church tower on its bluff, enclosed by the substantial remains of a chequered stone-and-flint retaining wall.

Alternatively, you can take the winding steps up to and around the base of the church tower emerging into the churchyard, past the attractive brick-and-flint 19th century entrance porch and out into St John's Street to be confronted by simple but attractive entrances to the Victorian cottages opposite.

On the wall of the church a plaque (replaced) recalls that the first church is partly of 12th century construction and the south window is 13th century geometric tracery. It also records the fact that the church was used by the scholars of Winchester College for services before their chapel was completed in 1395, and that Bishop Thomas Ken, the hymn writer, was in charge of this church for a period.

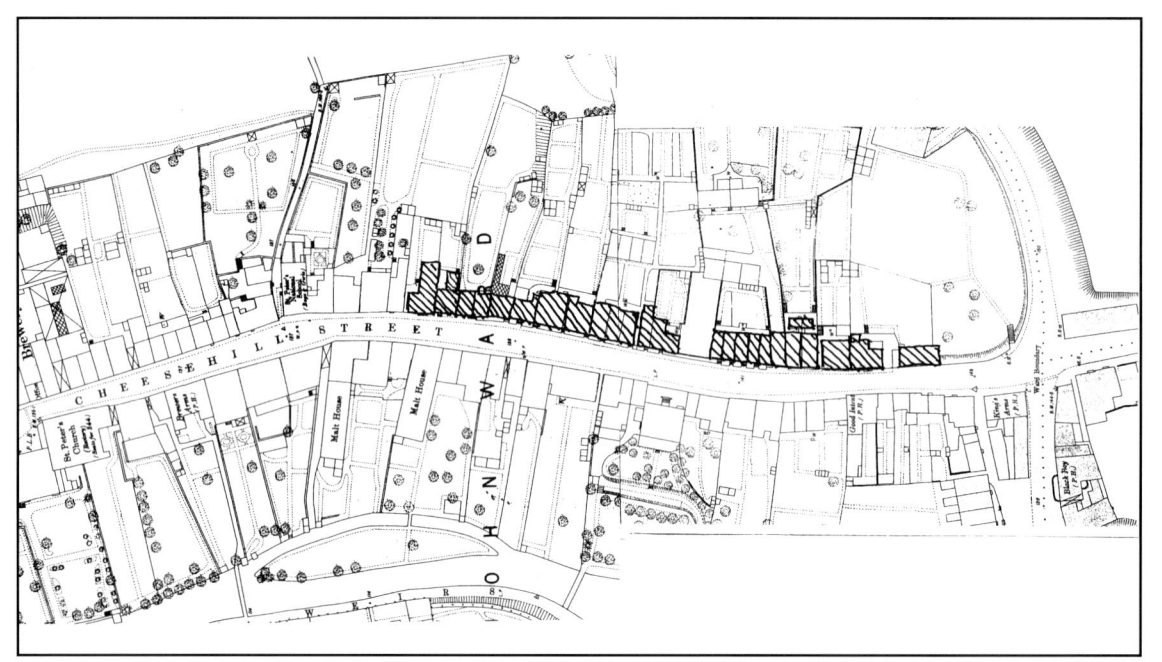

Houses pulled down in Chesil Street in order to build the railway.

Chesil Street before 1885

Chesil Street

Chesil Street or Cheshulle (on a gravel bank) is an important part of the medieval suburb of the Bishop's Soke with two Roman roads leading to the bridge point and the walled city's east gate. It had its own church, St Peter Chesil, and in the 19th century its own school, shops and public houses. The discovery in 1997 of a timber-framed roof structure dated to 1293 clearly underlines the street's medieval importance. Properties of wealthy people have always been built directly onto this narrow, busy road with the compensation of having fine gardens either facing west down to the river, with views of the Cathedral, or towards the downland of St Giles' Hill.

Allotments on site of the present car park in Chesil Street. Photograph by W T Green

By the 18th century small-scale industrial enterprises had crept in, including pipe manufacturing, maltings and a brewery. Then in the late 19th century it was seriously disrupted by the construction of the railway line from Didcot and Newbury to Southampton, boldly tunnelled under St Giles' Hill and then proceeding via a cutting behind Chesil Street to Bar End goods yard. This led to the destruction of seventeen properties at the northern end of Chesil Street to provide construction access and sidings, and one property at the southern end to accommodate the bridge under East Hill.

The GWR station, built on the up line in 1885, was for much of its life in a sylvan setting surrounded by conifers and set against the beauty of St Giles' Hill. Tucked away as it was at the lower end of the city, not everyone was aware of the station's existence. Those who were recall an individual character and quiet charm impossible to find amidst the bustle of a main station complex.

Bar End looking southeast to St Catherine's Hill with track and rolling stock of DN&S railway c.1891

To create the Station Approach, two houses were demolished next to the Chesil Rectory Restaurant and large enamelled signs were put up on the gable wall of No 3. Its fine garden was replaced by a brewery (later a laundry). This paved the way for other buildings associated with modern transport, in the form of three garages for the King Alfred Bus Company. In the 1950s a petrol filling station replaced cottages on the west side of Chesil Street. All of these changes were disastrous in townscape terms.

Old Chesil Rectory and Station Approach c. 1893

In Victorian times, Magdalen Hill was also upgraded to make a better route out of town to the east, bypassing the narrow St John's Street, and this led to the demolition of houses on the north side of the Chesil Rectory Restaurant so that it now remains an isolated building. The restaurant is a graphic demonstration of how road levels in towns have built up over the years as they are made up, so that now access to the building is several steps down. Based in Chesil Street the family business of R Chisnell & Sons Ltd started the first regular bus services in 1922 to Twyford, Flowerdown and the new council estate at Stanmore. It was one of the few privately owned bus companies to run a municipal service which served most areas of the city plus country routes to Fishers Pond, Basingstoke, Stockbridge and Broughton, and had a café and office on the ground-floor of St John's House in The Broadway.

Chesil Street is now predominantly residential with offices at the northern end, and secondary shops, eating establishments and public houses in the adjoining Bridge Street.

The approach from the south has been adjusted to enable the railway to pass under the road at the junction of Chesil Street and Wharf Hill. Chesil Street itself undulates and curves into town, now only having houses continuously on the west side at far as No 32. The east side which became allotments after the construction of the railway is now car parking. This lies behind a wall and small street trees, with a view to the sycamore trees along the railway embankment behind and St Giles' Hill beyond.

Kingsland House

View from the multi-storey car park looking towards Chesil Street. The road on the left was the old railway line

Walking northwards, after the 18th century King's Head public house (now the Black Rat), there is an Edwardian terrace, with characteristic first-floor bays and dormer windows, originally built as shops with living accommodation. This is followed by new flats and some Victorian houses which conceal Chesil Terrace, a double line of houses situated on backland to the west, which can only be reached by a footpath. Chesil Terrace commands good views of Wolvesey Palace.

Kingsland House is now the most important house in this section of the street by virtue of its attractive garden and the fact that it is set back from the frontage in order to accommodate the magnificent 18th century railings salvaged from Mildmay House, when it was sold and demolished in 1847. The ugly garage and gap site have now been disguised by the insertion of a new brick terrace house that contributes a gabled elevation to the riverside.

The next group of modest cottages have 18th century frontages which disguise the fact that they are timber framed houses in origin (this is revealed by observing them from the Weirs). No 42 has the oldest domestic king-post roof found in the city and quite possibly in the whole of Europe, and dates from 1293.

Where the street bends, the old King Alfred Bus Company premises has been transformed into a tyre service centre and the adjacent garage has been replaced by two parallel blocks of flats, known as Watersmeet, with an inner garage court between them. The adjoining site has been the subject of a recent planning permission for an extension to the theatre, some houses and a pedestrian route through to a new bridge crossing the River Itchen.

The next section is built up on both sides, starting on the east side with the flint-and-brick school with its gothic windows and a bell-tower. This makes an attractive feature not only in the street but also in the section of footpath that leads up to St Giles' Hill over a pedestrian bridge recently imaginatively reconstructed by the County Architects. The brick-fronted, timber-framed buildings adjoining it still have gardens rising up to the old railway cutting.

St Peter Chesil church tower is seen full height from the pavement, with its tile-clad, timber-framed top storey and three stone-and-flint gables attached. This building, now adapted to house a theatre, forms the knuckle point around which the rest of the street is organised. Opposite the church there used to be a hideous single-storey bus garage, which has been replaced by Avalon House, a three-storey office building with tiled roof to fit into the townscape when seen from the St Giles' Hill viewing point. By studying the streetscape in model form, the architects arrived at a three-storey building by setting back the frontage, introducing two principal gables with two hipped roof elements between and modern wrapround windows. This massing, combined with patterned brickwork, enabled them to achieve a building of considerable bulk which emphasises the knuckle point without destroying the townscape value of this small-scale church tower seen from either the street, the river or from St Giles' Hill.

The old bus garage, now Avalon House

The Soke from the rear

St Peter's church and The Soke

Beyond this the street widens reflecting the imposing presence of the three-storey 18th century front to The Soke (one of the most important houses in Winchester) together with its former warehouse neighbour. William of Wykeham sold a monastery site here in 1387 after the Black Death for the erection of a house. At the Reformation, the courtyard between this property and St Peter Chesil had been roofed in to extend the church and because of the law of 'ancient lights' one window of the house remained looking into the church and a pew was created in the thickness of the wall so that services could be observed. This is now incorporated into the present house. By the time of Sir Robert Fleming, Recorder, MP for Winchester and Chief Justice of England 1603-1605, The Soke was an 'E' shaped timber-framed house (shown on Bucks' 1735 View from St Giles' Hill) with a stone back wall, and the rear chimneys that one sees today. The ornate tomb depicting him and his wife and children is to be found in St Nicholas church, Stoneham, where he was buried in 1613. This house was then owned by the Earle family for three hundred years and was modernised in the late 18th century, with the existing brick front, parapets, inset sash windows and lovely doorcase and steps.

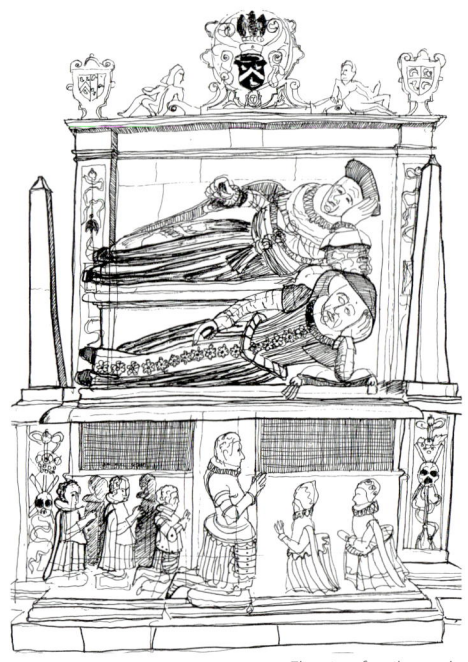

Fleming family tomb

The Chesil Rectory c. 1850, watercolour attributed to A Godwin, c. 1850

The 18th century street character is strengthened by adjoining buildings, Nos 7 and 8, the latter having shop windows which contrast with the bolder 19th century shopfront of Nos 5 and 8 opposite.

The street is closed by the three gables of the Edwardian Cricketers' public house built at a time when the Victorian Lion Brewery in Eastgate Street would have been seen above it. Around the corner in Bridge Street there is a varied group of 18th century two-storey buildings leading down to the river bridge crossing.

Standing on the corner of the roundabout there used to be an ugly flat-roofed garage and two-storey flat-roofed shops, over which could be seen the Cathedral when coming into town or from Station Approach. When the undertakers acquired both Nos 6 and 7, a new scheme was implemented which strengthened the street form by building a three-storey building on the garage site, with a gable over the entrance in place of the flat roofs.

Returning southwards in Chesil Street, the distinctive double-gabled Chesil Rectory dating from about 1450, marks the opposite corner. However, it looks uncomfortable as the original adjoining houses have been removed, leaving unsuccessful spaces either side. The scale of the buildings behind tends to overpower this important building, a condition redressed to an extent by the new alder tree on the corner.

Chesil Street looking south, c. 1893

Looking southwards, the most important building in townscape terms is St Peter's church with its main entrance and window facing north. Its tower appears over the top of the roofs so that the church with its weather vane is seen in silhouette against the strong southern light. The buildings on either side provide a strong supporting framework and, beyond the church, the street curls round with trees replacing the buildings that would have been there in medieval times. Beyond Chesil Rectory on the eastern side, No 3, a fine listed building, has been restored to its pre-railway days with the entrance detail put back in the centre of the building and the shop window removed. On the north elevation a modern balcony and French doors have been inserted to take away the starkness of the party wall. No 3 is followed by a shop with offices above, a 1980s development of offices, a row of attractive cottages and the converted school, all making an interesting sequence of buildings despite the narrow pavements and an extremely busy road.

Beyond St Peter's church the street winds up the slope to a sort of 'pinch point' at Wharf Hill where buildings on higher ground close in. On the eastern side of the street the wall and trees disguise the car park so that St Giles' Hill appears to be part of the street. On the western side there is a variety of buildings which together form a successful townscape.

There are two other constituents of this area which are integral to it, Bridge Street and Station Approach.

Bridge Street

Bridge Street has two-storey buildings on either side forming an appropriate scale for the attractive early 19th century bridge with its high stone balustrades that cast such a strong shadow on the road in winter sunlight. The restaurant on the north side is particularly important by virtue of its position looking out onto the river, the mill race and island, with its attractive judas tree.

View looking down to Bridge Street

In townscape terms, the corner by the Chesil Rectory Restaurant is visually weak and much depends for improving this on the success of the new alder tree planted next to it. There used to be a compact prunus tree making an effective screen in this situation and unfortunately a flat-roofed extension to No 17 was allowed on the basis that it was hidden behind it. When the tree was blown down by a storm the replacement cherry was totally unsuitable in scale and form for a position that was so important looking down the High Street.

There is now a good group of buildings rising up the hill on the south starting with the Rising Sun public house, a listed building whose cellar was possibly used in medieval times as a prison for offenders on St Giles' Hill. Inserted next to it are offices, probably the first ones in Winchester designed with an air-conditioned interior. These step up the hill successfully by virtue of staggering the frontage, varying the eaves line to the parallel hipped roofs and having a glazed atrium containing staircases in between.

The small two-storey building next door with its half-hipped tiled roof, which is very prominent coming into town, also has an extension which helps to step up the hill, towards the original station master's house. On the corner just beyond this was an idiosyncratic building (now replaced) created by the refugee metalworker, Jack Schrier, with its own landscaped courtyard, containing exotic trees and a light-hearted pergola. On the west side the redundant shop and the small cottages made a corner of appropriate scale. This site, too, has been redeveloped as town houses with parking below, which form a block, with prominent balconies and windows. The paint colour that has been used, however, is unfortunate and prevents people seeing it as part of a group.

Station Approach

This is now the principal pedestrian route into town from the major multi-storey car park, built on the site of the GWR station in 1983. Its makes use of the old railway line to bring traffic in and out of town without blocking up Chesil Street

This site was the subject of a major debate in 1983 when a larger 960-space car park was designed to a different orientation in horizontal layers; the type of construction that was common for car parks and offices at that time, as can be seen at Friarsgate. Associated with this was a proposal for a 10,000 sq.ft. glass office block at an angle beyond the old school in Chesil Street and a 139 bed hotel beyond at the south end over the railway lines, that looked not unlike a stranded liner.

The Planning Department found in its assessment that the proposals would have a major impact, not only on Bridge Street and the Chesil Rectory (where geometry and rows of lights at night would dwarf and devalue the restaurant as a historic building) but also from the High Street, the Westgate, the Weirs, Wharf

Mill, Wolvesey Palace and St Giles' Hill. It was a big-town developer's solution that would have been very damaging to the townscape, however valuable to the city's exchequer.

Sketch of proposed glass office block and hotel

The scheme having been withdrawn, the present car park was then designed to fit in with the roofscape of the town from all directions. The staircase and lift housing were designed to fit into the townscape of Magdalen Hill as well as the background of St Catherine's Hill. It was also intended to provide a dramatic viewing point for visitors. Unfortunately, the designers of the adjacent residential building (which replaced a cigarette machine reconditioning factory) felt that the north east corner was the logical place for a circulation tower. This unfortunately blocks out the Cathedral view from the car park but at least there are some good views to be had at each floor level.

Chesil car park tower

The bottom of Station Approach is nicely detailed with concrete paving bricks and cast-iron bollards. There are trees which now draw attention away from the poor design of the back of the Rising Sun public house and the electricity transformer. The view is closed by the attractive 18th century buildings, Nos 5 and 7, whose painted finish makes them very prominent. Unfortunately the tree which was on the south side of this street, between No 3 and the residential building, was vandalised and not replaced. In the reverse direction, the view up Station Approach is quite dramatic, closed by the car park's circulation tower with its gabled, projecting viewing balcony at the top.

Chesil Street Station, beneath St Giles' Hill, c.1895

Wharf Hill

This was an important connection to the southern side of the walled city enabling the Bishop to cross the Itchen at Black Bridge and go in and out of his palace without having to go through the city. This applied to all the commerce associated with his estate including Seagram's Mill, Priory Mill and the wool warehouse. The high ground adjoining the street to the south called 'Rack Hill' was also used by clothmakers in this important medieval industry.

The name Wharf Hill indicates a trading connection associated with the Wharf, whose storage buildings to the south of Black Bridge marked the end of the Itchen Navigation. This was authorised by an Act of Parliament in 1665, designed to enable deeper barges to bypass mill sites on the Itchen, and was completed in 1710. Construction was undertaken using six barges carrying coal, timber and building materials from Coasters House, Northam. The canal ceased to function in 1869 because of the lack of cargo for the return trips and competition from the new railways. The manager's house and warehouse remain and are now college houses. The offices were sited behind Wharf Mill, together with four customs' officers houses.

There was a builders' yard attached to Domum House and various public houses adjacent to the Wharf Mill including the picturesque 'Dog & Duck'. These have all been demolished to create an open space and the area is now almost entirely residential. The only public house left is the Black Boy, with its converted stone-and-flint stable block and one of the most descriptive local inn signs in Winchester.

The townscape design of Wharf Hill now centres around the grassy open space incorporating tall, beautiful lime trees. The seat under these gives views of the Mill and the water. In the winter Wolvesey Palace can be seen on the right hand side and the College tower on the left hand side of the Mill. To the east are 1960s council houses which provide a fine environment for the tenants, overlooking a private open space by the river with formal rose beds. They step down the hill, have wide windows and concrete tile hanging with basic flat canopies over the front door, but lack interest as townscape.

At the bottom of the hill the large converted Wharf Mill has a modern eastern wing, which disguises its original blank east wall and allows cars to be tucked underneath. It is probably this wing that helped to make this conversion profitable.

Itchen Navigation, Black Bridge. Lithograph by F C Lewis from a drawing by T Taylor, 1805

Rural scene at Black Bridge, 1917

Adjoining it is a 17th century timber frame cottage with attractive fish-scale tiling on the southern side. The cottage is followed by Granville Place, a terrace at right angles to Wharf Hill built after the 1880s and proposed for demolition in 1976. In view of its townscape quality the Winchester Preservation Trust argued for the terrace to be retained. So, instead, the terrace was modernised using standard 1970s windows and lean-to porches which transformed these buildings into classical council housing with a paved central road.

On the eastern side of Wharf Hill is an almost continuous run of pleasant Victorian terraced housing, apart from one cleverly inserted set of three-storey infill town houses designed to exploit the wonderful views from top floor living rooms. The design of these buildings is interesting but let down by the impact of the garage door openings.

Tucked in behind No 7 is Matley's Yard, a good facility for small-scale service industry. There is a tendency for housing to push out this type of use in Winchester. In this case the proximity of industrial-type buildings to the rear walls of the town houses would be unacceptable in a newly created environment today.

Opposite the site of the Wharf are two attractive mid-19th century houses with rendered walls. On the north side of Black Bridge, a new residential development sought to provide picturesque townscape that carried the street round to the bridge whilst relating to the other, rather awkwardly proportioned property on the corner. Due to the necessity for an appeal against planning refusal, the architects lost control of the buildings and the detailing suffered accordingly. Note the lack of curved windows on the curved elevation adjacent to the bridge and the awkward staircase, all part of the economic retraction demanded by the developer to compensate for the financial costs of the appeal.

New house showing curved wall

Open space in Wharf Hill

Domum Road

Domum Road is a narrow curved road, beneath the tree-lined embankment of the old GWR railway that leads past the canal wharves, an 'L' shaped group of 18th century cottages and an extensive canal-side builders' yard, to the substantial Domum House. Domum House is an attractive brick-and-slate Victorian house in its own garden, with tennis courts and playing fields on College land beyond. The road provides a convenient pedestrian access to the 'park and ride' site at Bar End.

The builders' yard is now replaced with six semi-detached houses with first-floor patios over garages with distinctive triangular windows in their gables. The cottages were disfigured at the eastern end by unsatisfactorily proportioned modern windows. The College won an appeal to insert a new house here and, as part of the development, the window proportions were improved. The cottages are hemmed in by two substantial houses similar in form but much more pretentious in detail. These houses adjoin the wooden College boathouse with its shingle roofs. There are footpaths along the canal to Garnier Road on both sides. The eastern footpath runs close to the houses and around the field with regularly planted 140-year old plane trees. There is also a plane tree north of the boathouse over the little 18th century humped-back bridge and, along the grassy western side beside the College nature reserve there are poplar and willow trees following the river's edge. The canal with its swans, ducks and grebes is a peaceful environment so close to the centre of Winchester.

Winchester from Tun Bridge, drawing by W Westall c. 1840

Rackhill open space

Accessed from the junction at Wharf Hill at the north end, and the steps up the bank from Domum Road at the south end, this is a hidden area of grassy high land between the railway cutting and the river. It is now surrounded by ash, hazel and cherry trees, with a path down the middle and a lovely view towards St Catherine's Hill.

Riverside

The River Itchen has a catchment area of 400 square kilometres fed by aquifers in the underground chalk which produce a very pure stable flow of water throughout the year. Since Winchester became an established settlement in this valley in pre-Roman times, the position and use of water channels has been crucial to its health and economic development throughout the centuries.

The archaeological chapter sets out the changes to the river system made by the Romans and Saxons. There are still decisions to be taken within the town as to the changes that could take place to enhance the stream near St John's House at Busket Lane which has not yet been culverted. It is hoped that the new scheme proposed for the Silver Hill development will exploit these old water courses.

Chapter 1 highlighted the importance of the river valley north and south of the central area for the setting of the conservation area for wildlife of all sorts and as a place to walk.

It should be noted that over the last twenty years, the process of levelling the land to provide more playing fields has been stopped. North of the centre, the City Council used to have an active policy to allow builders to dump rubble from construction sites in order to create and extend the existing Recreation Ground. No doubt this has been beneficial to people's health and fitness but from an ecological and visual point of view it has produced a green desert, broken up by a few trees. For the time being the pressure for playing fields has moved to the south and west of the city following major development at Stanmore, Oliver's Battery and Badger Farm.

There have been proposals dating from the 1930s to create a new feeder road into the city through Winnall Moors (more recently relating to the M3) to relieve Wales Street and combine it with associated car parks. This was all part of a policy to provide parking on radial routes on the edge of the central area. But the policy would have been very destructive of wildlife habitats which, despite human activity, are remarkably productive around Winchester. Recently, for example, otters have been sighted on Winnall Moors.

South of the centre it was Winchester College which in the late 19th century reclaimed land to provide their need for playing fields for the expanding school. However, the College also recognised that the land between the canal and the Itchen was a valuable and rich nature resource for educational purposes and has managed it as such. The creation of the Winnall Moors Nature Reserve, managed by the Hampshire and Isle of Wight Naturalist Trust, has given the same possibility to the north, as well as being a potential source of inspiration on the doorstep of the Art School.

This does have management implications since, from medieval times to the late 19th century and beyond, there were mill owners who controlled the hatches. These landowners needed to maintain a good head of water to run their mills and this interrelated with farmers' management of the water meadows. Since the 17th century they had developed a system of minor water channels that separated drowners and drainers. Flooding the land in winter was carried out in order to fertilise it and keep it frost free, thus enabling early grass to be produced for animals in spring.

City Bridge and City Mill

The City Council, which controls the hatches, has as its primary responsibility the avoidance of flooding in the city. That can conflict with the maintenance of wetland habitats with their reeds, grasses, marsh flowers and associated mammal and bird populations, so characteristic of the River Itchen. Nineteen species of plant on Winnall Moors have disappeared since the 19th century and there is a real danger that Winnall Moors will be invaded and taken over by scrub if it were allowed to dry out. A habitat restoration project is currently being led by the Hampshire Wildlife Trust.

North and south of Garnier Road, Winchester College, with assistance from the Environment Agency, has carried out work to enhance the river habitat for iconic chalkstream wildlife such as salmon, brown trout, and otters, which are regularly seen at the City Mill. There is also the question of power generation from the water flow. It is now being recognised that we need to find ways of harnessing natural resources, which are renewable assets, to combat global warming; some of the abandoned mill sites may perhaps have potential.

It is still amazing that such good areas for wildlife come so close to the city centre and it remains important that a corridor is kept along the river so that wildlife can be interconnected. The rest of this chapter will deal with the riverside link through the town, which is only 966 metres in total length, divided into two sections, north and south of the City Mill.

This is an area that in Victorian times was becoming more and more filled in with buildings but since the earlier part of the 20th century has seen a major change in emphasis. As a consequence of the selective demolition of buildings (many of which must have been vulnerable to flooding), planned enhancement has turned the riverside through the town into a major amenity.

It is important to note that, although there are now three public houses with gardens on the riverside, commercial advertising has not been allowed to intrude into the character of the area. The two sections identified have different characteristics. South of the City Mill, the river has strong historical associations and virtually no direct access to dwellings. It is an important pedestrian and cycling route into the centre for adults and children from Highcliffe, Wharf Mill and the College area, and a starting point for recreational walks to St Cross, St Catherine's Hill and beyond. It is also used as the start for long distance walks along the South Downs Way. It is a place where residents come to relax and sit on one of the many benches that have been put up as memorials to relatives. And it is also a place for visitors to walk through and enjoy looking at the swans and ducks, which provide visual delight and endless entertainment.

Before analysing the townscape it is relevant to look at the three mills that come within this stretch of river, because the mills were important both to the medieval economy and to the townscape. Since they all lay outside the city walls in the Soke, after 1231 they could, in principle, come under the control of the Bishop and contribute to his exchequer.

City Mill

Situated at the end of the High Street, City Mill was established in the reign of Richard I around 1189-99 by the Abbess of Wherwell and was very profitable until the time of the Black Death in 1348, and the subsequently shifting of the wool trade to Calais. This reduced the economy of the town so that the mill had become derelict by 1417. After the Dissolution of the monasteries in 1538, it became the property of the Crown and was eventually given in 1554 by Queen Mary to the City Council in recompense for the entertainment they provided at her wedding in Winchester. However, it remained derelict until 1743 when a local tanner built the

Ladies bathing place, Y.H.A., City Mill. Sketch by J Ludlow Northeast

present mill reusing some of the 15th century timbers. In 1820, the Corporation sold it, plus some land, to John Benham whose family ground corn there until the 1920s. Competition from roller mills at the docks seriously reduced its profitability so that, by the time of the 1914-18 war, it had an additional use as a laundry. It finally came up for sale and potential demolition in 1928, but luckily a group of local benefactors purchased it and gave it to the National Trust, though without any endowment to pay for repairs.

In 1931 it was leased to the new Youth Hostels Association as one of their pioneer hostels. It was spartanly furnished and hostellers bathed in the river. The upper floors and machinery must have been stripped out to increase the usable area, yet even so it did not provide enough income for its long-term wellbeing. In view of its historic and architectural importance to the city, it was made a Grade II* listed building in the 1950s. It was not until 1994 that the National Trust used other resources and

The City Bridge, Heywood Sumner 1880

City Mill

grants to undertake the first stages of repair and presentation of the mill to a larger public. They opened up a shop in the women's dormitory on the west side, rebuilt the foundation arch, and repaired the machinery at a lower level prior to a scheme to add back enough structure and machinery at first-floor level to demonstrate the original milling process. They also opened the attractive northern garden. The mill is now well placed as an introduction to a tour of other mills and pumping stations in the area open to the public.

Durngate Mill

Durngate Mill to the north, founded in 1213, was at the head of the waterways through the town, and a profitable mill for the Bishop. It was rebuilt in the 18th century, acquired a Victorian mill house, had its machinery updated by a turbine and remained as a working mill for animal feed until 1946. By 1960 it had become derelict and, because it adjoined a very narrow road perceived as a link of growing importance for motor traffic, the mill was demolished in 1967 rather than moving the road north. It was, however, recorded in detail by the local model engineering society.

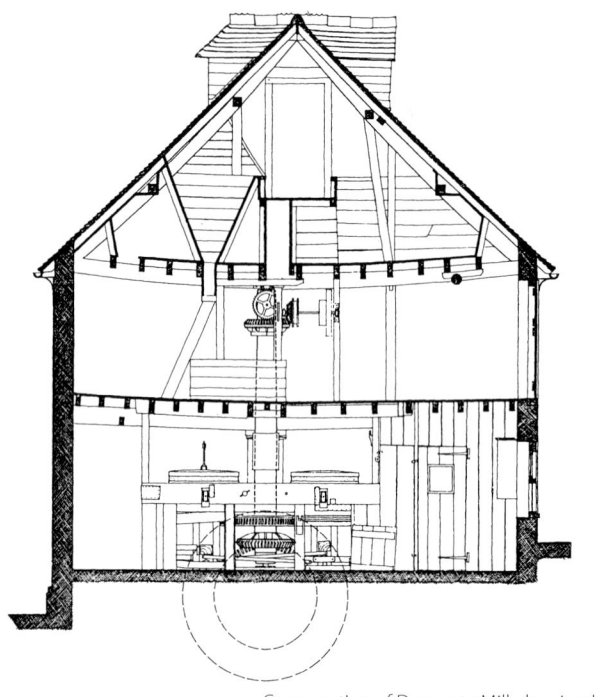

Cross section of Durngate Mill, drawing by John Reynolds

North Elevation Durngate Mill, drawing by John Reynolds

From a townscape point of view this destroyed a building which articulated the change between the countryside, represented by Winnall Moors, and the town, represented by the section through the Weirs. Now its site lies adjacent to a causeway bridge designed and built by the County Council to celebrate the centenary of their founding in 1888. The design is in a simple, robust brick style with Flemish bond and careful detailing to parapets. Round beds containing trees have been formed at each end together with a considered redesign of the pedestrian route into North Walls.

Mechanism from Durngate Mill installed in City Mill

The Weirs, from a postcard c. 1910

Wharf Mill

Wharf Mill, also known as Seagram's Mill, was originally founded in 1205, and later was a source of clean water for Winchester College. After the demise of the 17th century canal, whose wharf was located to the south of Black Bridge, and demolition of an 18th century mill, it was rebuilt in 1885 as a three-storey corn mill. This was owned and operated by SCATS and became derelict by the 1960s when it was acquired by local developers, Bendalls, for one of their housing projects. Since it was not restricting any road and had a marvellous location looking up and down the river, it made a viable conversion into flats with an additional wing added on over car parking on the eastern side. The old canal offices at the rear with attractive garden became a private house, adjoining an 18th century mill house with a garden containing many trees.

A significant aspect concerning the conversion (from a townscape point of view) is that the cast-iron windows of the working mill on the north side were removed and projected forward as oriel windows to the living rooms. This is an architectural device to overcome the utilitarian design of the industrial elevation and provides an architectural presence in keeping with its new use and townscape importance at the end of a vista. Imaginative use was also made of rooflights giving the mill group a distinctive silhouette which shows up well from St Giles' Hill.

At the turn of the century the riverside footpath north of this mill was only eight feet wide. A terrace of seven houses north west of the mill and fourteen other properties outside the mill were demolished up to the site of Scott Gardens, possibly because they had suffered from flooding. Adjacent to the city wall bounding Wolvesey Palace, a ditch and a small water channel called Lady Close were filled in.

Wharf Mill

It is fortunate historically for Winchester that Thomas Stopher, the Mayor in the 1890s, commissioned an art teacher, Beatrice Corfe, living in Canon Street, to paint a series of watercolours of 'old picturesque' buildings in Winchester for the Corporation before they were demolished. Her paintings of many buildings in this area, including the Dog & Duck public house, mark the start of the city picture collection, which has been added to over the years.

River walks: southern section

Walking the public footpath along the river valley past Winchester College, the river bends eastward and the path follows around the city wall to take you into the city. This walk opens up some fine townscape views around Winchester. Note that you are walking on old stone pavement, a reminder of the type of work undertaken by the 18th century Pavement Commissioners.

Medieval wall section alongside the River Itchen

Going north, the footpath leads around the eastern corner of the best surviving stretch of the medieval flint city wall, now an Ancient Monument. Responsibility for its maintenance is shared between the Church Commissioners and their lessees on the inside, and the City Council as adjoining landowners on the outside. In this section up to the Almshouses there are two lengths of wall which retain their battlements, some with dressed stones still in position. This is now a formal walkway in which large forest trees have been planted. In winter the pattern of tree shadows on the wall can add contrast and texture. Round the corner between the walls and the main river feeding the mill are well-planted garden beds either side of a noisy relief water channel, providing colour and interest. Looking across from the river paths to the west there are rewarding glimpses of the Cathedral, Wolvesey Palace and the chapel of the Bishop's Palace.

On the east bank of the river, a public house and terraced houses on Wharf Hill were cleared away and new council houses built in a key position overlooking the Weirs in the 1960s. However, in general it is private gardens that sweep down to the river, providing views of the backs of the mostly medieval buildings that front Chesil Street above, with the trees of St Giles' Hill seen in the background.

Kingsland House back garden with private bridge

The most important of these gardens is that of the late 19th century Kingsland House which has a private bridge at the point where there is a lovely copper beech tree and the path changes direction and character. This is now the only surviving bridge from the four shown on the 1870 Ordnance Survey map.

North of this open section, the almshouses of St Mary Magdalen, erected in the 1980s, have been extended on either side of a formal entrance with gates through the city wall. These have tile hanging and triangular oriels giving the residents views up and down the river. On the east bank an island provides the nucleus of a belt of trees that shelter the river and give screening and privacy to the houses in Chesil Street and hide the industrial-type buildings.

The final section up to City Bridge and Mill is parallel to Colebrook Street, which runs at a higher level within the walls. Here, terraced houses and a public house have been removed and two houses placed at right angles to the river with gardens between, the most important one being the garden in memory of Sir Leslie Scott PC, created in 1952. In 1942 he produced an important government report into rural land-use which recommend the setting up of national parks and the consolidation of a national grid of footpaths. The garden is approached by steps from the river with railings, salvaged from the workhouse at St Paul's Hill, seen in front of the 18th century armoury with its arched openings and idiosyncratic sculptures.

On the east side there is a wonderful old listed wall, making use of recycled bricks and medieval stone, which gives privacy to the gardens of buildings in Chesil Street while at the same time sustaining wallflowers and other plants. One of these gardens is a memorial garden alongside a converted malthouse associated with Steele's, the funeral directors. The most important is that of The Soke, a 16th century stone house adjacent to St Peter's church which has attractive trees and yew topiary in its garden.

The wall running along the east side of the river, built with medieval stone

The City Bridge, with its single arch and attractive balustraded top, effectively plays down the impact of traffic. This bridge, with the gable of the mill to the north, forms one of the most cherished views of Winchester. In addition, the flow of the water and the play of light under the bridge, the island beyond with its judas tree in front of the mill and the sycamore tree behind it, give it a rural character. What is important is that the two buildings that flank it on the east and west banks, while not being great architecture, are of an appropriate scale. This view has been threatened in the past twenty years with the possibility of high new development on land to the north of the mill at the back of Eastgate Street, ruining the skyline. This scheme would have led to a dramatic change to the whole area and was fortunately refused by the City Council. It indicates how much care is needed when considering changes within the city.

To be able to come up from the riverside, cross the road into the mill, see the great wheel turning, appreciate the noise and massive power of the falling water and then move on into the peaceful boat-shaped garden to the north of the mill and sit under the shade of the apple tree with the birds singing, is a truly wonderful experience.

Returning to the bridge, the noisy traffic is left behind to be replaced by the murmuring and splashes of the fast flowing river. It is extraordinary to recognise that this part of the river was positioned by Roman engineers. The single oak post-and-rail fence emphasises the curve of the river and carries on right down to Wharf Mill, linking the two ends of this footpath.

This walk, attractive in all seasons, has great variety of architectural detail. Unfortunately the flats that replaced the petrol filling station in Chesil Street lack the quality of material and attention to detail that is displayed in the design of the almshouses opposite.

Approaching the four-storey Wharf Mill the river 'disappears', but the noise of the water and of the bypass weir, is considerable. Here the path splits. You can either go back past the city walls and look out over playing fields to the east face of Winchester College, its chapel and tower, or go left into the triangular grassy space of Wharf Hill.

Passing Granville Place, the road leads to the stone Black Bridge built by Bishop Morley in 1680 at the same time as the new Bishops Palace. It provides slightly mysterious views southwards through trees to the weir where the canal with its little 18th century hump-back bridge breaks away from the main river and, northwards, along a densely tree- shaded series of channels towards Wharf Mill.

The road continues past Black Bridge House and the row of magnificent plane trees planted in the 18th century alongside a small water channel that separates the road from the water meadows. Across the channel is the site of the medieval St Elizabeth's College and St Stephen's Chapel. The route leads back to the 1960s

College New Hall, with its distinctive copper roof, and the 18th century mill and its mill cottage which form a picturesque end to this section of the path.

River walks: northern section

In contrast to the riverside area south of the City Bridge, in the northern section industry and small domestic buildings were mixed together in the gently curving Water Lane. Behind the Cricketers' public house, there was a timber yard and further north, adjacent to the public footpath through to St John's Street, was a brewery. Further north again, on the site of Riverside House, was a gasometer and associated buildings. In Eastgate Street there was the fine Lion Brewery, later acquired by the Co-op, who used it as a bakery. This was a very large building, clearly visible from Chesil Street and the water meadows north and south of the City. All these industrial processes produced strong smells.

The river alongside Water Lane

In the 1960s the City Council, under clearance scheme powers, removed all of these buildings together with twenty three properties on the west side of Water Lane and properties on the west side of the river as well, including the tall three- and four-storey Victorian buildings Nos 37-39, known as the Mazzini Arcade, and several other buildings in Union Street.

The council were preparing to implement a section of the Town Centre Plan of 1967, which would have built a dual carriageway down Eastgate Street with either a large gyratory round the City Mill as proposed in the Abercrombie Plan, or a subsequent proposal to put a roundabout across the river north of the mill with an extension through St John's Street and under Alresford Road to connect up with the site of Chesil Railway Station. A model was made of this scheme in the 1970s but, when it was tested with drawings, there was a violent public reaction to it and the scheme was abandoned. This paved the way for the rebuilding of Eastgate Street and Water Lane creating the present situation of a road with residents' parking opposite a grassy open space containing trees.

The footpath starts between the listed No 8 Bridge Street and the 1930s Cricketers public house. At the beginning there is a small section of street, which includes an extension to the mill which was the entrance to the Youth Hostel, plus two Victorian cottages and a yard. An ash tree in the old Youth Hostel yard frames the view into and out of this street. After the National Trust implemented their scheme to open the mill to the general public, an application was received from the Youth Hostels Association to build a fine new hostel. Despite being well presented with a model, this foundered on the need to demolish the cottages on Water Lane and remove the ash tree. From here the area widens out and the road on the east side is defined by a series of terraces which create townscape interest, principally by their irregular alignment and their age. There are three Victorian terraces with simple arched entrances, decorative lintels and sash windows, plus one Edwardian terrace with larger windows and a pair of 18th century cottages with orange tile hanging at the corner of Blue Ball Hill. These were saved from demolition by a change in legislation which required consent for demolition in conservation areas. The rest are infilled council buildings, including the three-storey block of flats on the gasometer site which have concrete pantile roofs.

18th century cottages at the foot of Blue Ball Hill

The first group of council houses, Nos 8-38, although providing good accommodation, were indifferently designed with large ground-floor windows at an angle to catch the sun, and with a central feature of railings and different treatments of windows and walls on the end houses. The effect is lost in perspective. The scheme would have been improved by using strong rhythmical design, such as can be seen in Eastgate Street, in order to do justice to this location. Between the council houses and the Victorian houses there is a little path that leads up to the 15th century tower of St John's church.

On the west bank of the river in this section, the land is higher and is defined by an unattractive wall, broken where there are private house gardens, and by sycamore trees which grow out of the banks and add character to the river environment. Here are three housing developments adjacent to the river, all having a central service courtyard and a frontage to Eastgate Street as well. The southern one adjoins the former Mildmay Arms in Eastgate Street and at its northern end has a terrace of three-storey town houses with gardens adjacent to the river. The middle terrace, built by the City Council for elderly persons, is a traditional form of building with powerful gables and rendered walls that lift the character of the area, though unfortunately the railings along the river bank have a weak rhythm with little visual interest. The northern group is a set of semi-detached houses in a modern idiom reached through Itchen Court, Eastgate Street, built in hard red brick and slate with rather angular balconies, heavy projecting windows and railings along the river that achieve appropriate massing but do not have any strong visual character. The large weeping willow trees at the southern end of this section almost touch the buildings and hang down over the water, softening the character of this area.

In the middle section there is grass on both sides of the river with a wooden bridge at either end and attractive trees which are backed on the Eastgate Street frontage by a thorn hedge that shuts out the sight of traffic. This is a popular area for people to sit in, to feed the ducks, for children to fish or swim and for pedestrians to pass though from Winnall and St John's Street en route to the centre. Opposite the green, the 18th century cottages which turn the corner have multi-coloured tile hanging that links up with the roofs and dormers of Rosemary Cottage. At this point Blue Ball Hill rises up to Chester Road and St John's Street.

For many years, groups of young people would come from a wide area with their canoes for competitions in this section of the river.

The last section leading up to the site of Durngate Mill is terminated by trees. The road reaches the riverside, separated from it by a fence. On reaching the causeway, there are attractive footpaths running behind the houses in Wales Street on the east bank and, on the west bank, connecting through to the Winnall Moors Nature Reserve.

On the west bank of the river, Durngate Place is a one-sided street consisting of some late 19th century terrace houses and good early 19th century houses, some with delicate window and door details. These houses lead up to the attractive Willow Tree public house. This has its beer garden on a triangular space between minor water channels.

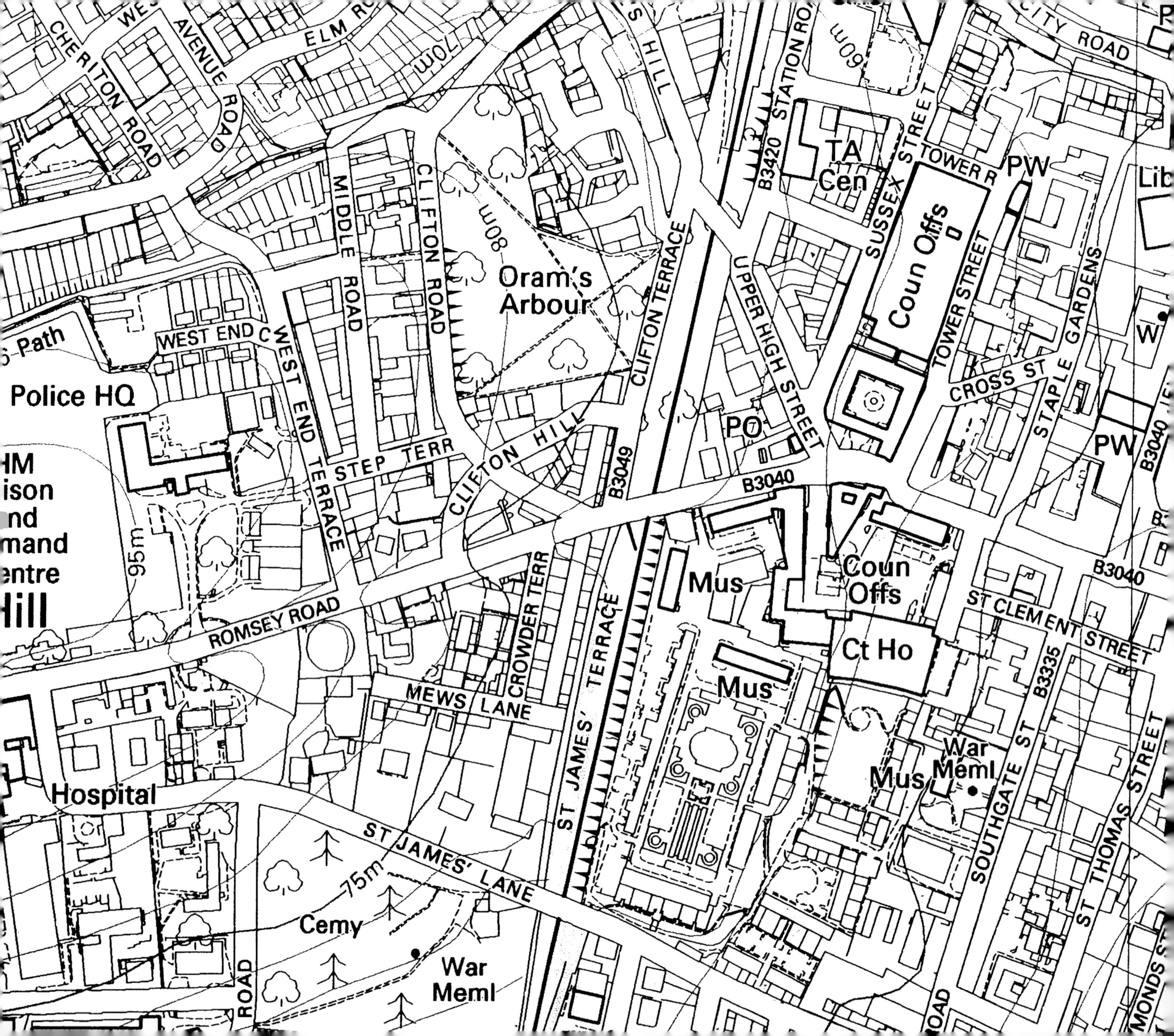
CHERITON ROAD
AVENUE ROAD
ELM RO
70m
S HILL
STATION RO
60m
CITY ROAD
B3420
TA Cen
SUSSEX STREET
TOWER R
PW
Lib
MIDDLE ROAD
CLIFTON ROAD
80m
Oram's Arbour
CLIFTON TERRACE
UPPER HIGH STREET
Coun Offs
TOWER STREET
STAPLE GARDENS
CROSS ST
Path
WEST END C
WEST END TERRACE
Police HQ
CLIFTON HILL
PO
PW
B3040
HM
ison
nd
mand
entre
Hill
95m
STEP TERR
CLIFTON
B3049
B3040
CROWDER TERR
Mus
Coun Offs
B3040
ROMSEY ROAD
ST CLEMENT STREET
Ct Ho
MEWS LANE
ST JAMES' TERRACE
Mus
B3335
Hospital
War Meml
Mus
SOUTHGATE ST
ST THOMAS STREET
ST JAMES' LANE
75m
Cemy
War Meml
ROAD
OAD
MONDS ST

CHAPTER SIX

Western Winchester – The Railway, Westgate

In 1831 the idea of linking Southampton's deep water port with London by rail was suggested in order to save the long journey around the coast by sea. This was seen to be more feasible than an earlier proposed canal link. In 1834 the London-Southampton Railway Act was promoted in Parliament for the substantial sum of £31,000, the work of constructing the railway to be financed principally by London and Manchester investors.

The line opened in 1840 after considerable earthworks were completed between Winchester and Basingstoke, including four tunnels totalling three quarters of a mile and embankments up to sixty feet high, at a time when the hills around central Winchester were open downland. This work proved arduous and dangerous for the navvies, many of whom had to be treated in Winchester County Hospital in Parchment Street where Sir Thomas Baring, a local landowner, contributed financially to their care.

The line of the railway took away part of the Oram's Arbour open space and cut off the barracks from the 'airing ground' land used for military exercises west of Romsey Road. The station was located as close to the old walled defences as possible with the result that space for the development of the station with sidings was cramped because of the local topography.

The First Passenger Train from London to Southampton via Winchester: watercolour by Richard Baigent, 1840

Railway looking south from Upper High Street

The new City Road and Station Hill had to be constructed to service the station and an underpass was created to connect with the existing Stockbridge Road.

In townscape terms, this meant that the railway was not a dominating feature in central Winchester, though like the river it was a key restricting factor. South of the station it had the effect of disguising the castle ditch. However, when the barracks Long Block was rebuilt along the ditch line, the ditch completely disappeared.

It also led to the creation of two of the longest terraces in Winchester, St James' and Clifton. These terraces made use of chalk from the cuttings as a structural material behind the rendering. A new material in the form of slate for roofs was introduced, brought in by the railway from Wales. If you look out over the town from St Giles' Hill in the east, clay tiles are a major component of the roofscape. If you look out from St James' Terrace or Ashburton Court to the west, slates are much more prominent than clay tiles, illustrating the impact this new form of transport had on the built environment.

South of St James' Lane the railway runs partly on an embankment which provides views out to St Catherine's Hill. It then proceeds under the footbridge crossing at the ancient trackway of Whiteshute Lane, and entering a small cutting east of the old Bushfield army camp where the Southampton road passes over it.

The railway introduced a much wider range of visitors to Winchester which helped the local economy. Entrepreneurs in town published postcards and guides to significant buildings. For example, Canon Humbert's 'History of St Cross', was illustrated with the earliest landscape and architectural photographs of Winchester taken by William Savage, a local photographer in St Michael's Road. Holiday snaps are also represented in the City Museum. Special popular excursion trains were laid on from Winchester station to Salisbury with horse transport on to Wilton and Stonehenge.

In 1870 the idea of putting a carriage works in Winchester was mooted by some sections of the city council, though there appeared to be little suitable flat land. In the event it was built at Eastleigh along with engine sheds and housing estates, creating what was to become a new commercial rival. In 1888 the collection of ad hoc huts that served the passengers and staff were replaced by the present station with its long wooden canopies. Provision was also made for cattle pens to service the local market which was adjacent to the new Corn Exchange (1838).

It is interesting to note that there have been several alterations to the railways to cater for particular needs. For example, during the Crimean War there was a platform to the army barracks in central Winchester linking with the Mons Hospital Block.

In the 1914-18 war an extension was made up to the extensive army camps based at Morn Hill, Easton Down and Avington Down to carry military supplies, coal and flour for the bakery, food for the horses etc., for the 270,000 men who camped there. Casualties were brought back from the front for treatment at the County Hospital in Romsey Road.

In 1920, the council paid £4,700 to create a siding on the west side of the rail bridge over Ranelagh Road in order to deliver building materials for the extensive new model housing estate at Stanmore.

From the railway's inception trees were deliberately planted on the embankment so that their roots could stabilise it and, as a result, the railway lines have become an attractive feature of the landscape. This has led to the current situation where,

Railway station

looking from the Romsey Road and St James' Lane bridges or from the Christchurch Road area, the cuttings and embankments are visually attractive and make good cover for a great variety of wildlife.

By the 1970s this had created management problems for the railway with trees that required surgery on lines that are permanently busy and with restricted access. This prompted the Hampshire County Council to join British Rail in undertaking a study of line-side vegetation to assess the ecological value of the railway estate and work out practical management strategies.

The planners of the railways did not have the foresight or finance to create strong pedestrian and road links across the track, so that with the development of the suburbs this has become a restriction on movement into and out of the city.

In 1960, a much-needed subway was created from the station forecourt out to Stockbridge Road. And in the 1970s the station forecourt was upgraded to make better links with buses and taxis, as well as improving the environment for pedestrians going either down to City Road or to the Upper High Street. This upgrade included the planting of trees which in a few years will have grown to enhance this area. The electrification of the line to London in the 1960s and the resultant service improvement created a huge demand for parking spaces for commuters which has been accommodated on the former goods yard.

Sussex Street

This street constructed outside the City wall has become a major traffic artery connecting Romsey Road and the busiest traffic junction in Winchester below the railway station at City Road. The northern end was widened when Ashburton Court was constructed as the first part of the 1960s proposed three-quarter ring-road scheme.

From south to north the road rises up and then drops down to the junction, providing good views northwards. At the southern end the stone plague monument becomes the key feature as the road finally turns towards the Castle complex.

The dominant townscape features are the three County Council buildings. Firstly, Queen Elizabeth II Court stands with its high red brick elevations and traditional windows; then the long four-storey, pre-cast concrete Ashburton Court, raised on columns over the finned concrete podium enclosing underground car parking. Finally, at the bottom of the hill, on the western side beyond extensive tree planting enclosing a temporary car park, the triangular three-dimensional Record Office was built in 1993. This introduces a totally different approach to solid and void in a building, with its prominent staircases, balconies, folded overhanging roof, giving it a rather nautical flavour. It all looks surprisingly modest when viewed from the higher ground to the south.

Hampshire Record Office

Starting at the northern end, the street contains the conservation area's only pedestrian underpass, a 'big-town' feature given some visual interest with patterned engineering brick on the approach ramps and a coloured internal mosaic representing the land use patterns of the Itchen and Test rivers. The red brick wall of the Record Office rears up from the pavement and is covered by the projecting roof of the glazed staff accommodation over. This forms a dramatic townscape feature.

On the east side of the street, the mainly two-storey Victorian/Edwardian houses interspersed with a modern three-storey block of flats, all step up the hill, hiding the tree-covered mound that marks the corner of the old city defences. This leads on to Ashburton Court which is currently undergoing a major refurbishment and recladding programme. On the east side of the street, the two three-storey villas, Nos 80 and 86, are the most distinguished buildings in the group with stucco ground-floors, two-storey pilasters strengthening the corners and good projecting balconies. On the western side, a modern terrace, with poorly proportioned windows, now remakes the corner into Newburgh Street. Beyond this are two good Victorian terraces with attractive brickwork. The first, built in 1857, still retains considerable detail and has a modest brick boundary wall in front; the second, even though attractive, has been compromised by insensitive alterations to windows, doors and dormers.

At the knuckle point where the street bends to the south, the Victorian corner house, once a restaurant, has been restored as flats necessitating a complete rebuild. The development behind, replacing a very insensitive 1970s flat-roofed extension consists of a three-storey block expressed as two pavilions with fashionable curved aluminium roofs with heavy-handed metal fascias. In between the pavilions are huge pvc windows, looking out onto triangular balconies.

Gladstone Street

This short, residential street slopes from west to east and is now part of a minor gyratory system that has affected the layout of the corners at the north west and east ends.

The main section of the street comprises two good Victorian terraces, the northern one being the older. It is distinguished by Flemish bond brickwork with dark headers and a continuous glazed canopy, supported on thin columns on a brick upstand, which protects the way down to the semi-basement below. The terrace is enhanced by good chimneys and pots on both sides of the ridge, sash windows and small but attractive gardens in front. The terrace on the southern side is plainer, with large pane sash windows and a variety of frontage treatments. Looking east, the road is terminated and overpowered by Ashburton Court. Looking west, it is closed by the bank and trees along the railway line. In the background is the new development that includes altered buildings of the former St Paul's Hospital.

On the southwest corner, there is a strong Victorian building where the flank wall rises from the pavement with a hipped double-height bay and central decorative cast iron porch, behind a small garden. On the north west side, however, the corner is disrupted by the Territorial Army Centre, set back behind its paved courtyard. This is a typical indifferent 1960s building.

To improve the character of the street, the Town Clerk in the 1960s tried to incorporate the re-erection of the stone arched entrance to the Debtors' Prison, but this was rejected.

Victorian terrace, Gladstone Street

Upper High Street and Castle Hill

The area outside the gate of a walled city is always significant in terms of activity and the area outside the Westgate is no exception. Whereas the lower trading end of town outside the Eastgate and the river is depicted on Winchester's earliest map produced by Speed in 1611 as having four converging roads lined with medieval gabled properties, the Westgate was significant as the defensive end with only the Castle buildings including a chapel. Outside it, however, this area has been transformed since the 18th century.

Godson's map of 1750 shows the principal roads from Basingstoke, Whitchurch, Stockbridge (Andover) and Romsey (Salisbury) meeting at a point where a market place had been sited until the time of the plague in 1666. One access road then entered through the Westgate with the Castle ditch as the major feature on the south side.

The only features that have remained virtually unchanged since then are the Plague Monument and the road pattern.

The coming of the railway in a deep cutting in 1840 blurred the road pattern, disguising much of the Castle ditch, and encouraged the town to grow away from the centre. Well-known pictures show buildings attached to the Westgate on both sides, reinforcing the idea of a walled town even though the walls as defensive structures were decaying. Despite having been largely destroyed after the Civil War, the Castle still had significance, because the 14th century Great Hall continued to be used as law courts.

The Plague Monument

First came the creation of offices next to the Westgate and later in 1893 the County Council offices and the Council Chamber, attached to the Westgate but built outside the wall in a picturesque flint-and-stone building designed by Blomfield. This was followed by buildings by TG Jackson on the opposite side of Castle Avenue which were eventually linked to the Grand Jury chamber by offices designed by Sir Herbert Baker.

The decision was taken in 1930 to improve the traffic flow into the city although this was not fully implemented until after 1945. Finally the Plume of Feathers public house alongside the Westgate was demolished in 1958, allowing traffic to filter around the Westgate; at the same time the new Queen Elizabeth II Court was built.

A 1937 proposal for the site to the north side of the Westgate by the architect C Cowles Voysey

This is a dominant four-storey brick building round a central courtyard with steeply pitched roofs containing attics. The courtyard is penetrated on the southern ground-floor by a powerful series of brick arches with a clock tower and a copper fleche over. This building was to meet the expansion of the County Council services. In effect it has shifted the visual bulk of the Castle northwards, thus completely disguising the position of the city wall.

Queen Elizabeth II Court in townscape terms extends a lower two-storey gabled wing towards the Westgate. The gap between enables traffic to bypass the gateway.

The gap has now been visually blocked by the complex design of Mottisfont Court. This includes a narrow gable with a stepped brick arch set on columns to catch the eye when entering the town from Romsey Road, as part of a design created to turn the corner and provide a pentice along Tower Street.

Queen Elizabeth II Court

The area now forms one of the strongest but most complex urban spaces in Winchester connecting five roads, four of which run uphill, with at its centre a mini roundabout. From this space you look south up Castle Avenue to the magnificent 19th century front entrance of the Great Hall with its complicated building texture. The whole street is an impressive essay in stone detailing on both the buildings and the floorscape and it possesses good railings which complement the buildings.

The County Council offices and entrance to the Great Hall

Westwards, looking up Romsey Road to the guardhouse at the main entrance to Winchester Barracks, the railway bridge beyond marks the edge of central Winchester, reinforced by the wonderful group of trees on the skyline and just a hint of the three-storey terraced houses which are such a strong feature of the other side of the railway line. On the south side, demolition of the Barracks' perimeter wall, and its replacement by railings and trees, has made visible the full elevation of the Mons Block with its simple but attractive façade, drawing the Barracks' entrance into the street composition. The Mons Block is now renovated as housing. On the north side is the Westgate Hotel, boldly turning the corner in a sort of regency fashion, attached to which is a rather severe three-storey terrace of residential buildings over shops. Beyond, front garden walls form a privacy screen for 19th century town houses set back from the frontage.

To the north you look past the very simple obelisk of the Plague Monument with its crumbling base, and up a predominantly 19th century street of slate-roofed terraced houses to the trees along the railway embankment. The houses on the left are rendered, those on the right are brick built and include one delightful former shop front, now a bay window.

North eastwards, Sussex Street starts with a respectable 19th century corner building whose front elevation has been incorporated into a housing scheme with fashionably curved roofs. These, however, are crudely detailed and jar. The street disappears from sight as the land drops away, much more steeply than any street inside the walls. This has the cliff of Ashburton Court behind Queen Elizabeth II Court on the right hand side with an important group of trees to alleviate the disjointed effect of the car park and the terraces on the left.

The Westgate Hotel at the junction of Romsey Road and Upper High Street

Walking in the other direction back into town, the view down Castle Avenue is unsatisfactory and ends on the weak Sussex Street corner. However, when you emerge to see the whole design of Queen Elizabeth II Court, it is a pleasant surprise and makes a powerful composition with the Westgate, adding to the townscape.

Coming down Romsey Road, on turning the final corner, the impressive medieval stone Westgate comes into view with its shields, sculptured heads, and machicolations. This frames the view through its principal arch towards the High Street, the projecting Queen Anne clock and the Buttercross with St Giles' Hill behind.

From the Upper High Street the complicated silhouette of the 19th century county offices closes the view past the attractive town houses with the Westgate beyond. The road then turns the corner past Queen Elizabeth II Court with its sculpture of

Westgate from the west

Westgate from the west, c. 1875

Westgate from the east

the Hampshire Hog. Moving downhill there are glimpses into the courtyard, before the view is closed by Mottisfont Court, which itself turns the corner revealing the High Street and the Frink bronze horse silhouetted black against the painted wall of No 73 High Street. A careful look at the north side of the Westgate shows how the position of the old town wall is marked by a change in stone texture.

From Sussex Street the Plague Monument stands out against the complicated texture of the county offices with Castle Avenue and the Great Hall behind. Recently, this space has been enhanced. The addition of trees in front of Queen Elizabeth II Court helps to soften the building's impact and provides welcome shade and colour. The Hampshire Hog, which adds interest at low level, appeals to children and has also begun to be used as a focus for demonstrations and a place to take photographs.

Oram's Arbour

As described in Chapter 10, the Oram's Arbour enclosure from the middle Iron Age (100 BC) was much larger than the St Catherine's Hill enclosure. The present Oram's Arbour space occupies only the western third of this enclosure, its massive ditch still reflected in the northern part of Clifton Road, with a gate close to North View and the southern gateway where Arbour Court on Romsey Road now stands.

Under the Normans the land outside the city formed part of the King's Forest of Bere which came up to the Westgate. Later, Oram's Arbour became part of the town's outer defences which were more vulnerable on the ridge than on the eastern riverside. The freehold of a significant part of this was given to the city at the time of Henry IV in 1408 and subsequently it was leased to tenant farmers. The leasing was subject to the public's right to roam and there was a footpath crossing to the farmlands and the church of Weeke. People were encouraged to practice archery, which they were unable to do inside the walls. Leases are in existence back to 1558, and from 1669 for a hundred years it was leased to different members of the Oram family and the name stuck.

View across Oram's Arbour looking north

It was also the recognised meeting place for freeholders of the whole county of Hampshire, especially for Parliamentary elections and the choice of Knights of the Shire. In the 18th century part of the land was used for the training of 'local militia', which the city was required to raise. In the 19th century it was used for an autumn sheep fair when 30,000 – 40,000 sheep would be brought in, hurdles being stored in a special hurdle house close to the present Clifton Lodge, and the land became very muddy and rutted. Celebratory bonfires were also lit here.

The usage changed in 1836 when land on the eastern side was sold to create a Union workhouse, and a further strip was sold for the construction of the railway line. Consequently the land between there and the Westgate was developed for housing and the railway also stimulated housing beyond the Arbour itself. The Hampshire Constabulary Headquarters and Prison were established above it in 1846-49.

Life in the Arbour could be rough and people indulged in fighting games in the northern ditch. The residential development led in 1864 to a petition to the City Council to lay out the land as follows: 'We, the undersigned inhabitants of Winchester, beg to call your attention to the condition of the Arbour or footfield and to request you to take some steps to render it more beneficial to all classes of the population, which is the purpose for which it has been for centuries confided to the care of the Corporation. The trees planted in it for the purpose of affording shade are rapidly being destroyed by cattle for the want of a railing, and its condition is very different from that of any other place devoted to the public in towns in the South of England, where the citizens take a pride (as at Southampton) in maintaining these in a state suitable for the recreation of invalids as well as the young'.

As a result the Corporation moved the sheep fair to Roebuck Field and the City Surveyor, William Coles, drew up plans for a gravelled terraced walk three hundred yards long by four yards wide, with ornamental plantations, platforms and public seats. Work was started but resulted in substantial riots, and the destruction of fences, by those who wished to uphold the right of working people to play lawful games there. This caused the City Council to take counsel's opinion and, after advice against putting a formal structure through the centre, only the southern path was created.

In 1874, the Corporation hired unemployed people in the winter time to level the western field and more trees were planted. In 1896 bye-laws were introduced governing the use of land here, together with the newly acquired St Giles' Hill and the pleasure ground of Abbey Gardens. Partly due to Council discussions in 1904 and the amendment of these bye-laws to exclude football on Sundays at the Arbour, it was recognised that proper football grounds were required in such a position that they would not cause offence. This led to the making up of land to form the recreation ground, North Walls, in 1901-1903. This land was given to the city by William Simonds, the owner of Abbots Barton farmland and adjacent abbey land.

After the Second World War, the custom of lighting a bonfire on or around Guy Fawkes Night was re-established with the procession forming in the Broadway, including floats, going up to the Arbour for the lighting of the bonfire before fireworks were set off, making a successful annual event. Due to police concern about public safety on the steep banks and attendance by thousands of people, this was discontinued in 1996 and moved to the recreation ground. Something of historical significance and characteristic of an ancient town has been lost in the process.

Nos 6-10 Clifton Road

Unlike St Giles' Hill, which is separated from the town by a steep climb, Oram's Arbour is a continuation of the western hill which feels very much part of town. Its visual contribution to the conservation area is much less dramatic but is nonetheless important as part of the tree-clad skyline of Winchester. The Arbour forms a backcloth to Queen Elizabeth II Court and its neighbour Ashburton Court, when viewed from St Giles' and St Catherine's Hills.

Oram's Arbour is now visually separated from the town by the railway cutting which, because it is deep and tree-lined, appears from a distance rather like the course of a river. Part of the Arbour's character, however, derives from the audible rumble of trains, the intermittent sound of street traffic and the chiming of the clock on the spire of Queen Elizabeth II Court.

Oram's Arbour has always been a suitable place for informal ball games, kite flying and so on. It also has curious banks which relate to its archaeological past. Due to its elevated easterly and northerly aspects, it seems much colder and less sheltered than St Giles' Hill, although it does pick up the early morning sun and strong shadows from the western evening sun.

As a space it is criss-crossed by paths giving direct access to the two bridge points. The oldest south east/north west path connects through to housing on its perimeter and further afield to the valley beyond, to Cheriton Road, Westgate School and Fulflood. This means that there is a substantial movement of people across the Arbour during the day, many going down to the railway station on the path which leads round the edge of Alison Way (the former St Paul's Hospital). As you cross Oram's Arbour in a north west direction the three-storey gabled houses in Clifton Road only gradually emerge to their full height as a townscape feature because they are set down behind the old defensive ditch.

Oram's Arbour

The north east/south west path connects the railway station area and Hyde with West End Terrace, the Prison, the Hospital and the University of Winchester's West Downs site. Walking across Oram's Arbour in this direction, a brief but attractive view of St Catherine's Hill can be seen at the Clifton Road crossing.

Corner of Clifton Terrace

Oram's Arbour's basic townscape character is of a grassy space surrounded on three sides by forest trees, with the old chimney of the former hospital as its one striking feature. This chimney is now the sole-surviving example of Winchester's Victorian industrial past. Further east, the three-storey red-brick houses with gabled roofs that form part of the dense redevelopment of the former hospital site are visible in a gap in the trees and relate well to the houses in Clifton Road, giving this end of the Arbour an urban feel. On the eastern side, the Gothic stone Littlehales drinking fountain, moved from Upper High Street in the 1930s, is a feature. This commemorates one of the most important medical families in Winchester, Dr John Littlehales and his son, who practised at the Council Hospital in Parchment Street during much of the 18th century.

However, the Arbour is also an open space with diagonal views from the north western side to the Cathedral seen against the background of St Catherine's Hill, then Queen Elizabeth II Court seen against Cheesefoot Head and St Giles' Hill and the Guildhall Tower. Moving round, the view is towards Ashburton Court, to the tower-blocks at Winnall and then to the line of the beech trees running along the edge of the motorway. Looking past St Paul's chimney, there are views to the woodlands north of the Itchen valley and the copper roofs of Peter Symond's College against its background of trees in Bereweeke Road. Less attractively, to the south west, the Police Headquarters building is seen over the houses in Clifton Road.

Clifton House

St James' and Clifton Terraces

The most striking features of the western suburb beyond Oram's Arbour are the three-storey terraces, with sash windows and iron balconies. These terraces were constructed after the railway was completed. St James' and Clifton Terraces form the largest domestic townscape feature in Winchester. It should be noted that from the bridge point, the land rises up to north, south and west producing different design responses in each of the terraces that radiate from that point.

On the north side, Clifton Terrace, attributed to Owen Browne Carter (1846-51) is designed like one of the Regency terraces in Bristol, Bath or Cheltenham, as a grand, horizontal design of town houses with pavilions at the end but a virtually continuous roofline punctuated by chimneys. It has a stone pilasters and window trimmings, a horizontally rusticated base and similar coloured pale yellow bricks. These are

St James' Terrace

enlivened at the first floor level by highly decorative but standard balconies. They have front garden walls of brick punctuated by decorative stone details. This terrace was quickly extended at both ends in the same manner, the southern end being wrapped round the corner and up Clifton Road. At the north end a separate villa was added with details and complicated enrichment unique in Winchester.

South of Romsey Road, St James' Terrace was, in contrast, developed in sections. The northern houses step up the hill, having varying eave heights, some with parapets, some without. Those at the south end have central gables, some with brick-and-flint details, some with bays. The tallest building is at the highest point. Most buildings have rendered fronts over chalk with brick-and-flint walls at the back. Some of these houses at the north end have delightful delicate iron balconies joining two houses into a wider design with supporting iron pilasters. Others have small balconies for each window. The metalwork casts attractive shadowing over the wall face.

The garden walls in front of the north end run with the land and the gates reflect changes in level, some properties with railings although most with brick gate posts and hedges. Beyond this terrace, brick-and-flint garden walls run downhill with the land to St James' Lane.

St James' Terrace consists of individual linked houses. Despite the variations of colour, materials and details, the terrace is satisfyingly cohesive. The front gardens, boundary walls and railings reinforce the quality of this terrace. It is further enhanced by having a footpath access only along its front, cars are accommodated via a service road well to the rear of the properties.

Clifton Road

This is a residential loop road which marks the westerly and northern edges of the Oram's Arbour Iron Age settlement. At its southern end it climbs steeply uphill past a corner building on the west side, whose northern extension has an idiosyncratic design by Comper. It is overhung by trees to the north and south, including a copper beech tree which is suffering from having its roots area covered by a car park.

As the road turns northwards there is a remarkable series of individual Victorian buildings that collectively make good townscape. Firstly there are two pairs of five-storey rendered, gabled, semi-detached buildings that show up across town from St Giles' Hill. These houses have projecting first-floor bays with battlemented tops and hood-moulds to upper windows, topped with decorative bargeboards. The later link between these houses is set back, but is so bland as to be disquieting, and it is interesting that the southern one has an Edwardian extension in a totally different style that is sufficiently three dimensional to look reasonable.

Houses at junction of Clifton Hill and Clifton Road

Town houses, Clifton Road

St Mary's House, Clifton Road

Continuing northwards there is a series of five buildings of different styles, which end with a pair of semi-detached buildings similar to those described above. These houses succeed in townscape terms, firstly because they do not rigidly follow any building line and have considerable setbacks, secondly because they have been intelligently linked in detail, and thirdly because of the planting in the front gardens together with the boundary treatment. The best examples of this are the two pairs of tall gate piers to No 10 which have strongly modelled tops. These complement the dignified entrance which is emphasised by the attached cast-iron railings over the top of the porch.

The next section of road runs gently downhill with Oram's Arbour opening up under the line of forest trees on the east side and a series of villas on the west side. Old St Thomas's Rectory is in a prime position and then a pair of rather delightful semi-detached gabled buildings at Nos 18 and 19 which illustrate the difference that can be made to a basic design by facing a building in brickwork or render.

The northern part of this road goes on steeply downhill using formal 1884 three-storey townhouses stepped in pairs so that changes in level can be accommodated. The building style changes further east into conventional wide-fronted houses with ground-floor bay windows, simply stepped at the party wall position. The depth of the front gardens decreases from west to east with the land in front of the north westerly houses being sufficient to accommodate cars off the road without losing the substantial greenery that separates gardens. The lower buildings are narrow with a variety of low boundary wall/railing treatments, some of which have particularly good cast-iron railings of a pattern found in profusion in the Fulflood area to the north east.

At the lower eastern end, management of the very high bank below the Alison Way development site is crucial to the enjoyment of reasonable light in the ground-floors of the houses opposite. The situation has worsened over the last ten years with the growth of sycamore saplings. Clifton Road ends abruptly at a dangerous junction with St Paul's Hill, with the substantial bulk of the Railway Inn to the north and the steep wooded bank to the south.

In townscape terms, the view is closed off by St Paul's House set against the dark trees on the railway embankment. This is a decoratively remodelled 1930s Pickfords warehouse, now converted to office use, with a first-floor balcony over the entrance, roundels at the top of the pilasters and artificial stone balls above the parapet, adding interest to the silhouette. The walls are rendered and painted with two colours.

Proceeding back up Clifton Road, the character of the old workhouse bank is important to the area, and, at the upper level of the Arbour, the individual character of the different houses becomes apparent. One example is a 1960s developer's house that is inappropriate in massing, materials and detail. Next door but one is St Mary's House, an example of what was once a totally inappropriate infill for Winchester, but which, having been extended and transformed into a modern building, fits surprisingly well between its very different Victorian neighbours. An attempt to play safe and copy the buildings next door might not have worked so well. Along the west side, there is a fine view under the lime trees across the Arbour. Towards the south end of Clifton Road is a glimpse of St Catherine's Hill, before the road descends sharply between overhanging trees and terraced flats to Romsey Road. From this point there is a view across the Barracks site to the austere outline of the Great Hall of the Castle.

Clifton Hill

This steep, curving residential road starts on Romsey Road beneath a high bank to the west covered by trees between large modern villas with rendered walls and timber-clad first floors. The modern Arbour House provides flats which have replaced a standard Victorian terrace. The banks surrounding it have been planted with trees that are important to the townscape, but are likely to create light problems as they increase in size.

At the top of the hill are two pairs of five-storey, gable-ended, rendered villas with flat-roofed links, described in more detail under Clifton Road. On the other side of this road is a good group of Victorian cottages at the corner of the Arbour. On the south west side is a block of five 1960s houses with integral garages. Possibly because of post-war shortages, they are built with quite inappropriate pale bricks and concrete pantiles. On the south side, in order to make the most of the spectacular view, they now sport two floors of wide flat-roofed dormers with very prominent white fascias. The only redeeming features are rather decorative balconies.

West End Terrace

This is both a residential street and an important road connecting through to Cheriton Road and Fulflood. The street also serves the Hampshire Police Headquarters. This tall building is sited largely amongst the beech woodland that crowns the skyline when viewed from St Giles' Hill. Tree management necessary to provide a succession to this important group of trees will be difficult. In fact, a gap has appeared opposite the end of Step Terrace which makes the nine-storey end elevation of the Police Headquarters more visible from the viewing point on St Giles' Hill.

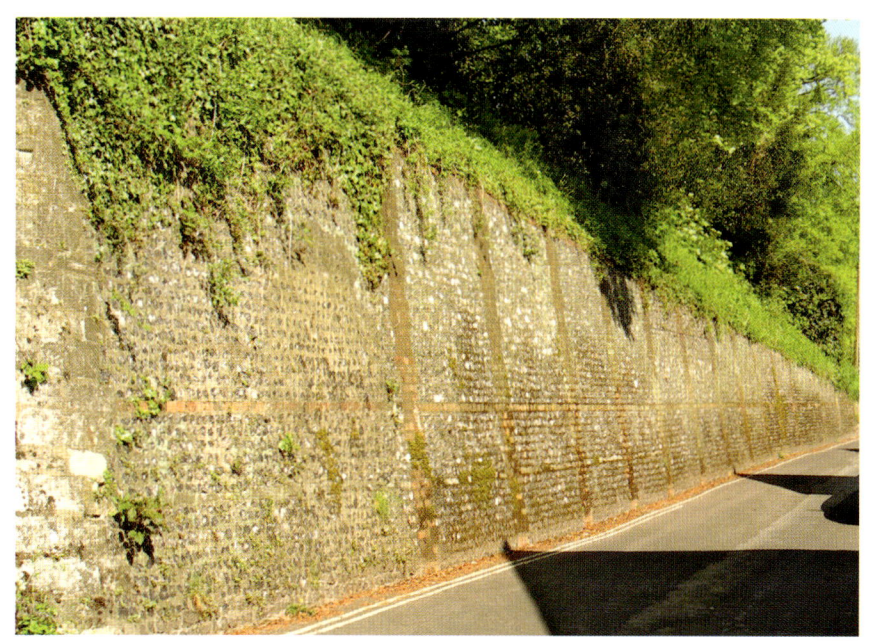

Flint-and-brick wall, West End Terrace

At the southern and northern ends, these trees grow on a bank above a flint-and-brick retaining wall whose courses run with the land. This tree belt shades West End Terrace, which is the highest residential development that can be seen from St Giles' Hill.

Osborne Place, West End Terrace

Door canopy, West End Terrace

Clearly, West End Terrace has been created in stages and is a combination of two- and three-storey rendered buildings with slate roofs. The tallest buildings, Osborne Place, are Italianate in flavour, having a rendered base to an area containing a semi-basement, yellow brick first and second floors with applied rendered mouldings over the heads of the windows and closely-spaced decorative eaves brackets, with brick-and-flint as a walling material at the rear.

These terraced houses have strong paired porches topped by low decorative cast-iron railings, repeated in front of the main windows. The upper floors feature narrow windows linked by decorative mouldings over a central recessed panel that spans the party wall.

At the northern end, the houses are more varied, one having a delightful cast-iron entrance detail, another continuous top-heavy dormers. There is one half-hearted attempt at providing a modern gabled infill building. The road drops away sharply beyond South View with the staggered gable ends of the terraces making an interesting townscape. Beech trees line the other side of the road as it turns the corner.

At the south end, the buildings stepping up the hill are mostly modern, but they do form an attractive group with sufficient modelling to make them interesting. These buildings complement the three-storey building at the end of Step Terrace. Of great importance to West End Terrace are the generous front gardens separated from the pavement on the eastern side by brick pillars and railings.

Step Terrace

This is a sloping narrow street, terraced on its north side with an end view of the prison tower rising up above trees to the west and an Indian bean tree to the east.

Step Terrace

At its west end, it starts with a terraced three-storey rendered house (No 1, West End Terrace) which has a strong two-storey bay over the front door. No 1 is set back behind brick-and-flint garden walls with an idiosyncratic use of coping bricks that have been turned at right angles to the way they are normally laid, giving an interesting pattern. Further east is an attractive brick two-storey terrace, with slate roofs and good brick chimney-stacks stepping down the hill. The terrace has blank window openings over the front doors, and is enriched by a two-storey bay with arched sash windows at its western end. These houses have thin strips of front garden to create privacy with low walls topped with railings detailed to swoop down adjacent to each gate, reflecting the change in levels. Sadly they are being devalued by poorly-detailed added porches.

At the eastern end, a shop has been skilfully transformed into a house by attention to details of glazing and mouldings. The south side of the road is occupied by a garage court enclosed by a good flint-and-brick wall which continues on to make the boundary of the five-storey gabled housing fronting Clifton Hill. The contrast in scale is worth noting.

South View

This is an attractive narrow, level street with a south facing terrace of small two-storey Victorian slate-roofed houses, with period porches and small front gardens. These face the side gardens of West End Terrace with its flint wall.

North View

This comprises two rendered slate-roofed Victorian terraces within the conservation area. The western one is approached from the north via a narrow footpath, along the outside of which is a dramatic change in levels. These houses have long back gardens and vehicular access to the south and as a result they have a splendid view over Fulflood to the beech avenues along Chilbolton Avenue and towards Peter Symonds College.

Along the footpath are small front gardens set up on a bank, planted with shrubs that emphasise the illusion of being near a cliff edge. The eastern terrace is set down over the edge, making the treatment of its roofs, which are at eye level when seen from the south, more visible than would normally be the case.

Projecting out from North View is a steeply sloping piece of ground containing mature trees and the former Western School. This is a large building with a degree of architectural detail that makes it a focal point in an area of ordinary 19th century terraced houses. The school is now converted into flats. Alongside this, there is a public flight of steps by a terrace that climbs the steep hill out of Fulflood into Oram's Arbour.

North View

Looking south from the playing fields of Peter Symonds College, the build up of painted houses and slate roofs that form North View makes an attractive view despite the Police Headquarters seen at the top of the hill.

Romsey Road (Wudestret)

The Romsey Road was known as Wudestret (street leading to the wood). This has been continuously used as a route since before the Romans made it their way to Salisbury and seems to have taken the form of a 'hollow way' as the result of the constant traffic eating into the hillside. This has now been formally enclosed in bricks and mortar.

Romsey Road, looking west

On the northern side, starting at Clifton Road, buildings partly disguise the change of level but, by the time West End Terrace is reached, the beech trees enclosing the Police Headquarters become prominent.

Higher up again, the prison is set up on a bank that still contains forest trees. This is retained by a brick wall with a carefully detailed top, using special bricks that give it a greater significance as a townscape feature. This wall was rebuilt a few years ago, faithfully reproducing the original details.

On the southern side is the St James' public house and adjacent 19th century terrace. This terrace now contains two modern infill buildings leading up to the fine listed house, built originally for the 'water manager', which hides the much higher land behind. This is followed by the characteristic battered brick walls some six metres high that surround the water reservoir (previously used as a Crimean war graveyard) and their continuation into the walls round the Roman Catholic burial ground. Beyond this are two more two- and three-storey terraces. It is this combination of steep sloping ground with substantial trees on top and the standard workaday 19th century terraces, with a scattering of shop windows and railed areas, that makes up the predominant character of the road.

Winchester Prison

East end of the chapel, Royal Hampshire County Hospital

This approach into Winchester frames the end view of the Queen Elizabeth II Court with its orange pantiles and clock tower set against Easton Down. Going westward out of town, Romsey Road reveals Butterfield's brick hospital building of 1866. The building has been compromised by the removal of its chimneys and by the additional clutter of unsightly buildings round its periphery. The tree-lined road beyond continues out to the edge of the built-up area.

Fortunately the nine-storey Police Headquarters, which is so dominant from across the valley, is tamed by the mature trees seen from the entrance in Romsey Road. As a result the building becomes less significant than the five-storey Queen Elizabeth II Court at the bottom of the hill.

Mews Lane

As the name implies, this steeply sloping lane originally contained stables and service buildings for the group of fine early Victorian houses in St James' Lane. On the north side is the waterworks at the top, dating from 1849 (with some of the few remaining cast-iron windows left in Winchester), together with some adjacent terraced cottages. Lower down is an interesting school building with decorative brickwork built in the late 19th century.

Corner of Mews Lane and Crowder Terrace

From the top there is a spectacular view over the Barracks site and the Cathedral tower to St Giles' Hill and Cheesefoot Head beyond. Over the last few years it has turned into a fully residential street with the conversion of the stables, the insertion of some new houses, and the rebuilding at the top end of a sheltered hostel. The school too has been converted into individual dwellings accessed off a courtyard, with a prominent three-storey building on the corner with Crowder Terrace, making good use of the change in levels.

Crowder Terrace

This is primarily a service road for St James' Terrace with a whole range of back gardens and garages, all of which slope down to Romsey Road, alongside the St James' Tavern. Crowder Terrace also provides, on the western side, a car park and two small Victorian terraces on back land. Part of the frontage was developed with three unattractive three-storey town houses which sit uncomfortably with the neighbouring smaller house.

St James' cemetery

The entrance is marked by the delightful single-aspect Lodge, with attached railings and boundary walls, which were erected in 1829 by James Farquarson, to protect this ancient spot. This followed its acquisition by the Roman Catholic Church when St Peter's Parish was re-established in 1802. It was in fact the first building to be built in Romsey Road.

The whole site, originally that of the Saxon Church of St James, was one of three parish churches recorded in medieval times as having attached graveyards, and a staging point for pilgrims making their way to the shrine of St James at Compostella in Spain. In 1399 Pope Boniface permitted the church to be demolished as a result of the Black Death. Later Cardinal Beaufort transferred its endowment to St Cross. It was, however, re-established as a burial place in Elizabethan times (1587) when Nicholas Tichborne died in Winchester Castle where he had been imprisoned for adherence to his Catholic faith and, as a result, was refused burial inside the City. Shortly afterwards, the chaplain to his country house in Tichborne was similarly imprisoned and buried here. It has been used by the Roman Catholic community from many parts of Hampshire ever since.

The cemetery, with its two small mausoleums made with stone and rendered walls, has been deprived of any views across town, both by the fine trees in the grounds of the old Rural District Council offices (now the site of the nurses hostel), and by the 1970s circular concrete reservoir. Its elevated sunny position however, above the busy Romsey Road, makes it a peaceful spot of great character.

The beauty of the serried ranks of simple patterned gravestones, with their decorative tops and accumulated lichen, separated by mown grass paths, is emphasised in autumn when the bright orange of the turning beech trees seems

St James' cemetery

to enhance the light that outlines the stones. Near the entrance is the distinctive grave of Archbishop King, who in his later years researched and recorded the people buried here.

As with many other cemeteries, but particularly notable here because it is so full, the change in fashion from the use of limestone to shiny black granite, often with decorations in colour and attached photographs, is regrettable. Granite will not mellow over the years like Portland stone and will damage the character of this cemetery.

West Hill cemetery

West Hill cemetery
This was created in 1840 by the Winchester Cemetery Company established by an Act of Parliament and chaired by C W Benny, a Winchester grocer and financier who became Mayor in 1834. West Hill cemetery used to contain a Church of England mortuary chapel on its high point near the present cross and a Non-Conformist chapel lower down on the south east side, in addition to the current entrance lodge. These were all designed in Tudor Gothic style by Owen Browne Carter.

In townscape terms the cemetery commands extensive views eastwards to Cheesefoot Head, Deacon Hill (with the College chapel tower beneath it), St Catherine's Hill and southwards to St Cross chapel, which from here appears to be set in a wood. Important to its character is the closure given by the mature trees west of Sparkford Road surrounding the University halls of residence, the pine trees in St James' Lane, and the trees to the east which hide the Cathedral in summer.

The cemetery has an additional use as a major pedestrian route from the University of Winchester to St James' Lane and on to the town centre. This pedestrian way helps to create continuous life and movement without detracting from the quiet enjoyment of the other circulating paths of which the lower path gives access to individual soldier's graves. The northern path provides the best viewing point, centred on a 1914-18 Memorial Cross, one of a standard design used on many sites in France and adapted here by Sir Herbert Baker, architect of Winchester College's War Cloister.

Emphasising the strong Victorian flavour of this space are several important buildings, including Christ Church and its spire, built in 1859 by the architect Ewan Christian, and the extraordinary 'Pagoda House', designed in Chinese style in 1844 for Richard Andrews, Mayor of Southampton, possibly by the Southampton architect William Hinves. To the west are the main buildings of the University of Winchester campus; of these the original Gothic building of the Winchester Diocesan Training School was designed by John Colson in 1859. The north boundary of the cemetery consists of fine iron gates and railings (part of O B Carter's design of 1840), set between brick piers and through which one can see the stuccoed houses of St James' Crescent, built by James Robbins, the Winchester publisher and bookseller, in 1840-43. There are flint-and-brick boundary walls on the other sides, of which the west wall in particular is an extreme case of a wall built with its courses running with the slope of the land. It forms a dramatic foreground view looking to the University and in the reverse direction from Sparkford Road looking to Christ Church spire and the Cathedral tower.

The memorials contain interesting information about local people. The cemetery has as its focus a significant cross in granite, with a Celtic top and eight gabled panels at its base. And the evergreen planting includes cedar trees, with their distinctive branch structure, Irish yew and holly trees. The cemetery, taken over by the City Council in the 1930s, has proved expensive to maintain and many gravestones have been destroyed. After grappling with this problem in the 1970s, a number of trees and shrubs have recently been planted to enhance its character. A mowing regime to encourage development of downland flowers, butterflies and wildlife has also been agreed. It is important that the Victorian character of the area should not be lost, while its value as a wonderful open space close to the city centre is retained.

St James' Lane (formerly Barnes Lane)

Connecting with Canon Street and College Street, this would have been an important bypass route in medieval times. It climbs gradually up to the western ridge at Romsey Road.

In late Victorian times and the early 20th century the land near the junction with Southgate Street was a service area for the town with a brewery, stables and later a motor garage. The latter was developed around Radley House which was subsequently refurbished as an office and snooker hall. Next to Radley House is a tyre depot and, just inside the line of the city wall, a car dealership. With the demise of the brewery and the increase in domestic development, the residual industrial use of this area now seems out of place.

On the north side, the corner with Southgate Street is formed by a three-storey 18th century listed building with its projecting first floor window bay, followed by modern town houses with two-storey gabled bays that visually continue the line of the old city wall along St James' Lane to a distinctive 19th century cottage.

Rendered terrace on north side of St James' Lane

On the south side is an attractive rendered terrace with slate roofs and railings at the start of Edgar Road. These catch the eye across the tyre service site and turn the corner to continue up St James' Lane, with a break for St James' Villas. Important to this attractive composition are the holly and yew trees which punctuate the vista. This is in an area where chalk from the railway cutting was used to construct walls of the houses which were then rendered.

By the time the road reaches Edgar Villas the new brick and cast-stone residential block, erected in place of the 1960s barrack building, looms up on the Castle mound. The development looks down on the slate roofs and rendered details of the new terraces built at Constable Gate as part of the 1997 redevelopment of the barracks site. An effective archway draws you visually through the pedestrian way to the space beyond.

Rendered house in St James' Lane

Christ Church Vicarage

St James' Lane closes in with garden walls on both the south and north sides, split by the short cul-de-sac of attractive cottages known as St James' Villas. St James' Lane is visually enhanced by the 19th century gabled yellow brick-and-flint Vicarage at the start of Christchurch Road. This has sweeping brick-and-flint boundary walls with a background of trees on both sides of the road marking the position of the railway line. It signals the start of the leafy Christchurch Road and the strong design of Christ Church spire rises up to provide a focus looking south.

St James' Villas on the corner with St James' Lane

The Pagoda House

The position of the deep railway cutting is indicated at the end of the barracks site by the bridge parapets.

The walls continue up to West Hill cemetery with its lodge, gates and railings. The lane climbs on up opposite the graveyard, closed in to the north by brick-and-flint walls that rise with the land, topped with a mixture of large forest trees that hide an attractive group of individual, set back, mid-19th century houses, formerly know as St James' Crescent.

Fine trees inside the cemetery can be seen through a good set of railings, which are punctuated by brick pillars with Gothic stone caps, before reaching the Pagoda House already mentioned. This is a three-dimensional composition of great spirit and amazing detail, complemented with cylindrical brick-and-flint entrance columns of different heights and cast-iron railings manufactured at Lankester's foundry in Southampton in 1844.

The house is beautifully sited to look across the cemetery to St Catherine's Hill and the chapel of St Cross and roughly closes the junction with Sparkford Road which plunges down to the University of Winchester and beyond. In medieval times, this route was used for processions between St Faith's church and St James' church and the cemetery on Romsey Road. After this point the road is closed in by fine trees seen over walls on both sides. The final bend brings you out onto Romsey Road opposite the former prison gateway.

In the reverse direction, the indifferent buildings that occupy the hospital grounds frame the distant view of trees. However, on the corner where the road turns east, there is a fine arts and crafts house, Marlfield. The road opens up at the turning into Sparkford Road where, from a patch of open ground outside the cemetery railings, there is a wonderful panorama of Winchester College and the east side of the valley.

The 15th century College chapel tower can be seen against St Catherine's Hill and the panorama extends as far south as the Hospital of St Cross (still miraculously isolated in its parkland setting), taking in the spire of Christ Church with the trees and gravestones of the cemetery in the foreground. On the north side of the lane the walls backed by trees, which are such a feature of St James' Lane, plunge down into town linking with the trees along the railway cutting.

View down St James' Lane towards St Catherine's Hill

Once through the trees, the walls continue, now enclosing the large barrack block on the left and the patterned tiled roof of the Rectory, typical of the latter part of the 19th century. This, together with large yew trees, marks the start of Christchurch Road with its rendered walls and slate roofs.

Continuing down into town past rendered mid-19th century terraces and Constable's Gate, the College chapel tower again comes into view. With the wall of two-storey gabled bay windows on the left and the Queen's House at the end, you have arrived close to the site of the Southgate, the Roman entrance into the city.

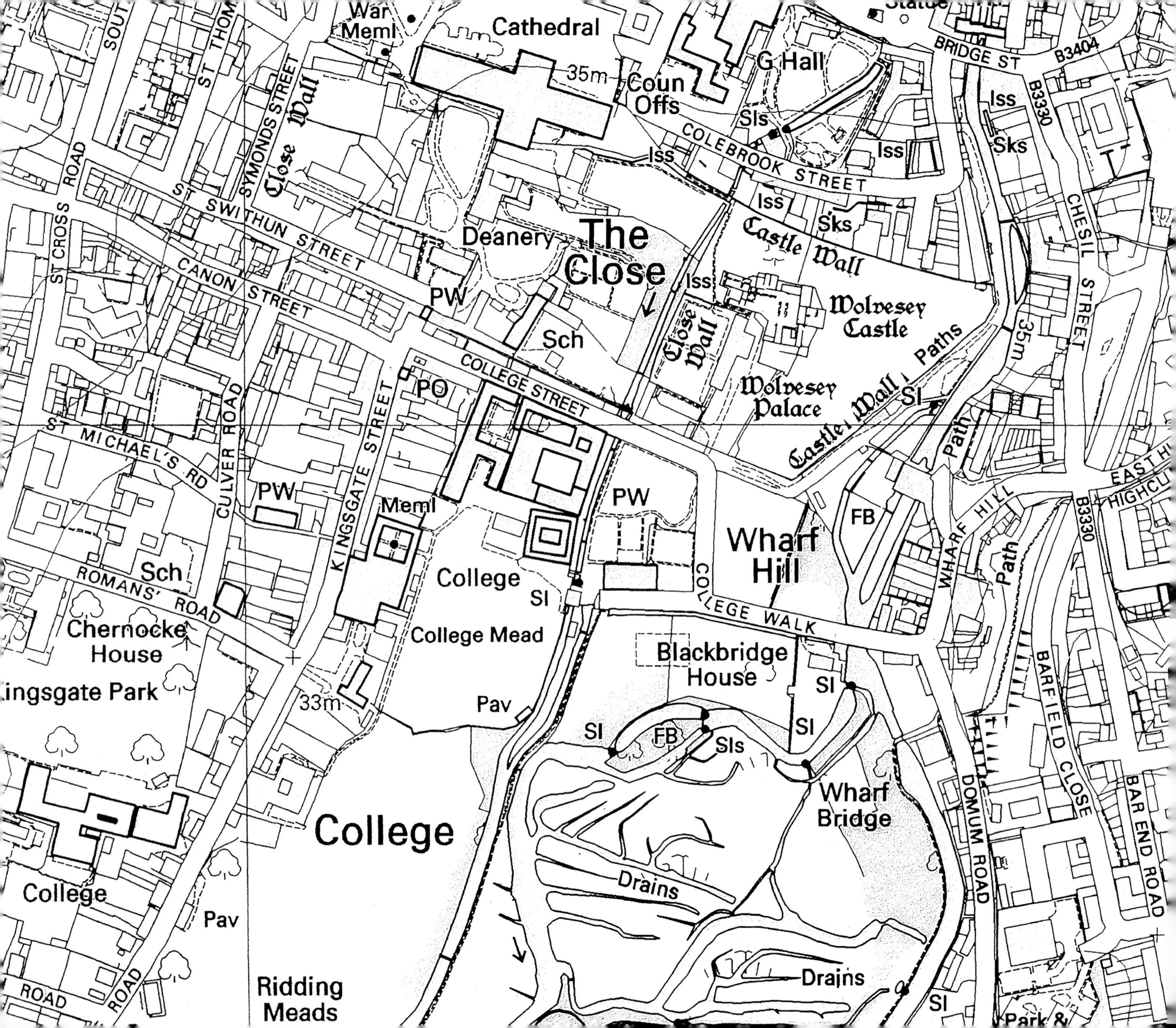

War Meml
Cathedral
35m
Coun Offs
G Hall
Sls
Statue
BRIDGE ST
B3404
B3330
Iss
Sks
COLEBROOK STREET
Close Wall
SYMONDS STREET
ST THOMAS
SOUTH
ST CROSS ROAD
ST SWITHUN STREET
CANON STREET
Deanery
The Close
Castle Wall
Wolvesey Castle
Paths
CHESIL STREET
PW
Sch
COLLEGE STREET
PO
Wolvesey Palace
Sl
Path
ST MICHAEL'S RD
CULVER ROAD
KINGSGATE STREET
Meml
EAST HILL
HIGHCLIFFE
WHARF HILL
FB
Wharf Hill
ROMANS' ROAD
College
COLLEGE WALK
Chernocke House
College Mead
Blackbridge House
Kingsgate Park
33m
Pav
Wharf Bridge
BARFIELD CLOSE
DOMUM ROAD
BAR END ROAD
Drains
Ridding Meads
ROAD
Park &

CHAPTER SEVEN

Winchester College

This medieval group of educational buildings was designed by William Wynford for William of Wykeham. It is complete with service facilities developed around three irregular courtyards of different dimensions. It originally replaced seven properties in College Street, probably timber-framed buildings of narrow frontage. This core has then been expanded into the surrounding townscape, as the needs of the institution have developed over 600 years.

The College has always instilled great loyalty and affection amongst its pupils, many of whom have gone on to secure a range of jobs in high places. This has been reflected both in appeals for money for development plans and in individuals' benefactions to the College including land round St Catherine's Hill. It has also maintained a high standard of architectural and townscape quality through changing architectural fashions as well as managing careful modification of the original buildings to suit particular needs.

Examples of this careful attention to detail can be seen in the repair to the sculpture on the north side of Middle Gate and in the additions both to interiors (like the Library in the Old Brew House), and to exteriors such as the north doorway to College Chapel.

Winchester College

View towards Winchester College chapel with backs of Kingsgate Street houses

As a consequence, the College has ended up owning a quarter of the most historic part of the conservation area. This places a great responsibility on its governing body for the care of a very complex set of historic buildings which are costly to maintain. It requires a particular philosophy towards the maintenance of the buildings which is crucial to keeping a balance between respect for historic fabric, sound repair, sensible modernisation and creative additions. It has also led to an investment in land and property outside Winchester for its upkeep.

Winchester College is particularly fortunate in its siting adjacent to the old recreation land used by the Priory of St Swithun. At its foundation it was just one of several medieval institutions in the area, most of which have subsequently disappeared: St Elizabeth College, College Street, founded in 1301 as a large charity for secular priests with a staff of choristers and a priest; St Stephen's Chapel near Black Bridge; and a Carmelite Friary (White Friars) in Kingsgate Street, acquired by Winchester College in 1543.

Its position allowed it to keep in touch with the centre of town and the Cathedral but, being outside its walls, to stay independent of the town's taxes. The one major drawback was that foul drainage coming through the town from the Brooks passed through and under the College, via the Lockburn and other streams, a difficulty unresolved until the late 19th century.

As a consequence of expansion and the gift of land to the College by two dons, Murray Hicks and Maurice Platnauer, development threatened in the 1930s was prevented. The College now owns a complete section of the chalk landscape from the river valley with its fine water meadows and canal up to the summit of beech trees on top of St Catherine's Hill, with its 17th century mizmaze. Many of the school's activities are set against the backdrop of the Cathedral, St Catherine's Hill, St Giles' Hill and West Hill.

This in turn imposes a responsibility of a different sort for the management of habitats and trees. The College has been fortunate that there have been dons, from the 19th century onwards, with particular botanical interests who have collaborated with a local family, Hilliers, in bringing back botanical specimens from many parts of the world. Grounds and private gardens in Kingsgate Street have been enriched in this way. For example, in the 1970s the College Art master, Graham Drew, designed an interlocking townscape and landscape stretching from Water Close in Colebrook Street, through the Cathedral Close and the College courtyards to the playing fields. Here he envisaged a great ring of chestnut trees linking the riverside landscape with the topographical feature of St Catherine's Hill as a background for cricket matches.

The College was founded by William of Wykeham, Bishop of Winchester and Chancellor of England. In 1382, after the Black Death had taken its heavy toll of the clergy, able people were needed for government and influential positions in England. The foundation was for the education of 70 scholars, 16 choristers, plus 10 commoners from wealthy parents, all entering between ages 8 and 12, with access afterwards to the parent institution of higher education, New College Oxford, founded by the Bishop in 1379. This link was unique at the time.

The original buildings did not have to be fortified; nevertheless access was controlled by putting service buildings, such as the granary, brew house, stables

than either of the medieval great halls of Wolvesey Palace and are equivalent in length to the east end of the Cathedral. The chapel glories in its great east window, magnificent vaulted wooden roof inside (which is a forerunner of the stone fan-vaulted perpendicular roofs as at King's College Chapel, Cambridge) and its stone tower first built between 1474 and 1480, then rebuilt by Butterfield in 1862-3 after foundation problems. Butterfield reused the stone without altering the design.

The Chapel tower shows up above the general roofscape over a wide area, both inside and outside the city walls, from Wolvesey Palace to Bushfield and Whiteshute Ridge, Great Minster Street, Colebrook Street and Dean Garnier's Garden. It also has a key visual role within the College grounds.

The buildings have all the medieval characteristics of stone buildings with string courses, strongly modelled windows with hood moulds, windows and doorways of

The buttressed wall of the Warden's Lodgings

and kitchens, which only required small window openings, and the cloister (which obtained light internally) on the outside. The introduction of gatehouses into the walled courtyard reinforced the feeling of fortification.

The College now represents one of three medieval building groups in Winchester, which have not only survived but retain their original use, thus contributing to the town's essential character. Unlike the Cathedral Priory it was one of only four national institutions (Winchester and Eton College and two university colleges) which escaped physical damage at the Dissolution in 1540.

In describing the townscape of the College it is worth keeping in mind the constant kaleidoscope of colour and movement at different times of day between these buildings – including scholars with black gowns, and the choristers in red and white cassocks and surplices in Chamber Court and chapel.

In addition to the outbuildings (built of flint with dressed stone details and stone-slate roofs) are the former brewery and the entrance gateway in College Street, Chamber Court behind (which originally housed the Warden in the Middle Gate, with his assistant Fellows on the upper floors and scholars below), the great east/west building of the chapel/dining hall with a buttery and the original classroom (known as Seventh Chamber) under its west end. These latter buildings are built in dressed stone with a low-pitched lead roof behind bold parapets. They are longer

College Chapel tower

different size and scale, all united under great roofs. The courtyards are stone-paved, with corner stairs to the dining hall starting outside in stone and finishing in wood where enclosed. There are strong contrasts of light and shade through the sequence of arched gateways. These gateways have stone-vaulted ceilings, incorporating carved stone bosses, wonderful oak doors and the silhouette of parapets, stair turrets and buttresses, together with a great wealth of stone carving in niches on principal elevations.

Fromond's Chantry

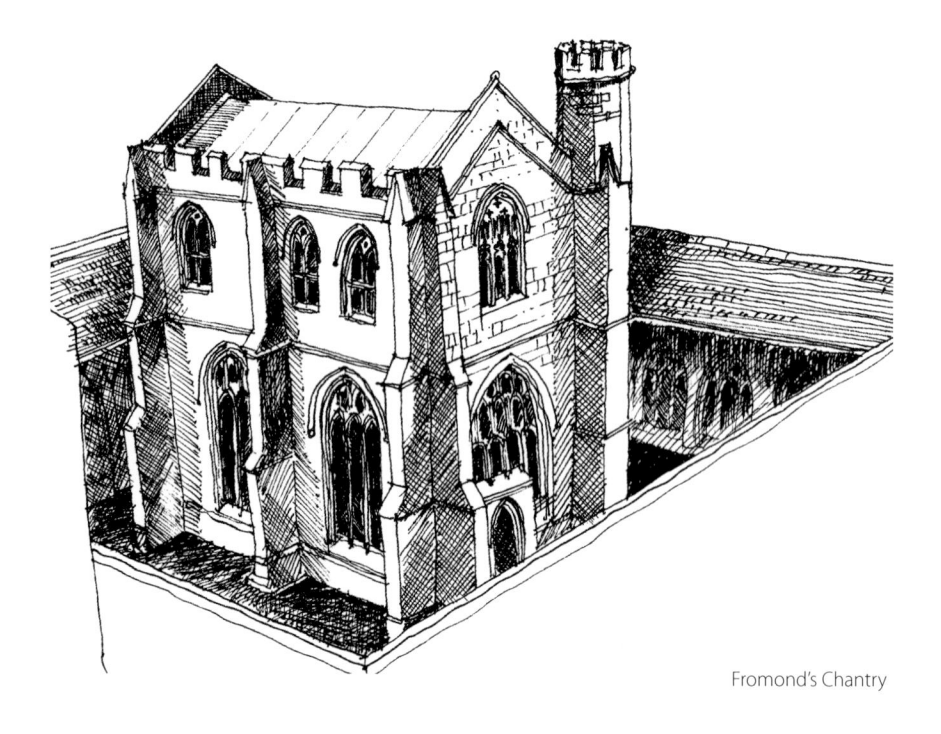

There is a complete quadrangle of stone cloisters whose decorative stone windows are seen in silhouette against sky or trees, creating patterns of light and shade on the red clay floor tiles inside.

This cloister around Fromond's Chantry was consecrated as a burial ground by 1395 and has acquired a range of memorials on the inside of the plastered outer walls which illustrate the evolution and characteristics of design and taste over 500 years. The cloisters were originally used for recreation and also as a place for summer study for the boys, as can be seen from the worn inner seats and the historic graffiti. The recent discovery of arches in the outer walls to south and north raises questions about previous use, still to be answered. This cloister has a remarkable roof with arched ribs of chestnut like an upturned boat, with very little to tie the roof together. This is one of the reasons for the waviness of the inner wall. Fromond's Chantry, in the centre of the cloister, is a two-storey stone building erected in 1435 to enable masses to be sung for John Fromond, a College Bursar. The Chantry contains wonderful stained glass, heraldic roof bosses, and carvings of heads on the outside. After the Dissolution it was subsequently used as a granary, a library and, recently, a chapel.

The College changed little in size until 1830, but in townscape terms those changes that happened were significant.

In 1544 the College acquired stone from the demolition of the Nunnaminster in Abbey gardens to construct an outer wall round Meads to the south of the College.

In 1597 the Warden moved from Chamber Court to a new lodging on the east side.

In 1657 a brick and stone building for the treatment of sick children was built on part of the land acquired from the Carmelite Friary off Kingsgate Street.

In 1673 Outer Court was subdivided by a screen incorporating a fine brick arch.

In 1683 a fine sophisticated brick school building, known as 'School', with tiled roof, classical pediment, heavy eaves modelling and classical metal windows in stone surrounds, was constructed in the fashion of Wren churches. This was created by Warden Nicholas, aided by public subscription, to mark the 300th anniversary of the College's foundation, and to meet the need for a new schoolroom to cater for 79 commoners to be taught alongside 70 scholars. Its windows face north, marking the start of a new quadrangle and, since the early 19th century, this has had diagonal stone and flint paths constructed close to the College tower.

In 1692 Warden Nicholas refaced the Warden's lodging in brick with generous windows looking out east into the beautiful spacious Warden's garden through which the millstream runs. The transition of this building from medieval to 17th century design, with even later replacement windows, can be seen to the left of the main College gateway. In the 1980s one of the sash windows was altered, to provide a door with fanlight above, for the visit of the Queen.

In the 1760s further work was done to the wall round 'Meads', an area of parkland used for the recreation of the Fellows. This wall is interesting in detail, showing different shapes and materials, including flint, freestone, worked stone from old buildings and even the use of thin Roman bricks in some sections.

Elaborately carved fireplace in Warden's Lodgings

In the 1770s the plane trees which are now such an important feature of the Winchester landscape were planted in the Meads and the Warden's garden. They have now reached a height of some 30m and are still growing. (One of them has swallowed an iron seat).

In 1739 the land of the medieval Sisters' Hospital to the west of the College was purchased and a brick building to contain 100 commoners and a house for the headmaster on College Street was built.

The Cloister Gallery and Headmaster's House built by John Burton 1739

In 1839 the headmaster, George Moberly, built the new imposing Headmaster's House in College Street next to the brewhouse. This was designed by G S Repton in squared knapped flint and stone, in the Gothic style, topped with great chimneys. However, streams ran under this building and it proved unhealthy for habitation, convincing the headmaster that in principle the commoners would be better split up between the houses of members of staff, such as Chernocke House in St Thomas Street, Moberly's in Kingsgate Street and Du Boulay's in Edgar Road, just south of St James' Lane. Repton also rebuilt part of the Warden's lodging on the north side of Outer Court in the same materials and style as Headmaster's House.

In 1862 a brick wall to the west of School, which had been restricting the area in which the commoners could play, was removed, opening up Meads to all students.

Headmaster's House, College Street

This decision was so popular that it was celebrated with a bonfire and candlesticks stuck into the walls. It was the start of the traditional festival of 'Illumina' at the end of the winter term, for which little niches for candles have now been carved in stone all round the walls of Meads creating a magical night-time effect seen through the trees on Bonfire Night.

In 1867 George Ridding took up his appointment as headmaster, more or less coinciding with the 1868 Act of Parliament on public schools which curtailed the power of the Warden and Fellows who, from now on, were only part-time appointments. It started a remarkable process of change.

In 1869 Ridding purchased six and a half acres of Culver Close, on the other side of Kingsgate Street, and divided it into four equal lots on which masters built boarding houses. He was also responsible for draining the water meadows south of Meads to provide the current sports field.

In 1870 Butterfield reordered and extended Repton's building to create classrooms with a room for concerts and exams. The chapel was later reorganised to increase seating by removing its fine 17th century panelling and inserting a gallery. One by one new buildings gradually followed toward the south.

In 1871 the medieval brewery was converted to house the school library. Its details include a carved owl at the bottom of the staircase to the gallery and a decorative clock on its east wall. The separate Fellows' Library in the Warden's Lodgings contains an important collection of books dating back to its foundation which, unlike the Cathedral Library, was not pillaged by Cromwell's soldiers, probably thanks to the officer-in-charge, Nathaniel Fiennes, being a Wykehamist.

In 1902 Lord Roberts laid the foundation stone for the South Africa gateway on Kingsgate Street.

From the stone Chamber Court the view out past School to Meads with its grass and tree trunks is most enticing. The same paving pattern of light grey stone for the paths inset with grey flint re-establishes itself, one path leading diagonally to the entrance of School with its sculpture of Wykeham above. The other straight path leads to an old, gnarled lime tree, which acts as a 'message tree' advertising forthcoming meetings and productions in the school. From here the path changes direction southwards, through a calm green space surrounded by walls that cut noise and low-level views. There is just one arched opening to the south of Ridding Gate, seen through the tree trunks and the shadow of their foliage.

Moberly Library

Typically, since this is Winchester College, much of the lettering on the walls and gateways is in Latin, the basic language for teaching at the school for hundreds of years. Walking south along the path by the enclosing wall to the gardens of Kingsgate Street, buildings on the western side become incorporated into the stone-roofed cloister building, which has a single central gabled entrance.

This is the entrance to the 'War Cloister', the only part realized of an expensive and ambitious scheme, a memorial to the 500 Wykehamists who died in the First World War. Built in 1924, it was designed by Sir Herbert Baker, and landscaped by Gertrude Jekyll. Sadly, within 20 years it had to double up as a memorial to the Second World War and continues to be added to.

This is a totally different sort of building with its round classical archway (mirrored by the sculpture niche over) framing an axial central cross, flanked by evergreens. It is also used as a way through to Kingsgate Street to and from boarding houses.

up a theatrical façade. This was intended 'as a group resource for the presentation of Wykehamist antiquities, the encouragement of architecture, natural history and sciences'. It failed as an appropriate building for teaching but became a dons' common room some 90 years later, with the careers department on the ground-floor.

The south façade of Museum is a flamboyant neighbour for the much humbler Sick House. The building is constructed in 17th century brickwork with stone window dressings set back within its rather fine formal gardens. Opposite, the 19th century gymnasium is now converted into a theatre workshop whose celebratory two-storey gabled entrance faces south onto an area of gravelled drives and parking.

Beyond the Sick House are the round towers and conical tiled roofs of the High Victorian sanitorium built as two separated pavilions. In the 1980s these were brilliantly connected into an art school with natural lighting to studios in the roof through glazed rooflights along the entire ridge. This was designed by the architect Edward Cullinan who joined the two halves by a gabled, black red and yellow tiled 'jewel box' on stilts, with a shiny aluminium roof over decorative gabled windows. It frames views out between Meads and the 18th century domestic buildings of Kingsgate Street over a perimeter wall and the South Africa gateway facing Romans Road. This gateway is linked with the Art School by a formal pleached tree avenue in the French manner, which disguises a parking area.

The War Cloister

Inside, the cloister has a totally different atmosphere to that surrounding Fromond's Chantry. Paired classical columns support Portland stone arches under grey stone roof tiles constructed with courses diminishing to the ridge. These arches cast a deep unbroken shadow, made more intense by the pairing of the columns. Within the cloister, the roof is supported by a strong rhythm of oak trusses whose solid tie beams are supported on corbels above the paired columns. The rear walls have a strong dark texture made of knapped flint tied together by a continuous frieze of decorative lettering, under which are set colourful heraldic devices and coats of arms. The result is a space of great tranquillity for a perambulation, but with no encouragement to sit or meditate. The gates on the east side are similar in design quality to those in the south transept of the Cathedral.

Further down the path immediately beyond the War Cloister is the tile-roofed 'Museum', designed by Basil Champneys to celebrate the 500th Anniversary of the College on the site of what had been the Victorian racquets courts and two blocks of fives courts. This building has similar classical arches, making a covered loggia on the ground-floor, looking out at Meads, with a virtually windowless first floor in which niches containing sculptures of Queen Victoria and other notables make

College Sick House built by Warden John Harris in 1656-7

On the west side the skyline is broken by the strong silhouette of Butterfield's County Hospital building and, in the foreground, by the 1930s two-storey cricket pavilion which is rather stodgy for such a fine setting. In the south east corner, tall poplar trees fronted by evergreen holm oak trees successfully blot out the view of the Garnier Road pumping station.

Looking north towards Meads, the view is of a group of trees enclosed by light stone walls with only glimpses of the College tower and the Art School being possible in summer. Ridding's gateway appears dark in this landscape. Through the gate the straight path leads past the trunks of trees until it reaches the message tree. Here you look into Flint Court with its central arched entrance under a three-tiered stone oriel window, before entering the attractive space enclosed by School, the dining hall and the College tower. This is located at the end of the diagonal path with just glimpses of the trees beyond. Through the arch under the dining hall, Chamber Court is the only remaining outdoor space in Winchester with a stone floor and enclosing walls and no trace of greenery.

There are other ways of enjoying Meads. For example, from the side staircase door of Butterfield's classroom block, a diagonal view of St Catherine's Hill is framed by the giant plane tree on the right and the very simple wall of School enlivened by the detailing of quoins, doorways and eaves.

The Ridding Memorial Gate

Heading back towards the playing fields, the dramatic Ridding Memorial gateway opens the way through the Meads outer wall, with its flowing Celtic-inspired gates which cast fascinating shadows onto the path. Through the gates is a different, less controlled world where the playing fields and their trees link up with the much wilder water meadows beyond. The last big building in this sequence, the red brick and tiled Science Building, designed in 1904 by Henry Hill with white window surrounds, makes a handsome contribution to the setting. This building is a strong feature when seen from the public footpath along the millstream from Garnier Road to New Hall which is crossed by little arched bridges linking the inner and outer playing fields.

These playing fields must be among the most beautiful in England, ringed as they are by a large variety of trees and presided over by the changing light on St Catherine's Hill (with its 18th century beech trees in the centre of its Iron Age ramparts) and the long white nave and tower of Winchester Cathedral rising above the College buildings.

Drawing by Richard Baigent of a game of Winchester Football, 1838, looking towards St Catherine's Hill.

View of Meads across to the College

On the south side beyond the trees is New Hall, a self-conscious building designed in 1961 by Peter Shepheard to accommodate the whole school for concerts, plays and assemblies. Shepheard had the added complication of having to display the beautiful panelling, probably designed by Pierce for the College Chapel in the 17th century, discarded in the 19th century and then returned from Hursley House in the 20th century.

The design of New Hall sets out to incorporate some of the details of brick and stone on earlier buildings around the College and it provides a loggia facing the trees and the central lawn of the Warden's garden. However, by rejecting the strong parapet detail used on the Chapel and failing to use some of the palette of materials already in existence, it is visually disappointing externally. The decorative brick-and-stone chequerboard to the gable of the entrance elevation seems strangely hard.

Walking round the outside wall to the cricket pavilion, the silhouette of the Art School can be seen and, adjoining it, the roofscape of Kingsgate Street set against massive trees in St Michael's Road and the trees in front of Museum, the War Cloister and School. It is worth noting how satisfying simple architectural forms can be if they are made out of good natural materials that weather well, complemented by good detailing. In winter, when far more of the College buildings are visible, the tree shadows falling across these simple forms are even more exquisite. And in summer, when there is a cricket match on Meads, there is the pleasant contrast of whites against the green surroundings.

In the far north east corner there are two gates, the 14th century gate, adjacent to the brick mill building, leading out to the roadway beside New Hall, and the 19th century Stewart memorial gateway. This gate has a complicated repeating pattern, and leads through to the Warden's Garden and the entrance courtyard to New Hall.

The Warden's garden is a peaceful brick-walled space containing a lawn, with a slightly raised grass walk on its northern side. Magnificent trees on the eastern and southern sides frame a view of St Giles' Hill in winter. The Lockburn stream, coming through from Abbey Gardens and the Cathedral Close, flows down its western side. There are bridges over to the red brick Warden's Lodgings with steps up to a balcony at first floor level. Above is a projecting stone dormitory block and the end of the Chapel with its great east window, its set back tower and the long wall of the cloister with its doorway. Leading to this is a plank bridge made from a single tree.

The Warden's Garden 1816, from Ackerman's Winchester College

The southern suburb (within the Soke)

The Garten report of 1962 described the area of Kingsgate Street, College Street and Canon Street, 'This, outside of the Cathedral Close is the area of the greatest concentration of unspoiled architecture of the past in Winchester. It does not mean that it possesses finer buildings than can be found in St Thomas Street or St Peter Street or elsewhere, but what I do mean is that as a concentration of buildings mostly contiguous with each other and generally unspoiled, it is second to none. A further point I wish to make is that this area is singularly free from advertisement clutter, unsightly street furniture or aggressive street lighting'.

Kingsgate Street

This narrow flat street is the most urban of all the residential streets in Winchester, increasing in scale the closer it gets to the city walls. It is also the most 18th century in character.

This can be examined by looking at the number of buildings with parapets, and decorative string courses, the character of the brickwork, the arches and enrichment around windows, consistent use of sash windows, panelled doors and a wonderful range of doorcases, which give the buildings their individuality, within a given design theme.

They range from Nos 62 and 16, which have full-round wooden columns supporting a decorative entablature and flat hood moulds with deep panelled reveals which match their six panel doors, to No 13 which has the same idea but with only flat pilasters, and No 15 with stone steps and railings, narrow pilasters supporting a pedimented hood. Others like No 8 have only thin pilasters with a decorative fanlight (to let more light into the entrance passage) with decorative timber mouldings and a place for a glazed lantern.

In addition to these there is a double bow-fronted shop window with its sinuous fascia, double-leaf glazed doors and a pretty fanlight above. Unusually, this has a major oriel window over the door, one of three similar in the street which have decorative modillion tops. There are also other details such as window shutters, boot scrapers and early insurance signs, and many chimneys have decorative Fareham pots.

A great deal of ingenuity has been put into the design of these fine houses which replaced earlier timber-framed buildings. They were commissioned by a range of eminent middle-class families, doctors, lawyers, shopkeepers who served the town from the 18th century onwards. Some of their gravestones are to be found in St Michael's graveyard. No 9 has a decorative plaque recording that 'Sebastian Wesley, 1810-1876 lived here and was organist to the Cathedral and College between 1849 and 1865'.

The general architectural theme persisted into the 19th century so that brickwork varies, from the highly sophisticated early 18th century buildings, which have sash windows close to the surface and thicker glazing bars, to duller later buildings with sash windows set back four and a half inches from the face concealing weight boxes. There are also dummy windows similarly recessed and using header bond disguising internal features like staircases, different room layouts and party walls. Each house does repay individual study.

In fact the street is likely to be Roman in origin issuing from what is now known as 'Kingsgate' to link up with Sparkford (now St Cross) and Southampton. Later on this would have been the gate that gave access to the Saxon and Norman palaces. Kingsgate Street developed over time as a subtly curved medieval street with three churches, the only surviving one being St Michael's with its 16th century tower set away from the street.

Gateway to College Art School

Houses in Kingsgate Street

In 1278 a Carmelite Friary was established where the College Art School now stands, and in the 15th century Henry V is believed to have led his army out through Kingsgate to Southampton and Agincourt after receiving the French ambassadors in the Castle's Great Hall. It is clear that, as in other parts of the Bishop's Soke, Kingsgate Street contained many important timber framed houses, of which it is considered that only No 66B has survived. It now sports a central 19th century gable, but has the characteristic first-floor overhang of medieval buildings and recent work revealed massive internal timbers including arch-braced open trusses indicating an early 16th century hall house or semi-detached pair, much altered and disguised.

Next to it is Moberly's where Walter Stempe erected a house in 1571. This is now a complex house with twin gables end-on to the street in the way that a substantial timber-framed house might have been constructed at that date with 17th century gable windows. It still has one or two heavily modelled stone windows, stone quoins and parapet dated 1571 together with early patterned brickwork normally associated with the 17th century, an 18th century asymmetrical stone entrance porch with a 19th century extension. Unfortunately its characteristic early brick diagonal shafted central chimney stack has been lost. This house was occupied by George Moberly, a prominent College master in the early 19th century, who started the trend of having external Commoners' boarding houses.

By the early 19th century there was an important inn, now the Wykeham Arms, on the corner of Canon Street, and several shops and small manufacturing businesses like that of Henry Gunner, a hatter at No 4 in 1875, and the nearby cabinet maker

Moberly's, Kingsgate Street

and upholsterer whose sign can still be seen painted on the brickwork. Most of these shops and businesses closed when the College acquired the buildings for the use of the growing number of school staff in the 20th century. Recently, the old Post Office (which used to have a bakery behind) with its Victorian post box has been resurrected as a community shop with the house next door serving as a bedroom extension to the public house.

In townscape terms Kingsgate Street has many surprises and subtleties, one of which is the way the Cathedral appears and disappears. It starts with low-density buildings opposite the trees at the south end in the College playing fields by the Altham gate. Then there are two-storey buildings either side of the road with 19th century decorated bargeboards and, on the left, a lovely view into the College's Kingsland Park. This runs alongside the three-storey Kingsgate House with its wide inset entrance loggia and Ionic capped pillars. Just by its entrance gates there is the first view of the Cathedral. The next section has interesting houses opposite a fine 19th century flint-and-stone wall with tiled capping in which is set the gateway to the Art School, supporting a purple wistaria. The wall leads on into the Priors Court with its three gables and the armoury before the South Africa War Memorial gateway, or Commoners' entrance to the College. These stone buildings turn the corner where you just get a glimpse of the Cathedral tower.

Kingsgate Street looking north to the Cathedral

After the South Africa gateway the buildings are all red brickwork on both sides (although some of them have been painted). By its nature the street appears to close in until the double-fronted shop window with the oriel above, at which point the 19th century building in the distance appears to close off the Cathedral entirely. By the Wykeham Arms, however, the Cathedral tower emerges again over the central arch of Kingsgate, only to disappear entirely a few yards further on behind Kingsgate, with the windows of the south elevation of St Swithun's church above. Walking through Kingsgate and Prior's Gate and turning left into the Close, the Cathedral tower reappears again in all its glory.

Returning down Kingsgate Street, more details of the historic buildings are noticeable, such as the remarkable brickwork of No 5, the composition of the first floor oriel to the door at No 6, and the complicated development of windows, brickwork and stonework at Moberly's a little further on to the east. On the left hand side note the unusual Mansard roof of a stable block, now converted into living accommodation, set back behind a boundary wall. It has two pedimented brick entrances, next to No 15 which, with its neighbour No 16, has an extraordinary number of blind windows.

At the South Africa gateway there is a tantalising view into the War Cloister, followed by the long area of curving flint-and-stone wall, drawing attention away to the west side with the asymmetrical composition of No 52 now colourwashed. Through the Art School gateway is seen the little tiled 'jewel box' centrepiece which connects two wings of the old French chateau-style sanatorium. Note the built-in tile shadow representing a real shadow at mid-summer.

After this, opposite the cliff-like proportions of Kingsgate House, the buildings become smaller in scale, interspersed with low-eaved, stable buildings. Here are situated cottages with 17th century windows followed by a rather inelegant brick science laboratory and the white Meadow House beyond. Set into low brick-and-flint walls are the modern Altham memorial gates to the playing field with a diagonal view of St Catherine's Hill beyond.

Opposite this, the new school maintenance yard repeats the same low walls for its entrance and is followed by two groups of cottages with first floors projected forward on heavy wooden beams with eight gables. Finally, set back behind a small front garden is the Queen Inn, a small country-style public house with a traditional painted sign of playing cards and an extensive garden behind.

There are some 19th century buildings inserted into these frontages. Of particular townscape interest is Quiristers, dated 1883, a large boarding house with an interesting design of two scales of windows with refined terracotta details to string course and eaves and decorative panels under windows. No 74 adjoining the Wykeham Arms has narrow windows arranged in different groupings with stone heads, mullions and sills in a brick wall, culminating in a powerful low-pitched gable with strong modillion eaves. Finally, at the northern end two old cottages which projected out into the street (whose ghost is reflected in the line of the pavement) were removed in the 1960s and replaced with set-back college staff flats designed by Peter Shepheard. This has revealed an interesting section of wall on the Kingsgate with blocked openings. In the diagonal view down Kingsgate Street, the two-storey splayed bay windows fit quite well, although the building itself is very utilitarian, particularly at ground level.

Quiristers

Kingsgate Street is paved with diagonal concrete blocks, reused stone gutters and kerbs, trying to establish priority for walking and cycling rather than for cars. The street lights are set on the buildings themselves to avoid bulky columns.

College Street

This is a straight, level street that runs over a bridge erected in stone in 1327-8 which spans the Lockburn. This stream runs from Abbey Mill in Colebrook Street through the Deanery garden to College Street, where there had been a mill on the north side, and on through the Warden's garden to the College mill and out past the playing fields.

The northern side, which used to be the town ditch up to 1649, had shops built on it, with residential accommodation above at the Kingsgate end, and a 17th century house to the east. In the 1930s the shops were demolished and replaced by a series of garden spaces, backed by a section of the City wall.

At the east end, where there are large trees set in a gravelled area outside the stone wall surrounding Wolvesey Palace, glimpses of the Cathedral and the Palace can be gained. To the west a grass garden is confined by the high flint city wall and a brick wall with cambered coping bricks leading up to a garden entrance to No 7, a 17th century house at right angles to the street. This is now the College Bursary.

Garden on the northern side of College Street

Beyond the flank wall of No 7, the city wall continues with many patches in it due to alterations over the years. Buildings for Pilgrims' School are set hard against the wall on its northern side. Eventually it reaches the three gables of Cheyney Court which now has many windows punched through the wall dating from medieval times. The wall includes an 18th century Venetian-style window. There is also a patch of 17th century brickwork with a 17th century window adjoining Kingsgate.

Along the street the garden is defined by tall vertical brick piers with balls on top (that used to have railings between) which were built shortly after the houses here were demolished. In the central part adjacent to the back wall of No 7 there is a lawn, the remains of a pergola, a magnolia tree and an Indian bean tree.

On the south side, starting from the east end, is a fine prospect of the three-storey red-brick Warden's House of the College, the chapel with its east window and tower followed by Fromond's Chantry and the cloisters. All these buildings are seen over the brick 18th century wall with its shaped brick capping. Opposite is a glorious view of the Cathedral and Wolvesey Palace.

Approaching the College, it is possible to see how the medieval stone buildings have blank 13th century windows at the base, merging into brickwork with 18th century windows and a 17th century eaves detail for the roof and the dormer windows. There is an interesting heraldic plaque indicating the dates of some of the changes.

The College entrance and tower are in a fortified medieval style. This in part is the perimeter flint wall to the former College brewery. The main entrance, flanked by buttresses, leads through into stone quadrangles.

Over the front entrance arch there is a most delicate and well-preserved statue of Madonna and Child. Adjoining is the rather forbidding four-storey stone and squared knapped flint building, in Gothic style, which is the 1839 Headmaster's house. On its west side is a vehicular entrance furnished in 1994 with original wrought iron gates designed by Charles Normandale, a Hampshire blacksmith.

The next section of street has a fine collection of houses, the first one being where Jane Austen died in 1817. The next one, set back, is of 17th century design with steps up to the entrance. This is followed by Wells Bookshop with an art nouveau shopfront between

Shopfront, Wells Bookshop

terracotta pilasters added in 1891. There has been a bookseller and bindery here since at least 1724 when Andrew Holloway, the College writing master, supplied books, pens and ink as well as antiquarian books. The business was taken over in 1806 by James Robbins who published the Hampshire Chronicle here for six years. The end terrace building, with 'Cornflowers' shop on the ground-floor, jetties out over the pavement, suggesting that this is really a set of timber-framed buildings at heart, restyled with sash windows, including an 18th century first-floor oriel.

The terraced houses ending with 'Cornflowers' shop

This is the one street in Winchester where a whole section was redecorated in a co-ordinated scheme devised in the 1970s by Winchester City's Conservation Officer. The colours were selected from earth-based pigments to relate to the colours of the building materials. The idea was to assist the visual transition from the yellowy-grey stone at the eastern end of the street to the plummy red brick of the Victorian building at the western end. The bay containing the oriel window was picked out in a darker colour, both to emphasise the attractiveness of its design and to break up the façade into separate buildings.

The street is closed by a 1960s residential building, designed by Peter Shepheard, for College staff, in replacement of some 18th century cottages. The architect has respected the overhang of the building opposite, articulated the building with two-storey reasonably high bay windows which have a vertical proportion, and kept its overall scale appropriate to the adjacent buildings. It is a 'hard' building with metal windows rather than a 'soft' building and, in such an important visual location, inevitably something more is expected in terms of detail and materials.

Canon Street (*Paillardestwichene*)

This is a fine medieval street just outside the city walls and ditch with subtle curves along its length and a steep gradient rising up the hill to Southgate Street at its western end.

Canon Street

Despite numerous changes in its history it has kept its townscape integrity. It became a street of ill repute in the 19th century with Hamilton House becoming a women's refuge. It saw the start of the Salvation Army in Winchester in 1884. After the second world war it was designated as a slum by the City Council which by 1955 had decided that many buildings were in an advanced state of dilapidation and decay. Demolition was considered to be the only economic answer and even the Ministry of Housing and Local Government withdrew the listing on eleven properties in February 1962. That is why the acquisition of No 25 by the Winchester Preservation Trust, to demonstrate that houses could be economically repaired, was so important. Improvement grants were made available, encouraged by the Garten Report's statement 'that the lower end of Canon Street is generally speaking worthy of protection and repair…'

Looking up and down the street it has remarkable integrity, made up of brick walls, vertically proportioned windows, tiled roofs with dormers, good chimney stacks, many with fine Fareham chimney pots.

Canon Street once contained a number of shops and public houses which have all disappeared, with the important exception of the Wykeham Arms. It has now become a residential street.

In townscape terms, starting from Southgate Street the road is narrow with the sheer walls of Queen's Lodge on the right, and, on the left, a terrace of modern buildings. Rounding the first bend there is a wonderful view down to the College chapel and tower set against the plane trees of the Warden's garden behind, and the wooded Deacon Hill beyond Chilcomb in the background.

As Canon Street winds downhill, on the left a series of terraces steps down, their chimneys and doorways making a strong rhythm against the trees behind. On the right, terraces of formal three-storey town houses with parapets also step down the hill to link up with two-storey slate-roofed Victorian buildings.

On reaching the old primary school of Friary Rooms, the College tower on the skyline has disappeared and, with the change in direction of the street, is replaced by the powerful three-shafted stone chimney of the Headmaster's house of Winchester College and the three-storey brick bulk of Hamilton House midway down Canon Street, its chimneys dominating the smaller houses round about.

At the junction of Culver Road and St Swithun's Villas, the sheer bulk of Hamilton House is quite startling and it is a surprise to find two-storey houses so close to it on the south side in what used to be its garden. Looking left a little 'green lane' leads past two-storey Victorian houses to a view through the garden of St Aethelwold's in St Swithun Street to the outer flint Close wall and the Cathedral beyond. The gables of this house seen on the right are built onto a remaining fragment of the city wall at this point, whereas the rest of the wall has been robbed of its material.

The next section of Canon Street is by far the oldest with brick-faced houses, mostly listed, crowding the road. Terminating the view is No 22 Kingsgate Street with its shop window and Victorian post box still intact.

Many of these houses are not what they might seem and in fact disguise older timber frames, of which No 62 is the most notable. It was probably a 16th century hall with a 17th century panelled interior together with massive chimney and twisting staircase.

Returning uphill the houses are consistent in their appearance and, as the street bends, a Victorian house is revealed with its flint wall, strong gable and barge boards. This visually closes off the street beyond Hamilton House which marks the Culver Road junction.

The next section of the street contains Victorian or later buildings with one or two exceptions. For example, No 28 is an attractive earlier building whose windows have architraves attached to the brickwork. On the eastern side is an insensitive infill building. Added on is an extension with a garage door and a mock Georgian bay above, which is no better.

Nos 26 and 27 have delicate arches over doors and windows and simpler proportions.

Opposite on the left are two Victorian houses, set well back which have well-planted bays that make a welcome space in the street.

A view of the Cathedral from a house in Canon Street

On the north side there are two 20th century terraces that step down the hill, one of which has restrained door cases and sash windows with good reveals, giving a strong vertical emphasis, and the other with casement windows. An attempt has been made to give variety to this pair by having different materials for the ground and the first floors though this gives a strong horizontal emphasis.

The last building, which was commercial, has been replaced by a two and a half-storey residential building with car ports and a pitched roof with dormers. Although the windows lack detail, the building form and colour of the bricks make this a positive addition. At the top of the street, the garden of Queen's Lodge provides welcome relief just where the street turns round the corner into Southgate Street.

Canon Street has been repaved with diamond pattern concrete paviors, stone kerbs and drain channels, and cast-iron bollards have been positioned to restrict parking and reduce vehicle speed.

Two front gardens in Canon Street

Winchester College Music School

Culver Road

According to Godson's map of 1750, Culver Road did not exist but was part of a great meadow that extended as far south as Romans Road. It had garden land on the east side, the Norman St Michael's church with its 16th century tower and graveyard, and a pond and garden area on the western side (later to become St Thomas's and St Michael's Rectory) with Hamilton House and its stable at the north end in Canon Street.

As Buck's Panorama of 1735 shows, St Michael's church was at that time a significant townscape feature in Winchester. Milne's map of 1791 shows no change but by 1869 the Headmaster of Winchester College had purchased six and a half acres of this meadow on which four large College boarding houses for commoners were erected, with access into the College through the narrow-walled St Michael's Passage leading to Kingsgate Street. In 1880 Butterfield remodelled St Michael's church adding a new chancel and porch.

By 1895 the northern part of Culver Road had been built up on both sides with Victorian terraced housing and, rather surprisingly, included the garden of Hamilton House, with a factory on the backland. Hamilton House, with its panelled interior, had become a women's refuge within the red light area of Canon Street. An Edwardian terrace, with distinctive orange pantiled roof, is built on backland to the west adjoining what used to be the school. The 'L'-shaped Culver Lodge was built close to the junction with St Michael's church in a characteristically late Victorian style. This was set within its own orchard and has now been infilled with pitched-roofed cottages.

In 1903 Winchester College built its music school on the junction with Romans Road, designed by E S Prior. This is a striking stone building with a high conical roof surmounted by a lantern. On the east side are three carefully composed gables, the central one rounded, and all made out of stone dressings with pebble inserts. It is surrounded by a battered boundary wall to the street, which for the first time introduced rounded pebbles into Winchester as a walling material rather than using flint.

Detail of Music School

The bicycle sheds that adjoined Music School have now been replaced by an interesting and successful addition. The new three-storey building by architects Nugent, Vallis & Brierley, with its top floor studios, is a sensitive addition which takes into account the townscape views and its relationship to the older part of Music School.

With the development of the College boarding houses came forest trees on the west side of Culver Road, complemented by others in the walled garden of No 62 Kingsgate Street, next to St Michael's Passage. As a consequence the southern section of Culver Road, ending with a view out over Kingsgate Park, is dominated by trees which now dwarf the church as a townscape feature.

In 1936 land belonging to the rectory on St Cross Road was given to the Friary Bowling Club and a thin sliver on the northern side to the City Council as a public open space. This peaceful space contains a children's playground, a sitting area, a flower area and has a thatched roof shelter at its western end. The Bowling Club has a valuable view of Winchester Cathedral, the flat-roofed clubhouse visually dominated by a huge copper beech tree.

In 1970 the unattractive factory site behind Hamilton House was redeveloped as garages with flats above.

Subsequently the College has developed narrow sites on either side of Culver Close as housing, on the east side with two terraces designed to link together two parts of the street. One of them has a gable that marks a lowered entrance to a garage court behind and an external pergola structure which helps to create privacy. On the western side of the road, more traditional cottages with tiled roofs have been built in between the trees, with modern corner windows to make the best use of views up and down the street. This scheme is of lower height than that shown in the planning application, and this has allowed the College tower to remain dominant in views from the west.

College houses in Culver Road

At the junction with St Michael's Road, there is a panorama of two College boarding houses apparently joined together to create one of the bigger residential buildings in Winchester. They have a totally different window pattern to that of normal domestic premises and a range of brick gables with a scattering of chimneys.

The north end of Culver Road is closed off by the back of buildings in St Swithun Street and a view of the trees in the Cathedral Close beyond.

St Michael's Road (*Sevetuichne*)

This ancient medieval street is now a wide residential road which slopes down from St Cross Road to St Michael's church. It marks the border line with the land on the north side. This area was once dominated by the medieval Augustinian priory and, later, a rectory for St Thomas's and St Michael's church was built on its southern side amongst some very fine trees, extending from the Culver Close area of the College boarding houses.

At the St Cross Road end is the strong gable of Hawkins, a College house on St Cross Road. To the east, the road apparently ends with a huge copper beech tree, but in fact it curves at this point and the true termination point is St Michael's church, flanked by trees. It has in front a local war memorial and, at the side, a redwood tree that dominates the discreet graveyard.

On the north side, the road is flanked by high residential buildings hard against the pavement. The gable end of the terrace to the north has many windows to overcome the shadowing of its College neighbour across the road. To the east is a 'cottage ornée' style building set right back from the road with three steep carved gables and similar dormer windows, flamboyant chimneys with flues set at an angle, decorative arch to windows with niches and a ground-floor pergola. This house was the home of William Savage, an important early Winchester photographer. He ran a successful souvenir shop in the Square and according to local historian Barbara Carpenter Turner was 'the first Winchester citizen to realise that much of Winchester's future would depend on its importance as a tourist centre'.

The site next door was developed in 1996 as two pairs of semi-detached rendered townhouses with slate roofs, using the device of covered balconies and steps to disguise the semi-basement garage. With low garden walls and chunky gate-piers they represent a form of development that has become popular in Winchester, in this case having its image reinforced by adjacent mature trees.

Past these buildings, there is a view over the wall of the bowling green and, beyond, a view of the Cathedral nave, tower and south transept over trees, and the tiled roofs and chimneys of Hamilton House and its lower neighbours in Canon Street. This is one of the few places where this view is still possible, and is made more special by the huge copper beech which separates it from Culver Lodge.

Culver Lodge is an 'L'-shaped building with its entrance in St Michael's Road that marks the corner with Culver Road.

Semi-detached houses, St Michael's Road

entrance repeats the design of the chancel gable. Following on round the tower a new view of St Michael's Road opens up with Culver Lodge beyond backed up by the magnificent copper beech tree.

St Michael's church is now owned and used by the College and a large number of students and staff pass along this route.

St Michael's Graveyard

This is a quiet grassy area tucked away with extensive tree planting. It provides views out to the cottage gardens at the backs of houses in Kingsgate Street, glimpses to the Cathedral and St Thomas's spire in Southgate Street. It is a place to sit quietly on the hidden seat or look round the old gravestones, many of which have ogee tops and delightful carved lettering from the late 18th or early 19th century.

Romans Road

This wide residential road slopes down from St Cross Road to Kingsgate Street. Its character is partly determined by the College boarding houses and their open spaces that allow large forest trees to become major townscape features.

St Michael's Passage

St Michael's Passage

This narrow passage passes the church of St Michael in the Soke through to Kingsgate Street. On the south side is a garden wall with a wide entrance gate to the back of the new Music School. The terminal view at the east end is of an 18th century house on the east side of Kingsgate Street framed between Nos 61 and 62 Kingsgate Street.

In the other direction, the 19th century gable of the chancel with Butterfield's chequer-board stone-and-flint patterns is very distinctive, rising up over the passage, the view closed by beech trees just beyond the tower. At this point the

Romans Road looking towards Kingsgate Street

Seen from the western end are the trees on the other side of St Cross Road in the attractive garden of No 30. On the north side the decorative brickwork on the boundary wall of Morshead's makes a strong corner backed up by the four-storey brick building and, further down the street, there are wooden fences broken only by the Gothic entrance railings of Sergeant's. Beyond this is a glimpse of the gable end to the boarding house.

On the southern side, the most recent of the College boarding houses, Chernocke House, is stone-built with a slate roof and selective red brick embellishments. Its grounds contain fine trees, surrounded by a brick wall, which slopes with the land down the street to Culver Road and is set on a level flint base whose height varies with the slope of the road. This wall is divided into shorter lengths by piers which set up a strong visual rhythm. It encloses Kingsgate Park, whose northern edge is defined by a fine row of trees which frame the view over the open grass to St Catherine's Hill.

At the junction with Culver Road, the street takes on a new character with the striking elevation of Music School. On the south side is the bulk of Kingsgate House and its 1980 extensions which include a covered ball-play area adjacent to the road and some small service buildings abutting the street.

The street is closed off by the splendid 19th century gateway in the stone perimeter walls of the College in front of the Art School. A specimen tree on the north side balances the bulk of Kingsgate House on the south side.

Kingsgate Park

This playing field contains substantial perimeter trees stretching from the back of Kingsgate House to St Cross Road. Cut out of the south west corner is Chernocke House, a distinguished building with stone walls and slate roof (both 1905), to which has been added at its south east corner one of the most insensitive additions to any of the College houses. It is the result of trying to add a mock Mansard roof to create a light extra storey over an existing building. Beyond Chernocke House the tree-lined ridge on Romsey Road and the tower of the prison can be seen.

From the vantage point of the raised footpath under the trees adjacent to Romans Road there is an attractive diagonal view through to the Cathedral to the north east and St Catherine's Hill to the south east.

Along the southern boundary is a range of Winchester College service buildings. These include a simple pavilion with a shingle roof, the design workshops, the double pitched roof of the laundry and the two large covered spaces of the gymnasium and the swimming pool, both of which have flat roofs and heavy fascias. On St Cross Road is Antrim House, a Victorian building that became the College sanatorium in 1979. All these buildings are made relatively unobtrusive by the colour and quality of the materials chosen and by the row of individual forest trees within Kingsgate Park which break up the skyline. There are also important trees adjacent to the eastern boundary.

Hidden away behind the College swimming pool is a small garden, containing a delightful copper statue of an athlete sitting on an old tree stump.

Norman Road

This is a wide, straight residential road on the east side of St Cross Road sloping down to Kingsgate Road. The view is closed at the east end by the fencing and trees in Winchester College playing fields and at the west end by an attractive Victorian villa which is framed by the pine trees in St Cross Road on the east, and a beech tree in Edgar Road seen to the south.

1930s semi-detached houses

The northern side has three pairs of semi-detached houses from the 1930s built of brick and tile and projecting tile-clad bays with early metal windows of some distinction and tiled porched roofs supported on timber posts. These houses are followed by Jubilee Cottages, brick and slate with chamfered brick detail, which have a good example of a late Victorian style for gates and railings.

The College tennis courts then border the road behind a brick wall and, at the eastern junction, the villa in Kingsgate Road has been extended towards the corner in similar style and has a high density development of town houses hard against the trees adjoining the tennis courts. This is out of character with this part of the conservation area.

On the south west corner of the road there is a striking, large three-storey brick building with steep gabled roofs that was a hotel and is now flats.

On the south side is a three-storey scheme of flats set back from the road behind a grass area planted with cherry trees and served by a wide bell-mouth entrance. These 1960s flats have brick walls, a pantiled roof with panels under certain windows making up four groups of vertical columns, together with exposed horizontal floorlines. This 'style' looks incongruous and is an example of the town planning of the period, which had little regard for context or street frontage.

To the east of this is a substantial house with a concrete-tiled roof and extensions that link it with its own garages and the brick gable-end wall of the corner house in Kingsgate Street.

St Michael's Gardens

This was the site of St Thomas's and St Michael's Rectory and contains a set of mature trees in the garden that show up from many vantage points including St Giles' Hill. Because of the heavy traffic on St Cross Road, the City Engineer insisted on enormous splays set back from the road, a feature foreign to the townscape of Winchester and which took out a number of trees.

St Michael's Gardens

The boundary of the sightlines is lined with brick walls that incorporate honeycomb panels that help to create privacy and some degree of lightness.

Within the estate there is a detached garage block close to the major cedar tree, and terraced town houses on the northern and eastern boundary (where there is a steep change of levels) making a hard three-storey edge to the adjacent bowling green. These have inset garages to allow space for the trees within the site. The overall effect is attractive so long as the trees remain sound but there is little room for new trees to grow as eventual replacements for these mature specimens.

In townscape terms, the effect of the Engineer's 'hole' is mitigated to a large extent by the enormous copper beech tree growing within the garden of The Friary behind a high brick-and-flint wall to the north. This tree hangs out over the road and is one of the more important trees in Winchester. The 'hole' is also mitigated by the strengthening of the terrace opposite and by the addition of a block of houses with projecting two-storey gabled tile-hung bays and underground parking. This is located between an attractive 19th century terrace and Hawkins boarding house. Consequently, the entrance to St Michael's Gardens is closed off by substantial buildings and this helps to maintain a reasonable townscape.

The townhouses within St Michael's Gardens have been carefully detailed to disguise garages by using doors which look like windows. The good quality entrance doors do give a lift to what is otherwise a rather mundane design copying 'Georgian' details in a haphazard way, without using the same proportions or the correct materials.

The Friary

The main house and outbuildings have been swept away and replaced with a high-density scheme consisting of a replacement three-storey block linked to a series of staggered slate-roofed houses with integral garages stepping down the slope adjacent to St Michael's Gardens, ending with a two-storey building. These have columns of corner windows exploiting views over Canon Street to the Cathedral. In the centre is a lumpy block with balconies offering views on both sides. The development has good quality hard landscape but no amenity land and it looks indifferent when viewed from Culver Gardens or in views between houses in St Michael's Gardens. However, seen from Southgate Street, the retention of the windowless old cottage hard against the road, with its charming elevation turning into the site entrance and the retention of the copper beech in its own raised garden (which one hopes is big enough to support it), is a real bonus.

No attempt has been made to give a new coping to the important flint boundary wall that includes the pedestrian entrance canopy.

Next door the former Oriel Hotel has been extensively repaired and converted for a housing association. As part of the development a block of eight back-to-back, two-storey houses, with pitched roofed outer bays, has been added. Both the clay-tiled roof and the brick walls complement the original building in a quiet way by a good choice of colour – and a modern 'L'-shaped bungalow, with a low-curved zinc roof, closes off the extensive car park at the eastern end.

The Friary development

(priv)
College
PENINSULA ROAD
ERSKINE ROAD
SWITHUN STREET
CANON STREET
CHRISTCHURCH RD
ST JAMES'S VILLAS
ST CROSS
COMPTON ROAD
MILNTHORPE LANE
s Hill
SPARKFORD ROAD
ST MICHAEL'S RD
CULVER ROAD
KINGSGATE STREET
PW
BEAUFORT ROAD
SPARKFORD CLOSE
GEORGE EYSTON DR
PW
Sch
ROMANS' ROAD
GRAFTON RD
EDGAR ROAD
Chernocke House
Kingsgate Park
PER'S HILL
WENTWORTH GR
AIRLIE ROAD
Gov Off
33m
dns
RANELAGH ROAD
Coll
PO
LISLE CT
OCTAVIA HILL
CROMWELL ROAD
CHRISTCHURCH ROAD
College
Pav
65m
50m
Recn Gd
NORMAN ROAD
Ridding Meads
KINGSGATE ROAD
Pav
YWCA
WINCH
ST MARY STREET
STUART CRESCENT
45m
LANSDOWNE AVENUE
SI
CROMWELL RD
PAULET PL
KINGS AVENUE
PRINCES PL
32m
Cross (rems of)
FB
FB
Gate
e
PW
round
FRANCES WAY
SIs
BARNES CLOSE
ST FAITH'S ROAD
CLAUSENTUM ROAD
43m
School
GARNIER ROAD
OOD CL
LOWER STANMORE LANE
SI
OOKS DOWN ROAD
WREN CL
BARN CRESCENT
WHITESHUTE LANE
EDWARD ROAD
Sch
Drains
Dra
Playing Field
Path
CRISPSTEAD LANE
Path
Drain

CHAPTER EIGHT

Christchurch Road and St Cross

A number of factors explain why this part of Winchester developed during the latter part of the 19th century: firstly, the railway line linking to Southampton and London was constructed in 1838, mostly on an embankment sloping down to the south, bringing noise, but also trees on the embankment. Chalk from the railway cuttings was used for building in Winchester at that time.

Secondly, as a result of reorganisation of diocesan finances, the Board responsible for the Bishop's lands in the Soke decided to change its policy and sell land on the west side of Winchester for development.

At the same time, the military needs of empire led to an expansion of Winchester Barracks with a demand for accommodation for army officers outside the Barracks in surrounding streets.

Winchester College, too, expanded its intake of fee-paying boys way beyond the original expectation of its Founder, and boarding houses were constructed in the eastern part of this area, Du Boulay's (1862), Turner's and Hawkins in addition to the development of Culver Close in 1869 and Chernocke House in Romans Road in 1905 (replacing the original Chernocke House in St Thomas Street).

Meanwhile, the Anglican Church, having put a lot of effort into the establishment of primary schools in central Winchester, decided in the 19th century to move its embryonic Diocesan Teacher Training College from Wolvesey Palace to Sparkford Road, where a fine new building was designed by the architect, John Colson and completed in 1862. This became King Alfred's College and is now part of the University campus. Once again this created a demand for houses in the area for teachers.

A new dynamism in the 19th century Anglican church led to the creation of the parish of Christ Church and a fine church was built in 1861 in Christchurch Road, designed by Ewan Christian in the style of the time. This had wall paintings in the apse at the east end, now covered by curtains as the result of reorientation of its interior to focus on a redesigned baptistry at the west end.

View towards Christ Church

ST CROSS ROAD/CHRISTCHURCH ROAD
BOUNDARY TREATMENTS

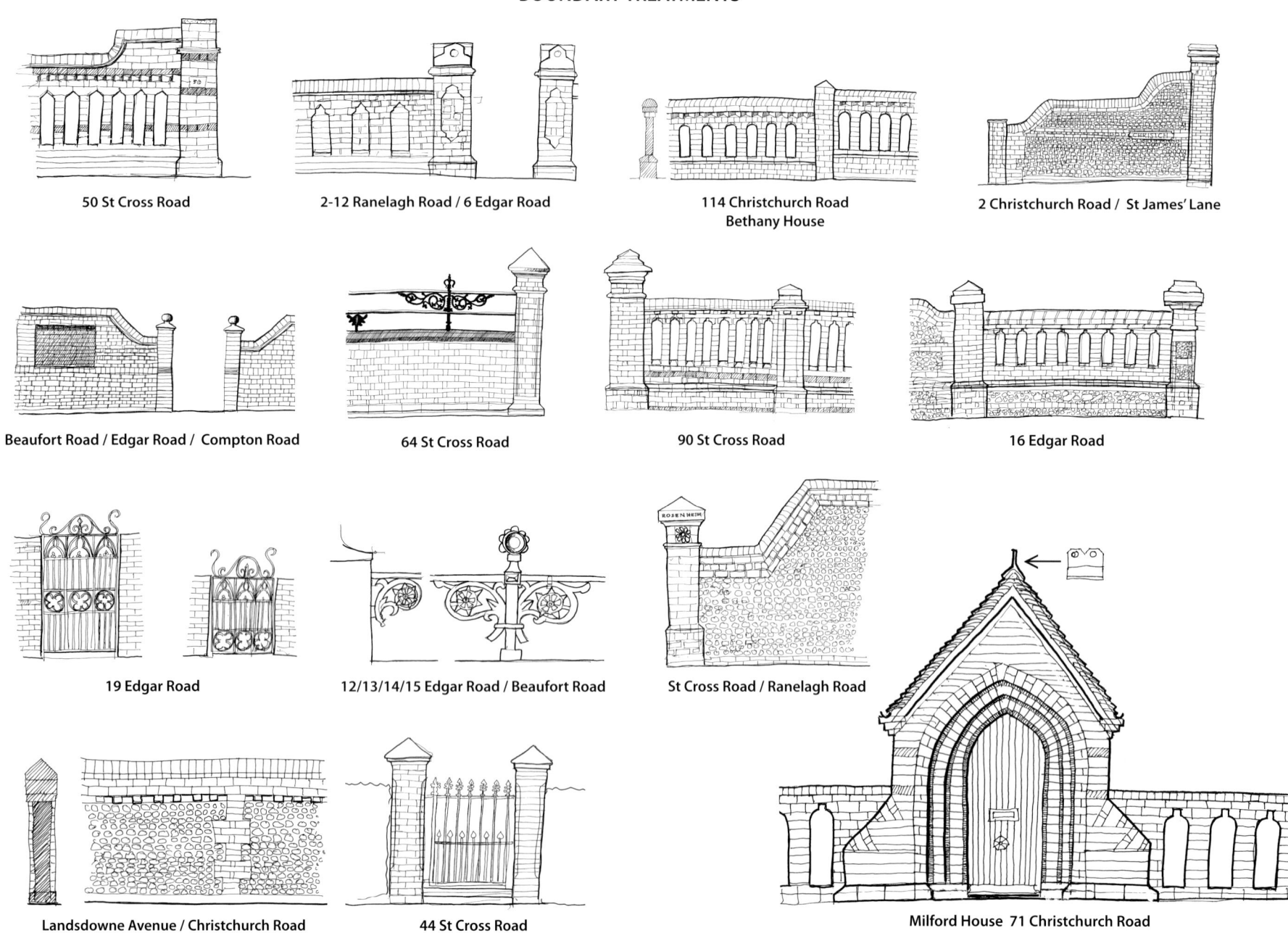

50 St Cross Road

2-12 Ranelagh Road / 6 Edgar Road

114 Christchurch Road
Bethany House

2 Christchurch Road / St James' Lane

Beaufort Road / Edgar Road / Compton Road

64 St Cross Road

90 St Cross Road

16 Edgar Road

19 Edgar Road

12/13/14/15 Edgar Road / Beaufort Road

St Cross Road / Ranelagh Road

Landsdowne Avenue / Christchurch Road

44 St Cross Road

Milford House 71 Christchurch Road

View towards Winchester from St Catherine's Hill

Finally, the introduction in 1875 of a new main drainage system for Winchester, with a pumping station at Garnier Road, allowed the development of Christchurch and St Cross Roads as attractive residential areas for professional people.

The area of open fields immediately beyond the old Southgate was laid out on a grid that was appropriate for the sale of plots for speculative development. These plots changed considerably in size by the time the houses were built. The roads vary in level, with Christchurch Road to the west having two ridges running through it whilst Edgar Road to the east is more gentle, and St Cross Road is flatter still.

There was little conscious idea of 'civic design' in the layout, although in practice the spire of Christ Church does have a significant visual effect in the north section of Christchurch Road itself, from West Hill cemetery, St James' Lane and the Barracks, as well as contributing to the distant townscape of central Winchester, seen from St Catherine's Hill. It cannot, however, be readily seen from most of Christchurch Road, south of Beaufort Road, because of trees and buildings.

Edgar Road, at its northern end, terminates roughly on the line of the spire of St Thomas's church; this may be no more than a happy coincidence.

Some houses are placed at the end of roads ensuring that they have a townscape significance, even though this is not a formal device. Two farmhouses remain from before the Victorian development, and the line of Landsdowne Road derives from a previous country lane.

The buildings in this area were built at a time when speculative builders and architects used traditional pitched roof forms on quite complex plans which incorporated bay windows as a typical feature. These were often roofed with slates brought in by the newly constructed railway, making them an economical alternative to clay tiles. They incorporated windows with large unobstructed glass areas, encouraged by the lifting of glass tax and the new technical ability to produce large glass sizes.

The developer-builders favoured a considerable amount of decoration, different coloured bricks, and stone render details that often have mouldings or designs on them. The buildings were detailed with decorated barge boards, chimneys and decorative features at the front doors.

All this added up to a consciously picturesque approach to residential design which is complemented by decorative boundary walls and gate posts often incorporating rough coursed flint work, harvested from the surrounding fields as a cheap building material.

This approach is reflected throughout the area in different ways according to the ideas of particular developers and the types of market that they were aiming at, so that some houses are terraced, some closely-spaced, semi-detached properties with deep gardens, and others are individual villas in large grounds.

Houses were originally set out along road frontages built well back from the pavement but with generous back gardens. During the latter part of the 20th century some houses have been demolished allowing several houses or flats to be built back in their place, and some have been converted into multiple occupancy. Despite the gradual erosion of the quality of the area and the devaluation of some of the landscape setting the original character of this 19th century part of Winchester is still apparent. It should be recognised that the continuous chipping away at the area's character could eventually lead to losing the interest and vitality of this important part of the city.

St Cross

The suburb of St Cross is similar to that of Hyde in having a main street containing many varied buildings along an important historic route out of central Winchester. It once was, and still feels like, a separate community and still has its public house, primary school, church hall, local car-repair garage, graveyard and flourishing allotments. St Cross has a mixture of housing and cottages dating from medieval times in a late Victorian suburb, with a major religious foundation set back from the main highway within its own enclosure and surrounded by open parkland.

Beaufort Tower, the entrance to St Cross

St Cross, however, differs from Hyde in many ways. First of all, the Hospital of St Cross and Almshouses of Noble Poverty, which gave it its identity, remains remarkably unchanged. Its brothers can be seen in distinctive black or red gowns with a symbolic cross that is also incorporated into several buildings.

Functioning since the middle of the 12th century as an almshouse and a place of daily worship, its large, beautiful medieval buildings and park provide a unique experience. A fine separate, late 19th century Master's House stands opposite the almshouse entrance.

Secondly, this area has not been subject to the industrial development that had such a powerful influence on the character of Hyde, although the full weight of modern traffic still passes along its main street. (St Cross Road was once called Fore Street contrasted with the lesser Back Street.) Several larger houses still have a variety of grand trees within their boundaries.

Situated a mile away from central Winchester, the surroundings of St Cross remain rural. The wide valley supports a fishing river that can be followed southwards. Its several channels run between water meadows growing a wide range of water plants. The land is actively farmed and livestock graze within the park right up to the walls of the Hospital.

St Cross Mill is still in existence as an isolated group of buildings created by William of Wykeham and served by a wide channel from the Itchen, fringed with reeds and full of swans, geese and ducks. It is still possible to enjoy a countryside walk all the way to the centre of Winchester past Priors Barton. This was the Winchester Priory farm at Garnier Road, a moated site with a fulling mill. The moat was filled in by the 17th century.

Returning from Garnier Road this path passes the 600 year old Winchester College and enters the walled town and, finally, the Cathedral precinct.

St Cross stands below St Catherine's Hill, the western outpost of the designated South Downs National Park. The hill changes its character with differing light throughout the day. It also provides, via the footpath across the river valley, a local beauty spot from whose slopes and heights can be seen this medieval building group almost in isolation against the backdrop of Bushfield Down which has remained undeveloped. From the opposite side you can walk up Whiteshute Lane to the edge of Bushfield Down (at one time occupied by Bushfield Army Camp) to see St Cross in the context of the Cathedral, Winchester College chapel tower and the panorama of the chalk down stretching away to the east.

The area is bounded by the railway line to the west which has its own tree-lined landscape that sets it apart from the extensive housing developments of Stanmore and Badger Farm.

In many ways St Cross is a microcosm of Winchester, with repose and beauty, linked to the Iron Age beginnings of Winchester. Yet it is not disconnected from the modern world, as the busy St Cross Road and the restless traffic on the M3 and the aeroplanes descending to Southampton Airport emphasise.

St Cross Hospital

This Norman charitable foundation was established in 1136 by the generosity of Henry de Blois, grandson of William the Conqueror, made bishop in 1129 at a time when Winchester had a population of some 5,000 and there was widespread poverty. It was situated at Sparkford, on the site of an earlier Saxon religious community, which had its own mill and was probably semi-derelict following Danish raids.

In April 1536 there were, scattered throughout England and Wales, more than 800 monasteries, nunneries and friaries, housing some 10,000 monks, canons, nuns and friars. They occupied the wonderful stone buildings that were the most striking aspect of the English medieval landscape. By 1540, the process of destroying Winchester's Nunnaminster in Abbey Gardens, St Mary's Abbey in Hyde, St Catherine's on the Hill, the four friaries, the cloister, dormitory and chapter house of the Priory of St Swithun had begun, although the Cathedral building itself was one of 14 that were spared. The Bishops Waltham palace became a ruin; and in nearby Romsey the abbey church of similar proportions to St Cross was sold to the town.

Fortunately the hospital of St Cross was saved thanks to its having been one of the stopping places for pilgrims coming from the continent going on to the shrine of St Thomas à Becket at Canterbury. The incumbents were able to prove that, as a lay foundation with a master not a prior in charge, it did not come under the terms of the Act of Suppression of 1536. So it was able to continue its core work of looking after 13 poor men, 15 men of noble poverty and providing a daily meal for the poor in the Hundred Men's Hall, and a dole for wayfarers.

St Cross church

Unlike Winchester Cathedral, which had been substantially built in 15 years, St Cross church took at least 255 years to complete, starting at the east end with its massive Romanesque masonry and decorated round-headed windows, continuing with a nave in the Early English style with pointed arches, and finishing with a rebuilt tower. This makes it, in architectural terms, one of the finest transitional Norman churches in the country. Again, unlike Winchester Cathedral, it has remained unchanged apart from repairs, minor embellishments and enhancements, and some 19th century work in the chancel by Butterfield.

As a building group, St Cross Hospital has evolved over seven centuries. The Beaufort Tower and surviving almshouses date from Cardinal Beaufort's work in 1450; the entrance gate and ambulatory date from the 16th century, including the original almshouses and schoolroom and a substantial wall round the south eastern graveyard (this was demolished in 1760). The southern leg of the almshouses was removed in the 18th century (when the ambulatory survived a threat of demolition) and was replaced by a fine set of railings by Butterfield in the 19th century which divide the major courtyard from the park. A new Master's house in flint, stone and tile, designed by Sir Arthur Blomfield, was built opposite the north side in 1899, releasing the Master's previous residence in the northwest corner of the quadrangle to become brothers' accommodation.

Today these buildings provide a group that is distinctive against the background of chalk downland and riverside landscape. The simple high cruciform mass of the flint and stone church, roofed with lead, is organically related in colour and tone. This is topped by a tower that has a plain unbroken parapet encircled with five recessed arches on each face and complemented by the lower stone tower of the original Master's Lodge with its access turret and sculptured niches.

The very simplicity of the tower, without, for example, the external buttresses and pinnacles of the 15th century Winchester College tower, means that it is particularly vulnerable in townscape terms to competition from building development on the high ground, which forms its essential setting; every effort must be made to resist such development on Bushfield Down to the west.

South of St Cross the river valley retains its parkland landscape setting on three sides, so that it is possible to appreciate its pure architectural forms in different lighting conditions. These accentuate the colour and texture of its building materials, so that, even in winter or evening light, the flints glow against the dark trees. All this is in a setting which contains lime and beech avenues, plane trees, horse chestnut, sycamore, thorn and copper beech trees. There is also the north/south Saxon millstream that Beaufort diverted around his almshouses for sanitary purposes. The stream near the lime avenue produces a fine reflection of the church tower. To the east is the broad sweep of the Itchen millstream making this the only medieval building in Winchester to have a waterside setting.

Externally the long low lines of the Hospital are accentuated by flint external walls with tiled capping, in many places containing crested medieval ridge tiles; it also has the longest single sweep of tiled roofs in Winchester. The small-scale windows of the east side of the flint-faced church give little hint of the richness of detail within its courtyards. However, if you circle round beyond the graveyard and approach from the south west, the view into the main courtyard reveals the full elevation of the Beaufort tower, flanked between the western range of almshouses and the west end of the church.

The essence of medieval institutional planning lies in the arrangement of courtyards, each with their own particular character. There are arched gateways which frame views as you pass from one space to another, with porches marking the entry point into the principal rooms. At St Cross, approaching from St Cross Road, after a walk round the northern flint walls, past the hipped roof of a garden building, the impressive gable of the guest quarters and the clipped yew hedge, you enter through a 17th century gateway into the service courtyard. After passing the 14th century Hundred Men's Hall to the left and the magnificent 15th century kitchen to the right, with its impressive central chimney, you see the three-storey stone Beaufort Tower guarding the entrance to the main courtyard. It is only from the earlier Master's House that there is internal access on the east and west to the 1340 Great Hall. This is built over an earlier vaulted cellar, with its impressive arched chestnut roof, screen

Lime walk at St Cross

Brothers' quarters, Hospital of St Cross

passage and minstrels' gallery and simple large windows containing stained glass decorations. On the south side of the gatehouse lodge there is access at ground and first floor to the two-storey timber-framed ambulatory leading directly into the north transept of the church.

It is only in the main courtyard that the wealth of domestic detail becomes apparent, with its monumental set of 14 projecting chimneys, ground- and first-floor stone windows, arched entrance doors, large dining hall windows and even larger ground- and first-floor windows to the nave of the church with its great west window.

This courtyard with its smooth lawn, gravel paths and two well-placed specimen trees, softening the bulk of the church, seems to pick up the sunlight and embrace this church and, at the same time, offers a view through the railings to the parkland beyond. Small entrances lead through to the garden areas between these buildings and the enclosing outer wall, of which only the old Master's garden on the east side is open to the public.

The garden contains a rectangular fishpond, now home to lilies and dragonflies, clipped yew and box hedges that define different spaces, and three specimen trees. Nearby is the site of an old dovecote situated on the corner of the wall at the north end of the fishpond. This lovely garden is one of the most magical and peaceful spots in Winchester.

The courtyard

St Cross Park

The path by the Lockburn southwards from Garnier Road pumping station passes through a shady woodland area with views under the canopy of trees across the water meadows to St Catherine's Hill. There are allotments on the west side, before finally you turn the corner by a great plane tree into the wide meadow of St Cross. This is framed by trees across the mill stream to the east, in the park to the south and along St Cross Road to the west, with a specimen lime tree in the foreground.

It is worth viewing St Cross in its tranquil water setting by walking eastwards to the mill stream, where the meadow is divided up by old water-meadow drainage channels which contain wild flowers. This provides a classic view of the church and its range of buildings. The path goes hard against the garden wall which hides the main building until, at the end of the garden enclosure, there is revealed a sudden dramatic view of the east end of the church rising up out of its graveyard, framed once more by large trees. Southwards is a lime walk joined by the stream that flows round the almshouses and now goes on through the field beyond, past the modern farm buildings to arrive at Five Bridges Road.

The sequence is equally dramatic returning south to north. Beyond the church can be seen the important, but rather strange, elevation of Brookside in Back Street, before the path leaves the meadow back into the shady walkway along the Lockburn. Lockburn means 'filthy stream' because it served as the sewage system for many of Winchester's monastic establishments.

There is a footpath from Five Bridges Road, leading eastwards up to the entrance of St Cross Mill between recently planted chestnut trees, and then along the west side of its feed channel. This part of the old mill, seen beyond the fence, is a less distinguished Edwardian replacement for a charming 18th century building. The private mill garden has a fine brick, mid 19th century mill building, with deep inset windows and half-hipped slate roof spanning the stream and, beyond it, attractive outbuildings in brick-and-flint with tiled and slated roofs. They show up as an important group of buildings seen from the hillside to the east. Today the millstream is used to generate electricity.

From the Mill there is a narrow footpath that leads northward along the mill stream emerging into the field south of St Cross church before joining the lime walk.

The big field to the south of St Cross contains a beech avenue, a row of limes along the main road and strange depressions along the western side marking what is believed to be the line of the original channel of water which ran the mill of the Saxon community. The view of the church and almshouse buildings opens up until you can see right into the courtyard before going out to St Cross Road.

To the south, there is a cricket field surrounded by horse chestnut trees. The

St Cross Mill from the west

cricket ground has three pavilions which sit unobtrusively in their parkland setting. The real focus at the centre of the parkland is the stone St Cross church and its almshouses.

Five Bridges Road (previously Hockley Road)
This was a busy road linking through to Twyford from which, with the construction of the motorway, the traffic function has been removed but, sadly, not the constant roar of the traffic. Now it is an attractive route for walkers and cyclists.

In townscape terms it is closed off by higher ground and trees at either end and its appearance has slowly changed as the grass has crept out from the hedges to reduce its width. The hedges are punctuated in five places by the white painted cast-iron bollards and rails of the bridges, the most noticeable being the wide Itchen bridge. The western section gives wide views over the fields in both directions.

At this bridge very wide panoramas open up. Northwards the Mill shelters behind a wood and is framed by trees in the garden. The river meanders through the water meadows apparently coming from the distant wooded St Giles' Hill, presided over, on the east, by St Catherine's Hill and its Iron Age earthworks. Here there is no view of Winchester even though the city is only a mile away. To the south the river curls round to the 27 rhythmical red-brick arches of the old Great Western Railway line's Hockley viaduct. Fortunately this shields all but the westernmost part of the M3 where lorries can be seen climbing the hill. Five Bridges Road continues through open fields until it reaches the tree-lined embankment of the old railway line where it passes through the gap of the dismantled bridge.

Hockley Viaduct

St Cross Mill from Five Bridges Road

233

The Grange

This private area of garden contains a wonderful collection of trees surrounding a large Edwardian house, with decorative porch and gables and fine chimneys that has been extended rather well to the north, but not attractively to the south. The building is now a nursing home. The northern extension, though to a different scale, is sufficiently bold to complement and hold its own with the house. Recent changes in Government policy have resulted in a new access road and a housing development within the grounds. The drive up from the Lodge on St Cross Road to the house has been arranged so that there is a large stretch of lawn on the eastern side of the house, isolated from St Cross Road by a belt of attractive planting.

Mead Road

This wide residential street runs up from St Cross to the railway-crossing bridge leading to the ancient Whiteshute Lane, down which the body of William Rufus was brought from the New Forest to its resting place in the Cathedral. This is now part of the Clarendon Way from Salisbury to St Cross and joins the riverside footpath into central Winchester.

Mead Road

The houses on the south side reach down to the Edwardian St Cross Mede, now converted into flats, with recent extensions which fortunately retain space for trees in its communal garden. On the north side of Mead Road there are magnificent trees in the garden of Bindon House and its lodge. For walkers coming down the Clarendon Way the principal feature they will see is the 19th century Master's Lodge with its stone chimneys, steep-gabled tiled roof, stone and flint walls and windows, set against the background of St Catherine's Hill. Having reached St Cross Road, there is a view to the south of the Bell Inn, and the roofs and towers of St Cross behind,.

St Cross Road (Fore Street)

Approaching St Cross from the south over the hidden main railway line and down the slope past houses on the right hand side, the road flattens out and is dominated by fine trees. On the western side there are the trees of St Cross Grange and, on the eastern side, the large chestnut trees and the weeping limes of St Cross Park, with more trees beyond. These partially cut off views of the Hospital and its church from the road.

St Cross Grange has an unusual decorative Edwardian gatehouse with a half-timbered single-bay window and a decorative chimneystack. It is the first of a distinctive group of listed buildings. These are set back behind a wide pavement of which No 134, St Cross House, an 18th century building with header-bond brickwork, is the centrepiece, with its much older farmhouse neighbour to the north. After two taller set-back Victorian villas the trees and the low flint-and-brick walls of St Cross Mede and Bindon House, on either side of Mead Road, close in. This sets the scene for the centre of St Cross, along what was Fore Street, with houses built right up to the pavement.

Villas on St Cross Road

Houses on the west side of St Cross Road

After the garden wall of Bindon House, a large house set back and glimpsed through the gate, the road is closed in by a flint-and-brick building, with decorative barge boards and latticed windows, and its associated flint wall hard onto the road with no pavement. This is followed by two groups of 18th century buildings and a converted Edwardian public house.

Returning, on the eastern side there is an early Victorian terrace followed by an Edwardian one and the distinctive Bell Inn, that uses the St Cross sign. This old timber-framed building, whose elevation has been 'Georgianised' with an inserted 19th century bay window, makes a distinctive entrance to the lane leading to St Cross Hospital. To the north, alongside a low wall to the Master's garden, are the wooden bus shelter, a telephone kiosk, and a shop (once the Post Office) marking the village centre.

Characteristically, this bus shelter, like the others in this section of the road, is solidly made out of oak that has weathered grey, with a shingled roof. This design fits the character of the area in contrast to the modern 'advertisement' shelters creeping in elsewhere which would be particularly alien to this conservation area.

The east side of St Cross Road contains a whole line of interesting buildings of different ages that creates a strong group character with its many chimney stacks, despite the varied building styles. Landau House with its 18th century first-floor oriel window over the entrance is the most distinctive but there is also Bishop Sparkford's house, partly 18th century (which has had a 19th century external wall added on with windows looking up and down the road), and the converted White Horse public house, still with three simple attractive horse signs. This section ends with Goodworth House, set back from the road with fine brick details round the windows and doors. This is followed by a section of road with many trees and the excellent Victorian house, No 51. In the reverse direction, going south out of town, the tall Victorian infill steps down to the two-storey 18th century houses and the street is visually terminated by the eastern 'end stop' of the Bell public house with its welcoming bay window,.

Cripstead Lane (Water Lane)

This is a narrow, slightly winding lane leading from St Cross Road to the pedestrian river bridge over the Lockburn where there used to be a medieval mill called Crepestre. It is divided into two sections either side of the important 15th century farmhouse, which hints at the original medieval character of the village of Sparkford. The western section continues with the side view and outhouses of Goodworth House, enhanced by its cedar tree and a weather vane. Beyond is a cottage and a car repair garage, with its green painted corrugated-iron walls and roof and painted lettering – a lone surviving village industry.

On the south side, set back, is a group of undistinguished local authority flats,

St Cross Road

St Cross Garage

with a distinctive entrance designed to disguise the four rubbish compartments under a canopy. A block of terraced houses are being devalued by changes to the windows and doors.

The eastern section comprises mainly a single Victorian terrace, looking south over a low round-topped flint wall onto the allotments site, with a building set back at the west end opposite the farmhouse, with good clay-tile hanging. To the north the tall cedar tree in Goodworth House garden is the centrepiece of a group of large trees which visually dominate the lovely old roofs and chimneys of the farmhouse.

The allotments

Entered from Cripstead Lane, these occupy an open, sunny, fertile area bounded by an important low flint wall that lacks any sophisticated coping and is therefore liable to crumble unless repaired by a skilled workman.

The allotments, which are in demand from people all over Winchester, contain little sheds, trees and seats to mark the individuality of the holders. St Cross Hospital is seen beyond a late 19th century red brick parish hall. This was designed with a steeply pitched clay tile roof which is bold but simple in form. From the allotments there are views of varying styles of terraces in Cripstead Lane and Back Street, which show up the banality of the bungalows built opposite the parish hall.

St Cross allotments

Back Street

This is an ancient narrow north/south street connecting the main entrance of the Hospital, via Cripstead Lane, and St Faith's Road. It is characterised by frontage development on alternate sides.

At the southern end is a glimpse of the Master's Lodge between the dense trees overhanging the flint wall, followed by low timber-framed cottages (which used to be thatched) and the high unadorned gable wall of No 10 which directs the eye out over the meadow to the river.

On the east side a white end wall, and tile-hung gable, with its idiosyncratic window placing, captures the eye at the end of a row of five houses, built as a terrace, most of which have an outlook over the garden of No 10 on the west side. These houses are followed by the glazed entrance porch and the bulk of St Faith's Hall, built in brick-and-flint with its joinery stained black. The view here opens up over the allotments to St Catherine's Hill. Development now returns to the western side where there are five bungalows, all screened by large shrubs along their frontage. These are followed by a terrace of seven 19th century, flint-walled, slate-

The Master's Lodge, St Cross

roofed cottages with strong chimneys. They all have original cast-iron gateposts and wrought-iron railings and gates in front of their miniscule front gardens. Mercifully these railings, imported on the railway from the Midlands, have so far escaped devaluation by alteration.

15th century farmhouse on the corner of Cripstead Lane/Back Street

On the east side, at the end of the allotments, the 15th century farmhouse, with its strongly projecting brick-and-stone chimney frames views in and out of the street opposite the terrace in Cripstead Lane.

In the reverse direction these features frame the view of St Cross church tower which becomes more prominent as you walk down the street. The wide north elevation of No 10 is noticeable with its distinctive 19th century porch. The tower then disappears from view as the road passes the Master's garden, with the railed-off meadow on the left. The road diverts to serve the 17th century entrance to the Hospital between walls to left and right, aligning with the substantial Beaufort gatehouse tower.

St Faith's churchyard and environs

This ancient raised site is located in the north eastern corner of the junction of St Cross Road with Kingsgate Road. The church of St Faith stood here until 1509 when it was destroyed by fire and parishioners were then permitted to attend services at the private church of St Cross, which now serves as the parish church of St Faith. It is roughly enclosed on two sides by buildings and tall trees and, to the south west, by a hedge and small trees. It contains good yew, holly and other trees, interspersed between Victorian gravestones, the chief townscape feature being the prodigious columnar redwood tree seen from the end of Lansdowne Avenue. The graveyard is well looked after, with a mown path around the redwood tree, but it lacks any real focus. One would expect views out to St Catherine's Hill and St Cross tower, but these are hidden by development. To the south of this site are good examples of houses set back behind a building line designated by the Highway Department. These are designed in neo-Georgian style with steep-pitched pantiled roofs, stretcher-bond brickwork and decorative brickwork over the heads of the windows. The sash windows with exposed boxes have rather squashed proportions, due to the lack of storey height, but the front doors and door cases are well detailed. The houses have weathered well over the years.

St Faith's Road

This is a wide, undulating, residential road with room for car parking on both sides. It slopes slightly from north to south, lined for the most part of its length by Edwardian terraced houses, with small gardens at the front and long gardens at the rear reached by service alleyways. In townscape terms the eastern side has more consistency with two-storey bay windows surmounted by gables. The western side has more variety.

The whole street is characterised by a minimum of alteration, even extending to the colour of the paintwork, so that the intended balance of colour and repeated detail has maximum effect. At the north end, the street is terminated by the southern gable of South Hall Lodge and the large forest trees in Kingsgate Road and the magnificent chestnut tree at the junction with Clausentum Road.

Looking south past this tree, the three-storey Dean Lodge frames the view down the street to St Cross Hospital. Next to Dean Lodge a modern two-storey house, with boarded finish and louvres, has been inserted behind a white garage. This is

Modern two-storey house

visible from Kingsgate Road from where its low, flat-roofed design, by keeping low, complements its neighbour while allowing a view to St Catherine's Hill over the top. Before the rhythm of the terraces with their chimneys and two-storey bays starts, there is, on the western side, a single-storeyed house with decorative, almost arts and crafts railings. On the eastern side, the first house has a splayed bay on the corner, with its entrance in Clausentum Road. There follows a group of four houses, the end ones having splayed bays with side entrances, their bays taking advantage of the views up and down the street. Along the terraces there is consistency of footpaths to front doors, using either red tiles or red-and-black tiles. Sadly, the original railings and gates have mostly disappeared and, as a result, there is now no consistency in the treatment of front boundaries. Instead there is a mixture of railings, fences, block walls and shrubs. Fortunately the gardens are too small to permit conversions into parking bays.

St Faith's Church of England School

At the south end, the road turns gently east past the corner where St Faith's School is located on the western side. Originally a small, characteristic flint-and-brick building with a tiled roof, set back behind the recreation area, the school has recently been much enlarged with an assembly hall and a series of staggered rooms in front, matching the original in materials and style. This is in a sympathetic style, though losing the charming small scale of the original. In front there is a simple railing enlivened by a good strong nameplate, using cut-out lettering. On the eastern side next to the Lockburn there is a hedged-off playing field and an attractive wet environmental study area. This section of road leads on to the much narrower Back Street at the junction with Cripstead Lane where the townscape is dominated by the 15th century timber framed house and cross wing. Most striking is the powerful gable, with projecting first floor. The cross wing had 19th century hipped dormer windows inserted when the house was earlier subdivided into smaller units. This house in Sparkford (St Cross) is of similar historic importance to the Old Blue Boar in St John's Street and the Chesil Rectory.

East terrace in St Faith's Road

Clausentum Road

This loop road comes off St Faith's Road opposite the school, where the St Cross sign (originally identifying a shop) on the splayed end wall remains a feature. The road runs parallel to the river and returns past the important 18th century boundary wall to Priors Barton at the northern end of St Faith's Road.

It is a flat road with simple terraced houses on the west side only. These have ground-floor bays linked by a continuous roof at first-floor level, and with gables to provide an end stop to two sections of terrace. There has been a modern infill at the south end, a pastiche building that does not take particular advantage of its position.

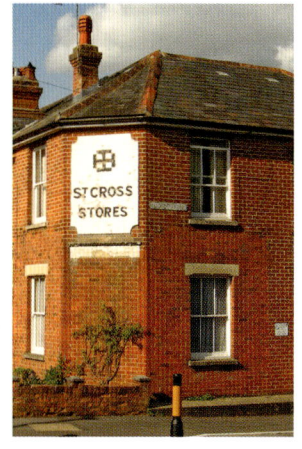

Many of the houses retain interesting original doors, though many windows have been altered, and there is even less continuity of boundary treatment. The house at the north end, however, has an attractive clipped privet hedge, with simple topiary either side of the gate, which gives the corner a lift. This terrace looks out onto an important area of wetland, Carr Fenn, with a good range of cover and trees, which makes it particularly rich in insect, mammal and bird life. This complements the Site of Special Scientific Interest in the river valley the other side of the Lockburn and should be seen as an important wildlife habitat. Attempts by developers to turn this into building land have been rejected more than once.

Priors Barton

The name relates to the home farm of the original Priory of St Swithun, the equivalent to Abbotts Barton, north of Hyde, which was the home farm for the monks of Hyde. Priors Barton is shown on an early 16th century map as a moated site (the nearest equivalent ones still in existence being at Otterbourne and Marwell). An important Saxon Cross, now in the City Museum's collection, was discovered here. There also used to be a medieval mill close by in Garnier Road.

Entrance to Priors Barton House

The present L-shaped brick house and surrounding wall dates from the 18th century with the principal elevation and double bays facing north, perhaps to command views of the Cathedral and College tower. However the views are now restricted by tree planting. The principal entrance is to the west. The house is subdivided into flats which has led to some unfortunate alterations to the roof, and devalues its townscape importance as a north end-stop for Clausentum Road, although it remains an important building in itself.

Vestiges of its outbuildings remain including the 18th century cottage on Kingsgate Road which, with its extensive old tiled roofs, makes an attractive entrance feature. Other outbuildings have been converted into flats above garages whose doors are intrusive.

In the 1970s the land attached to Priors Barton was developed with large detached houses separated by flat-roofed garages. The use of concrete-tiled roofs and first-floor tile hanging, white fascias, window reveals and modern windows makes no attempt to complement the listed building of Priors Barton in either plan, section or materials. However, the house owners have taken a pride in their front gardens and the recently planted cedar tree, if allowed to grow, could become one of the townscape features of this area. There is also a first-floor games room over one of the garages which, by its position and by virtue of the nature of its projecting bay and simple design, enhances the central space even though it has broken normal city planning criteria.

Garnier Road

This road is much used by pedestrians en route for walks along the canal and over St Catherine's Hill. However, it is also used as a local distributor road for the south side of Winchester relieving Kingsgate Street, College Street and Wharf Hill of traffic that was damaging their many historic buildings. Because of its proximity to an exit road from the M3, it has been redesigned with width restrictions and deliberate switches of priority to slow traffic. Recent rebuilding of the road bridges has been carefully done, apart from one poorly designed timber footbridge over the main river.

At its western end the road is enclosed by the garden wall of Priors Barton and the high wooden fence of the Winchester College playing field. Northwards there are views across the playing fields to the red and white science building of the College and the silhouette of the Cathedral nave and tower, framed by large trees. On the south side of the road is the wood associated with the wetland area of the valley. The road then crosses the Lockburn, wider to the north, where the banks are planted with cornus and other wild plants growing alongside the footpath, whereas to the south the shady footpath runs alongside the narrower Lockburn to St Cross

Converted pumping station

Hospital. Along this stretch experiments are being carried out with bundles of osiers to increase speed and wash the silt off the gravel bottom as a means of improving the habitat for wildlife.

Also on the south side the pumping station, recently converted for office use preserving the machinery, is a good example of Victorian architecture, erected in 1875. This pumping station was built with its associated water mains and biological treatment plant on the north west side of St Catherine's Hill to solve the problem of sewage disposal in the centre of Winchester when piped water became available. It is one of the few industrial buildings left in the conservation area. Facing the pumping station on the north side is a fine row of tall poplars which shimmer in the light, backed by evergreen oak trees. These adjoin the main River Itchen and were sited to screen off the pumping station from the College buildings and playing fields. They also perform a strong landscape role in views from St Catherine's Hill. Nearby is the site of Bull Drove, an open air swimming pool, where many Wintonians learnt to swim until it was closed by public health officials. Beyond the Itchen the hedged road crosses between the College playing field and adjoining wild area to the north, and a well-maintained keeper's cottage with its outbuildings in front of water meadows to the south. The road continues to the 17th century Itchen Navigation canal before reaching the one remaining brick bridge and embankment

Garnier Road pumping station from the footpath

of the old GWR line. This is the closest the road comes to the steep rounded sides of St Catherine's Hill.

A small car park on the south side provides an excellent viewing point for the tower of St Cross seen against the background of trees lining the railway and Bushfield Down to the west. This is a popular starting point for a wide range of walks in the area.

It is salutary to remember that under the original M3 proposals this canal would have been moved west and replaced by eight lanes of noisy traffic.

Christchurch Road

This long, wide, predominantly residential road runs parallel with the railway line from St James' Lane to Stanmore Lane. For much of its length on the west side, the railway embankment and trees form a backdrop to houses. Visually the road divides into five sections.

The first, northern section slopes down from St James' Lane, levelling off after Compton Road before turning sharp left into Beaufort Road and then turning right again as Christchurch Road. At its northern end, the view is closed by the high brick boundary wall of the Barracks and, rising above it on the Castle mound, the recent three-storey block of flats. The boundary wall is pierced by a crude opening which gives access to a flight of steps and pedestrian archway through the building to the great parade ground. Many large trees help to frame the views.

This section comprises mainly substantial Victorian detached classical style villas, two-to three-storeys high, mostly stuccoed and set well back in private gardens with prominent gate piers, shrubs and trees, many of them evergreen. Within this townscape, the spire and apsidal end of Christ Church rises dramatically to create the dominant element. To the north, a good modern church hall extension (by the Sawyer Partnership) thrusts its boldly projecting glazed entrance toward the road, providing a useful meeting space between church and hall. One of the most attractive houses in the street, the vicarage, forms the corner with St James' Lane.

On the east side, one of the villas was replaced with a block of flats in the 1960s before the area was designated as a conservation area. Towards the south, No 24, Clevedale, is a large brick-and-flint house with prominent chimneys and club-tiled gables; it is one of a number of houses in Winchester to be decorated with substantial modelled trusses outside the hanging tiles – a Thomas Stopher trademark. Adjoining it to the north are two incongruous little infill houses, whilst to the south is an excellent modern house that is traditional in form with good clay tile roof but with modern fenestration and detail.

The second section rises uphill from Beaufort Road, passing Grafton Road before sloping downhill again. The modern Church of the Latter Day Saints with its campanile in pale grey bricks, is set back within a big car park, behind a wall, topped by railings. Unlike Christ Church, the combined effect adds little to the townscape. This section of street contains a variety of houses, those on the west side at the northern end set discreetly behind frontage trees. More prominent are two pairs of three-storey houses on the east side with strong gables and ground-floor bays which frame the northward views. Due to the change of levels the view across to the sloping gardens of Compton Road (with Turner's and adjacent houses having ground-floor verandas and superb trees) is interrupted by the white lodge in the foreground. Other noteworthy houses on the east side are a substantial 1930s house of good design with a covered way leading from the road to the front door, a small mono-pitch '70s infill and a recent and well-executed replica of the Grafton Road houses designed by Michael Warren for Bendalls on the corner.

The Church of the Latter Day Saints

Stuccoed villas, Grafton Road

The third section from Grafton Road dips down and then up to the Ranelagh Road crossing and on up to the ridge-line trees beyond where Lansdowne Avenue joins. Most striking are the group of double-fronted, stuccoed villas on the east side with prominent bays and entrance porches set back from a white boundary wall with gate pillars

Opposite, on the west side, No 50, now a hotel, is a large yellow brick house with tiled roofs and gables and good architectural detail closing the view from Grafton Road. On its south side is one of the few remaining Victorian conservatories and a walled garden, containing lime and copper beech trees. Beyond it there is a less appropriate three-storeyed block of flats with glazed balconies. Garages are hidden discreetly behind trees and there is a lane leading to a series of houses on backland below the railway embankment.

The remainder of the road was once a nursery garden with pollarded lime trees on the frontage behind which are now the Ministry of Transport driving test centre and a 1980s two-storey sheltered housing scheme behind railings. The design is somewhat whimsical, with tiled roofs ending in gables, finials and roofs over projecting two-storey balconies, brickwork with matching joints, and brown-stained windows.

The corner with Ranelagh Road, perhaps the densest corner in the area in terms of buildings, is dominated by a cedar tree behind which a square Victorian villa commands views of the Barracks, St Thomas's church, Winchester College and St Catherine's Hill. A slate-roofed double garage now stands in a corner of its southern garden space.

The next section of road goes uphill to the trees on the ridge line. Cedar House is followed by two Victorian villas, the only ones with pyramidical slate roofs behind parapets. A modern scheme that replaced a third is in the form of two semi-detached blocks with strong gabled roof form and conservatory-style porches giving a slight glimpse of the copper beech tree between them. These buildings will become integrated into the street when the small trees grow up to reinforce the new boundary walls and gates.

Its southern neighbour, Lantern Court, is the most damaging development to the Victorian townscape in the area. It is set far back into the site, has no modelling or character in silhouette, ugly-shaped windows, insipid bricks and no landscape detail to continue the street character. Fortunately the building is softened by evergreen trees to the south.

The next Victorian house is an interesting three-storey villa with two-storey stone bays with decorative gables on either side and a central three-storey entrance lobby with battlemented top. Beyond this is a group of substantial semi-detached houses with gable attics, ground-floor bays with colonnaded entrances, all having decorative walls along the frontage.

120 Christchurch Road

On the east side is a varied set of houses, some original, some newer. Halfway up the hill is a leafy lane leading to backland development whose enclosing sycamores are a townscape feature.

The bungalow garden immediately to the south of this lane is dominated by a huge copper beech tree and the road narrows after the YWCA hostel. Now devoid of chimneys but still with its decorative ridge, this has a substantial extension set behind trees. Its distinctive feature is the long tiled porch reaching right out to the pavement with triple inset Gothic arches in brick. The quality of the original building has been devalued, but not beyond retrieval.

The last section starts at Lansdowne Avenue on top of the hill which, for a short distance, is a much narrower road with good brick topped flint walls on one side and a fence on the other and large trees on both sides that make a complete arch over the road. Between pine and chestnut to the north, and beeches to the south there is a view over evergreen hedges to the magnificent trees in the gardens towards St Cross Road and on to St Catherine's Hill beyond. No 106 on the west side is a good flint-and-brick house with slate roof and one of the finest 'conservatory type' entrances in the area.

The road then dips down steeply to Barnes Close and up again to Stanmore Lane at the southern end. Looking north or south the view is terminated by trees on the skyline so that in perspective trees predominate. On the east side Christchurch Gardens is a modern infill development with the houses flanking the cul-de-sac having no real townscape presence and hidden away behind foliage. Only No 1 Christchurch Gardens shows that a chalet bungalow can have a positive character when well designed, and this one is enhanced by a good front entrance. Looking west out of this road, the view is terminated by the double gables of a large house with a heavily-decorated porch in need of support. This house has a dreadful flat-roofed extension to the north with aggressive white fascias at two levels emphasising its inappropriateness. A gabled first floor has been added, repeating the front balcony details which, although not outstanding, shows how indifferent design can be improved. Next to this house is an unmade road leading to a railway arch into the Stanmore estate with trees on the north side. There is a modified coach house with projecting three-dimensional window bays and this is backed by a flint boundary wall with a fine arch in the middle.

Barnes Close

This straight, wide, east/west residential road is closed at the west end by Wykeham House, a late Victorian brick-and-flint house with striking double gables and a long, decorative conservatory leading from the pavement to the front door, seen very effectively from an angle. The architectural effect of this house has been compromised by a wide balustrade between the gables above the two-storey bays. It is interesting to note that, while a south side extension to this house to provide flats uses the same gable form and central entrance, the proportions of the windows and the lack of modelling and architectural detail make it poor by comparison. The main feature of the road are the fine trees on the north side, in particular the copper beeches between Nos 5 and 7. There is also a series of fine semi-detached Victorian houses, with wide bays at each end and first-floor balconies looking out over deep gardens. On the corner with Christchurch Road at the west end, Palmerston Court is a modern block of flats in yellow brick in two sections, with garages tucked underneath; although of no particular interest it nonetheless fits into the townscape by virtue of its perimeter wall and trees.

The houses on the south side start with St Lawrence House, now a clinic, with a strong corner bay with conical roof partly hidden by conifers. No 4 is a good red brick house with carefully considered details.

Lansdowne Avenue

From its junction with St Cross Road, where it starts between two most distinctive groups of four-storey Edwardian houses, it curves north westwards, breaking the rectangular pattern of the Victorian development. The curve follows the line of a former country lane. The first section, before Edgar Road, runs between three-storey, semi-detached houses with curved bays which have brick garden walls with recessed panels stepping up the hill. The trees in the grounds of White House in Edgar Road (previously Prince's Mead school) provide an end stop looking north west; in the other direction, there is a fine view of St Catherine's Hill over the top of Victorian houses in Kingsgate Road.

Landsdowne Avenue, showing the curve of the road

Edwardian houses on the corner of St Cross Road / Landsdowne Avenue

The second, longer section of Lansdowne Avenue starts with a pale modern block of flats that ends Edgar Road in a disappointing fashion. The road continues uphill to the Victorian houses in Christchurch Road and the trees on the railway beyond. On the south side there is a mix of houses, the most notable being 'Flint House', built straight off the pavement, and a curious new V-shaped house with two garages incorporated; beyond these, towards the end, there are two pairs of semi-detached red-brick houses set back behind boundary walls and shrubbery. On the north side from west to east there is, first, the flank wall of the YWCA Hostel, then a typical small post-war infill house and, lastly, a new development of three-storey houses. These have a central gable and the ground-floor projects to provide a first-floor balcony topped with a glass balustrade to capitalise on south facing views. Because these are serviced from Edgar Road, the frontage has a run of railings, which are kind to the mature trees.

Edgar Road

This long, wide, residential road is characterised by its undulating topography and the grid layout of the area. Its houses were all once on the western side with the eastern side made up of garden walls and stables and coach houses to properties fronting St Cross Road. The surviving coach houses are of some townscape importance. Increasingly, however, the larger gardens have allowed the development of small houses fronting on to Edgar Road, resulting in very confusing house numbers. To the north this road aligns with the spire of St Thomas's church in Southgate Street, views of which come and go when walking northwards. It becomes a townscape feature of considerable importance in the northern section when starting up the hill towards Du Boulay's Winchester College boarding house, where the view opens up. The terminating feature then becomes the modern, three-storey terrace in St James' Lane.

The view southwards from Du Boulay's appears to be primarily one of trees with the buildings largely hidden. The last section at the southern end is closed by a very disappointing block of modern flats in Lansdowne Avenue, built in pale bricks with awkward shaped windows, whose mass fails to make any townscape contribution.

Moving north between Lansdowne Avenue and Ranelagh Road, the trees make a big impact on the east side starting with pines and a red leaved prunus and a copper beech in the gardens of Nos 43 and 44 respectively. The frontages on the east side are generally weak, with a collection of shabby garages, though there is a growing trend to rebuild these in brick with pitched roofs. Opposite No 36 is a development of a pair of three-storey gabled houses and a single house in St Cross Road, set behind trees, with its access from Edgar Road. This takes the form of two pitched-roofed brick garages and a boundary wall forming a feature on either side of a courtyard. A new plane tree has been planted to replace a chestnut tree that had to be felled. There are poor infill buildings until the walled rear garden at the Ranelagh Road crossing. Here an original coach house of good character has recently been converted for residential use and a matching, mock coach house built in the same garden (Rosenheim in St Cross Road). This was one of the more important houses in the area and has been devalued by poorly considered development.

On the western side, the variety of square detached and semi-detached houses form a terrace when seen in perspective. The roofline varies considerably, as does the elaboration of detail to eaves, quoins, window modelling etc. with a painted stucco wall. Nos 42-48 are a 1970s infill scheme which introduces garages and semi basements. Although they are stuccoed buildings, they do not have the substance or detail to complement their location and lack interest in silhouette. However, next to them, the recent brick-and-tile infill house is much more successful having enough modelling and detail to enhance the street and the adjacent 1930s houses. The remaining houses before Ranelagh Road make an attractive group of semi-detached Victorian stuccoed villas.

Between Ranelagh Road and Grafton Road there are two pairs of wide-fronted, semi-detached houses with strong gables, decorative bargeboards and some remaining plaster details to windows and cornices, plus good frontages with trees and brick walls. Opposite these, there is a valuable series of walls, some with unfortunate garage insertions.

Edgar Road looking towards St Thomas's spire

Between Grafton and Beaufort Roads the most important house is No 16, built in 1874, with brick-and-flint walls, tiled roof and good details. The walled garden has several trees of townscape importance. This is followed by two pairs of stucco houses with good details to entrances, windows and eaves.

Opposite this on the east side there is now a group of modern, brick houses in the garden of a site originally reserved for a planned western ring road around the central area. These have good brick-and-flint boundary walls that, in perspective, keep the feeling of the street continuity. The most northerly wall in squared knapped flint joins up to the converted coach house of the listed white-painted house, Freelands, which preceded the Victorian development of the area.

From Beaufort Road to Compton Road the gradient steepens. The eastern boundary has pollarded limes outside the boundary wall of Hawkins, a College boarding house, with service buildings hard onto the pavement. There follow two developments of three houses each. The northern one established the road frontage providing garages and cycle storage, the latter in response to a planning requirement.

Two developments of red-brick houses, Edgar Road

The southern one is set back behind parking bays and this gives prominence to the gabled block behind Hawkins. A framing device is used to emphasise the wood-clad two-storey bays set asymmetrically over ground-floor windows and entrances. These striking red brick houses enliven the alleyway between them that leads between garden walls to St Cross Road. On the west side, immediately after Beaufort Road, is a development of town houses on College land adjoining Turner's, with small gardens and garages tucked behind. These buildings have formal design characteristics reinterpreting the Victorian theme. Small trees, bushes and climbers help to integrate the scheme into the area, and No 3 has replaced its gate with an interesting one of central European design.

At the top of the hill, the stripy brick-and-flint retaining walls of Du Boulay's garden form a striking corner feature enclosing magnificent beech trees. Du Boulay's itself rises three storeys sheer from the pavement with strong gables, chimneys and interesting window details.

Beyond Du Boulay's is a two-storey terrace set back behind small gardens; it was constructed in three sections from 1840-80s. Numbers 10a-d are red brick houses with two-storey splayed bays, large pane windows and Gothic entrance recesses. These look out onto the high wall enclosing the site of Radley House and the converted garage workshop behind.

Nos 5-10 are earlier, yellow brick houses with small pane sash windows, attractive entrances with good railings in front, while 1-4 are stucco houses with good moulded details similar in design to those in St James' Lane. All these look out across the tyre services depot on St Cross Road, and the interesting row of town houses beyond in St Cross Road with a glimpse of the Cathedral over their roofs.

Ranelagh Road

This is an important traffic route leading to Stanmore, Sleepers Hill, the University and the Hospital through an arch in the railway embankment. Looking east, the view is closed by the mature pine trees on St Cross Road, beyond which the downs can be seen.

At its north east end there is a modern flat-roofed building with white cladding to the first floor that successfully advertises the presence of a veterinary practice that has become a local landmark. On the south side is Rosenheim, a carefully detailed house with a copper beech in its front garden and a flint wall leading round into Edgar Road where it forms the foreground to the semi-detached Victorian houses on the west side of that road. The garden has been greatly reduced by the development of a new house on the St Cross Road frontage and an additional house and wing at the back.

Between Edgar and Christchurch Roads, the north side is occupied by narrow, painted stucco, semi-detached houses with semi-basements and steps up to front doors, two floors of splayed bays and simple slate roofs with prominent chimneys. These give way to higher and deeper red brick houses at the west end, some with decorative walls and gateposts. Opposite, on the south side, there are just four detached villas with gables and double height bays in red brick. The two outside houses have been painted, devaluing their detail, and their frontages are being opened up to provide additional off-street parking.

The junction with Christchurch Road is dominated by Denstone and its corner cedar tree, beyond which a two-storey extension rises up sheer from the pavement, signalling a small paved courtyard beyond in which are set back two new town houses with a 1950s infill house further back. On the north side is the sheltered housing scheme set well back behind its trees.

Grafton Road

This short, wide link between Edgar Road and Christchurch Road is visually closed off at its west end by the strong form of the hotel and the trees along the railway line beyond, and at the east end, by small 1970s infill houses of little townscape value that are seen against the trees in Kingsgate Park beyond.

The most notable feature is the remarkable group of houses, linked by conservatory entrances, that have delightful Regency fronts with decorative window hoods and ironwork that are unique in Winchester. A very recent, painstaking and successful matching house has been added at the west end, let down only by its poor cornice. To the east is a most unfortunate infill bungalow, out of character within this setting. On the opposite south side, a house is curiously attached to the Edgar Road houses;

Painted stucco houses with semi-basements, Ranelagh Road

2-8 Grafton Road

No 3 is a modest double-fronted villa set back with attractive railings in front. No 5 is a pre-war house behind trees, which until recently had pebbledash walls but, with a new extension to the east, the walls have been smooth white rendered. The last house on this side is a 1960s addition with little to commend it.

Beaufort Road

This east/west road connects St Cross and Christchurch Roads. It is terminated at its west end by a garden wall and a tall redwood tree, and at its east end by Hawkins. The tree-lined east end of the road is wider because it was designed to have a cab rank to serve the houses in the area, very few of which were built with coach houses. Its eastern end starts with trees behind the walls of Hawkins to the north and to the south with Freelands, a white painted farmhouse which predates the Victorian development of the area.

Timber-boarded house, Beaufort Road

To the west of the junction with Edgar Road on the south side are the flank walls of the principal houses in both Edgar and Christchurch Roads and, in between, a semi-detached pair of large three-storey Victorian houses with steep roofs, gables and prominent chimneys. Their upper floors have a pattern of rough and smooth rendering, imitating half-timbering. The pair have been devalued by the replacement of clay tiling on one with concrete tiles. The fences adjacent to the pavement are a poor townscape addition.

On the north side, there is a new timber-boarded house which has been built to replace a College squash court. It is an interesting design with a central gutter – which stands like a pavilion – deliberately contrasted with its setting. A high brick wall encloses Turner's garden leading to the White Lodge, an infill from an earlier period.

Compton Road

This link between Edgar and Christchurch Roads is terminated at its west end by the white painted house of St Faith's Mede with its Ionic entrance porch, framed by trees.

The road is distinctively different in character from its adjacent streets as most of the houses, including the great width of Turner's boarding house on the south side, use the same formula of slate roofs, strong chimneys and generous eaves. The houses also include ogee gutters, paired decorative wooden brackets, dormers with curved heads on the top sashes, and in some cases, decorative scrolls. They have painted stuccoed faces, rusticated on the ground-floor with inset sash windows, and plaster decorations around the door.

St Faith's Mede

Turner's boarding house is the only one to have been painted. It also has modern additions using similar materials which, by staying low-key, do not detract substantially from the overall design. They do, however, divide the frontage into two sections.

On the north side, next to St James' Villas, is a red brick house with gables on top of splayed bays and a reasonable modern entrance porch that is aggressively different. Nevertheless, in this situation it does act as an introduction to the powerful stepped brick-and-flint walls of Du Boulay's garden.

St James' Villas

This is north/south residential road links St James' Lane to Compton Road. At the north end the terraced houses of St James' Lane turn the corner to provide two substantial frontages and there is a prominent copper beech tree on back land to the west.

Houses on the west side of St James' Villas

The most distinctive aspect of the street are eight pairs of painted rendered semi-detached houses. These have low pitched slate roofs, enrichment around sash and French windows, and distinctive square chimneys. They have been subject to various attempts at 'improvements' which have affected the space between the buildings but, because they are still set back, the original townscape interest remains intact.

The boundary walls and railings have been devalued to accommodate off-street parking.

'Rat trap' bonded walls

At its southern end the road drops down to Compton Road between red brick walls that, on the west side, are built in 'rat trap' bond, in front of a rendered house. On the east, the wall is divided by piers with prominent tiled caps, to accommodate the change in levels and a kitchen entrance to Du Boulay's.

Winchester College Chapel viewed from the roofs of Winchester College

CHAPTER NINE

Importance of Detail

This book seeks to provide a framework for managing the conservation area and its setting. The concluding chapter aims to set out aspects of the administration of an urban environment. However, this does not include the management and design of the road system. Not that the appearance of roads is considered unimportant – clearly the design of surface levels, pavements, lighting, signs and street furniture are among the key components of any townscape – but it is beyond the scope of this book.

Since conservation area legislation was introduced thirty years ago, there have been a great many changes to highway design and no doubt new rules will continue to have an effect on townscape. Listed below are the more important recent highway legislation regulations, some of which have had a detrimental effect on streets within the conservation zone:

- Attempts to improve the lives of people with disability; personal electric vehicles introduced
- Introduction of measures to calm the speed of traffic
- Introduction of cable systems underground with new junction boxes
- Changes in lamp posts as old systems wear out; new lamps for greater energy efficiency
- New parking controls and bicycle paths, with a plethora of signs stemming from regulations
- Introduction of CCTV cameras

View from above Priory Gate, looking up St Swithun Street and Christ Church spire in the distance.

- Introduction of new artificial paving materials (which have not proved to be as long-lasting as expected)
- Many of the traffic-calming measures have introduced features and colours which are discordant; they do not reflect the modest tradition of qualities of materials that are compatible with the best architecture and townscape of Winchester.

If even a small part of the budget for all these activities was available to Conservation Officers for the repair and enhancement of the townscape, the cumulative effect would be dramatic.

Some of the most important ingredients that add delight to the overall context of an urban setting are materials, well designed spaces and links, details such as doors and windows, street furniture and the setting in which the city is situated. There are a number of key elements and contributions that give a city such as Winchester its identity.

DESIGN OF TOWNSCAPE AND BUILDINGS

Design in and around the conservation area is an important consideration in any planning application. Successive governments have issued advice to local authorities in an attempt to help the application process. It is important that this advice be given adequate consideration because commercial pressures often belittle the contribution and role of a good designer or architect. Many developers take little interest in the importance of detail and quality control, giving scant recognition to the contribution they should be adding to the sensitive organism that is the heart of the city.

The City of Winchester Trust

The Trust was founded in 1957, as the Winchester Preservation Trust, after the destruction of fine buildings in Upper Brook Street for development, with the immediate aim to oppose similar demolition proposals in Canon Street. In a letter to the Hampshire Chronicle written in 1981, the then Chairman set out certain principles which form a good starting point for any discussion or decision on design:

The Trust is not opposed to new development in the city because an essential part of Winchester's character derives from the patchwork of history which should stretch into the future as well as the past. But we argue that in order to maintain the character, change must be as firmly controlled now as it always has been. Once it was the limitation of available materials, the constraints of the city wall, the pattern of land tenure and many other things. Now at a time when anything is possible, planning control has been invented so that what should remain is protected, and what may be new is in keeping.

Opinions will vary about individual examples, but we do believe that if certain principles are followed change in general will not harm Winchester.

These principles include the size of new buildings, and the spaces between, the materials used and the scale of their detailing. Mostly we are concerned with the satisfactory relationship of new buildings with their surroundings. This may be restful or stimulating, but never uncaring, discordant or offensive. In addition we hold that any old building has squatters' rights by virtue of history and familiarity, besides which being by nature irreplaceable should not be disposed of lightly.

Similarly, new buildings, though to be enthusiastically encouraged where appropriate should be proved to be acceptable before joining the collection, especially where intended to join an old inhabitant. Consequently we argue that nothing should be demolished without the quality of its replacement having been adequately proved.

We hope the planning authority will have regard for the principles set out, and will not fall for the plausible arguments on many sites which claim that a clean sweep is the only viable solution, that inconvenient old buildings are beyond repair and that modern designs cannot be improved by discussion.

Houses in Canon Street rescued by the Winchester Preservation Trust before refurbishment

After refurbishment

Silhouette

Every town has a characteristic silhouette instantly recognisable by those who know it. As the city lies in a river valley, Winchester has several characteristic silhouettes: the Cathedral, the supporting towers and spires, St Catherine's Hill, St Giles' Hill and, at the level of the High Street, the statue of King Alfred, the Guildhall, Queen Elizabeth II spire, Christ Church, St Thomas's church – often seen in combination with each other.

It will be observed that these silhouettes can be dark against a light background or light against a dark background. Winchester has examples of both that can be observed from various directions and this is one of the key visual characteristics that adds to the city's attractiveness.

The uncharacteristic eight-storey-high flats at Winnall appear below the horizon, whereas the nine-storey Police Headquarters dominates the skyline. The scale of new buildings should not be allowed to compromise the silhouette any further.

Silhouettes add considerable townscape value well beyond their immediate area.

While buildings with a small plan area are not likely to be a problem, large buildings in a walled town can have a damaging effect. It is fortunate that Ashburton Court has a north/south axis and this has had a less harmful effect when seen from St Catherine's and St Giles' Hills. Recently Ashburton Court has been refurbished and refaced with vertical panels of brickwork. It is remarkable now how this building has been assimilated into the townscape when seen from across the valley. There was a narrow escape in the 1970s when two proposed tower blocks for nurses were refused permission near Romsey Road because they would have challenged the view of the Cathedral tower from St Giles' Hill. The Cathedral silhouette is currently being challenged by horizontal glinting metal-roofed industrial buildings on Winnall when seen from Whiteshute Lane. At a detailed level, chimneys contribute to the silhouette of an area, but many Winchester buildings which had distinctive silhouette features, such as St Lawrence church and the old Guildhall tower, are being overtaken by higher buildings.

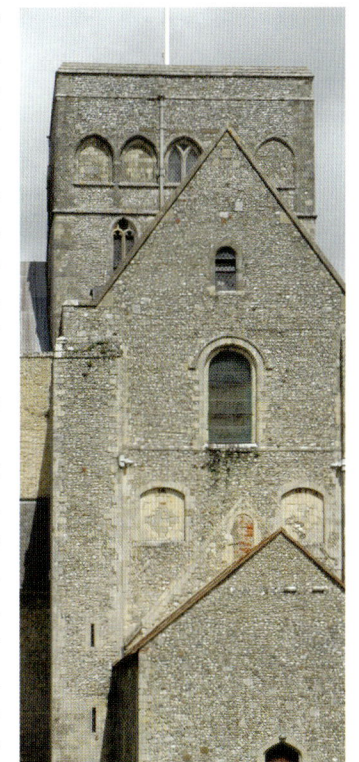

St Cross church

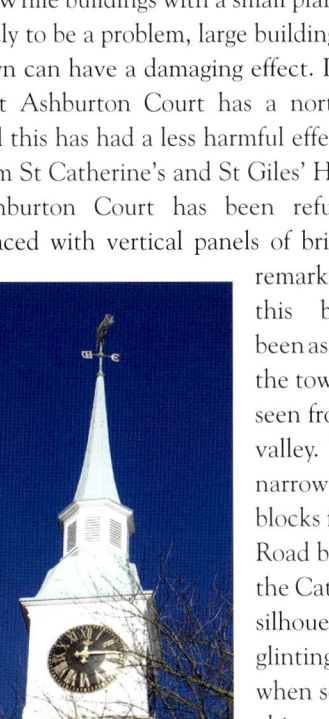

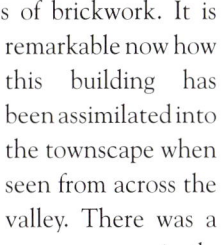

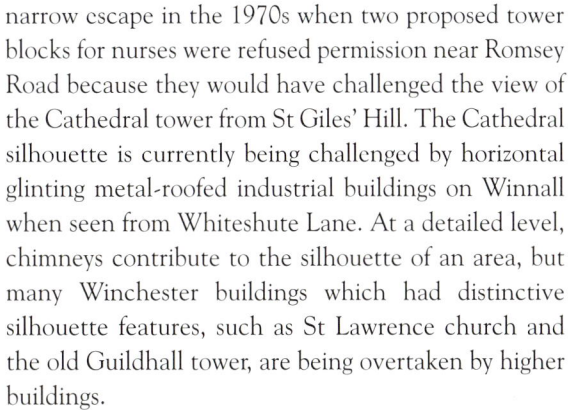

Queen Elizabeth II Court spire

Briefs

A responsibility of those commissioning a building is to provide a good brief and an adequate budget. Consultations with the planning department should then inform the brief of requirements contained in approved policies and proposals.

On the whole, buildings within the conservation area have a vertical emphasis and occupy narrow frontages and this should be born in mind when designing additions. Where there are examples of a horizontal grain, one can judge how inappropriate the building is. Horizontal layered buildings with a hard skyline were fashionable in the 1970s but they look intrusive in the Winchester conservation area, as do deep, white fascias.

Long horizontal bands conflict with the vertical grain seen throughout most street scenes

Building Design

This section considers buildings that have not taken account of their particular place in the townscape. Many modern buildings appear to be diagrams of buildings with a lack of detail, making them uninteresting and bland. Copies of old buildings generally pay scant regard to the original style so that storey heights and proportions are incorrect and often fail to include the correct detailing. Inappropriate materials for roofs, walls, balustrades and gutters are often used, thus devaluing the conservation area.

It is not a matter of style, but rather consideration of the relationship of parts to the whole, detail at eye level and the use of appropriate materials. Good design also requires analysis and sensitivity; it cannot be the product of the mechanical application of 'rules' by the planning system.

Modern architecture, with the freedom that structural systems and a wide range of materials offer, has the ability in the hands

Award winning rear elevation to Slug and Lettuce, Little Minster Street

of a skilled designer to produce solutions in ways that were not always available to previous generations. Odd-shaped sites and informal plan relationships can be used where strictly formal methods of designing would be impossible.

The nature of Winchester's topography and the position of important public spaces and buildings with an outlook over the town, mean that any design should be considered from a variety of viewpoints. The public and the planning authority are entitled to see proposed buildings accurately demonstrated in a planning application.

It is not always understood that Winchester is small in scale; it is the tension between the Cathedral and the generally smaller-scale supporting buildings that provides its character.

Winchester's roofscape

Sizeable projects should be shown to have been tested for context from various viewpoints within and without the city, bearing in mind that central Winchester can be seen from many viewpoints above.

For this reason roof design is important. Large, completely flat roofs are generally ugly. Health and Safety regulations require that railings be erected on flat roofs to protect workers servicing mechanical plant, and these in themselves add to the ugliness. It does not mean that all roofs have to be of hand-made clay tiles with a steep pitch. However, roofs should be designed to look attractive from above.

There is no reason why all open spaces in the conservation area should be anything other than attractive, even if normally seen only by the occupants of the building. There is also no reason why people inside buildings should have to look out on unattractive views. Streets should not become facades as in a film set; what happens all around is just as important. In making this statement it is recognised that not all land uses can be 'tidy', and there must be room for artisan activities. However such areas can still be made acceptable.

Another characteristic of Winchester's historic streets is that the heights of eaves vary considerably. This gives many streets their particular character, and it is important that it be retained. If there are proposals to raise the height or lengthen a building, then consideration must be given to the visual impact on the character of an area.

Terraced housing

The Winchester conservation area has a number of terraced house groups all of which are important within the urban grain. Winchester does not have a national reputation for terraced development. It has none of the attractive squares or crescents that went with substantial developments in the early 19th and 20th centuries. Nonetheless it does have some good examples of terraced housing. These illustrate a variety of designs resulting from the use of different materials and structural systems, as well as varying components, such as windows and balconies, all reflecting the period in which they were built.

Typical terrace in Hyde area

Terrace in Little Minster Street

Terrace in Southgate Street

Clifton Terrace

The terrace form is a resilient one that can be adapted to cater for changing needs. Winchester has many examples from different periods.

Today's developers tend to avoid terraces, assuming consumer resistance. However recent government directives are demanding higher densities in order not only to utilise available building land more efficiently, but to provide a wide range of different sized dwellings. In order to meet the density requirements, developers have had, in many cases, to re-introduce terraces. Apart from the density issue, the demand is also for a more efficient use of natural resources. Terraces and flats certainly provide a far more efficient use of land, materials and heating than individual properties.

Windows

Winchester College

Great Minster Street

Colebrook Street

Little Minster Street

Windows are of particular significance in building design not only because they allow light into interiors, but also because they affect the external appearance of buildings as well as the character of whole streets.

Windows are only part of the total design of a building, but nonetheless they repay individual study for they illustrate taste and technology through the centuries. Properties within the Winchester conservation area contain a wonderful range of windows in both listed and unlisted buildings. For centuries, windows have obeyed certain principles of proportion and subdivision, giving an overall harmony, while attempting to cope with the practical problems of providing light, ventilation and security. Most of these windows have a vertical overall proportion; if not they have usually been subdivided into units with the same vertical proportions sometimes emphasised by deep moulded mullions.

These principles have remained good over the centuries despite changes in materials and new technology. In addition, the development of glass and the introduction of upvc in the 20th century has offered new, but often misused, freedom for designers. It is only comparatively recently that asymmetrical window designs, combining panes of widely different character, have been introduced, upsetting the integrity of individual buildings and occasionally whole streets.

Relatively small changes in dimensions of glazing bars can affect the appearance of a window. Windows that are set back from the face of a wall can add vitality to an elevation and also help with weathering.

It is only during the latter half of the 20th century that windows are being mass manufactured and this takes little heed of basic principles. They often have a crudeness of section that looks odd, with window panes that are quite unrelated in shape to each other, thereby damaging existing buildings and the visual aspect of streets. The percentage of money spent on windows as a proportion of the total budget for a building is probably too low.

There is no reason why windows designed for double or triple glazing should either be ugly or ignore proportions which have worked successfully over the centuries.

Entrances

As with windows, entrances cannot be separated from the overall design of a building. Their significance makes it appropriate to highlight their evolution through history. Their importance in the past can be seen by the amounts that house-owners were willing to spend on them and this was matched by the ingenuity and skill of designers and craftsmen. Winchester is rich in examples from all architectural periods.

Chesil Street

Portico, Symonds Street

Great Minster Street

Hyde Street

Colebrook Street

Dome Alley

Railings

Railings were a considerable feature of 18th/19th century Winchester, marking boundaries along streets and keeping people away from windows and areas in front of semi-basements. They give a finish and a demarcation between buildings and the pavement, and apart from their functional purpose they add interest by casting shadows when the sun is out.

Unfortunately, many railings went for scrap in World War II in the mistaken belief that the metal could be re-used for the war effort. Railings that were spared in Winchester were those that prevented people from falling into water, those by the railway embankment, basement areas as in Southgate Street, St Peter Street or Castle Hill; also burial grounds and war memorials as at Hyde, St James's Lane, St Michael's Road, St John's Street and the Cathedral Close. The quantity of railings remaining may not be great compared with some other towns, but there is still a variety of railing designs within the conservation area, some surviving from the 17th century like those in front of Kingsland House in Chesil Street. The most splendid example of a cast-iron railing is by Abbey Gardens in the Broadway, donated in 1888 by Richard Moss, MP. The panels have strong decorative qualities, as well as reducing the impact of traffic on the gardens. The railings extend past the Mayor's residence to the entry gate which incorporates the city coat of arms.

For new railings it would be better to design good contemporary ones than make weak copies of old styles. Often new railings are made of standardised thin metal, lacking longevity and visually weak. Good new examples are unfortunately rare.

Late 17th century gateway at Kingsland House, Chesil Street

Modern railing and gate, Arthur Road

Gates

Winchester College has a range of memorial gates dating from the mid 19th to late 20th century. Good gates were also added to Queen Elizabeth II Court.

The internal gates between the Great Hall and the law courts were placed to commemorate the wedding of Prince Charles and Lady Diana Spencer in 1981. Not only do they provide an important security device but, in using stainless steel, a 20th century material, they also make a sculptural addition of great power and originality to Henry III's magnificent building.

Hampshire County Council gates

Brewery Gates, Hyde Street

Milner Hall, St Peter's Street

Most ready-made garden gates are fussy in design, use thin sections that rust easily and are inadequate. Good new gates have, however, been added in St Peter Street (Milner Hall), St Clement's Street (at the Dolphin entrance), St Giles' Hill (the glass house) and a passageway between two shops in the Square.

Boundary Walls

Walls are an important part of any environment, but they are not often given enough design consideration. They define property boundaries, provide visual continuity in streets, give security and shelter, enclose space and provide many other functions. Winchester conservation area is rich in different examples.

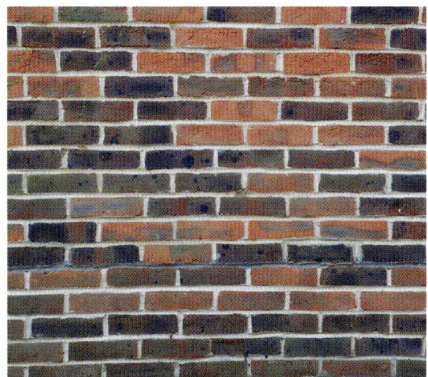

Stretcher bond

Re-cycled stone with brick

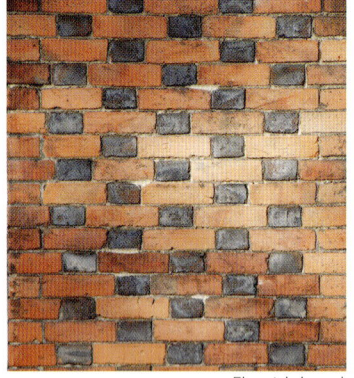

Banded brick with stone flint panels

Flemish bond

Blank walls of any size arouse suspicion because of their bland and uninteresting appearance. Yet many modern buildings require high blank walls; for example, large shops, the gable walls of domestic buildings and boundary treatments. Walls can be improved by the quality of the materials used and the skilful use of modelling.

With brick walls the jointing is important and the particular bond of brickwork used makes an enormous difference. Commonly used stretcher bond is the least attractive while Flemish bond and English garden wall bond produce a richer effect overall.

The conservation area is rich in historic examples, where stone, flint, brickwork and render offer inspiration. After much destruction in earlier centuries, building materials were often recycled; stone from the abbeys taken down after the Dissolution has enriched the quality of boundary walls of which there are many examples in the conservation area.

There is a design tradition in Winchester that walls (and railings) run with the slope of the land and this produces a simple, calm effect. Walls not only run downhill but can flow round a corner. Modern craftsmen faced with sloping ground tend to lay their brickwork or stonework horizontally and this results in a wall having a stepped top, rather than one that runs with the land.

Building materials and painting of buildings

The principal character of historic buildings in Winchester comes from the use of natural materials, stone and flints, with lead or slate roofs for public buildings, blue-red and yellow stock bricks, plain tiles and some slate for domestic buildings; all these materials have a natural affinity for blending with the local landscape.

Locally fired bricks and tiles, using clay from the Hampshire basin, provided the richness of colour and texture in the 17th and 18th centuries, and these are highly prized today. Strong coloured hand and machine-made bricks were brought by railway in the second half of the 19th century, together with Welsh slate for roofs. There was a scattering of pale yellow Beaulieu bricks in the early 19th century. In medieval times Devon slate was imported by sea. Bricks predominantly from the Sussex Weald with its similar clay belts have been used more recently to maintain colour and quality. Over time these materials have gained a patina from weathering that adds to their character. This includes the lime putty pointing with which they were put together, particularly in the 17th and 18th centuries, and it is a mistake to disturb this by re-pointing or cleaning the surfaces. During much of the 20th century hard cement pointing has been used which often harms the soft stock brickwork, though the use of lime mortars is now coming back into fashion.

It is often a mistake to paint over brick wall surfaces creating a regular maintenance regime. It can also be destructive to the fabric and become over-dominant in a street scene.

The repointing or cleaning of a listed building may require Listed Building Consent. The correct consideration and specification needs to be given to such a project. There are some listed buildings, however, that have already been painted, or designed with stucco walls that were intended to be decorated. There should be some policy guidance on this, because long-term damage can be caused by the incorrect application of paint or paint type.

Colour wash, Chesil Street

Colour wash, St Swithun Street

Colour is an important element in the street scene and care should be taken to ensure that the right quality of decoration is achieved. This stems from an appreciation of the natural lighting conditions in the Itchen valley. This is a soft and variable light as compared with the stronger light that is found at the seaside, where stronger colours look better.

In principle, therefore, modest soft colours are appropriate, based on earth pigments which traditionally have a longer life span than colours such as green or blue. Acceptable colours are off-white, pale cream, buff, warm greys, pale ochres and terracottas; whereas strong greens, blues, pinks, bright yellows, red or purple, dark grey and black are inappropriate. In many situations, buildings reflect the light and this means that dark colours in a narrow street are generally depressing.

Historic Signs

Fire mark, Kingsgate Street

Painted sign above Prior's Gate

Parish boundary sign

In different parts of the conservation area there are signs painted on walls, not always artistic, but sometimes interesting because of the information they provide about earlier times. Some examples of these are:
- The beautiful lettering in Kingsgate Street advertising a hatter and a cabinet manufacturer
- The sign of the Old Wykehamist Bakery in Canon Street
- The sign on the south wall of Gieves in the Cathedral Close indicating the medieval church parish boundaries
- The SWS sign in limewash on the almshouses in Colebrook Street (and other places) to indicate, during World War II, the direction of temporary water reservoirs for fire-fighting (and their distance)
- Garage sign on No 71 Parchment Street.

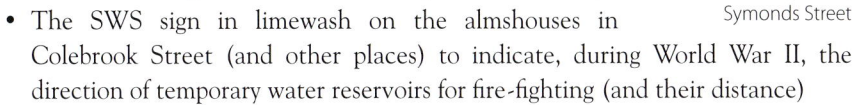

Almshouse, Symonds Street

CONSERVATION PLANNING

A key to the success of any historic town is finding imaginative uses for buildings that are valued as part of the townscape but, for whatever reason, have lost their original purpose. Current advice is that buildings are best used for the purpose for which they were originally built; new uses may create all sorts of problems, such as new floor loads and fire escapes. These can sometimes so compromise the integrity of a building that conversions become questionable.

When a town loses its status, buildings can become redundant and lose their original purpose. This happened to the Great Hall of Winchester Castle, when Winchester ceased to be the capital of England. After its functions were moved to London, they were replaced by Crown Court trials. Finally, when legal cases became more specialised in the late 20th century, the Hall reverted mainly to use for entertainment and touristic purposes.

The medieval town gates that have survived are those that have acquired new uses for their upper floors. Thus in the 16th century the Kingsgate acquired a church on the top of its 14th century structure. The Westgate was once used as a prison, later became an entertainment room for an adjoining public house, then the City muniment room in 1836, before becoming a City Museum in the 20th century.

These are just three of several prominent examples of the use of historic buildings evolving sympathetically. Buildings within the conservation area frequently have to be evaluated bearing in mind that a building has to be economically viable, and that the use to which it is put is a sympathetic one, with the minimum possible interference. This is often an extremely difficult process to achieve. Not only are historic buildings vulnerable to insensitive operations but so also are the vulnerable small details such as carved signs, metal fire insurance discs, tiling, even historic painted signs, all of which are part of Winchester's and the buildings' long history.

In an historic town there may be a case for well-considered structural changes to provide a new amenity. In general, however, it is important that planning policies and decisions do not create uneven site values, as can easily happen when a large built area is demolished. This often leads to a demand to replace buildings whether or not they have any architectural or historic value. It is not just a matter of protecting statutory listed properties, for there are many buildings making up the character of the streets that do not satisfy the national criteria for listing and yet are valuable locally. There are many such examples within the conservation area.

There is another important consideration, and that is one of resources. The effect of two World Wars and financial recessions set back craftsmanship and design because so many skilled operatives were lost to the building industry. A building represents an investment in resources, but different parts wear out and need repairing or renewing at different times, requiring a regular maintenance programme using skilled craftsmen.

Buildings that are built to good standards of space and proportions tend to keep their value, as has been demonstrated clearly by Georgian properties. Money spent on maintenance after sixty to one hundred years tends to be thought of as high expenditure, the years of satisfactory service forgotten. The economic effect of good maintenance is a price well worth paying for.

The character of Winchester depends much on the city's defensive and Close walls, gateways and many miles of flint-and-brick walls whose maintenance is dependent on a buoyant economy. In an historic town there is a need to be aware of the intrinsic value of a building, and its contribution to the whole area, so that a local authority can exercise sound judgement and provide good advice where necessary.

The University of Winchester has compiled a list of the historical uses of buildings in the Winchester Conservation Area. Pilgrims' Hall, for example, which has one of the earliest hammer-beam roofs in the country, lost its function of accommodating pilgrims at the Dissolution of the Monasteries. Later five of its eight bays were enclosed by a 17th century house. The northern section was neglected for years, before becoming the Dean's garage when motor cars first became fashionable. In the mid 20th century it was converted into a school hall.

Pilgrims' Hall

Over its long history Winchester College has broadened its educational requirements and has been able to satisfy them by the conversion of existing buildings. The 14th century brewhouse, no longer required as such by the end of the 19th century, has now become a library. The 19th century gym found a new use as a theatre in 1981 and the 19th century sanatorium, formerly in two blocks, found a new use as an art school in 1983.

Milner Hall, named after a prominent historian and priest, was originally erected as a Roman Catholic church in the 18th century until 1927 when the new St Peter's church was built nearby. The hall became neglected and the decorative interior, badly damaged by dry rot, was removed. A crude new floor and windows on the west side were added when it became a television repair workshop for a Jewry Street electrician. With growing prosperity and with the help of a grant, the building was restored in 1986 and became a hall used for a variety of purposes.

The medieval church of St Peter in Chesil Street was made redundant in the 1960s, and its lack of maintenance posed a serious threat to its future. The Winchester Preservation Trust found an organisation that was willing to undertake sensitive repairs and to use it as a theatre with the help of town scheme grants. It is now an established home for the Winchester Dramatic Society.

Milner Hall

St John's House in the Broadway has survived some 700 years, seeing many changes since it was originally founded as a hospital with an attached chapel, one of three to serve the medieval town. The medieval guilds met upstairs where, amongst other business, property transactions in the walled town were formalised. In the 18th century the upstairs was rebuilt as an assembly room used for a variety of purposes. (Paganini played there in the early 19th century.) It was later used by the Corporation of Winchester until the new Guildhall was built in 1873. Later it became a cinema and then a museum. During much of the 20th century, the King Alfred Bus Company had its tea and rest room on the ground floor and there were temporary law courts upstairs. Other parts of the building were used for an architect's office and for political party rooms. In 1980 the building was leased as a restaurant, and the principal rooms were restored. Today it is once again a place for receptions and functions of different sorts, a classic case of recycling a building.

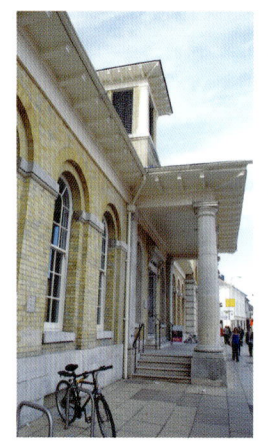

The Corn Exchange in Jewry Street is a fine building by Owen Browne Carter, a noted Winchester architect. The building makes an important contribution both to Winchester and its immediate surroundings. It was constructed as a market in 1838. Since then it has had many uses but the basic design has always shone through. Today it forms the centre-piece of its latest reincarnation, a library and discovery centre.

The Corn Exchange illustrates the changes which any historic town has to contend with as it adapts to changing requirements. Such changes keep a town alive. Indeed, this is what conservation is about. For good conservation to succeed, however, it is essential that architects and planners with vision are attracted to work in this field.

The Corn Exchange

TREES

There are some spaces important to the character of Winchester conservation area which are without trees: for example, the long central section of the High Street, the central quadrangle of Winchester College, and the Square, all spaces of high architectural value.

These are exceptions, however, and this study has highlighted the visual value of trees both as individual specimens and as groups. It should be recognised that trees create an environment often more important than buildings. Trees have much more importance than just their appearance and shape; they add a richness to urban spaces that is beneficial to all. Unfortunately their contribution to the setting of Winchester is not always fully appreciated by some inhabitants, developers and even local and statutory authorities.

The question therefore has to be asked whether the tree cover that exists is sustainable. If we do not accept advice from those who understand the natural environment of Winchester and the surrounding landscape, then the environment for future generations will be impoverished.

There are some trees which make a special contribution within the conservation area; the size, shape and colour of copper beech trees is an example. There are few of these left, all large, old, and occupying sites where if they had to be felled they would be difficult to replace.

Several of the tree belts that form the structural planting around the town are of beech trees; many are ageing, some are over a hundred years old and potentially vulnerable. The County Council's landscape study of 1981 highlighted this as a problem. Many of these belts run along the ridges and the principal access roads to the city.

For planting to have a structural role in the townscape there needs to be sufficient land available close to tree belts for new trees to be planted alongside the old rather than having to clear fell and start again. Although these tree belts lie outside the conservation area, nonetheless they make a major contribution as a backdrop to the city. For example, consider St Giles' Hill, Sleepers Hill, Chilbolton Avenue and Bereweeke Road without trees! Within these areas all trees are under threat due to concentrations of new development which often provide insufficient space for trees.

In the less developed areas such as parks, the river valley, burial grounds, and large gardens and school sites, there is room for the planting of individual forest trees to provide continuity of this important element. In many urban and suburban situations trees need to be cared for by skilled tree surgeons to ensure their survival as a valuable asset. This process is often expensive, but surely worthwhile.

Street Trees

More consideration needs to be given to the maintenance and replacement of street trees before they cause damage to paths and walls. Highway engineers are not always sympathetic towards trees and more appreciation is needed of the contribution that they make to Winchester as a whole.

Street trees are also vulnerable to pressures brought about by road safety and traffic requirements, and provisions for new development. Their value must be given due weight when undertaking these measures. Fortunately British Standard protection requirements offer useful guidance to avoid risk to trees.

On new building sites where trees are already growing, the actual process of building can affect the drainage situation by virtue of trenches being dug for services, foundations and the provision of hard standing. This can affect the long-term health of the trees, resulting in their eventual removal. Public authorities need therefore to have both knowledge and a long perspective.

Extensive tree cover seen from West Hill Cemetery

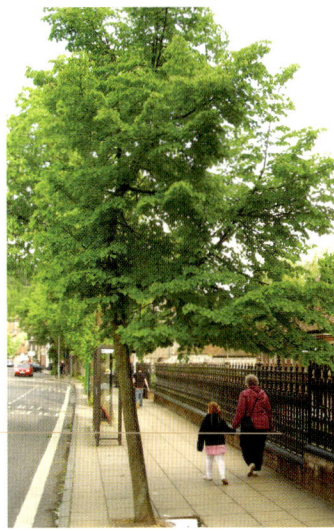

The Broadway

Trees in the Cathedral Close

Tree Preservation Orders protect important trees and tree belts. However, good strategic policies need to be drawn up not only to preserve trees that exist but to consider planting for the future to replace the ageing stock of important forest tree belts. Without such trees there could easily be a dramatic and detrimental change in Winchester's character.

A tremendous amount of educated thinking and planning will be needed if the present tree-enhanced character of Winchester is to be sustained into future centuries. It should be recognised by all the authorities concerned as well as the general public that we have a responsibility for maintaining and improving one of the great features of Winchester – THE TREE.

SCULPTURE

Several years ago during his time as County architect, Sir Colin Stansfield Smith drew attention to the fact that, since the time of the Greeks, one of the important features of European cities has been public sculpture.

From its medieval past, Winchester has had sculpture on the outside of many buildings, for example the lovely Madonna over the outer gateway to Winchester College. There are also the figures on the gateway to Chamber Court, the outside of Fromond's Chantry, the Westgate with its gargoyles and shields, the Buttercross with two tiers of sculptures (many replaced in the 19th century), the Beaufort Tower at St Cross (a Madonna on one side and sculpture of the benefactor on the other), and the gargoyles and heads on the Cathedral itself. The beautiful headless statue found near the porch of the Prior's Lodging can now been seen by the entrance to the Lady Chapel in the Cathedral. And the Cathedral has a superb set of carved stone bosses in the ceiling, too high up to be damaged in the Civil War, and carved wooden misericords in the choir stalls.

Statues on the Buttercross   *Madonna, Winchester College*

Later on came the statue of William of Wykeham on the outside of the 17th century School in Winchester College; the plague memorial that is such a feature of the Upper High Street; an early 18th century statue of Queen Anne on Lloyds Bank (the old Guildhall) and the magnificent clock on the same building with its ornate and distinctive case creating a singular silhouette. There are also three carved keystones on the late 18th century building at 108 Colebrook Street; heads on either side of the entrance door of what was the 19th century Dolphin public house in the High Street; sculptures on the outside of Mead Museum and on both sides of the War Cloisters in Winchester College; the head of a woman over the door of Abbey House; statues on the first floor of the Guildhall; statues of bishops on the early 20th century building for Boots; other figures under the first-floor windows to W H Smith which replicate carvings on medieval timber framed houses; the heraldic devices on Barclays Bank and Queen Elizabeth II Court; and the statue placed recently in the little niche at the east end of St John's church in St John's Street. A large statue of Queen Victoria was originally set up in Castle Yard, then moved to Abbey Gardens, and is now located in the Great Hall; the prominent statue of a First World War soldier stands as a war memorial near the west front of the Cathedral; and the statue of Lord Seaton was brought from Plymouth and is now close to the entrance of the Barracks.

Queen Anne, Lloyds Bank

First World War soldier

King Alfred

Horse and Rider by Elisabeth Frink

Hampshire Hog by David Kemp

The image which most visitors to Winchester associate with the city is the statue of King Alfred put up by public subscription in 1901, 15 feet tall and weighing 6 tons. This powerful statue dominates the Broadway. The subject of King Alfred caught the public's imagination at the beginning of the new century, and a national committee chose Winchester as the most appropriate site. It changes dramatically under different lighting conditions and is a prominent landmark.

The City Council should be encouraged to develop the idea of promoting more public sculpture to enhance the conservation area. It is something that other European countries have understood and practised for years. More recently it has been taken up in this country in urban areas like Sunderland, Kilmarnock and Swansea where it has been part of their strategy for regeneration. Hampshire County Council has organised major exhibitions of sculpture by Elisabeth Frink, Henry Moore and David Pye in the terraces outside the Great Hall and Law Courts.

During the last twenty years, at the instigation of the County Council, the Elisabeth Frink Horse and Rider and the Hampshire Hog have added to the character of the upper part of the High Street. A Woman and Child has been placed in the Records Office garden. A distinctive stone falcon sits on top of the water feature in Queen Eleanor's Garden behind the Great Hall and a memorial seat has been commissioned by the Hampshire Sculpture Trust on St Giles' Hill. An excellent statue has been placed outside Winchester College's swimming pool.

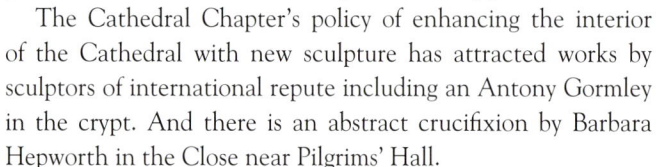

The Cathedral Chapter's policy of enhancing the interior of the Cathedral with new sculpture has attracted works by sculptors of international repute including an Antony Gormley in the crypt. And there is an abstract crucifixion by Barbara Hepworth in the Close near Pilgrims' Hall.

Other interesting local features are the three-dimensional shop signs in the High street, such as the two good 'boots' and a 'clock' that have been on display for at least twenty years. They have been joined by others – crossed pens over Warren's stationery shop, the clock and teapot in Parchment Street and the globe in the Square.

Sculpture in the crypt of Winchester Cathedral by Antony Gormley

Crucifixion by Barbara Hepworth

CHIMNEYS

Chimneys, apart from being a practical provision for homes and other buildings, are also an important design feature. They provide a counterpoint to the long roof ridge-lines. See how bland modern housing estates are without the all important uplifting feature – the chimney.

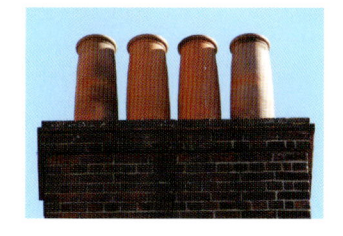

St Catherine's Hill from St Cross

Chapter 10

Archaeological & Historical Development of Winchester

Richard Whinney

This chapter provides, subject to any new discoveries, a general picture of our understanding of the development of Winchester from its earliest origins over 2,500 years ago to the present. As such, it sets the background, and provides a context and historical setting for the more detailed appraisal of the buildings and street scenes of early 21st century Winchester.

Geology and Topography

Winchester occupies a position in central-southern Hampshire where the valley of the River Itchen cuts through the gently undulating chalk downland. The site is constrained by two opposing hills; St Giles' to the east and St Paul's to the west, which constrict the otherwise broad floodplain. At this point in the valley bottom is an 'island' or area of raised ground in the floodplain, and together these features formed the principal ford of the River Itchen. Since the beginning of human habitation in the area, east/west movement focused on this ford, and the relationship between the site and the river is fundamental to the understanding of the origin and development of the city.

Figure 1 is a schematic section, immediately to the north of the High Street, of the city's underlying geology across the Itchen Valley. The valley sides reveal a number of terraces. Each represents different stages of the Itchen's paleo-channel created by the interglacial and postglacial melt-waters ending some 10,000 years ago. Although these have been greatly exaggerated by later human activity, archaeological excavations have revealed that they are of natural origin.

The base of the paleo-channel, extending between Parchment Street and Water Lane, lies some 17 metres below the modern surface. This is filled with river gravels, peats, and silts. Resting on the upper deposits is an area of raised ground made up of tuffaricious chalk. This chalky deposit was formed by a vertical spring that pushed small fragments of the underlying chalk to the surface, where they were deposited to form a mound. Also known as marle- or malm-hills, these were once common features of Hampshire's chalk streams. Although having the consistency of dry pudding rice, it formed a mound sufficiently raised to remain above water throughout the year.

Schematic section across the Itchen Valley at Winchester

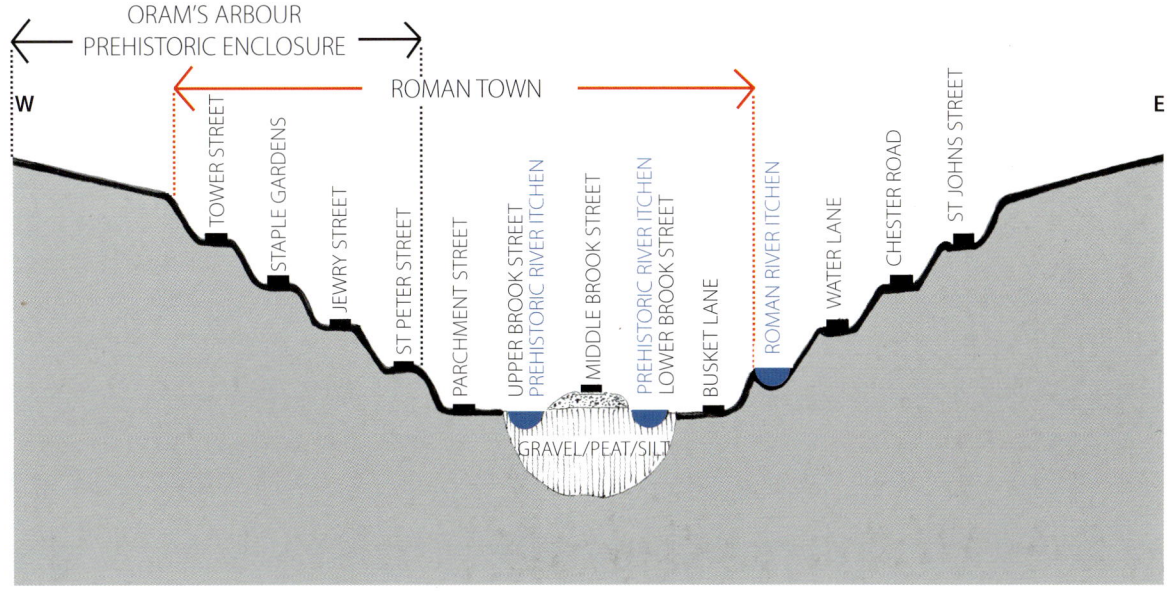

Figure 1

To date, the outline of the 'island' (**Figure 2**) has been traced to the north of the High Street only. To the south of the High Street it has been identified on a number of sites overlying silts and a gravel terrace that extends from the west. Silted prehistoric river channels indicate that prior to the establishment of the Roman town, the Itchen flowed in two channels: the principal channel to the east of the island and a secondary channel to the west.

Prehistoric Winchester (c. BC250)

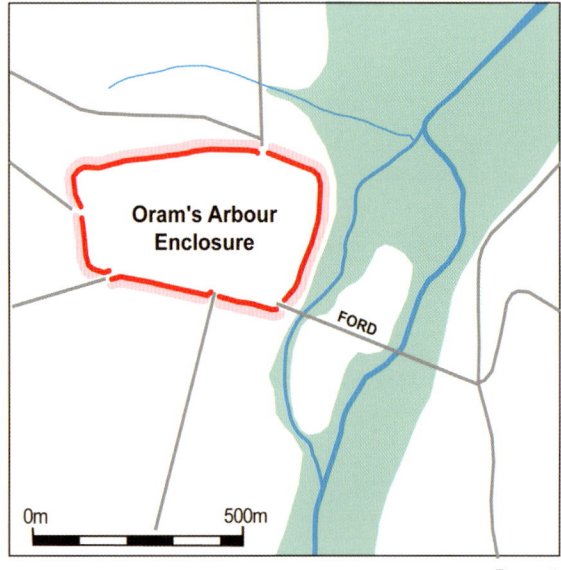

Figure 2

The Ford

Winchester's oldest and arguably most important monument is the High Street, originally the approach to the ford. Movement along this line has formed a sunken track or hollow-way that can be traced westward along Romsey/Old Sarum roads for over 2km. In the centre of the city, at the junction of High Street and Jewry Street, it was deep enough to hide a double-decker bus. Excavations on the upper part of the High Street have shown early Roman buildings extending down into a pre-existing hollow-way. Further west, it appears that the ditches of the Romsey Road entrance to the prehistoric Oram's Arbour enclosure (see below) had been specially manipulated to cater for it. If so, it was already a significant feature in the landscape by the middle Iron Age. The lower part of the High Street, now the Broadway, has had several names over the ages, but perhaps most telling was its medieval name of 'le causeway'. This was the site of the prehistoric ford.

PREHISTORY
Early Activity

The evidence for man's presence in the Winchester area prior to the late Iron Age is very fragmented and thus difficult to characterise with any certainty. The first indications of settled communities are of Neolithic date (3500-2500BC); these comprise a few burials, either in long barrows (burial mounds) or in pits on the chalk downs to the north and east of the present city, and scatters of flint and stone tools. To date there is no direct evidence for settlement or agriculture in the vicinity, although the presence of small agricultural communities may perhaps be inferred from the limited evidence.

For the ensuing Bronze Age, the evidence is somewhat more substantive, but is still limited to the chalk downlands around Winchester. Remains indicate small isolated communities, practising mixed farming – arable and stock raising. Houses and other structures were generally round and built of timber, thatch and daub. Burials took place either in round barrows (burial mounds), or in small cemeteries. The burial rites were either cremation or inhumation.

Iron Age

A similar situation existed for the early Iron Age in the area, with the chalk downlands being occupied by small farmsteads and settlements, in enclosed and unenclosed communities. Again mixed farming was the order of the day with the landscape probably fully exploited for the raw materials that it could provide – pasture and grassland close to the rivers, arable farming in small 'Celtic' fields on the slopes of the chalk downs, further pasture and grazing together with woodlands on the higher downs and steeper slopes.

At Winchester there was perhaps a settlement of some type becoming established on the western slopes of the Itchen Valley above the flood plain. Fragmented remains have been discovered in excavations from time to time, but these are not sufficiently extensive to allow any serious attempt at the reconstruction of the community.

Winnall Down

Extensive archaeological excavation of the site of an Iron Age farming community took place prior to the construction of the M3 Motorway interchange, on Winnall Down at Easton Lane (Junction 9). Here continuous occupation from the Middle Bronze Age through the Iron Age to the Romano-British period was discovered. The Iron Age phases of the settlement are well understood and can be divided into a number of discrete phases, based on stratigraphic and ceramic evidence. In the early Iron Age the settlement comprised a D-shaped enclosure, with a number of circular structures, grain storage/rubbish pits, post-built structures – granaries etc. By the middle Iron Age, the enclosure ditch had been filled in, and the settlement was essentially open. All around were 'Celtic' fields for mixed farming arable/stock raising agricultural activities.

St Catherine's Hill

Located some 4.5km to the south east of Winchester, this hillfort with the entrance to the east, is in many aspects typical of the type of site found all across the chalk downlands of Southern England. The only archaeological exploration of the site has been very limited, and little is known of the nature, extent and chronology of the interior. It is possible that a small community lived on the hill and other communities in the surrounding smaller farmsteads from the 4th to the 2nd century BC.

Oram's Arbour

Around 250BC (the middle Iron Age), there was a major shift in the area's settlement pattern with the construction of a defended enclosure, now known as Oram's Arbour (**Figure 2**). It lies buried below the modern city, and is known only from archaeological excavations. It was positioned to take advantage of, and perhaps control access to, the ford. Thus, it influenced movement over a wide area.

The Oram's Arbour defences were similar to those of other contemporary enclosures and hillforts, but the enclosure was sited on the western slopes of the river valley and, although strategically placed, it did not physically dominate its surroundings. The defences comprised a single ditch with an internal bank constructed from the upcast of the ditch. The line of the enclosure defences is known on the north, west and south, but is conjectured on the east. It is possible a bank and ditch was not required here as the flood plain of the Itchen may have provided a natural boundary or barrier. An area of about 20 hectares was enclosed in this manner. Four entrances have been identified and a fifth is postulated.

Little is known of the community which constructed the enclosure. The effort required in digging the defensive circuit perhaps suggests a large and centrally controlled population, but there are some indications that the enclosure was only occupied on a seasonal basis. Although recent excavations have revealed typical Iron Age features – circular structures, pits, postholes – their density perhaps suggests that occupation of the enclosure was seasonal and intermittent. It may have served as a central gathering- and market-place for the surrounding rural communities, where people could meet for the exchange of both commonplace and more exotic luxury goods.

When describing settlements like Oram's Arbour, archaeologists use awkward terms such as the borrowed Roman word 'oppidum' or the modern term 'proto-urban'. This recognises that the culture and economy of pre-Roman Britain was on the way to becoming 'urban'.

The Roman Town

There is no evidence that either St Catherine's Hill or Oram's Arbour were overrun and captured by the Romans in 43AD, as they were both apparently already abandoned by that time. The focus of late Iron Age occupation appears to have drifted to the south of the enclosure, while evidence of early Roman activity is confined to its south east corner. It appears that this latter area formed the nucleus around which a new town was founded, around 70AD. In establishing this new town, the Romans carried out major alterations to the existing landscape.

Early Roman Winchester (c. AD70 - 200)

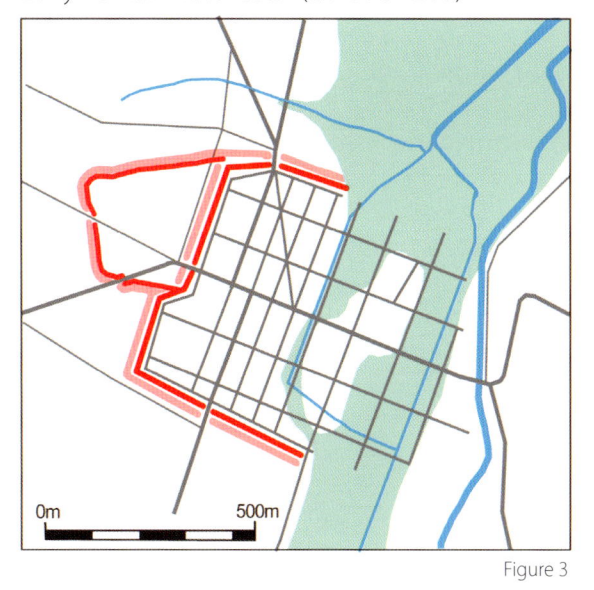

Figure 3

Figure 3 shows our current understanding of the early Roman town. Four main elements can be identified, all of which are broadly dated to the late 1st/early 2nd century. Firstly, the eastern part of the Oram's Arbour enclosure was removed, while the western portion was retained. Excavations have shown that the retained ditches were redug, and perhaps the ramparts strengthened.

The second element is the early earthen defences. Excavation at Southgate suggests that the early Roman gate, and earthen defences, were in place by about 70AD. To date the defences have been traced on the western side of the valley only. The Roman defences appear to be positioned to control access to the ford from the west, with all traffic first having to enter the retained portion of Oram's Arbour before entering the town. Excavations have suggested that they had a short active life, but remained a feature of the landscape.

The third element of the early Roman town is the street system. This is poorly dated, but the principal elements are of late 1st or 2nd century in origin and to the west it is confined by the defences. There are hints that the alignment of the principal elements of the system was based on the entrances of the Oram's Arbour enclosure at Trafalgar House and Northgate. The system also reflects the natural landscape. To the west the streets form long narrow *insulae*, with each north-south street corresponding to a natural terrace. To the east, over the relatively flat floodplain and 'island', the streets form the more typical square Roman *insulae*. One feature uncommon to other *civitates* is the street that ran immediately within the defences.

To allow the extension of the street system over the floodplain, the pre-Roman river channels were diverted into a newly dug channel located hard against the eastern side of the valley, in effect the present course of the Itchen. Associated with this were new channels dug to drain the low-lying areas.

Taken together, these early elements of the town reveal much of the then current status of the region. At the conquest, the late Iron Age Atrebatic kingdom was allied with Rome and retained a degree of independence under King Cogidubnus who was based at his palace of Fishbourne (Chichester). AD 69 was a year of rebellion in Rome, known as the Year of the Three Emperors and was certainly a period of instability. At about this time King Cogidubnus died and the Atrebatic kingdom was absorbed into the Province of Britannia and divided into three, with *civitates* established at Winchester, Chichester and Silchester. These three towns are the only *civitates* in Britain known to have early defences. What threat necessitated these defences is unknown, but Winchester's suggest that it was perceived to be coming from the west.

It may have been at this time Winchester was elevated to the status of a *civitas* or tribal capital called *Venta Belgarum* or '*the marketplace of the Belgae*'. Who the Belgae were is far from certain. They may have been newcomers to the region, or perhaps a sub-group within the wider Atrebatic tribe.

The extensive engineering works associated with the diversion of the river into a new channel had lasting effects on the development of the city. Placing the town in the floodplain in such a manner is unique in all Roman towns north of the Alps and was to pose special problems associated with the growth and development of the city. In origin the streets and drainage system can be seen as primary elements of the Roman town, but occupation was confined to higher ground and the 'island'. It took more than 100 years before areas of the former floodplain became suitable for permanent occupation.

Figure 4 shows the later Roman town. In the late 2nd century the town defences were reinforced with a new earthen bank and ditch which for the first time fully enclosed the urban area. These ramparts were strengthened again in the early 3rd century with a masonry wall three metres thick. On completion of these works, *Venta* became the fifth largest town in Roman Britain and was a focal point for communications, trade and local government.

Late Roman Winchester (c. 200 - 410)

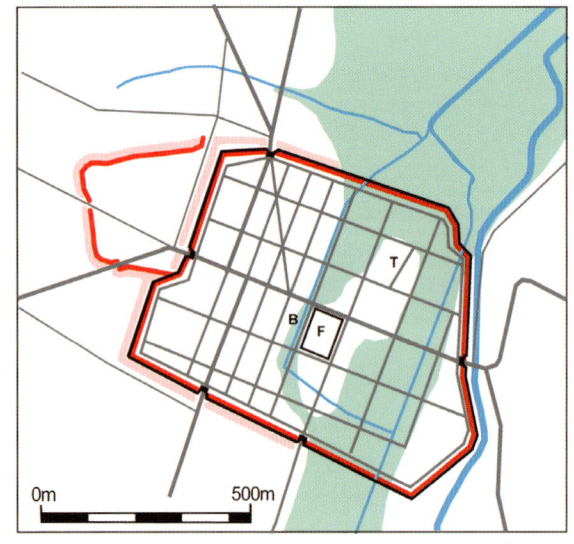

F – Forum **B** – Basilica **T** – Temple   Figure 4

Public buildings, such as the forum-basilica and temples were constructed within the street grid. The road leading to the ford acted, with the forum, as the principal market area of *Venta*. The location of other public buildings is far from certain. Our limited knowledge suggests that the baths occupied the *insula* immediately west of the forum, served by water from the pre-existing pre-Roman western channel of the Itchen. Away from the High Street were private dwellings. A Late Roman document refers to an imperial cloth manufacturer in *Venta*, and it is possible that the eastern stream powered associated mills, but to date no direct evidence for this has been found.

Too little is known of *Venta*'s public buildings to allow objective analysis of the public spaces. Only limited excavations have occurred on the High Street, and although they suggest it was densely built up, little is known of the character or use of these buildings. The greater part of the defended area was taken up by housing. Excavations have shown that in the 1st and 2nd centuries the High Street frontages were divided into narrow properties, giving Early Roman *Venta* an almost medieval feel. Since much of the lower part of the town continued to flood, these early properties were confined to the eastern and western banks, and on the island. During the following centuries, a process of change occurred. The early properties were replaced by larger ones containing fine stone-built townhouses surrounded by orchards and gardens. Excavations just inside Southgate provide a ratio of early to late properties of four to one, while at the Brooks the density was two to one. This implies fewer properties occupying the same area of land, all this occurring at a time when large areas of the floodplain were becoming suitable for occupation for the first time.

The town's cemeteries would be the first indication of settlement that visitors would see on any of the main approaches to the town. The northern cemetery, focused on the Cirencester (Andover) Road, is the best understood. It extended out from the Northgate along the Cirencester Road for over half a kilometre. The eastern and western cemeteries have been sampled, but little is known of the southern cemetery. Recent theories suggest that not all the people here were town-dwellers, but that *Venta* acted as a centre of religion and burial for the people of its hinterland – *Venta* here being seen as a tribal centre and a tribal burial ground.

The End of *Venta*

By the mid-4th century, major changes in *Venta* signal the demise of the Roman civic authority. From about 350AD no new town houses were built. Those already in existence fell into disrepair and large areas inside the walls were taken over for industrial activities, particularly iron-working. The drainage system began to collapse, the low-lying areas once again became uninhabitable, and occupation was confined to the island and the drier western slopes. Despite these signs of collapse, repairs to the street north of the Forum and at Southgate suggest that occupation and a degree of authority continued into the 5th century, although the makeup and function of the town at this time is uncertain.

5th to 7th centuries

Following the Emperor Honorius' refusal to give military aid to the peoples of Britannia in 410AD, urban life gradually decayed in *Venta*. However, the location of the town with its control over the river crossing, ensured a continuing occupation and over the ensuing centuries the appearance of new peoples, the Anglo-Saxons with a new language and culture, marked the gradual change of Roman *Venta* to Saxon *Wintanceaster*.

By about 450BC the Roman town was all but abandoned, the river management systems had broken down and parts of the Itchen returned to its prehistoric course. The island once again became a prominent feature in the local landscape. The Roman defences were in poor repair, but still formed a substantial barrier – the ruins of Roman buildings may have stood as much as ten metres high in places. The orchards and gardens belonging to the townhouses had gone to seed.

The long-distance Roman roads continued in use, at least close to the town, though at some time before the 8th century, the Roman Southgate was blocked. Traffic from the south was forced to use either Kingsgate or Westgate for access into the town. The abandonment of the roads immediately outside the Northgate indicates that it was similarly blocked. This suggests that there was still some form of authority in the city that controlled access to the ford.

The character of any occupation in the ruinous town is difficult to assess. What little evidence we have consists of a thin scattering of hand-made pottery. What occupation there was seems to be of a low level. This is in direct contrast to the upper Itchen valley where there are a number of pagan Saxon settlements and cemeteries (Kingsworthy, Itchen Abbas). These attest to a stable and relatively large population in the area.

Mid 7th to late 9th centuries

During this period, there is evidence to suggest that the old Roman town of *Venta* was undergoing a quiet revival, firmly connected to the introduction of Christianity and the creation of the Kingdom of Wessex. The make-up of the local Saxon population and any tribal or political divisions is difficult to assess. Bede's History informs us that in the early 7th century the Isle of Wight was held by a people of Jutish origin, whose influence extended into and beyond the Solent. A second people, called the Meonware, were centred on the Meon valley. A third people, called the Geuissae, were located to the north, but the extent of their territory is far from clear. It would seem that it was from this latter group that the West Saxons would emerge. With the arrival of Christianity, the earliest bishopric of the West Saxons was Dorchester-upon-Thames founded in 635, suggesting that the centre of their territory was the Thames Valley. Their influence extended southwards and in c. 648AD King Cenwalh established a church, later known as the Old Minster, in Winchester (**Figure 5**). By 662AD, the see was transferred from Dorchester-upon-Thames to Winchester. In the 680s King Cadwalla of Wessex annexed the Isle of Wight and the Meon valley, and the historic core of the kingdom of Wessex was formed.

Although the status of Winchester as a bishopric is well attested, the character of any associated settlement is far from clear. The main discoveries in Winchester consist of a small graveyard of mid 7th century date, excavated in Lower Brook Street, which included a richly furnished 'princess' burial. This was overlaid by a masonry building that by the late 10th century became the church of St Mary in Tanner Street. In addition, evidence has been found of ironworking dating to the 8th century (Guildhall), and late 9th century bronzeworking (the Square), leather and glass working (the Brooks).

A useful comparison can be made with the contemporary settlement of Hamwic (Southampton).

Mid 7th - 9th century Winchester

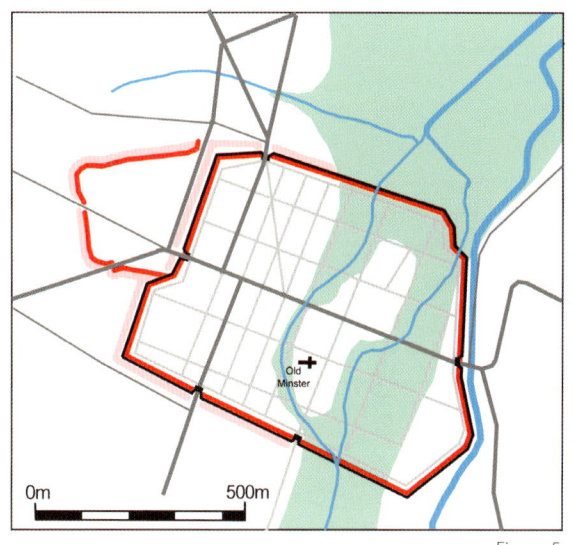

Figure 5

There, evidence has been found of a large settlement with a planned street system, a diverse community carrying out a wide range of industrial activities, and with access to locally produced and foreign products. Contemporary deposits in Winchester have only produced a small amount of local pottery and a handful of imported wares. This material is difficult to assess, but the absence of any evidence of housing or a trade function may indicate that whatever its population makeup, it was based on a monastic rather than a secular community.

Even the presence of a royal palace at this date in the city cannot be taken for granted. It is now argued that the *villa regalis*, or principal royal residence, was located at Hamwic. The site must have had considerable administrative importance, as by the middle of the 8th century it had given its name to the shire – *Hamtunscire*. Closer to Winchester was the royal *tun* of Kingsworthy, some 2.5km to the north. This suggests that Wessex had two principal sites fulfilling different functions; Hamwic the administrative and trade centre, and Winchester the ecclesiastical centre.

This physical division of the roles of church and state is paralleled in other middle Saxon kingdoms such as Kent and East Anglia.

The 9th century was characterised by Viking incursions. At first these were only raids, but they were later followed by settlement. The Vikings raided Hamwic in 840 and 842, and this, along with the disruption to the wider continental trade network, eventually brought about its end. It is one of those perverse aspects of history that the factors that led to Hamwic's demise in many ways brought about Winchester's next and perhaps best known phase of development, the establishment of the Alfredian burh.

Late Saxon Winchester

There are hints that in the second half of the 9th century the character of occupation in Winchester began to change. Between 852 and 862 Bishop Swithun had the first recorded stone bridge constructed over the Itchen, just outside the Eastgate. Whatever the character of Winchester at the time, it was sufficiently tempting to attract a Viking raid in 860. Yet despite these signs of activity and ecclesiastical patronage and support, life in *Wintanceaster* had not yet reached a truly urban state.

When Alfred the Great was born in 841, England was divided into seven kingdoms, but when he was crowned in 871 all save Wessex had fallen to the Vikings. Following Alfred's victory over the Viking King Guthrum, the resulting treaty divided England into two. North of a line drawn roughly between London and Chester became the Danelaw, while Alfred became overlord of the lands to the south.

To protect Wessex, Alfred created some 32 defended settlements called burhs, the largest of which was Winchester. As a site it had two major advantages. Firstly, there were the Roman town walls that were repaired and ditches redug. Secondly, it was the focus of the surviving Roman road network, and its control of the ford of the Itchen. This meant that by redefending the site, it had a controlling influence over movement throughout a greater part of southern/central Hampshire.

Winchester is first recorded as a defended site in a document called the *Burghal Hideage*, which is thought to date to c.886. It calls for each hide (a land unit) to provide one man to defend the city's wall. Winchester was assessed as 2,400 hides. At first these men served only in time of need, but later in Alfred's reign they became a permanent garrison. If we allow for wives, children and dependants, the population may have been as high as 5,000.

Late 9th - 10th century Winchester

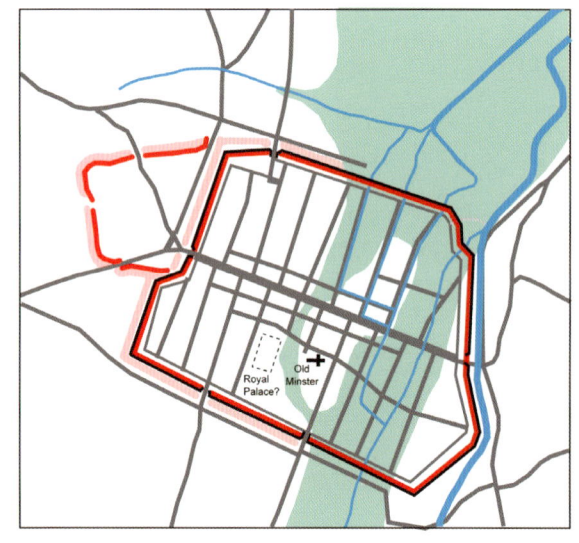

Figure 6

Drainage Pattern

Figure 6 shows out current understanding of late Saxon Winchester. As in the Roman period, the re-founding of the city required major alterations to the existing landscape. A new street system was established, but before this could be done the post-Roman abraded water channels had to be rationalised. Over the next 1,000 years, the drainage system was altered, so that its precise layout in the late Saxon town is uncertain, but it appears to divide into two distinctive parts. To the west were the Brooks, consisting of the Upper, Middle and Lower Brooks. Once open channels, they now flow in culverts buried below their respective streets. The Upper Brook may be Roman in origin, for its projected line reaches the possible site of the Roman baths. The streams converged on the High Street near Colebrook Street (West), and then continued south to serve the Old and New Minster precincts. In the mid 10th century, Bishop Ethelwold tapped into this system to form the Lockburn – a system of culverts that served the Old Minster and later the Cathedral. The second system was the Coitbury/Abbey Mill Stream, which entered the defences near Durngate, its flow serving Nunnaminster (later St Mary's Abbey) and the bishop's residence at Wolvesey.

Street System

Once the drainage system was in place, the street system could be laid down. There is documentary evidence for the presence of some streets south of the High Street by c. 900AD. Other main elements can be shown to have been in place by c. 950AD. Although the Roman street system had long fallen out of use, it has become increasingly clear that there is a far higher correlation between it and the Saxon street system than previously thought. Therefore, it may be best to compare and contrast the two systems. As in the Roman period, the late Saxon streets to the west respected and utilised the natural terraces of the valley slope – one per terrace. Unlike the Roman streets, this narrow spacing was continued eastward across the floodplain, but the two systems converge at Middle Brook Street. One obvious difference is that all the Roman east/west streets away from the High Street were left out of the Saxon system, but the Roman intramural street system was re-imposed.

The correlation between many of the Saxon and

Roman streets is perhaps not surprising. Many of the Roman streets would still be recognisable as corridors running through the ruined and overgrown town. It is important to recognise that when the Alfredian burh was being laid out, they were not working with a blank piece of paper, but with a site that had its own natural constraints, and one that still preserved physical elements of an earlier town.

Properties

Excavations at the Brooks suggest that once the street system was laid down the land was divided into properties, each 2 perches wide (10.5m). There are hints that this form of division was repeated throughout much of the city. The typical property consisted of a timber building on the street frontage, with yards and ancillary buildings to the rear. Evidence of a large range of industrial activities has been found throughout the defended area, with water-based industries such as cloth making, dying and tanning concentrated in the low lying areas.

On Staple Gardens, the remains of two buildings were found that had been destroyed by fire around 950. The charred remains preserved a moment in the life of the building. It appears to have consisted of two rooms set back from the street frontage. The back room contained a hearth and other features. Material recovered from the hearth indicates that it was used for iron smithing. Nearby was a bag of burnt beans and domestic pottery, suggesting the hearth, and therefore the room, was used for both industrial and domestic purposes.

Suburbs

The growing economy led to the expansion of the suburbs. In particular the western suburb continued to thrive and prosper up to the Norman Conquest. Smaller suburbs grew outside the remaining gates.

Principal Monuments

A royal mint was in operation by about 895 and King Alfred is recorded as being in Winchester in 896. The royal palace, located outside the west front of the Old Minster may have been established by this time, although it was not specifically referred to until the late 10th century.

Two new monasteries were founded in the city in the first decade of the 10th century. New Minster, founded by Edward the Elder around 903, may have served as the congregational church for the growing city. Queen Ealhswith founded the 'little timber monastery' of the Nunnaminster around 908. Under royal patronage, Old Minster continued to grow on the site of Cenwalh's original church.

Late 10th - Late 11th century Winchester

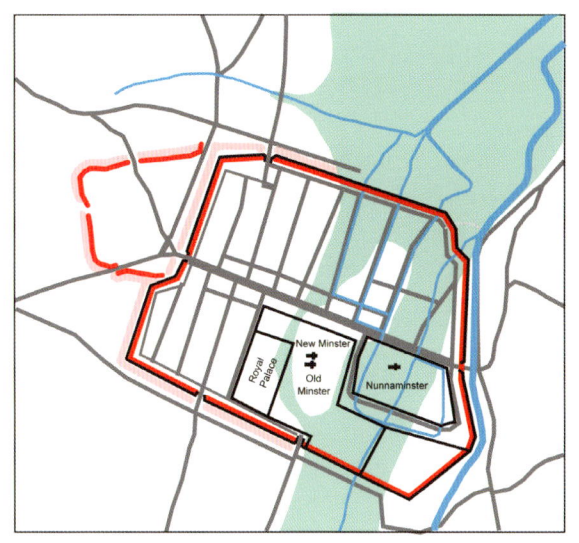

Figure 7

In the second half of the 10th century, Bishop Ethelwold reintroduced Benedictine rule to the city's religious institutions. With this came changes to their structure. He extended Old Minster, and enclosed the tomb of St Swithun, which by then had become one of the most important places of pilgrimage in southern England. He reformed New Minster and rebuilt Nunnaminster. He also began work on a new residence at Wolvesey. One aspect of Ethelwold's reforms was to have a lasting effect on the fabric of the city. He enclosed the monastic houses within a wall, to shield the religious inmates from the bustle of the growing city. This resulted in the removal of earlier streets and secular housing from the south eastern corner of the city (**Figure 7**). By doing so, he created, along with the Royal Palace and Wolvesey, a royal and ecclesiastical enclave occupying almost a quarter of the urban space. This was to remain a feature of the city up to the Reformation, and its presence can still be seen today.

By the end of the 10th century, the town had become a centre of religion, royal power, manufacture, trade and commerce. Winchester was no longer the 'Capital of Wessex', but the 'Capital of England'. The history and archaeology of the period reveals that by then it had become a lively, bustling, cosmopolitan place with a population perhaps as high as 8000 in 1056. Winchester for the first time in its long existence, had become a truly urban place.

Medieval Winchester (1066 – 1350)

Queen Edith opened the city's gates to William the Conqueror in November 1066, and Winchester experienced immediate and important changes. So many new elements were either introduced, or existing ones modified, that for the next fifty years the city probably resembled more of a building site than the capital of England (**Figure 8**).

The Castle

In the south west corner of the defences, a street and its associated properties were taken over as the site for the castle. Little is known of the first castle complex, but it was probably built of earth and timber in the motte-and-bailey style. Over the subsequent centuries the castle was rebuilt in stone, and modified to become one of the foremost medieval castles and royal residences in England. One important aspect of the castle is that, although it was within the city defences, it was not of the city, for there was no direct access between the two. One had to exit the city through either Southgate or Westgate before entering the castle through its own gate. There are sally ports at its northern end, but these are not true entrances. This concept of an enclave was repeated throughout the subsequent history of the site up to the modern day; from its intended use as Charles II's palace, its military phase as a barracks, to the present development.

Medieval Winchester

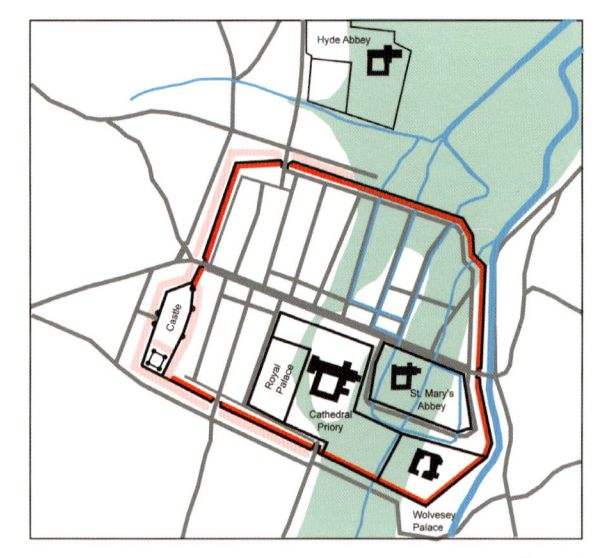

Figure 8

Religious establishments

The Normans had a distrust of the Saxon church and its saints, and to express this they not only carried out reforms but also rebuilt Old Minster. Bishop Walkelin began the construction of the Cathedral in 1079, and in 1093 the formal dedication of the east end of the new building took place. This new work may reflect the Norman church's wish to combine the earlier royal and ecclesiastical functions of Old Minster with the congregational role of New Minster. If so, New Minster became redundant and in 1110 its monks moved to a newly built monastery in the northern suburb of Hyde. By 1108, Nunnaminster had also been reordered and rebuilt in the Norman style, and its earlier dedication to St Eadburgh was changed to St Mary. Bishop Henry de Blois founded St Cross Almshouses in 1132, and work started soon after on the expansion of the Bishop's castle of Wolvesey.

By 1148 the city not only housed the three monasteries, but also 57 parish churches, each of which served as a centre of its own community. Later, these religious establishments were augmented by four Friaries.

There are four documented hospitals known within the medieval liberty of Winchester – St Cross and Sustren Spital in the southern suburb, and within the walled area St John, and a small hospital maintained by the nuns of St Mary's Abbey. A fifth hospital, St Mary Magdalen (for lepers), was located immediately east of the city on Alresford Road. Their existence is evidence that the city, with its many monks, nuns and parish priests, provided great care for the poor and needy, the old and infirm, and the impoverished traveller.

Medieval surveys

Winchester is blessed with a number of important surveys that allow us to appreciate the dynamics of the medieval city. The first is the Winton Survey conducted in 1110. This incorporates an earlier assessment carried out during the reign of Edward the Confessor (c. 1056), so in fact it is two separate surveys. There followed another survey conducted in 1148. Later Tarrage Surveys and other records highlight the changing fortunes of the city. One aspect, revealed in the surveys, that is shared with the modern city is that it had a very lively property market.

In 1110, the population is estimated to have been between 8,000 and 11,000, a figure that remained more or less constant until the Black Death in 1348. The surveys reveal a densely populated city with a confused mixture of houses, cottages, shops, workshops, yards, all linked by the surviving Saxon street system, interconnected by narrow back lanes and alleys. In these areas the business of a thriving urban centre was transacted. There is ample evidence not only of normal commerce, but also of pottery manufacture, working of bone ivory and leather, and metal working. The Brooks area functioned as a textile production and finishing centre based around the watercourses in the north east quarter of the town.

St Giles' Fair

Outside the city to the east, St Giles' Fair, one of the great annual medieval fairs of Europe, was held for 16 days early in September. Such was its success that it developed its own street system around St Giles' church, and become known as 'villa nova' or New Town. The peak of its prosperity occurred before 1200, and this level was maintained until the last decades of the 13th century when it suffered a rapid decline, probably associated with the overall general economic decline of the country. Beginning as an outlet for local agricultural produce, by the 13th century the range of goods traded had expanded considerably – wool and cloth, livestock, leather goods, furs, spices and gold were all extensively traded. There was a lesser trade in wax, wine, knives, metal vessels, mercery, haberdashery, nails and pig-iron.

Such was the Fair's status and importance that, within the street system, many of the buildings were arranged in groups or rows according to the wide range of specialised trades – for example Fullers Street, Grey Cloth Street, Wool Street, Skinners Row, The Drapery, Spicers Street, Cutlers Row – or, according to the origin of the traders – for example Hereford Street, Leicester Street, French Street, Spanish Row.

Some streets, especially those around the church,

were probably very like those in the city below, containing a range of permanent and semi-permanent buildings with shops, upper rooms, cellars and open land behind. Most of these properties were only occupied while the Fair was in progress. Land further away from the church was used for the erection of temporary stalls, parking of carts and tethering of animals.

The suburbs

As the population grew, it expanded outside the town walls and extensive suburbs grew up outside the main gates of the city. The eastern suburb was the bishop's principal Soke of Winchester. Under his jurisdiction and patronage, it was the most prosperous. Archaeologically, the western and northern suburbs are the best understood, and each reveals different patterns of development. The western suburb, contained within the banks and ditches of the ancient Oram's Arbour defences, was well established by the time of the Norman Conquest. Principally part of the king's fief, it contained amongst the housing the royal hunting or hawk mews. At the Norman Conquest the northern suburb was a much smaller affair, probably extending no further north than the Fulflood stream, an area roughly corresponding with the Bishop's northern Soke. The arrival of Hyde Abbey acted as a spur to its development and it rapidly expanded northwards. By the end of the 12th century, the western and northern suburbs were linked together by a new suburban defensive ditch.

During the Civil War of 1141 between Matilda, the daughter of Henry I and legitimate heir to the throne, and the usurper King Stephen, great physical damage was caused in the town, including the destruction of the royal palace. In spite of this, there is little evidence that the prosperity of the city suffered unduly. However, the 13th and 14th centuries saw a gradual decline in economic activity and prosperity in Winchester, a local reflection of national and international trends. Another influence on the city's declining prosperity was the gradual removal of royal functions to London. The Jewish community, a powerful influence in the city since the Conquest, as witnessed by its own cemetery in the Mews Lane and Crowder Terrace area, was expelled in 1290.

The Palace and the Pentice

The urban dynamics of the medieval city can be seen all around us in the modern cityscape. This is well attested in the very heart of the city, in the area of the Buttercross. Here the principal players of the time, the church, the crown and the merchants, met. The push and pull between their interests to occupy and control this space resulted in a remarkable group of buildings. Together they are known as the Pentice, a name derived from the covered walkway, or pentice, they all shared. If we think of this in terms of street scenes, then when Alfred reordered the High Street it was some 75ft wide. Its principal function was as the city's main market place, hence its Saxon name of Cheap Street. It would have been flanked on either side by a near continuous row of shops and booths. Those on the south side would have backed onto Bishop Ethelwold's monastic enclosure wall.

Soon after the Conquest, William extended the royal Palace northwards up to the High Street. The Winton Survey tells us that 12 High Street properties were removed to make way for the Palace. Now the street scene had changed: instead of rows of shops, the south side of the High Street was the blank wall of the Palace.

One common thing about merchants of all times and cultures is that if you give then a blank wall, they will set up a stall against it and carry out business. This appears to be the origin of the Pentice. Over time the booths were replaced with tables, then in turn replaced by permanent structures. At each stage, they encroached further into the High Street, primarily to extend their floor space. In due course an upper floor was added and extended to form the covered walkway. The result of this is a group of buildings that almost blocks the High Street. Something had to give and it appears that it was the buildings on the north side of the High Street. Today, the alignment of the High Street shifts north at the Pentice, only to return to its original alignment once past this obstacle. The date of construction of one of the buildings of the group (35 High Street) suggests that this process was well under way, if not completed, by 1340. A similar process can be seen in buildings on the north side of the Square whose staggered frontages are a telltale sign of encroachment into the market place.

The Wool Trade

During the 12th and 13th centuries, Winchester was a major collecting centre for English wool for export to Flanders via Southampton. Taking advantage of long established trading associations and shipping connections, the city was well located to act as a staging post for wool exports from the south west, from the Welsh Marches, from Berkshire, Buckinghamshire, Oxfordshire and Wiltshire. Much wool was exchanged each year at St Giles' Fair. Winchester was one of the English wool staple towns and, outside the Fair, exchange took place at the wool staple, close to the Westgate. The Bishop also had wool house(s) at Wolvesey Palace, to store wool from the episcopal manors.

Late Medieval Winchester

In 1348, the Black Death came to Winchester, and it was to revisit the city on a number of occasions up until the 18th century. It is thought that on its first visitation the city's population was cut by half. If Winchester had entered a period of gentle decline some 150 years before, this was to make it worse. Other factors were certainly involved, most importantly the economic disruption caused by the Hundred Years War with France, and later the Wars of the Roses, interspersed with a succession of poor harvests. There were bright periods, so decline was more akin to a roller-coaster ride than a nose-dive. By the end of the period, the city's medieval industrial base had largely collapsed and the main economic activity was the buying and selling of agricultural produce.

Sometime after 1350 the Norman west front of the Cathedral, with its two towers, was demolished and replaced with the west window in the Perpendicular style by Bishop Edington. The rebuilding continued under William of Wykeham who remodelled the nave in the Perpendicular style that we see today.

In contrast to the great works on the major ecclesiastical and religious houses, by the end of the 14th century half the parish churches in and around the town were deserted or ruined, although those churches that survive show signs of rebuilding and refurbishment in the Decorated and Perpendicular styles.

The decrease in the population appears to have resulted in changes to properties and buildings. For example, the manor of Godbegot was broken up into smaller units and let out. This subdivision was repeated in several of the city's larger tenements, suggesting the crowding together of poorer people in places once reserved for the wealthy. A similar fate befell John de Tytyng's house on Upper Brook Street. Built in 1299 by one of the city's wealthiest cloth merchants, by 1354 it had been divided into three. One part was occupied by Hugh le Cran, a prominent merchant and Mayor of the Winchester Staple, while in the same building lived the families of the poor and destitute. This may suggest that initially the Black Death was a levelling influence on society, though other factors were at play. John de Tytyng's house was demolished by 1377, the principal reason being the return of flooding to the greater part of the low-lying areas of the city. Therefore, much of the population shift may just have been the result of poor people seeking higher ground. There was still wealth in the city, for houses like Blue Boar in St John's Street, Chesil Rectory in Chesil Street and Godbegot in the High Street were all built after the Black Death and before 1500. Nevertheless, it is the population figures that tell the story. By 1525 there may have been as few as 3,500 people living in Winchester, the lowest number since the days of Alfred the Great.

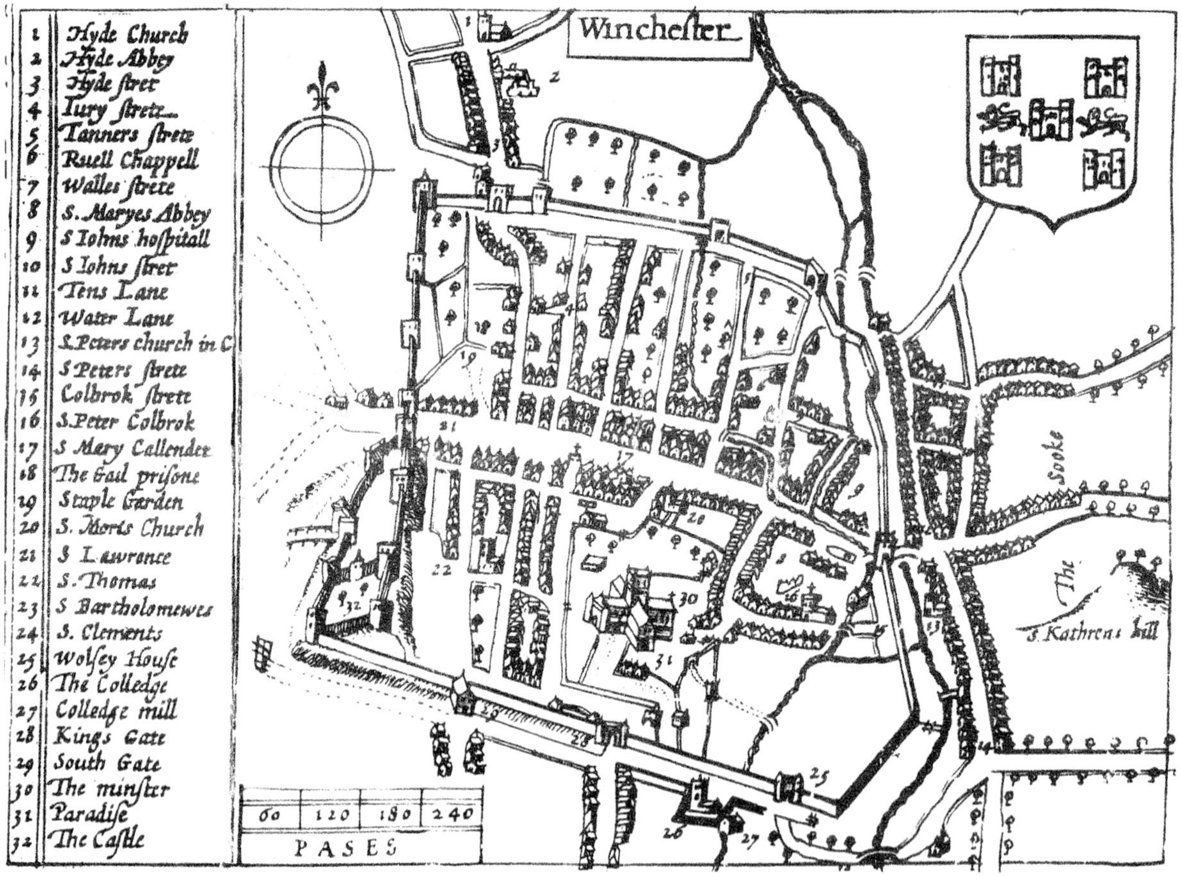

Speed's Map, 1611

Figure 9

16th and 17th century Winchester

The 16th to 18th centuries brought major changes to the city, not only to the topography, but also to the religious and political landscape. By the end of the 18th century the city was to re-emerge as something quite different – rather than a vibrant industrial medieval city, it became a gentrified town. Three important documents graphically show Winchester's early modern appearance – Speed's Map of 1610 (**Figure 9**), Buck's Eastern Prospect of 1736 (**Figure 10**) and Godson's Map of 1750 (**Figure 11**). Each tells the same story, one of a city at the end of a period of decline with glimmers of hope for the future.

Speed's map is the earliest depiction of the post-Black Death and post-Reformation city. Although there are a number of inaccuracies, generally it represents a fair picture. It shows the transition between the medieval and early modern city. The castle and city defences appear in good condition whereas the once extensive western suburb had all but disappeared. The southern and northern suburbs had contracted, the latter to its Late Saxon limits. The exception to this was the Soke of the eastern suburb where the bishop's patronage and interest ensured a degree of prosperity.

Within the walls, the effects of the Reformation of the mid 16th century and the dissolution of the city's monasteries can clearly be seen. Some of the abandoned areas south of the High Street equate with the dissolution of St Mary's Abbey, while the Cathedral medieval cloisters have been removed. The medieval bishop's palace of Wolvesey was by now abandoned and in ruins, and is not even shown.

North of the High Street, the Friars Minor and Black Friars, together with the houses of the Austin Friars and the Carmelites were dissolved in 1538 and their former sites lay abandoned. Their lands and possessions were all granted to Winchester College in 1543.

However, it is the absence of housing on the northern end of the streets that reveals the story. In the low-lying areas, occupation had retreated to the island. On the western side of the city, the former wool staple on Staple Gardens was by now the city's dumping ground.

The majority of the monastic buildings of the Cathedral Priory – Great Cloister, Little Cloister, Chapter House, Dorter, Infirmary, Almonry – were all demolished in the years after the Dissolution. Of the few original buildings that survive, the best-preserved is Pilgrims' Hall, thought to have originally served as the priory guest-house. Now partially incorporated with the late 17th/early 18th century Pilgrims' School building, it comprises a mid-14th century timber-framed hall with an important 3-bay hammer beam roof, reputedly the earliest such roof so far identified. The medieval Priors Lodge, now the Deanery, adjacent to the south side of the Great Cloister, was largely rebuilt in the 17th-century.

After its dissolution, Hyde Abbey and its holdings were granted to Thomas Wriothesley in 1538, who caused their immediate destruction and sale. Eventually William Bethell built a fine townhouse on the site, including courtyards and gardens extending east to the river meadows. His complex utilised the 15th century gatehouse as a grand entrance.

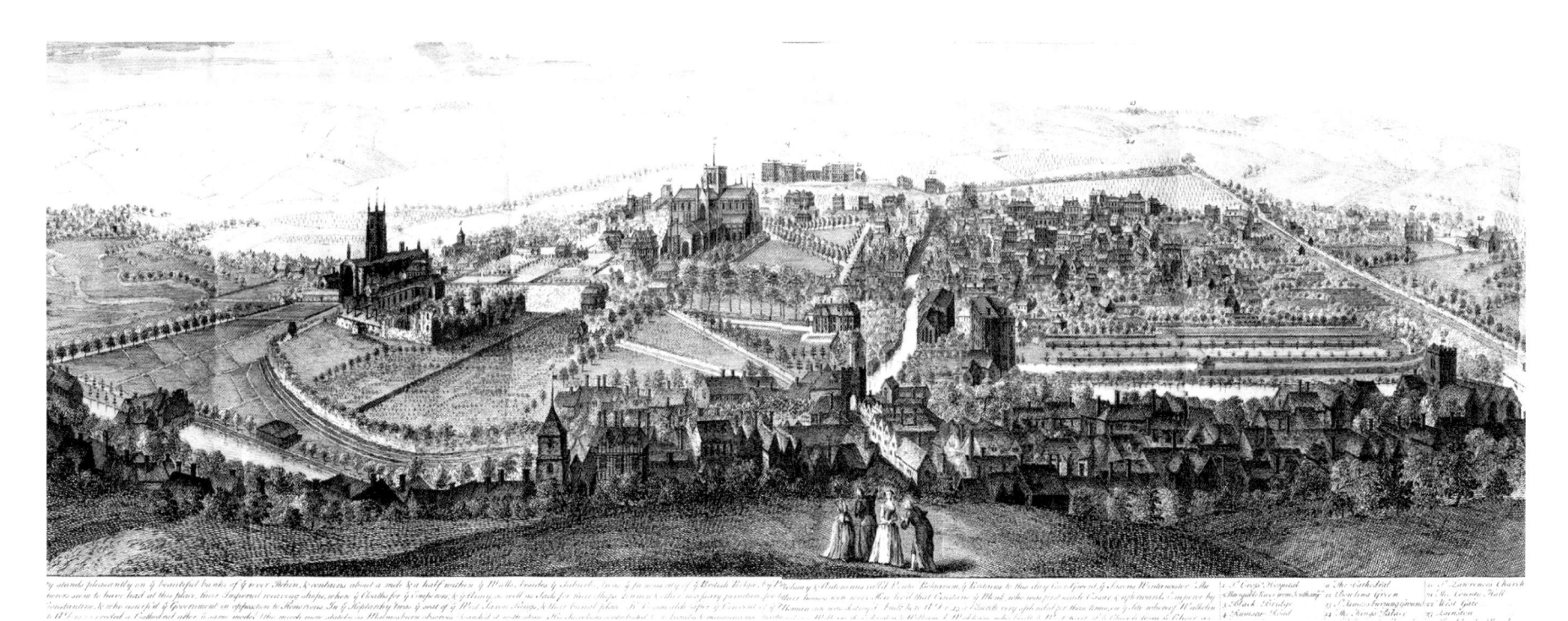

Bucks' Eastern Prospect of Winchester, 1736

Figure 10

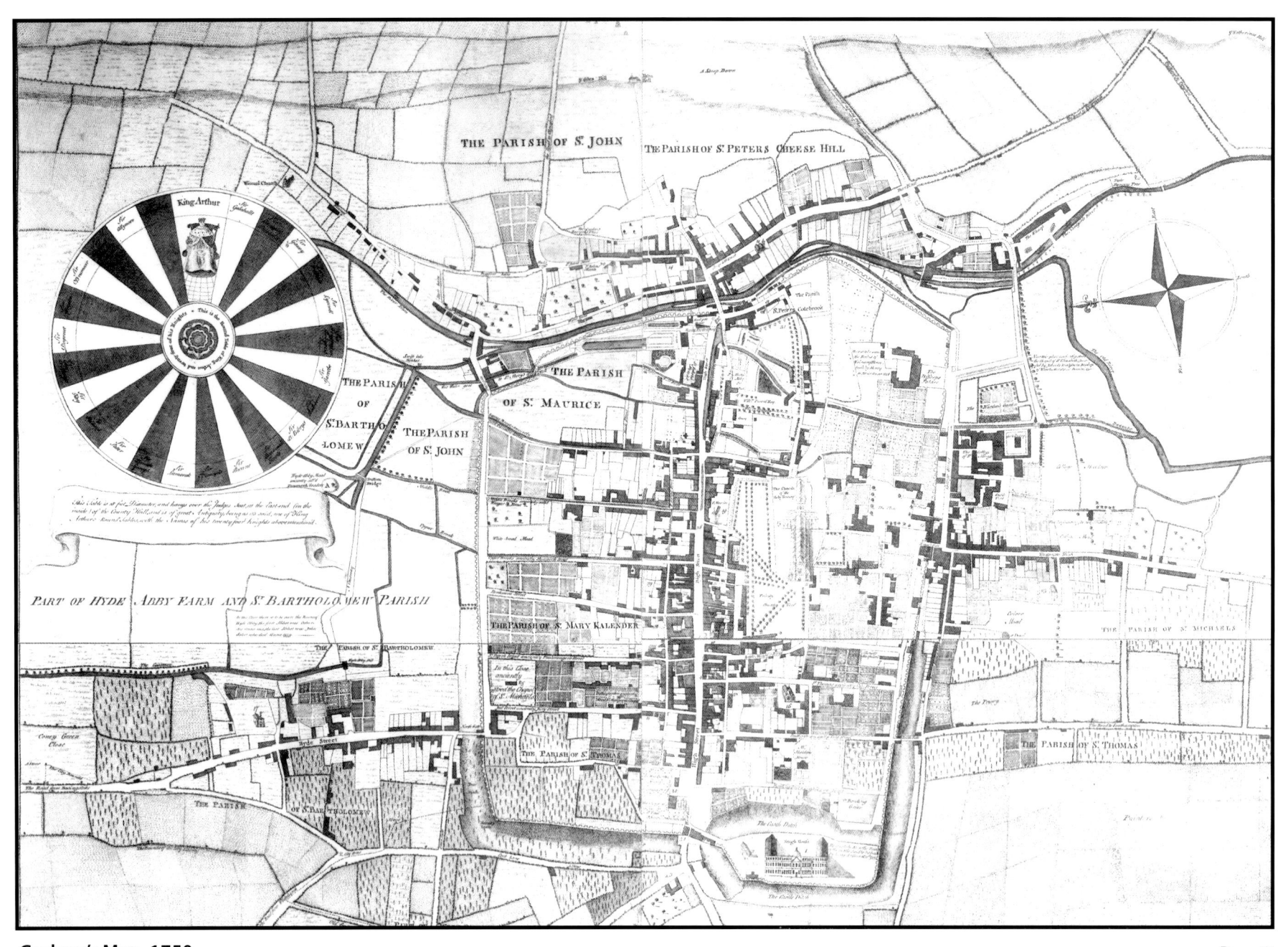

Godson's Map, 1750

Figure 11

The wedding of Mary Tudor to Philip II of Spain in Winchester Cathedral in 1554 brought short-lived prosperity, and the City Corporation benefited from Mary's grant of the former monastic properties in the city. Fine Tudor houses were built, including Moberly's House on Kingsgate Street, showing Renaissance influence, William Bethell's Hyde House, on the former site of Hyde Abbey, the Mason family's Eastgate House on the former Black Friars site, 26-7 St Swithun's Street, Avebury House in St Peter's Street, and Abbey House in the Broadway. Within the Cathedral precincts, 9 The Close was built of stone quarried from the ruined conventual buildings, whilst 1 and 11 The Close were constructed in brick.

The 17th century saw further changes. During the Civil War, the castle was a Royalist stronghold. The Parliamentarians captured the city in 1642 but it was retaken by the Royalists in 1643. The town and castle finally surrendered to Oliver Cromwell in October 1645, after suffering great damage. Soon after, the castle was blown up with gunpowder. The Cathedral suffered hugely at the hands of the Parliamentarians, who caused great damage to the fittings of the church, and destroyed the library. Many of the surviving medieval churches also fared badly under the Protectorate (1649-60).

It was during this period that the city's poor health conditions were first mentioned. Visitors were warned that they might suffer 'a sharp, but short fever'. The Great Plague of 1666 devastated the industrial and commercial life of the city. The plague victims were buried in communal graves to the south of St Catherine's Hill.

At the south end of Sussex Street is one of the city's great social monuments. On it stands an obelisk recording the community's response to the Great Plague, and in many ways reveals how contemporary Wintonians viewed themselves. Two local societies took it upon themselves to raise funds to care for the orphaned children. One was the Society of Natives, made up of prominent local people. The other was the Society of Aliens, made up of people who originated from as far away as Alresford.

There were some new additions to the city. The castle had been demolished and in its place stood Charles II's palace, known as the King's House (1683). Designed by Sir Christopher Wren to rival Louis XIV's palace of Versailles, the original plan was to clear housing to create an avenue between it and the west front of the cathedral. The character of Winchester today would be very different if Charles had not died before the building works were completed, and if his successors had chosen Winchester instead of London as their principal residence. But this was not to be, and this 'fine house on the hill' lay empty. The King's House served as a prison for French soldiers from 1757 to 1764, and again for French and Spanish prisoners from 1778 to 1785. From 1792 to 1796, it housed refugee clergy from the French Revolution.

The bishop's new baroque palace of Wolvesey (1680's) had also now appeared. Once based round a courtyard, it was soon neglected and today only the west wing survives.

18th century Winchester

A more detailed map of Winchester was published by William Godson in 1750 (**Figure 10**) depicting a city in a period of quiet prosperity and economic growth. Where it can be compared with other evidence, it appears to be highly accurate. In many ways, it shows the city in a similar state to that shown by Speed, but major differences reveal that the city had entered the early modern era.

During this time the city's defences were largely removed. Eastgate was taken down in 1768, closely followed by the north and south gates in 1771. Soon much of the circuit was demolished, and the raw materials were reused in other constructions. The suburbs were still in a depressed state.

Within the walls, the large expanses of open ground were used as gardens and orchards. To the west were extensive hop gardens, a reminder of the importance of the brewing industry, and that the city's water supplies were unfit to drink.

During this period, civic amenities appeared. The Guildhall (now Lloyds TSB Bank) was built in the High Street by 1713. The first hospital in Winchester occupied a site in Colebrook Street from 1736-1754, before moving to Parchment Street. The Theatre Royal dates to the 1780s, and Milner's Chapel in St Peter's Street dates to the end of the century (1792). The city was becoming a military centre, as the King's House was in use as a barracks by 1796.

The centuries of population decline and economic hardship had taken their toll on the city. As we have seen, the abandonment of the low-lying areas resulted in the crowding of higher and dryer areas. To see how poor economic conditions moulded the character of the city, we can return to the High Street. Earlier we considered how the economic and social dynamics of the medieval city created the Pentice. Look at the north side of the High Street and you will find something quite different. These buildings, at the commercial heart of the city, were not originally built to serve as banks, gameshops, or coffeehouses, but as fine townhouses. This is an indicator of the state of Winchester's social and economic condition. Indeed, in social and structural terms one can ask how different was late 18th century Winchester from the Late Roman *Venta*.

19th century Winchester

This was a period of great change in Winchester as elsewhere in the country. The population, estimated to be about 5,000 at the beginning of the century, had soared to about 19,000 by 1881. The earliest phase occurred as a result of the Enclosure Acts, carried out mostly between 1760 and 1830, which forced the dispossessed rural poor into the city and the only available space to accommodate them was long-abandoned low-lying areas of the city. The poor-quality housing made available to them resulted in conditions more medieval than modern. The second phase occurred following the arrival of the London – Southampton railway in 1839. Winchester was also connected directly to the Midlands at Chesil station on the Southampton, Newbury and Didcot line in 1885. The coming of the railways led to an increasing population, with many choosing to live in the city's newly created suburbs. By 1910 the suburbs extended far beyond their medieval limits.

Economic conditions improved, creating light industries in the form of brewing, soft drinks manufacture, bakeries, milling and small iron foundries, printing, electricity and gas works. A large wool warehouse was built close to the market behind the High Street. The railways also paved the way for the start of tourism in Winchester. A major photographic studio was set up in St Michael's Road and Warrens, a local printer, produced many guides. Accommodation for commercial travellers such as the Carfax and Eagle Hotels sprang up close to the station.

It was a period of rapid growth of working class housing in terraced form built together with associated public houses, shops and primary schools. Several new churches were built to serve the spiritual needs of the new population (St Thomas, St Martin Winnall, Holy Trinity, Christ Church, St Maurice, St Paul's, All Saints Highcliffe) together with Non-Conformist chapels (Congregational Church, Wesleyan and Methodist Chapels, the Baptist church and the Salvation Army Hall).

A workhouse was built at St Paul's and a new Winchester prison on Romsey Road by the middle of the century. These were followed by a new hospital designed by Butterfield in 1868 and West Downs school on Romsey Road. The first St Swithun's girls' school opened in Southgate Street in 1884, before moving to North Walls.

Such a population explosion required the continual implementation of modern amenities – a new cemetery at St James' Lane, pavements, piped water from a reservoir on Romsey Road, drainage and sanitation. As the central Brooks area became very unhealthy, a political struggle between the 'Muckabites' and the 'anti-Muckabites' supported by Winchester College and Dean Garnier went on from 1857 to 1875. Finally, a new trunk sewer connected to a pumping station was built at Garnier Road, to lift effluent to St Catherine's Hill for treatment by gravity. With the Brooks no longer used for the removal of effluent, they were buried in culverts below the streets to serve as storm drains.

In the 1870s, Winchester College went through a major expansion with new boarding houses in the Christchurch Road area. Notable public or rather grander private buildings were introduced – the Corn Exchange in 1836-8, almshouses at the Broadway, terraced houses at Chernocke Place, Southgate Street, St James' Terrace (1840-50s), Eastgate Street, the Market Hall (1857), Diocesan Training College, King Alfred's College (1862), the new Guildhall (1873) and the County Council buildings on Castle Hill (1895). The Barracks square was rebuilt after a fire wrecked the King's House in 1894.

In 1878 the Winchester Corporation bought land on St Giles' Hill for a 'pleasure ground' and planted trees on what had been a bare chalk hillside. This began the extension of the tree planting on higher ground that was to make the distinctive settings for Winchester conservation area in the next century.

20th century Winchester

In 1901 the statue of King Alfred by Hamo Thornycroft was erected in the Broadway at a millennial celebration, arousing interest in Anglo-Saxon history and attracting national donations. This was admired by a community numbering 21,702 according to the census figures of that year. The city created a recreation ground on the watermeadows at North Walls Park that included boating, and in 1903 erected the first purpose-built Museum in the Square.

In 1905 it was discovered that the foundations of the Cathedral were inadequate, leading the Dean and Chapter to search for national funding to save many parts from collapse. The rescue was a technical feat, completed in 1912 and celebrated by a Royal visit.

The Great War took a heavy toll of Winchester men and afterwards public housing estates, on the Garden City model, were built on ecclesiastical ground at Stanmore (1920) and Highcliffe (1926). The economic depression that followed stifled radical changes and led to the decay of older properties. However, in 1928 St Peter's Roman Catholic church was erected and the first large-scale stores (Woolworth's, Marks & Spencer) were opened in the High Street together with a bus station opposite the Guildhall.

Nationally Winchester was seen as a bottleneck for traffic bound for Southampton's port and the City Council pressed for western and eastern bypasses in 1938. A dual carriageway by-pass was built around St Catherine's Hill, with a landmark concrete bridge where it cut through the eastern ridge. This, and the widening of Southgate Street where it joined the High Street, the linking of Little Minster Street and St Thomas's Street, and a set back building line on the radial roads, presaged the problems associated with the domination of the car in the second half of the century.

Although the by-pass proved useful in preparations for D-Day, Winchester suffered little damage in World War II, apart from the self inflicted loss of many cast-iron railings.

In 1946, the City Council commissioned Sir Patrick Abercrombie to draw up plans for the redevelopment of much of the eastern end of Winchester. This had the aim of 'eliminating slums' by depopulating the north eastern corner of the city, in many ways returning it to its post-Roman and post-Black Death condition. Industry was resited further out, adjacent to the railway lines at Bar End and Winnall, adjusting the town to the needs of the motor car, opening up the river, and making the Cathedral more visible to motorists from the east.

The plan led to the demolition of many historic buildings, the creation of the car parks behind Marks & Spencer and the Guildhall, and many open sites throughout the city. For the first time in 1000 years, the late Saxon street system was altered by the insertion of new streets into the ancient pattern at Friarsgate and Cross Street. This was followed by the widening of St George's Street in 1953 (and part of the Jewry Street / High Street corner containing the George Hotel) as a bypass for the narrow High Street. It was complemented in the west by Hampshire County Council which built Queen Elizabeth II Court in 1959 enabling traffic to bypass the Westgate. A new Barclays Bank followed in 1960 on the High Street / Jewry Street corner, and a new School of Art and swimming baths were built at North Walls Park.

A number of small garages, to serve the needs of the motor car, developed in Southgate Street, St Cross Road, St Thomas Street, St Swithun's Street, Staple Gardens and Hyde Street.

Frank Cottrill, the museum curator, extracted what information he could about Winchester's past with very slender resources, as he tried to keep pace with building demolition work. But when in 1960 it was proposed to build the Wessex Hotel overlooking the Cathedral, to capitalise on the new tourist potential from America, it proved to be a key to unlock a new approach to archaeology in the city. A collaboration between Roger Quirke (who had researched the likely position of the Saxon predecessors to the Norman Cathedral), Trust Houses Ltd, the Ministry of Works and the City Council led to systematic excavations on the site under the direction of Martin Biddle. He introduced people with a variety of natural science skills to his team and this pioneering work revealed the enormous potential for the study of the evolution of Winchester as an urban community.

In 1962 the Winchester Excavations Committee was set up to undertake a 10 year programme of enquiry. This programme capitalised on the facts that the Assize Courts adjacent to the Great Hall were to be rebuilt, the offices of Hampshire County Council were to be greatly extended on the line of the western city wall, 29 acres of the Brooks redeveloped, and plans being prepared for the construction of a three-quarter ring road for the city.

Martin Biddle summarised the programme achievement as follows:

'During these years the Iron Age enclosure was defined and dated. The Roman defences were investigated in detail at five points, areas of the Roman town thoroughly examined for the first time including several streets, part of the Forum, a Temple, five town houses and a number of other buildings. The Anglo-Saxon Cathedral (The Old Minster) was fully excavated apart from the part underlying the present Cathedral. The New Minster was identified and its later buildings explored. The Royal castle was excavated at its northern end, and the Bishop's Palace completely explored. In addition, 20 parish churches, 3 chapels and 12 medieval houses were uncovered. More important perhaps was the demonstration that the street plan of medieval and modern Winchester derived from a deliberate act of urban refoundation in the later ninth century. All told 19 sites were investigated over eleven years at a total cost of £149,811 with the help of 3000 volunteers from 29 countries.'

This fieldwork programme was complemented by the creation of the Winchester Research Unit to process the data and back it up it by detailed studies of the extensive surviving documentary sources. This resulted in the publication of a series of research studies by the Oxford University Press.

In 1972, the City Council recognised that the work of recording Winchester's past must continue, by the appointment of a City Rescue Archaeologist. In 1976 Hyde House and Barn were converted into the Historic Resources Centre to house the museum and research staff, as well as records of all sites and artefacts from the excavations.

With the electrification of the railway to London in the 1960s making daily commuting viable, and the expansion of the suburbs north (Harestock), east (Winnall) and south west (Stanmore, Oliver's Battery, Badger Farm), archaeological excavations continued apace on numerous small sites, mainly in the historic suburbs. Major excavations were undertaken on Winnall and Twyford Down, the Nunnaminster, the site of the Brooks shopping centre in 1986 (visited by 75,000 people) and between 1995 and 2001 a series of community excavations at Hyde Abbey, and Oram's Arbour.

In 1962 the City Council also commissioned the Garten Report into which streets and buildings were crucial to the architectural character of Winchester. This led to one of the first UK town scheme partnerships between central and local government, to make substantial grants for the repair of listed buildings. The scheme, which ran for 30 years, rescued buildings like Chesil church, the Old Blue Boar, Gilberts bookshop, 35-36 the Pentice, 106-107 High Street, St John's House, and repaired many other buildings and walls in the Cathedral Close and other streets.

Post-war development introduced buildings with a far bigger floor area and scale into the urban fabric of the streets than in previous centuries, and steel and concrete frames made possible flat roofs (which were seen as a way of keeping down scale). Where concrete was exposed as a frame in the Police Headquarters, the Casson building in St George's Street, and the tower flats at Winnall, or even more as prefabricated cladding as in Ashburton Court, it was disliked. The new large multi-storey car parks that were built in the 1970-80s set quite new architectural and townscape problems adjacent to historic buildings.

In 1967 the County Council introduced a town centre plan which included two major elements. Firstly, a refined (from 1964) dual carriageway three-quarter road system down City Road, North Walls and Eastgate Street was proposed, to satisfy the traffic problems that were being fuelled by the demand for parking space for the shops and new office buildings. Secondly, a conservation area designation was drawn tightly round the listed buildings in the central area, with Hyde and St Cross as separate entities. In the 1980s Winchester Barracks was moved out to Littleton.

The ring road proposals included the demolition of all the properties on the north side of North Walls and the east side of Eastgate Street, a roundabout over the river Itchen behind the City Mill, cutting through St John's Street on the way to the Chesil station site, and a link from Durngate to the A34 at Winnall, with surface car parks on the watermeadows. When detailed attempts were made to implement these plans, objections were so strong that they were abandoned, thereby releasing land and property for investment. New movement and access proposals were substituted on an incremental basis resulting in the central one-way system, and leading eventually to the park-and-ride system, starting at Bar End, an idea first mentioned at a meeting in 1969.

At the same time, negotiations were going on for the route of the M3 past Winchester connecting into the A34 Kingsworthy link. The original proposal would have cut St Catherine's Hill off from the watermeadows by eight lanes of traffic and a huge whaleback south of St Cross to get over the railway. There was great opposition to this, with Public Enquiries in 1975 and again in 1987-88 into the final route using a cutting through Twyford Down. Despite national protests, this route, preceded by extensive archaeological investigations on Bronze Age, Iron Age and Romano-British sites, was implemented in 1990. The sewage disposal plant was relocated and modernised, finally eliminating the unpleasant smells that affected Highcliffe and Bar End.

The landscape over the old Winchester bypass was restored to its pre-1938 form, reuniting St Catherine's Hill with the city and incorporating a serious attempt to restore the chalk downland ecology.

The motorway has increased pressure for large shopping and industrial developments with uncharacteristic neon signs close to the northern junction at Winnall. The southern junction puts the future of Bushfield Camp and the unique setting of St Cross in the balance.

Following a city planning brief in 1985, the Crown Commissioners initiated the redevelopment of the Barracks in 1990, with a high-density classical scheme that included private underground car parking on the Lower Barracks. A serious attempt was made by the Planning Authority to house the increasing number of students at King Alfred's College and Winchester School of Art in the listed buildings of the Upper Barracks. This would have complemented the large open Barracks square, and a proposed new City Museum on the eastern side would have done greater justice to the wealth of material in its collections. Both sets of proposals failed for financial reasons. In 1996 'SAVE' spearheaded a campaign to value the complete Victorian Barracks. A lower-density conservation scheme designed by architect Huw Thomas was implemented by private developers that incorporated a formal landscape scheme on the parade ground, preserving the underlying archaeology. This led to a new residential campus for King Alfred's College being built on the playing fields of West Downs School on Romsey Road and a curved terrace of student accommodation for the School of Art on the disused railway line at Winnall.

The pressure continues to intensify development in the built-up parts of the city rather than damaging the historic landscape setting. The information gained from the archaeological exploration of the city is increasingly feeding through into museum displays, and into literature. Importantly, the Council is currently developing policies and strategies which recognise the importance of the city's past and the need for the active management and protection of this non-renewable resource.

Future Research and Enquiry

Winchester is one of England's most archaeologically investigated cities. The city is also blessed with a number of very detailed medieval surveys and other documentary sources. The combination of the data from these sources has enabled scholars to build up, over the past 50 years or so, a fairly full picture of the development and history of the city. However, this picture is still, and will always be, incomplete.

In general there is more information required to fill in the gaps in our knowledge and understanding of everyday life in all of these communities throughout the centuries. Each new item of information, be it recovered from either archaeological investigation or documentary research, adds to the overall picture The following significant gaps remain in our knowledge and understanding of the prehistoric, Roman, Saxon and medieval periods.

Prehistoric

Although we are clear that the Roman town was preceded by a large Iron Age enclosure (Oram's Arbour), there is still much that we do not know:

Where precisely was the line of the eastern defences of the enclosure, and how were they constructed?

What was the nature, extent, and duration of the occupation inside the enclosure?

When precisely was the enclosure constructed and how long did it survive?

What was its relationship to the apparently contemporary hillfort on St Catherine's Hill?

Roman

The location and layout of the Roman town of *Venta Belgarum* is well understood, but:

Was there an early Roman military garrison in Winchester, before the civilian settlement was established? If so, where was the garrison located? What was its nature and extent?

What was the reason for the salient in the southwest corner of the urban defences?

How was the town supplied with clean water?

What were the locations of some important public buildings, common to all Roman towns – public baths, religious temples, amphitheatre?

Post-Roman

We are woefully short of any information about the period between c410-650 – almost any new data will give further insight on any aspect of the settlement and occupation of the town in this period.

Saxon & Medieval – Royal Palace

The Saxon and Norman Royal residence, close to the town centre, is known virtually from documentary sources alone. We know practically nothing of the precise location of the palace, its buildings and their configuration.

Medieval Friaries

These religious houses in general are poorly understood, Their sites are known, but except for the Austin Friars, whose site was partially excavated recently, we have precious little knowledge and understanding of the arrangements of these complexes, their buildings etc.

It seems likely that only further archaeological excavation and research will be able to provide the answers to these and to other questions about the detailed development of many aspects of Winchester's complex and absorbing past. It is hoped that the tremendous advances in the understanding of the origins and growth of the ancient city made largely since the Second World War, will continue for the foreseeable future.

The Pentice   The Buttercross   Passage to The Square   Little Minster Street

How to make a space of a real architectural quality in an unpromising space between two three-storey buildings. Royal Hotel, entrance from St Peter Street

Gazetteer of Interiors

CELLARS

St John's undercroft, The Broadway

Many of these are not generally accessible to the public but may open on special occasions.

11th century: The crypt of the Cathedral, 1078; stone vaults supported on round columns and a well. There are cellars associated with the Norman palace under the Square.

13th century: No 10 The Close; vaulted stone undercroft of the cellarer's wing of the old monastic building.

St John's undercroft, the Broadway.

14th century: Arched stone cellar under the Vine public house, No 8 Great Minster Street. Stone barrel-vaulted cellar with two double-mullioned stone windows and Tudor-arched door, in the Rising Sun public house, Bridge Street (originally the prison of the Bishop's Court). Vaulted cellar under the Brothers' dining hall at St Cross.

17th century: Long, brick, barrel-vaulted cellar under Nos 40/41 High Street, containing a good contemporary stone fireplace and doorway.

Brick-arched cellar under the south wing of Avebury House, No 8 St Peter Street, with access door from the street. Also a brick-arched cellar under No 27 St Swithun Street.

BUILDINGS AND FURNISHINGS
11th century:
North and south transepts of the Cathedral (1079-1093), built by Bishop Walkelin. They give a good idea of the rugged character of the original Norman Cathedral.

Holy Sepulchre Chapel under the tower in the Cathedral with original wall paintings of 1180, uncovered in 1963; they show the deposition and entombment of Jesus.

12th century:
St Cross chapel, built by Henri de Blois, with powerful columns, carved Norman window openings, and good stained glass.

Two-bay stone undercroft to the south wing of No 24 St Thomas Street, believed to have been originally used as a mint, with room above altered in Tudor times with magnificent stone fireplace, mullioned windows and panelling.

13th century:

The retrochoir of the Cathedral (1189-1204), built by Godfrey de Lucy in Early English style, with large areas of medieval floor tiles (c. 1260).

The Great Hall of the Castle, built by Henry III in 1232-40, and the Round Table of c. 1270.

The lower room of St John's House, the Broadway, with deep-set lancet windows and niches from its original use as a hospital.

14th century:

Pilgrims' Hall, The Close, 1300. Three bays of a larger building which was the Prior's guest house. This contains one of the earliest hammer-beam roofs, decorated with carved heads.

Stone entrance portico to the Deanery, 1385, now supporting stone Tudor wing.

The Westgate, a remodelling of an earlier structure with 13th century windows to first floor room; commands wonderful view down the High Street.

Choir stalls, 1308, under the Cathedral tower, with splendid carving of upper panels and misericords.

Winchester College Chamber Court 1387-94, with fine stone-vaulted gateway and excellent pair of oak doors with carved detail.

Winchester College Chapel of six bays, noted for its wooden lierne-vaulted ceiling, a forerunner of stone fan-vaulting, with some medieval glass.

Winchester College cloisters behind the Chapel. 132 feet square with open wagon-roof using two centred arches.

Winchester College first-floor dining hall and buttery; original long oak tables.

Nave of the Cathedral, 1394-1410. Perpendicular period remodelling by Bishops Edington and Wykeham; a wonderful set of ceiling bosses.

The Brothers' dining hall at St Cross. Five-bay arch-braced roof complete with minstrels' gallery on top of a screened passage linked to a complete kitchen; simple stained glass; staircase with a wounded pelican symbol at east end.

Blue Boar Inn, St John's Street. A good example of a timber-framed merchant's hall of 1380 with crown-post roof and side gallery.

15th century:

Fromond's Chantry, 1435, built into the centre of the cloisters behind Winchester College Chapel. Built of stone with lierne-vault ceiling decorated with good roof bosses supporting a lovely room above.

St Lawrence church in the Square with a wide-span king-post roof.

Cardinal Beaufort's great stone entrance tower of 1450 for the Master of St Cross, and the long line of stone almshouses.

Chesil Rectory. A two-bay timber-framed structure on two floors, now a restaurant.

St John's church, St John's Street. Interior with crown-post roof, carved timber rood screens and stained-glass east windows incorporating important 13th century south window and fragments of 13th century wall paintings; flint tower encloses a fine interior room of dressed stone.

Timber framed tower of St Peter Chesil, Chesil Street, a complete contrast to St John's stone-and-flint tower.

Presbytery of the Cathedral altered to form its present vaulted roof and decorated bosses; great stone reredos behind the high altar (1455-73.) (The remains of the original statues damaged by the Puritans are now in the Triforium Gallery.)

St Swithun's church above the 14th century Kingsgate; windows from 1500.

Chapel of Wolvesey Palace with five-light east window and three-light south windows all Perpendicular style.

16th century:

Lady Chapel of the Cathedral rebuilt c. 1500 contains contemporary wall paintings.

Chantry of Bishop Gardiner, the last Catholic Bishop of Winchester, on the north side of the high altar; an amazing hybrid of late English Gothic and Renaissance style.

No 62 Canon Street; probably a 16th century hall converted in 17th century, with massive chimney stack, panelled interior on ground and first floor, and twisting back staircase.

No 36 Middle Brook Street; a small timber-framed hall building, with added 17th century chimney stack and fireplace, and 17th century wall painting in the front room.

Nos 33 and 34 High Street; a pair of timber-framed buildings which can be appreciated by looking upwards inside the shops. No 33 has a good set of 17th century panelled features upstairs.

The Soke, Chesil Street; a large timber framed 'E' shaped house completed by 1583, with staircases at either end and tall chimney stacks. It is the oldest continuously inhabited building in the conservation area; Sir Thomas Fleming, one of the judges on the western circuit who presided over the trial of the conspirators in the Gunpowder Plot, lived here. A modern front was added in the 18th century.

Godbegot House, High Street; an impressive timber-framed building, originally subdivided into smaller units; the first-floor front room overlooking the High Street has a panelled interior behind the 20th century façade which replaced a Georgian rendered elevation.

17th century:
The Pilgrims' School, No 3 the Close, incorporating the southern bays of Pilgrims' Hall. The hall has a fine staircase with decorative ceiling; rear entrance door containing medieval stained-glass coats of arms.

The Priors Hall (Deanery), subdivided into three levels, the most important of which is the large 17th century room on the first floor reached via a grand staircase with richly carved balustrades.

Long Gallery built onto the east side of the Deanery by Bishop Morley with windows containing old stained glass.

Cathedral Library over the Slype at the end of the south transept; a vaulted room with oak bookcases with a carved cornice and vase finials, created by Bishop Morley; two thousand of his books replace the library destroyed during the Commonwealth; contains the medieval illuminated Winchester Bible.

Wolvesey Palace built by Bishop Morley, 1680; the one remaining wing with a set of grand domestic interiors lit by original 17th century cross windows.

No 11, the Close: a fine late 17th century staircase with richly carved panels and adjoining panelled rooms.

School, Winchester College, 1687: plaster ceiling, panelling, Renaissance windows and chandeliers of 1724.

Hyde Abbey House, Hyde Street (exterior modernised, 18th century) contains good 17th century staircase and panelling with a heavily decorated plaster ceiling with birds and scrolls, brought in from elsewhere.

No 9 Parchment Street; sequence of panelled rooms around entrance hall and staircase.

The Vine public house, No 8 St Thomas Street; open-well staircase and first-floor room with oak panelling.

No 21 St Thomas Street behind the graveyard; interior with panelled rooms and staircase leading from the entrance hall; attic with 17th century diamond-pane casement windows.

Avebury House, St Peter Street, 1690; entrance hall with Corinthian columns.

18th century:
The Hotel du Vin, No 14 Southgate Street, 1715; part-panelled interior.

Serle's House, built in 1730 for William Sheldon in the English Baroque style, with its original entrance in Bowling Green Alley (Gar Street); magnificent staircase set within the entrance hall.

No 12 Southgate Street; fine entrance hall and staircase, panelled rooms with 17th century open-well staircase.

Winchester City Mill reconstructed in 1746 using earlier timbers; contains a working water wheel.

Mulberry House, St Thomas Street; entrance leads through to a grand staircase lit by an arched window.

Wickham House, No 12 St Thomas Street; rooms on a square plan, some panelled, with south view onto a delightful walled garden.

St John's Rooms, the Broadway; first-floor 18th century banqueting hall with twin fireplaces, decorative plaster surrounds for large paintings (no longer there, having been moved to the Guildhall) and five replica brass chandeliers of 18th century Dutch design. Early sash windows command view of Abbey House.

Abbey House, the Broadway; a fine staircase hall and set of panelled rooms containing many interesting paintings.

St John's Croft, St John's Street; a gentleman's house with original stone-floored larder; one of the few Venetian windows in Winchester commanding a view of an 18th century summerhouse with Regency style windows and glazed door. It still has an attached stable block and a wonderful southern view to St Catherine's Hill.

Milner Hall, St Peter Street (back land): an early example of Gothic revival design by London architect John Carter for the Roman Catholic Church.

One of the rare survivors of Winchester's manufacturing past. The 'loft' of the Royal Hotel, St Peter Street. There was a silk factory here until 1793. The windows are cast-iron.

19th century:
Chernocke House, No 34 Southgate Street, dated 1832; designed by Owen Browne Carter, architect and part of a terrace of four that has remained in domestic use, with Egyptian-style detail to the interiors.

St Bartholomew's church, Hyde; extended and remodelled from a Norman building; contains fine sculptured stone capitals from Hyde Abbey, 1130.

St John's Hospital South, designed by William Garbett, 1833; a first-floor boardroom with a fine window commanding the view up Eastgate Street; contains the oak chimney piece removed by Thomas Stopher from No 1 St Thomas Street.

United Church, Jewry Street, designed by W F Poulton, architect, 1853; octagonal plan with a central rooflight above.

Pumping Station, Garnier Road, of enormous importance to public health in Winchester and one of the few 19th century industrial buildings left.

Christ Church, Christchurch Road, designed by Ewan Christian, 1870; a vigorous Gothic interior containing wall paintings in the apsidal east end, now covered by curtains as part of a re-focusing on the new baptistery at the west end.

Winchester Guildhall, by Jeffrey & Skiller, 1873, in heavy late Flemish Gothic style. The ground floor toilets and their fittings are a reminder of Victorian public provision at its most practical, solid and spacious.

Meads Museum, Winchester College, by Basil Champneys, 1898; a flamboyant baroque design with a ground floor loggia with double Tuscan columns; first floor designed as a background to display artefacts.

20th century:
College Music School, Romans Road, by E S Prior, 1903/4; an unusual high space containing an organ; overlooked by a gallery giving access to smaller rooms. It now has a fine extension.

Winchester Theatre Royal, Jewry Street, 1914; created out of the Market Hotel; with decorative proscenium arch and decorative curved balconies and boxes.

War Memorial Cloister, Winchester College designed by Sir Herbert Baker, 1924;

courtyard building with open colonnade, remarkable for its decorative lettering and the integration of shields, symbols and memorials into a continuous wall design.

WHSmith, High Street, 1927; based on an early 20th century reinterpretation of an oak-framed barn, using metal tie rods and fixings, with a complete set of painted murals upstairs on the theme of King Alfred's life.

Lloyds Bank, Nos 49/50 High Street, by Sawyer Partnership; banking hall with plaster details; distinctive arched windows between Doric columns.

St Peter's Roman Catholic church, Jewry Street, by F A Walters, 1926; modern reinterpretation of a Gothic interior; contains a Romanesque door and a statue of Mary from the Magdalen almshouses, St Giles' Hill.

14th century brewhouse of Winchester College, converted into a library by Sir Herbert Baker in 1934 and extended in 1996; exploits the spaciousness of the brewhouse and its fine trusses.

Queen Elizabeth II Court, designed by Brandon Jones, 1959-60; excellent brick barrel vaults leading to carefully designed entrances incorporating sculpture and prominent columns with oak leaf plaster cornices to Chute and Wellington rooms, and some interesting pictures.

Barclays Bank, Jewry Street, by Curtis Green, 1960; a double-height banking hall, with classic detailed cornice.

New Hall, Winchester College, College Walk, by Peter Shepheard, 1961; school hall with 17th century oak panelling; a decorative ceiling incorporating lights is characteristic of the Festival of Britain 1951.

Law Courts, by Louis de Soissons, 1974; has a wide formal curving corridor linking the 19th century openings in the east wall of the Castle Great Hall with a window that captures one of the finest views of the west front of Winchester Cathedral.

Former Historic Resources Centre, Hyde Street, by Donald Insall, 1976; conversion of an 18th century barn and malthouse for storage of public archives, with display space between the kilns; incorporates a carved head and column details from Hyde Abbey, hidden in the stone walls.

St Thomas's church, Southgate Street, designed by E W Elmslie, 1845 in the decorated medieval style, and converted by Ove Arup in the 1970s for office use. Chunky concrete staircase and balconies inserted in central space provide unusual views of decorative features including stained glass.

Art School, Winchester College, designed by Edward Cullinan, 1980s; two 1870 Victorian buildings in French chateau style erected as a sanatorium, converted into an art school, with many interesting details, from the top-lit studios exposing king post trusses to the central exhibition space, lit by high-level gable windows.

Cathedral Visitor Centre, the Close, designed by architects Plincke Leaman & Browning, 1993; a carefully designed exposed steel structure with a light airy interior.

Hampshire County Record Office, designed by the County Architect's Department, 1993; a public building, providing archive storage to exacting conditions, with public and working zones that integrate glazed interior and exterior landscape spaces.

Hampshire Register Office, designed by the County Architect's Department, 1994; reorganisation of a run-down Victorian public house to create a double-height room for weddings, with distinctive furniture and a new high bay window with abstract glass designed by John Pasquali.

Further Reading

Most of these publications are available for reference at the Hampshire Archives and Local Studies collection at the Hampshire Record Office.

A History of Winchester by Barbara Carpenter Turner (Phillimore 1992)

A History of Winchester Streets: Unpublished Typescript from Manuscript compiled by Thomas Stopher, begun 1895

A Survey of Street Architecture by T D Atkinson (Warren & Son 1934)

Beauty or the Bulldozer? Peninsula Barracks (SAVE Britain's Heritage 1994)

Collected Information on Winchester City Mills by Tony Yoward (Hampshire Mills Group Archives 1998)

Durngate Mill by J Reynolds, C Burrell and D Bignell (Proceedings of the Hampshire Field Club, Vol. 24, 1967)

Excavations near Winchester Cathedral 1961 – 1968 by Martin Biddle (Wykeham Press 1969)

Glimpses of Hampshire History by Miles Hodnett (Jacob & Johnson 1992)

Hampshire and Isle of Wight (Buildings of England Series) by Nikolaus Pevsner and David Lloyd (Penguin 1967)

Hampshire Houses, 1250 – 1700: Their Dating and Development by Edward Roberts (Hampshire County Council 2003)

Hampshire Industrial Archaeology, a Guide edited by Monica Ellis (Southampton University Industrial Archaeology Group 1975)

Images of England From the Sollars Collection, Winchester by Bob Sollars and John Brimfield (Tempus 2001)

Initial Survey of Victorian Buildings in Winchester 1850 – 1914 by Michael Morris (Architects Journal 1987)

Medieval Hall Houses of the Winchester Area by Elizabeth Lewis, Edward Roberts and Kenneth Roberts (Winchester City Museums 1988)

Period House Fixtures and Fittings, 1300 – 1900 by Linda Hall (Countryside Books 2005)

Preliminary Report on Ancient and Historic Buildings and Buildings of Special Architectural Interest S J Garten (City of Winchester Jan 1962)

Publications on Winchester's Streets & Neighbourhoods (City of Winchester Trust Publications)

Roads to the Past: The Prehistoric Site at Easton Lane, Winchester by Peter Fasham and Richard Whinney (Trust for Wessex Archaeology, City of Winchester 1985)

St Catherine's Hill Winchester by C F C Hawkes (Proceedings of the Hampshire Field Club Vol. 11, Warren & Son 1930)

St Cross, England's Oldest Almshouse by Peter Hopewell (Phillimore 1995)

St Giles' Hill, Place in History by Hugh Watson (1996)

St John's Winchester Charity by Barbara Carpenter Turner (Phillimore 1992)

St Nicholas Church, North Stoneham by Norman Norris (Eastleigh and District Local History Society 1984)

St Swithun's School – A Centenary History by Priscilla Bain (Phillimore 1984)

The Art and Architecture of Owen Browne Carter 1806 – 1859 by Robin Freeman (Hampshire Papers 1991)

The Castle Winchester, Great Hall and Round Table by Martin Biddle and Beatrice Clayre (Hampshire County Council 2000)

The History of the Royal County Hospital by Barbara Carpenter Turner (Phillimore 1986)

The History of Winchester Cathedral by Frederick Bussby (Paul Cave 1976)

The Itchen Navigation by Edwin Course (Southampton University Industrial Archaeological Group 1983)

The Parish of Hyde by Rosalie F Pennell (H M Gilbert & Son 1909)

The Railways of Winchester by Kevin Robertson and Roger Simmonds (Platform 5 Publications 1988)

The Story of The Brooks, Winchester Archaeological Excavations 1987 – 1988 (Winchester Museums Service)

The Study of Winchester: Archaeology and History in a British Town Martin Biddle – Proceedings of the British Academy LXIX (Oxford University Press 1983)

The Wainscot Book: The Houses of Winchester Cathedral Close 1660 – 1800 by John Crook (Hampshire Record Series 1984)

Warrens Guides to Winchester (Warrens)

Winchester Illustrated: The City's Heritage in Prints and Drawings by Alan W Ball (Halsgrove 1999)

The Waterways of Winchester by Elizabeth Proudman (Winchester Preservation Trust Magazine, Spring editions 1994 and 1995)

The Winchester Diver: The Saving of a Great Cathedral by Ian Henderson and John Crook (Henderson/Stirk Ltd 1984)

The Winchester Guidebook: An Historical Guide for Visitors by Barry Shurlock (Ensign Publications 1990)

Winchester 100 years ago by Barbara Carpenter Turner (Paul Cave 1979)

Winchester: A Pictorial History by Tom Beaumont James (Phillimore 1993)

Winchester: An Architect's View by Peter Kilby (WIT Press 2002)

Winchester Cathedral by John Crook (Pitkin Guide 1998)

Winchester Cathedral 1079 – 1979 by Frederick Bussby (Paul Cave 1979)

Winchester Cathedral Close by T D Atkinson, Proceedings of Hampshire Field Club (Vol 15 1941)

Winchester City and Its Setting (Landscape Design Associates 1998)

Winchester College: After 600 Years, 1382 – 1982 by James Sabben-Clare (Paul Cave Publications 1981)

Winchester Excavations, 1949 – 1960 Vol. 1 by Barry Cunliffe (City of Winchester 1964)

Winchester: From Pre-history to the Present by Tom Beaumont Jarnes (English Heritage 1997)

Winchester Studies 1: Winchester in the Early Middle Ages by Martin Biddle (Oxford University Press 1976)

Winchester Studies 2: Survey of Medieval Winchester (two vols.) Derek Keene (Oxford University Press 1985)

Winchester, Yesterday and Today by John Barton (Halsgrove 1998)

Wolvesey – The Old Bishop's Palace, Winchester by Martin Biddle (English Heritage 1986)

Archaeology References:

A Report on the Treatment of the Administrative and Cathedral areas of the City of Winchester Sir Patrick Abercrombie and Richard Nickson (Corporation of the City of Winchester August 1946)

Historic Resources Centre for Winchester (Winchester City Council 1976)

Peninsula Barracks Winchester, conceptual master plan Reports by John Taylor of Chapman Taylor and Partners and Derek Lovejoy and Partners (The Crown Estate, the Secretary of State for Defence February 1990)

Preliminary Report on Ancient and Historic Buildings and Buildings of Special Architectural Interest S J Garten (City of Winchester Jan 1962)

Report upon the City of Winchester and Winchester and District Town Planning Scheme P H Warwick AMPT, City Engineer and Surveyor; Thomas Hall, Clerk (Winchester and District Town Planning Advising Committee, Guildhall Winchester July 1930)

The Jutes of Hampshire and Wight and the Origins of Wessex, in *The Origins of Anglo-Saxon Kingdoms* S Bassett (ed.), B. Yorke (1989)

The Lower Barracks: Revised Environmental Statement Heritage Residential Developments Ltd (Drivers Jonas, London April 1993)

The Study of Winchester: Archaeology and History in a British Town Martin Biddle – Proceedings of the British Academy LXIX (Oxford University Press 1983)

Winchester Studies 2: Survey of Medieval Winchester (two vols.) Derek Keene (Oxford University Press 1985)

Winchester Town Centre Plan (Hampshire County Council 1968)

Winchester Traffic Plan – Public meeting 26th July 1964 G L Bannerman, Kingham and Co, 2 and 3 Middle Temple Lane (London 1964)

Acknowledgements

I would like to thank all the following colleagues, museums and other institutions who have helped to make this book possible.

Winchester City Council – for having the original idea.

Robert Cross – who said it should be a 'book' not a report.

Richard Whinney – for the Archaeological section ably assisted by Graham Scobie.

Members of the Editorial Team – who have made it work
Keith Leaman, Richard Baker, Robin Freeman, Gill Collymore & Carol Leaman
Matthew Huntley of P & G Wells for encouragement and proof reading.

Helen Lefroy – for the difficult task of undertaking the first draft
Michael Carden, Stephen Pacey & Richard Plincke for additional help.

The main Sponsor – I would like to thank Mr Albert Gordon of New York City for his support not only for this book, but also for his abiding affection for the City and Winchester College.

Pat Edwards and the City of Winchester Trust for encouragement, financial support and the provision of additional material.

Additional artwork – I would like to thank Nick Bourne, John Reynolds, Keith Leaman and John Crook for additional drawings and paintings. Also Hampshire Archives and Local Studies; Winchester City Council – Winchester City Council Museums; and Winchester College – Suzanne Foster, archivist, for access to their archives.

Iain Patton & Peter Radcliffe of The Winchester Trust – additional advice.

Lisbeth Rake – the Chesil Theatre Team – for publicity.

Sarsen Press – Tony Hill and Judy Blake – for their patience and guidance during the publishing and printing process.

Illustration Credits

Permission to reproduce the following illustrations is gratefully acknowledged. The abbreviation 'HALS' indicates an image from the Hampshire Archives and Local Studies collection at Hampshire Record Office, Winchester; 'WCCM' refers to an image from the Winchester City Council Museums collections.

P3 St Catherine's Hill, 1881 by Heywood Sumner: HALS (B1179)
P4 View south from St Catherine's Hill, drawing by Heywood Sumner: HALS (B1179)
P27 The Broadway: Nick Bourne
P28 Eastgate House from Godson's Plan, 1748: HALS (147M86W/1)
P30 High Street with Buttercross, F P Barraud, c.1880: HALS (215M85/49 fo. 16)
P31 Westgate from south east, c.1800: WCCM (A.140, PWCM 3551)
P32 Drawings of three street elevations: Nick Bourne
P35 Green Man public house post 1886 & pre 1886: WCCM (PWCM 3566 & PWCM 3754)
P43 Sketch of the old St Thomas's church: HALS (215M85/49 fo.130)
P59 South east view of the Cathedral, 1870: HALS (85M88W/13 fo. 51)
P60 Reconstruction of Cathedral Priory, c.1540. Judith Dobie: English Heritage
P62 Reconstruction of New Minster and the west-works of Old Minster covering St Swithun's tomb: Winchester Research Unit/Martin Biddle
P63 West front of Cathedral, 1882: HALS (85M88W/13 fo. 50)
Morley College before 1870: WCCM (PWCM 3626)
P65 Pilgrims' Hall range, 1310-11: John Crook
P69 Wolvesey Old Bishop's Palace 1171 by Terry Ball: English Heritage Library
P71 Wolvesey Palace by William Cave 1793: HALS (Wavell)
P74 Eastgate Street, 1907: Edward Roberts
P76 St George's Street looking east, 1955: HALS (Dine photo 297/2/4)
P78 Middle Brook Street entrance to Marks & Spencer: HALS (Dine photo 89/1/4)
Historical pattern of St Peter Street & Jewry Street: Barry Cunliffe/Winchester Excavations Committee
P84 North view of Benedictine Convent, St Peter Street: HALS (TOP343/2/180)
P89 Former Hospital, Parchment Street: WCCM (PWCM 3625)
P91 The Brooks from Lower Brook Street, 1956: HALS (W/CS/10/23/16/1)
23 Upper Brook Street, 1955: HALS (W/CS/10/23/62/1)
P93 Middle Brook Street by Samuel Prout, 1813: WCCM (A.190)
P97 North Walls looking east, c.1900: Warren's *Winchester Illustrated* 1905
P98 Odeon Cinema and St Swithun's School: WCCM (PWCM 5230)
Winchester High School for Girls, North Walls, c.1890: WCCM (PWCM 3613)

P118 Winchester Castle (1216-1272): John Reynolds
P119 The Barracks, Castle and Law Courts, 1983: John Reynolds
P120 The ruins of the King's House, c.1897: HALS (Winchester Scrapbook Vol 2 fo.164)
The Assize Courts by T H Wyatt, 1872: HALS (85M88W/13 fo. 69)
The Great Hall and Grand Jury Chamber, c.1849: WCCM (A.213)
P129 Hyde Street looking south, 1910: WCCM (PWCM 16560)
P130 Welsh's Brewery Hyde Street, c.1905: WCCM (PWCM 7368)
P136 Nuns Walk 1897, photograph by George Roger Brown: WCCM (PWCM 23075)
P144 Internal view of St Mary Magdalen Chapel by H Schnebbelie 1788: WCCM (PWCM 3514)
Hospital & Chapel of St Mary Magdalen: John Crook
P145 The first train through Chesil Station, 1885: HALS (85M88W/13 fo. 47)
P154 St John's Street, early 20th century: WCCM (PWCM 7356)
P160 Chesil Street before 1885, Edward Roberts/WCCM (PWCM 8873)
P161 Allotments on site of car park in Chesil Street: WCCM (PWCM 4332)
Bar End looking south east to St Catherine's Hill, c.1891: WCCM (PWCM 4332)
Old Chesil Rectory & Station Approach, c.1893: WCCM (PWCM 14355)
P164 The Chesil Rectory, c.1850: WCCM (A.182)
Chesil Street looking towards St Peter's church, c.1893: WCCM (PWCM 3563)
P166 Chesil Street Station beneath St Giles' Hill, c.1895: WCCM (PWCM 10147)
P167 Itchen Navigation, Black Bridge, 1805: WCCM (A.1398)
P168 Rural scene at Black Bridge, 1917: David Fry
P169 Winchester from Tun Bridge by W Westall, c.1880: WCCM (A.393)
P171 The City Bridge by Heywood Sumner, 1880: HALS (B1179)
Ladies' bathing place, YHA City Mill by J Ludlow Northeast: Miss Coral Northeast.
P172 North elevation and cross section, Durngate Mill: John Reynolds
P179 The first passenger train from London to Southampton via Winchester by Richard Baigent, 1840: WCCM (A.1562)
P183 A 1937 proposal for the north side of the Westgate by C. Cowles Voysey: HALS (Dine photo 195/5/5)
P184 Westgate from the west, c.1875: WCCM (PWCM 6402)
P207 The Cloister Gallery and Headmaster's House, 1739: Winchester College
P209 College Sick House built in 1656-7: Winchester College
P210 Drawing by Richard Baigent of a game of Winchester Football, 1838: Winchester College
P211 The Warden's Garden 1816, from Ackerman's *Winchester College*: Winchester College